THE STATE AND ECONOMIC LIFE

Editors: Mel Watkins, University of Toronto; Leo Panitch, York University

18 TED MAGDER

Canada's Hollywood
The Canadian State and Feature Films

The development of the feature film industry in Canada has been uncertain and difficult, with problems usually attributed to the country's small population and U.S. domination of the movie industry. Ted Magder goes beyond these obvious influences in his examination of Canada's state policies as they affected the production of Canadian feature films from the First World War to the present. He presents a study focusing on the interplay between government policy and the dynamics of the industry, and undertakes an examination of cultural dependency in Canada. State policies, Magder points out, are related to domestic forces that impinge upon and set limits to policy decisions and their implementation.

In the immediate postwar period, the tone for much of Canada's cultural policies was set by the National Film Board and the recommendations of the Massey Commission. Members of both organizations expressed distaste for films designed to entertain and deemed feature film making unworthy of support. A change of heart took place in the watershed year of 1967 with the passing of the Canadian Film Development Corporation Act, when Canadians finally entered the business of feature film production. Magder considers how this came to pass, what had changed within the industry itself to make feature film production viable, and why the state changed its position from one of neglect to one of support. In the last five chapters, he examines the contradictions and limitations that have bedevilled Canadian feature film production over the last two decades.

In his conclusion, Magder proposes that both the notion of cultural dependency and the goal of public support for cultural production to express national identity need to be re-examined.

Ted Magder is Director of the Mass Communication Program at York University.

Canada's Hollywood: The Canadian State and Feature Films

TED MAGDER

UNIVERSITY OF TORONTO PRESS
Toronto Buffalo London

© University of Toronto Press Incorporated 1993
Toronto Buffalo London
Printed in Canada

ISBN 0-8020-2970-1 (cloth)
ISBN 0-8020-7433-2 (paper)

∞

Printed on acid-free paper

Canadian Cataloguing in Publication Data

Magder, Ted 1959–
Canada's Hollywood : the Canadian state and feature films

(The State and economic life)
Includes bibliographical references and index.
ISBN 0-8020-2970-1 (bound) ISBN 0-8020-7433-2 (pbk.)

1. Motion picture industry – Canada – History.
2. Motion pictures – Canada – History. I. Title. II. Series.

PN1993.5.C2M35 1993   791.43'0971   C93-094268-X

Printed on
Recycled Paper

This book has been published with the help of a grant from the Social Science Federation of Canada, using funds provided by the Social Sciences and Humanities Research
Council of Canada.

For my parents,
Lottie and Jacob

Contents

Preface

On a Saturday morning in early September 1984, I ventured to the Showcase Theatre in Toronto to attend a screening of Claude Jutra's *Mon oncle Antoine*. First released in 1971, Jutra's treatment of everyday life in a small Quebec mining town in the late 1940s has been acclaimed as a masterpiece of Canadian cinema. The theatre itself was nearly empty (not a common occurrence during Toronto's annual film festival, the Festival of Festivals). As the final credits began to roll and I drained the last drops of cold coffee from a styrofoam cup, the house lights came up. Someone passed me in the aisle. It was Jutra. He was alone. I didn't stop to thank him, to tell him how moved I was by the magic of his film, or to ask his opinions on the history of the Canadian film industry. I followed him out to Yonge Street and then watched as he disappeared.

This book stems from a concern with the magic of the movies and with the distribution of power that helps to structure and to shape that magic in the institutional configurations known as the cinema. Unfortunately, the word magic may be a bit misleading. I am not thinking only of the cinema as a series of mechanical or aesthetic 'tricks,' the cinema as illusion, or the cinema as dream. Ultimately the magic that I am interested in has to do with the way in which the cinema, or for the matter any other form of social communication, plays a role in the process by which societies and individuals develop an understanding of themselves and of others. This process involves the relationship between social communication and the formation of identities, values, and attitudes, the relationship between social communication and the sense of order, and the production and circulation of meanings writ large.

Contemporary scholarship has spent a great deal of time trying to unravel the nature of this relationship. It is fair to say that we still know very little with absolute certainty. We can, however, say this: All societies are based upon networks of social communication. People who live in social groups need to communicate regularly and publicly with each other. In contemporary societies, especially advanced industrial societies after the advent of electronic communication in the nineteenth century, the networks of social communication have become far more varied and complex. We interact almost constantly with a barrage of mediated messages; there is little escape from the mini-narratives and images of advertising or the series and serials of television programming. We are saturated by the media. Most scholars would also agree that all of this social talk is more than idle chatter. Though different intellectual traditions use different concepts to make their case, there is widespread convergence around the notion that these networks of communication are fundamental to the way in which societies are reproduced over time and across space. As Raymond Williams once said:

Society is a form of communication, through which experience is described, shared, modified, and preserved ... [T]he struggle to learn, to describe, to understand, to educate, is a central and necessary part of our humanity. This struggle is not begun, at second hand, after reality has occurred. It is, in itself, a major way in which reality is continually formed and changed. What we call society is not only a network of political and economic arrangements, but also a process of learning and communicating. (1962:10–11)

Like politics and economics, the practice of social communication involves relationships of power. There are winners and losers in the process by which societies go about describing their experiences and understanding their realities. There is a constant struggle around the dominant ideas of a given time, the taken-for-granted, the common-sense, the rights and the wrongs. Ideas matter, even (perhaps especially) when they are packaged by institutions as a form of leisure and received by audiences as entertainment. We are not only saturated by the media, we are sutured by them.

As I thought more about Jutra's film that morning in September, I found myself thinking about the question of Canadian identity and Canadian nationalism. *Mon oncle Antoine* had given me an intimate feeling for Quebec and the Québécois. It was an odd sensation, since as a Canadian (and English Canadian in particular), I spend most of my time watching foreign, mostly American, films and dramatic television programming. If the cinema plays a role in the construction of social values and attitudes, what happens when the people of one country are audience to the culture of another? I thought then that the answer was simple and that I knew it. The constant inflow and consumption of foreign culture was destroying the possibility for a unique Canadian sensibility. If the media are American, as Jeremy Tunstall once put it, then the mind follows.

On the basis of that premise, this book began to take shape. Given that culture is a kind of social cement, and given that until the arrival of television in the 1950s feature films were the most popular new form of contemporary cultural practice, why was it that there was no Canadian feature film industry to speak of until the mid-1960s? This question led me to investigate the relationship between the activities of the Canadian state and the production and distribution of feature films in Canada. With the exception of the United States, national cinemas exist in large measure as a result of support from the state: subsidies, grants, and loans to underwrite the costs of production, and exhibition quotas to ensure that the films that are made have an opportunity to be seen. What role has the Canadian state played in the development of a national cinema?

I offer an answer that traces the Canadian state's initiatives from the period immediately following the First World War to the present. The first chapter is a discussion of some of the theoretical questions that bear upon this work, most notably the question of media imperialism and its relationship to the activities of the Canadian state in the sphere of cultural policy. I suggest that the history of Canada's dependence on foreign films was not a history written in Hollywood; instead, various forces in Canada have been instrumental in shaping its course.

In chapters 2 through 6 the principal underlying theme is the almost complete absence of indigenous Canadian feature film production. As we examine the structure of Canada's film industry from the early 1900s to the late 1960s, we shall uncover an extremely truncated production sector that, with few exceptions, did not engage in feature film production. We shall also examine the extent and manner of Hollywood's penetration into Canada's feature film market, including the emergence of Canadians within the film industry who allied themselves with major American producers and distributors. In the second and third chapters we shall begin to uncover the Canadian state's seemingly contradictory stance with respect to its film policy. On the one hand, we shall see how the state developed an early interest in state-sponsored production and on the other hand, how it served to facilitate and reinforce dependency in the feature film sector. The fourth chapter will continue this line of inquiry by examining the early period of the National Film Board and the recommendations of the Massey Report, which set the tone for much of Canada's cultural policy in the immediate postwar period. These two landmarks in the evolution of a policy designed to promote Canadian cultural production will be contrasted with the postwar continentalist orientation of the Canadian state and the deepening of Hollywood's dominance in the field of feature films.

The fifth and sixth chapters are pivotal. They examine the movement to create an indigenous Canadian feature film industry, which culminated in the establishment of the Canadian Film Development Corporation (CFDC). Changes within the structure of the industry itself, the emergence of filmmakers and other industry representatives firmly committed to feature film production, and a crucial shift in the underlying assumptions that guided state actions – each contributed to the end of Canada's 'featureless' film industry. We shall examine each of these in turn, concentrating on the conflicts that emerged over what form state support to the feature film industry should take.

Chapters 7 through 11 focus on the period from 1968 to 1988. Chapters 7 and 8 concentrate on the first phase of the Canadian state's attempt to develop feature film production in Canada, a phase characterized by the provision of equity loans to producers from the Canadian Film Development Corporation and by the growing recognition that support to production was not enough to ensure the proper exhibition and distribution of Canadian films, especially English-language films. As Canadian productions have increased in number, there has been no corresponding increase in the number of Canadian feature films on Canadian screens. Repeatedly, the design of Canada's feature film policy has had to face this problem, and a trenchant conflict has emerged over the proper means to achieve adequate exhibition and distribution for Canadian films.

Chapter 9 examines the shift toward the production of big-budget, American-style films through the provisions of interim financing by the Canadian Film Development Corporation and the use of tax shelters provided by the capital cost allowance. The production of Canadian films designed for distribution through the American majors was seen as a way of alleviating the problem of market access and profitability. However, the 'tax-shelter boom,' as it came to be known, was no panacea. Emphasis on production for the U.S. market seriously disrupted the production of films with a 'Canadian' look, especially the production of films by Québécois filmmakers. Ultimately too many films were produced, at too high a cost, and without adequate distribution. By 1981 the boom had collapsed.

Chapters 10 and 11 deal with the boom's aftermath to the present. In 1984, the CFDC was renamed Telefilm Canada, and, with an enormous increase in its budget, the agency redirected its focus toward the production of Canadian television programming. During this period, the Canadian film and television production industry became a junior partner in the growing international marketplace for audio-visual cultural goods. Canadian producers now routinely enter into co-production arrangements with foreign partners, and many wholly 'Canadian' productions are made primarily with foreign markets in mind. As well, Toronto and Vancouver have become preferred sites for U.S. film and television production (in part because of the relative value of the Canadian dollar). Canada has its Hollywood, but it is also true that the relationship between Canadians and Canadian cinema is still rather tenuous.

Acknowledgments

This work originated as a doctoral thesis completed at York University in the fall of 1987. I am grateful for the support of the Social Sciences and Humanities Research Council during my years as a doctoral student. I would like to thank Fred Fletcher, Peter Harcourt, and Reg Whitaker, who sat on my doctoral thesis committee and made that experience more than pleasurable. The committee was supervised by Leo Panitch. I hope that this work stands as a tribute to Leo's unflagging support and enthusiasm, his incisive curiosity, and his friendship. I would also like to thank Stephen Clarkson, Jane Jenson, and John Meisel for their encouragement and advice. From our days on Kendal Avenue, Joe Liscio has been friend, confidante, and adviser (painting the pipes red was only the first of his many bright ideas). For their assistance in the final preparation of the manuscript I would also like to thank Alysia Pascaris, Michelle Matthews, James Leahy, and Daniel Wolgelerenter. Most important, I am grateful for the love and support of my family, especially my brother Shelley who took me to see *Those Magnificent Men in Their Flying Machines* when I was five, and Alysia who has taught me things I could never learn from books. To Sappho, *efcharisto* for the walks and the tugs of war. And to everyone who has endured my endless monologues and anecdotal tales: my apologies and my thanks.

List of Abbreviations

ACMPC   – Association of Canadian Movie Production Companies
ACTRA   – Association of Canadian Television and Radio Artists
AICOMPD – Association of Independent and Canadian-Owned Motion Picture Distributors
AMPPLC – Association of Motion Picture Producers and Laboratories of Canada
APC   – Association professionnelle des cinéastes
APFQ   – Association des producteurs de films du Québec
ARFQ   – Association des réalisateurs de films du Québec
CAMPP   – Canadian Association of Motion Picture Producers
CBC   – Canadian Broadcasting Corporation
CFDC   – Canadian Film Development Corporation
CFTA   – Canadian Film and Television Association
CGMPB   – Canadian Government Motion Picture Bureau
CMPDA   – Canadian Motion Picture Distributors Association
CRTC   – Canadian Radio-television and Telecommunications Commission
CSC   – Canadian Society of Cinematographers
CCA   – Capital Cost Allowance
CCFM   – Council of Canadian Filmmakers
DGC   – Directors' Guild of Canada
MPAA   – Motion Picture Association of America
MPEA   – Motion Picture Export Association
MPDEC   – Motion Picture Distributors and Exhibitors of Canada
MPPDA   – Motion Picture Producers and Distributors of America
NFB   – National Film Board of Canada

Canada's Hollywood:
The Canadian State and Feature Films

1 Film, the State, and the Question of Dependency

Introduction

In 1902, James Freer, a farmer turned filmmaker from Brandon, Manitoba, toured the fair grounds, music halls, and lecture theatres of Britain with a film program designed to encourage immigration to the Prairie region of Canada. Audiences at Ten Years in Manitoba, the title of Freer's exhibition, were treated to a package of over ten films including: *Harnessing the Virgin Prairie, Cyclone Thresher at Work, Arrival of CPR Express at Winnipeg,* and *Canadian Mounted Rifles Cutting Off a Boer Commando.*[1] James Freer's trip was sponsored by the Canadian state's Department of the Interior.

As the first foray in the Canadian state's now long and chequered career in the film business, the promotional tour was less successful than government officials expected. But the experience led them to give up only on James Freer and not the motion picture. Indeed, throughout the early 1900s, sporadic support for films designed to meet specific political objectives – immigration, foreign investment, tourism, and later the war effort – attests to the Canadian state's early interest in film as an effective medium for the dissemination of information, education, and propaganda. In 1918, the federal government established the Canadian Government Motion Picture Bureau (CGMPB), the first state-sponsored production unit in the world. Its better-known successor, the National Film Board (NFB) of Canada, has gone on to receive world-wide acclaim in the production of documentary, animation, experimental, and feature-length films. In the formative years of the motion picture industry, in the period before Hollywood captured and began to reshape the world's imagination, it might be said that the Canadian state was something of a cinematic vanguard.

Yet, as Peter Morris aptly explains in his history of early Canadian cinema:

The operation of government film units was paralleled by a sweeping official neglect of private film production. Throughout this period, governments refused to accept the possibility that there might be measures which could protect and promote a domestic film industry as there were measures that protected and promoted other industrial and cultural enterprises in the national interest ... It is almost as if there was an unwritten policy which suggested that, apart from the production of films to promote trade and tourism and the occasional provision of services to foreign producers wishing to film location scenes, it was not somehow *proper* for Canadians to produce films, and certainly not fiction films.[2]

The Canadian Government Motion Picture Bureau was never in the entertainment business. Its short films were primarily designed to be 'a very important adjunct towards the development of Canadian trade'; at best they were informative, at worst they were propagandist.[3] Under the venerable leadership of John Grierson, the early work of the National Film Board expanded the horizons of the documentary form but eschewed entirely the feature-length narrative film. Although some Canadian entrepreneurs – most notably Ernest Shipman – ventured into the world of commercial feature filmmaking, their efforts went unsupported by the state. While the governments of Britain, France, Germany, and even the United States, introduced measures to assist the development of domestic feature film industries in the 1920s, the government of Canada did not. As we shall see, feature filmmaking in Canada was a feeble enterprise from the start; it withered further from government neglect.

Accordingly, the establishment and growth of a commercial cinema in Canada shared a characteristic common to many other sectors of the Canadian economy: a heavy, almost exclusive reliance on foreign capital and goods. The Canadian political economy has been, and continues to be, the prototype of dependent industrialization among liberal democracies. The internalization of first British and then American capital are the hallmarks of Canadian capitalist development. The history of the cinema in Canada is perhaps the clearest example of this dependent development in the sphere of cultural production. By the early 1930s, the emerging U.S. giants in the motion picture industry (firms such as Famous Players, Paramount, MGM, and Columbia) and their Canadian allies had established a branch-plant distribution and exhibition network that controlled the Canadian market through monopolistic practices and ensured the dominance of foreign – mostly American – films. For the most part, Canadian capital was satisfied to assume an ancillary role. Canadian theatre owners (or exhibitors) were quite happy to play American films and seek out permanent arrangements with the Hollywood majors; a good living could be made showing American films.

In the first half-century of the cinema, Canadian audiences seemed content to consume a steady diet of foreign films, most of which offered a very peculiar and parochial vision of Canada and Canadian life. By the late 1950s, Hollywood had produced more than 500 feature films purported to be set in or about Canada, conservatively estimated to be about ten times the number of feature films that Canadians had made about themselves. While European governments in the postwar period took increasingly aggressive measures to challenge Hollywood's dominance of their respective markets, the Canadian government signed a pact with the Hollywood majors, known as the Canadian Co-operation Project, which all but guaranteed that Canada would remain the second-largest market for Hollywood films outside the United States itself. As the Motion Picture Association of America (MPAA) declared in 1953: 'Canada has been one of the bright spots in the world for American motion pictures'.[4] It was an understatement.

Not until 1968 did the Canadian state make an effort to support the production of feature-length films in Canada. The Canadian Film Development Corporation (CFDC), now known as Telefilm Canada, was given a one-time grant of $10 million and told to 'foster and promote the development of a feature film industry in Canada' through the provision of loans, advice, and awards to private producers and filmmakers. Though the grant was meagre (if not measly), the establishment of the CFDC was a watershed event in the history of Canadian cultural policy. For the first time, the Canadian state was prepared to advance funds to produce Canadian 'popular' culture that was expected to earn its keep in the marketplace. At the same time as they turned a profit (or at the very least made ends meet), these Canadian feature films, developed with the assistance of the Canadian state, were expected to play a role in facilitating that elusive phenomenon known as national identity.

Over two decades later it is safe to say that such an enterprise was easier said than done. Telefilm's budget for 1989–90 approached $150 million, and in 1988 over $500 million was spent on film and television productions in Canada. The labour of Canadian filmmakers has brought forth a small canon of classic Canadian films; most years see the addition of one or two more. But the industry has not yet achieved economic stability. It is still very much dependent upon state subsidies, its boom and bust cycles driven by such extraneous factors as tax policy, the value of the Canadian dollar, and the corporate plans of the Hollywood majors. And even today Canada's cinema and television screens predominantly reflect the cultural products of another place. The large American distribution companies still consider Canada as part of their 'domestic market,' and Canadian films occupy only three to five per cent of total screen time in their own national market.[5] Much of the production work in Canada is either tailored for sale in the United States or driven by American dollars and the corporate strategy of the American majors. Some filmmakers and producers are more than willing to work on the margin of the U.S. industry, making film and television productions geared to the U.S. market or in cooperation with the Hollywood majors, but others have tried to produce an indigenous film and television culture. While we can now speak of a feature film and television production industry in Canada, it is not at all clear what relationship it has to the way in which Canada is articulated and experienced as a nation. Certainly, in cultural matters, and specifically in matters of mediated cultural production, the national question is a source of continuing frustration and debate.

Media Imperialism and Cultural Dependency

It is this issue – the penetration of foreign cultural products on a level unparalleled in other capitalist–democratic societies – that, in one way or another, has been at the forefront of cultural politics in Canada since Confederation. As the Federal Cultural Policy Review Committee observed in 1982: 'As a democratic and cosmopolitan country, we have thrown open our borders to foreign cultural products and not given ourselves sufficient opportunity to enjoy the fruits of our own cultural labour. It is a telling state of affairs that our broadcasting system boasts the most sophisticated transmission hardware in the world – satellites, interactive cable, teletext – while Canadian viewers spend 80 per cent of their viewing time watching foreign programs on television.'[6] Statistics from other branches of the cultural industries tell a similar story. Over 75 per cent of the books sold in Canada are imported, and close to 90 per cent of earnings in the sound-recording industry accrue to foreign-controlled firms that principally market imported music. Cultural autarky has never been a Canadian trait.

While many Canadians regard the overwhelming diet of foreign 'entertainment' with complacency or satisfaction, a smaller cross-section of the population has consistently argued that it has a debilitating effect on the values and attitudes – the national culture – of Canadians. The first major review of Canadian cultural policy warned of an 'American invasion by film, radio, and periodical' that threatened to 'stifle rather than stimulate our own creative effort.' 'Hollywood refashions us in its own image,' wrote the Royal Commission on National Development in the Arts, Letters and Sciences in 1951. '[We] must not be blind ... to the very present danger of permanent dependence.'[7] Some twenty-five years later, the president of the Canadian Broadcasting Corporation referred to the 'American electronic rape of Canada' and charged the United States with 'cultural colonization.'[8] Dallas Smythe has argue that Canada is no more than a 'colonial satellite,' primarily because of its dependence on the U.S. 'consciousness industry.'[9] In an article ominously titled 'Escaping Extinction,' John Meisel, former chairperson of the Canadian Radio-television and Telecommunications Commission, drew the following dire conclusions:

The greatest threat to Canada lies in the possibility (some might even say probability) that, as the result of the strong presence of American influences, our cultural development may be stunted. United States styles, ideas, and products are never far away. There is, alas, a well-grounded fear that as a consequence, our perceptions, values, ideas, and priorities will become so dominated by those of our neighbours that the distinctiveness of Canada will, to all intents and purposes, vanish.[10]

Canada's dependence on foreign cultural products is not in large measure unique. The commercialization and internationalization of culture in the twentieth century – the fact that we now have something called the 'cultural industries,' which are dominated by a small number of large transnational firms – has engendered widespread apprehension (or fear, as Meisel puts it) that the autonomy and integrity of various national and local cultures is under siege. From the international success of a prime-time soap opera set in Dallas, Texas, to the world-wide popularity of the latest Hollywood blockbuster, it would seem that we live on the threshold of a global cultural marketplace. More and more people now watch the same images and hear the same sounds; and the institutions that produce and distribute these images and sounds are creating a transnational network of communications and culture that threatens to bypass or marginalize previous networks of cultural expression or communication.

Media scholarship has been sensitive to this phenomenon since at least the late fifties. Some scholars hailed the development of an international cultural marketplace as a further instance of 'modernization,' another step in the ineluctable and progressive spread of Western values and ideas. From this perspective, the export of Western media products was an integral part of the process by which 'traditional' societies would become consciously and socially 'modern.'[11] Marshall McLuhan, perhaps the most famous Canadian media theorist, suggested that 'the electronic age of instantaneous communication' would create the conditions for a 'global village' in which the peoples of the world could communicate as one big (though not always happy) family.[12] Another branch of media scholars was not anywhere near as sanguine about the developments underway. They began to speak about new forms of domination and dependency engendered by the international flows of television, film, radio, print journalism, and advertising. Given that the new global conversation was distinctly one-sided, with some countries and some institutions sending most of the messages and most of the rest of the world cast in the role of passive receivers, the emerging global village looked to them like a rather undemocratic place. To capture the inequalities inherent in this global conversation, to provide a sense of the power that underlay the seemingly innocent flow of images and sounds, these scholars began to speak of media imperialism as a new and dangerous form of (typically) covert domination.[13] As J.O. Boyd-Barrett explains, media imperialism may be defined as 'the process whereby the ownership, structure, distribution, or content of the media in any one country are singly or together subject to substantial pressure from the media interests of any other country or countries without proportionate reciprocation of the country so affected.'[14] The definition fits the Canadian case to a tee; not surprisingly, the literature on media imperialism tends to make special mention of the Canadian case. In his discussion of media imperialism Anthony Smith reflects a wide consensus: 'The culturally and politically debilitating effects of media dependence are perhaps most eloquently illustrated by taking an example not from the non-aligned or developing countries but from the developed world itself. Canada has always been obliged to struggle to maintain a thriving indigenous culture because of the proximity of the United States with its enormous output of information and entertainment ... It has conceded the right of free flow and has suffered the consequences.'[15]

As regards the phenomenon of media imperialism, two distinct questions warrant attention. First, what are the particular social, political, and economic dynamics that establish, maintain, challenge, and modify media imperialism? Second, what effect do the practices of media imperialism have on cultural values and attitudes? The first question draws our attention to the structure and operation of the media. The second question draws our attention to the products of the media, their meaning as texts (in the broadest sense of the word), and the way in which they are received and interpreted (or read) by audiences. All too commonly, media analysts have collapsed these two categories of inquiry. In particular, the early literature on media imperialism assumed that high levels of penetration by foreign media led inexorably to cultural absorption. One needed only to document what we have termed media imperialism to conclude that a cultural transformation (or annihilation) had occurred. In other words, too much of the scholarship in the field of media imperialism has worked with a 'hermeneutic naïvety,' in which audiences are assumed to accept wholesale the message of the media and to change their values and attitudes accordingly. Contemporary communications research has taken this type of analysis to task, rightly arguing that the process of 'reception' – the way in which audiences comprehend, interpret, and incorporate cultural messages – is a separate process, far more complicated and nuanced than the simple equation: message sent equals message received. Recent ethnographic studies into the process of media reception have demonstrated that audiences are far more active, creative, and critical in their 'readings' of media messages than has been assumed. As Roger de la Garde has argued: 'To conclude after extensive study of the transnationalization of the production process, that transnationalization of the reception process follows logically, is to take an unwarranted conceptual shortcut.'[16] Consequently, the cultural effect of foreign media products on Canadian audiences, for example, has to be investigated on its own terms; it cannot be assumed on the basis of statistics that illustrate the heavy penetration of foreign media products.

In Canada, as elsewhere, considerable work needs to be done on the question of audience reception, but work also remains to be done on *the question of how the structures of media imperialism are established, maintained, challenged, and modified.* For if one of the errors of the media imperialism thesis was its unwillingness to consider the role of the audience, another was its willingness to assume that all power flowed from the imperial core, as if the 'target' nation were an innocent and helpless victim. Certainly, the otherwise incisive work of Herbert Schiller suffers from this tendency. Schiller's analysis of U.S. dominance over global information and cultural flows maintains that it is the result of some master plan conceived by an omnipotent U.S. government and corporate élite working hand in hand to teach (or impose) the American way.[17] Likewise, Canadians analysts have been all too quick to finger the United States as an unrelenting cultural behemoth.

Over time a more accurate and subtle, if also more complicated, version of media imperialism has been developed.[18] It recognizes at least four characteristics of media imperialism that the earlier versions overlooked or undervalued: first, that the imperialist centre (the United States or others) is rarely omnipotent; second, that the dependent periphery is rarely powerless to offset the dynamics and effects of media imperialism; third, that specific actors within the periphery (including on occasion state officials) may indeed benefit from and facilitate the process of media imperialism; and fourth, that the effects of media imperialism are often unintended and unpredictable. It is not enough to document the internationalization of culture in its various forms; rather the limits, conflicts, and contradictions of media imperialism must also be evaluated.

This is not just an academic exercise or a more acceptable method for apportioning blame. Like many countries, Canada remains committed (how much so is a question we shall have to address) to the development of indigenous cultural production – to 'escaping extinction,' as Meisel so dramatically puts it. In the contemporary period this entails state intervention to support the production, distribution, and consumption of cultural products. A free market in cultural goods in Canada as most elsewhere means a steady and unrelenting flow of foreign cultural goods, not solely because of the wise choice of consumers but in large measure because of the economics of contemporary cultural production. Large capital pools, economies of scale, oligopolistic practices, and saturation advertising now play a significant role in determining production and distribution priorities, before the consumer makes his or her choice. Clearly, to comprehend the dynamics of media imperialism, we need to understand the dynamics of contemporary cultural production and distribution, just as we need more detailed knowledge of the ways in which the state intervenes to regulate and steer this process.

Thinking about the State

One of the most distinctive characteristics of contemporary culture is the extent to which it is produced and distributed in a marketplace dominated by large transnational media corporations. In the twentieth century, culture has been, in a very real sense, 'commodified'; media corporations create and sell culture in much the same way that other products are created and sold. But the production and distribution of cultural products is not completely governed by market forces. The state, in particular, plays a crucial role in both the production and regulation of cultural products. This is not an entirely new phenomenon. State patronage has been an important catalyst of cultural production throughout history; and state regulation of the content and uses of cultural products has constituted an important element in the attempt to manage and to police social and cultural norms. Now, however, complicated regulatory, fiscal, and tax mechanisms have been designed to steer the course of contemporary cultural activity. This is nowhere more apparent than in Canada, where few cultural endeavours are not, in one way or another, deeply influenced by the policy decisions and administrative actions of the state.

Generally speaking, there are two distinct objectives that motivate state intervention into the cultural sphere. In the first place, the modern state, much like its forbearers, is concerned with the questions of image, identity, and values. As a statement of sovereignty and civility, the modern state seems to require a certain number of cultural edifices and a certain degree of philanthropy. Relatedly, but perhaps more controversially, all modern states take steps to facilitate certain cultural practices while hindering or outlawing others. The protection and development of proper values and attitudes is the implicit, if not explicit, aim of many state actions in the cultural sphere. In a number of cases, including Canada, particular emphasis is placed on the need to protect and nurture the values and practices that constitute a national identity. The second objective, typically of more recent vintage, is concerned with the question of

economic growth. Contemporary states have come to see the value in supporting the development of internationally competitive cultural industries. There is
money to be made, insofar as the media – and the communication and informa-
tion-services industries more generally – are regarded as a sector of economic
growth. States everywhere have taken measures to ensure that some of the
capital generated by this sector is accumulated by individuals and corporations
working within their own territorial borders. To be sure, the real world of state
activity is rarely so neatly divided. Goals and objectives are often hard to
define in concrete terms; they may overlap; they may even contradict one
another. In Canada, the attempt to address the question of national identity is
complicated by the dualism of French and English Canada, by regionalism and
multiculturalism, and by a ready acceptance of American popular culture on the
part of the most Canadians. Moreover, the problem of developing a suitable set
of state activities is only exacerbated when cultural goals are linked to the goal
of economic growth (or vice versa). For one thing, economic goals are much
easier to pin down and quantify. Cultural goals resist easy classification and
measurement. For another, cultural goals, such as an increase in Canadian
feature film or dramatic television production, may exist precisely because the
marketplace itself has failed to deliver the desired material in the desired
amount.[19] The attempt to resolve these competing objectives is a bureaucratic
nightmare of the first order.

The ways in which the Canadian state has formulated and executed its goals
and objectives in relation to feature film production is a central focus of this
work. But what needs to be recognized is that the state is not protected by a
cocoon, cut off from the society over which it exercises authority.[20] Moreover,
it is not enough to say that the decisions of a democratic state, in one way or
another, reflect the priorities and values of its citizens. This is only true to a
certain degree. It is much better to say that the contemporary state must mediate between conflicting values and priorities that reflect particular and unequal
interests. The majority of citizens may be important in setting the general tone
of state actions, but specific policies typically emerge from more intensive and
sectional power struggles. At the same time, different policies may collide; for
example, spending priorities often have to be established in an overall context
of fiscal restraint. It follows from this that the policy process itself, and the
internal structure of the state, are characterized by flux, disunity, and struggle.

Although the form and activities of the state are important variables in the
process by which the formative conflicts and decisions in society are played
out, the principal dynamics behind this process are to be found within society
itself. From this standpoint, the state should be seen as the locus through which
an examination of social and political power may take place. Indeed, precisely

because the state is the target of most social and political interests, analysis of its forms of representation, intervention, and internal organization helps orient the study of the dynamics of contemporary culture and communications around the power struggles which, to a large degree, determine the specific nature of development in this sphere.

For our purposes a number of important points must be kept in mind as the analysis proceeds. First, we need to recognize and explain the divisions and conflicts that occur within the state itself during the production and implementation of Canada's feature film policy. While such conflicts often manifest themselves as bureaucratic struggles between various departments, agencies, and personnel, it will become increasingly clear that they represent the conflicts and disputes that obtain within Canadian society as a whole. Second, as we examine the nature of the social forces that bear upon Canada's feature film policy, it will become equally clear that they do not manifest themselves in simple class terms. It is in fact extremely rare that the issues and conflicts concerning the production of Canada's feature film policy manifest themselves as class conflicts or struggles, and it would be a serious error to try to reduce the problem in this way. As with other aspects of Canada's cultural policy, much of the debate turns on the national question and the issue of dependency, and it would be sheer folly to argue that there is a precise or objective class component to positions that defend the 'national interest.' To varying degrees, the demand for an alternative to Hollywood's domination of Canadian cinemas has emanated from each branch of the filmmaking community, and the general public; clearly, 'nationalists' do not have a necessary class position, nor do they necessarily have a common vision of what an alternative Canadian cinema should look like.

But this does not mean that class issues or class interests are not present in the development of Canada's feature film policy. In a fundamental sense, the development of Canada's feature film policy reflects the class nature of Canadian society in that the production and consumption of feature films has principally been oriented around the maintenance and promotion of feature films as commodities situated within the sphere of private accumulation. On many occasions and in varying ways, private interests in the film industry – most notably producers, distributors, and exhibitors – have presented themselves as representatives of capitalist production, and the values they employ have most certainly been internalized by state actors. Indeed, what often obscures the class dimension of the issues at stake is the fact that much of the conflict occurs within the capitalist class itself and along the plane of the national question. While they share a general interest in the maintenance of feature films as commodities, private producers, exhibitors, and distributors often have divergent interests with respect to specific policy decisions. Matters are only made more complicated by the pervasive presence of American capital in the Canadian film industry, and that fact that it has received significant political and economic support from representatives within the Canadian film industry.

Culture and the State in Canada

From the late 1920s, when the Royal Commission on Radio Broadcasting recommended the establishment of a state monopoly in broadcasting to ensure an adequate supply of Canadian content and equitable service across a sparsely populated country, the state has played an active role in facilitating Canadian cultural activity. Traditionally, Canadian nationalists have looked to the state to provide the necessary corrective to the onslaught on foreign culture. As Graham Spry, co-founder of the Canadian Radio League, put it long ago: 'It is a choice between the State and the United States.'[21] But this dichotomy, as Spry perhaps understood, is at best rhetorical. For the candid answer to the question, the State or the United States, is *both*: both massive dependence on American cultural products, and, on the face of it, a highly interventionist state trying to promote Canadian culture through the full range of policy mechanisms. In assessing the history and dilemma of Canadian cultural dependency we would be wise to focus our attention on the state and explore the forces that propel its actions and the consequences that follow in their wake.

The history of Canadian broadcasting highlights the central questions with which analysts of Canadian cultural policy have had to deal: How does one understand the nature of state intervention in the cultural sphere? Why and how has the state played a role in the development of Canadian cultural production? As often as not, analysis is framed around the limited nature of the Canadian government's intervention, the flip side of a massive dependence on foreign cultural products. As in most Western nations, the problems associated with the internationalization of cultural production – a growing homogeneity of cultural products and the ascent of transnational media firms – have been posed as problems for the state. More often than not the issue is framed around a nationalist strategy of protection and rejuvenation, as various Canadian interests struggle over the nature and extent of foreign cultural penetration.

Bernard Ostry, who in the early 1970s was deputy minister in the Department of Communications and more recently was the chairperson of TVOntario (a provincially owned non-commercial television network), provides us with a clear expression of the mainstream approach to the positive role of the state in cultural development. 'It seems obvious,' Ostry writes, 'that, apart from other considerations, the federal government has a clear responsibility – if we are to have a country at all – to encourage the growth of that missing sense of a common heritage and destiny. The federal task is to ensure that we "connect".' Economic prosperity and national unity have always been 'conscious goals' of federal administrations; it is only recently that 'the goal of fostering national identity has been added.' Culture, Ostry explains, is the basis of 'the integrity and spirit of the nation'; it is 'the essential element in any nation and ought to be seen as such by democratic governments and the citizens who elect them.'[22] For Ostry, the formation of a national cultural identity through the policy mechanisms of the democratic state is the final, and perhaps most important, act of nation building.

In the contemporary period, the need for an articulate cultural policy is especially urgent. Ostry is deeply concerned with the consequences of the internationalization of culture and the legacy of cultural dependency:

The need to create our own life and environment becomes more and more urgent as we feel the pressures to conform to the largely unconscious Americanization which acts on us through technology, advertising and other engines of commercial persuasion, as well as through the popular arts ...

The pressures of modernizing Americanization are toward uniformity, homogeneity and conformity. A policy of cultural development would seek to promote diversity and pluralism, correcting the tendencies inherent in mass marketing and mass entertainment to limit cultural choices.[23]

To offset these pressures, state policy must have two interrelated goals: First, 'it is the function of the central government in a genuine federation to try to build connections and link ... communities, provinces and regions into a larger whole'; and second, state policy must act toward 'the liberation of creative imagination wherever it is found, with support to those with the gifts to take advantage of it for their art.'[24] Without such support the regions of Canada will continue to drift apart and will thereby be unable to withstand the pressures of continentalism, and the individual creative worker will find it increasingly difficult to withstand the dynamics of corporate cultural production. Government action is seen as a corrective to market failures: 'It is probably only the federal government that has the power and resources to intervene and ensure the survival on a national scale of alternative cultural products. Canadians, to put it another way, need to be free to choose Canadian culture, and they cannot be free in this way if the culture they prefer has been bulldozed or fragmented out of existence.'[25]

Ostry's description of the dilemma that faces state officials and Canadian cultural advocates is telling, but his analysis of the nature of state intervention is somewhat naïve. The consummate bureaucrat, Ostry, in his review of Canadian cultural policy, reflects the optimism that his profession often places upon state steering mechanisms. 'The administration of culture,' he exclaims, 'has become a big beautiful machine. Only the mind in the machine is missing.'[26] In one of the most familiar traditions of Canadian thought, Ostry emphasizes the need for 'reason and order' around a policy that 'allows us to choose more rationally the possible courses, even the right course, for the Canadian confederation of the future.'[27]

It is a rose-tinted vision of the policy-making process and the nature of state intervention. Through its planning mechanisms, the state seems to stand above the fray of social forces, and by extension above politics itself. In *The Cultural Connection*, Ostry never systematically considers the possibility that specific social interests form the basis of the state's decision-making cues, or that at a given time there are real limits to the nature of bureaucratic calculations and the extent of state intervention. We are offered an analysis that abstracts the state's regulation of cultural practice from a systematic reading of the state's position within a specific historical array of social, economic, and political forces. State policy cannot be idealized as the practice of a neutral, rational-bureaucratic institution; less still can the policy process be situated above the contradictory dynamics of capitalist democracy. Ostry's intentions are honourable, but his mode of analysis does little to advance an incisive understanding of the Canadian state's cultural policies.

The perspective of an efficient and increasingly nationalist state intervening to correct the imbalances of the marketplace has been called into question by a number of critical works that argue that the Canadian state has acted in ways that have facilitated or, at the very least, failed to address the process of media imperialism. In his detailed historical study, Dallas Smythe sees the extension of American culture and communications into Canada as the necessary corollary to economic dependency. The 'consciousness industry,' in Smythe's words, functions to produce 'the necessary consciousness and ideology to seem to legitimate that dependence.'[28] For Smythe, the mass media in particular are the linchpin in the maintenance of monopoly capitalism: they produce audiences as commodities for sale to monopoly–capitalist advertisers; and they ensure a high incidence of consumer demand. Honed in the United States and exported abroad, consumer capitalism would collapse without the aid of the U.S.-dominated consciousness industry. The Canadian state, in Smythe's estimation, has facilitated this process; it is little more than a 'colonial satellite,' 'effectively part of the U.S. core of monopoly capitalism.'[29] Even the Canadian Broadcasting Corporation, Smythe argues, 'was converted by the Consciousness Industry into an indispensable adjunct to the profitable operation of private stations by 1948.'[30]

Smythe should be applauded for his insistence that the study of mass communications must address the question of the relationship between the dynamics of capital and the role of the mass media, but his main thesis is irredeemably reductionist.[31] Most important, for our purposes, is Smythe's one-dimensional caricature of the state's role in regulating the relationship between capital and the mass communications industries. Smythe's treatment of the state as the servant of monopoly capitalism inordinately simplifies the political struggles that impinge upon the state and affect its regulation of the cultural industries. While Smythe's argument may work best in the context of the U.S. communications industry, it is much less effective in explaining the public–private mix that characterizes the Canadian mass media. Further, Smythe seems unconcerned about distinguishing between the nationality of capital; yet the Canadian state has often found itself at the centre of disputes between national fractions of capital as it considers policy decisions that would discriminate in favour of Canadian capital. Finally, Smythe's argument is presented in a crudely ahistorical fashion: it depicts the forces of monopoly capitalism as being in control by 1870, and it offers little or no assessment of the substantive changes in the organization of the cultural industries in Canada and the way in which internal interests – which may or may not stand in alliance with American interests – are represented and mediated by the state.

Although rich in detail and insight, Susan Crean's pathbreaking work on Canadian cultural policy is similarly weak in its analytical perspective on the state.[32] Crean offers a comprehensive description of the Americanization of mass culture in Canada and argues that the state has aided and abetted this process by sanctioning the doctrine of commercialized mass culture and focusing its policies on the subsidization of high culture, which protects 'the arts' but makes little or no allowance for Canadian content. She writes:

Canadian culture is consigned to an underground where it cannot possibly function as a culture in the true sense of the word.

This situation is abetted by the continentalist approach to economics, including cultural economics, and by defeatist policy-makers who denigrate the creativity of their own compatriots; and, indeed, who do not value culture itself unless it shows a short-term profit and simply ignore the fact that U.S. investment in Canada has a stake in our continued cultural underdevelopment (and in the cultural receptiveness of the Canadian public) ... [F]unding policies have spawned a coterie of cultural corporate welfare bums (the official arts organizations) who are contemptuous of their benefactors and have turned our creative people into guerilla warriors. Meanwhile, as the techniques for distributing mass culture expand, Canada is bound ever tighter to the U.S. empire.[33]

Crean's argument that the Canadian state has had much less trouble rationalizing its support for high culture than mass culture is a very useful distinction, and one that, as we shall see, has a bearing on the development of Canadian film policy. But her discussion of the dynamics of 'mass' cultural policy is far less convincing.

Like Smythe, Crean offers a rather monochromatic reading of the development of Canadian mass culture under the aegis of American capital. Current efforts at 'Canadianization,' in the areas of book publishing and music recording no less than in filmmaking, cannot be situated within a theory of unchanging media imperialism and cultural dependency. Crean underestimates the range of indigenous interests that exist within these fields, and she has an unfortunate tendency to romanticize Canadian cultural producers (existing or potential) as budding cultural nationalists. Nothing could be further from the truth. In fact, many of the new Canadian cultural actors are primarily interested in developing products that will be attractive to the international, and especially American, markets. That this bias toward what Crean variously calls 'commercialized' or 'Americanized' culture exists cannot be ascribed to the intentions of 'defeatist' policymakers; rather it should be seen as a product of the dynamics of the cultural marketplace and, in this context, the rational decision of Canadian cultural producers. Ultimately, Crean has a tendency to idealize the 'invisible' Canadian culture as a vibrant 'popular' culture that springs from the everyday experiences of the people but is cut off from the main channels of cultural expression. As a vision of a critical, alternative, community-based culture, the sentiment is attractive, but as a yardstick by which to measure the activities of the state, it is far too unrealistic. With all due respect to the problems inherent in the notion of consumer sovereignty, it has to be said that the current mix of cultural practices in Canada does not exist because of some collusion on the part of American capital and the Canadian state, but because current cultural practices have been largely accepted and internalized by Canadians themselves. The state does not stand above society, either as the bête noir of cultural dependency or as the potential saviour of national cultural development. Crean offers a powerful critique of Canadian cultural policy, but does not provide a fully adequate explanation of its dynamics.

There is a tendency in Crean, as in Smythe, to remain trapped by the most fundamental error of dependency theory in its analysis of the state, that is, the tendency to reduce the activities of the dependent state to a strict function of the dynamic forces in the imperialist core. It is this perspective, more than any other, that fixes the stamp of functionalism and immutability on the activities of the Canadian state and thus loses sight of both the internal forces that impinge upon the policy process and the substantial changes that have occurred over time. The notion of dependency certainly remains relevant to the analysis of Canadian culture. But dependency must be analysed as a process of struggle and negotiation and not as a static relation of domination.[34]

The substantive argument of this study is that the history of Canadian cultural policy with respect to the cultural industries – and in particular its feature film policy – must be understood within the context of imperialism, but also within the context of domestic social relations and political conflicts. Whereas dependency theorists might see Canada's feature film policy as being produced at the behest of the American film industry and the American state, I see it as being determined by forces within Canada that are influenced by the process of dependent capitalist development. As we shall see, the example of the contemporary period in Canadian filmmaking illustrates a complex (and by no means uncontradictory) rearrangement of the terms of dependency through which the Canadian state has facilitated the development of large-scale Canadian cultural capital integrated into the expanding international cultural marketplace. That this strategy may not have created the spontaneous uprising of a truly Canadian cultural expression, as Crean would rightfully argue, does not mitigate the fact that substantive changes have occurred in the Canadian film industry and that the interests of important sections of that industry have been represented through the state. Through state initiatives, a Canadian feature film sector has been created. The manner in which this occurred, the characteristics of its production activities, and its ongoing negotiations with the Canadian state, offer us fertile ground on which we may explore the changing nature of the state's role in cultural production and the factors that have shaped this process of change. The apparent disarray of Canadian film policy is less the result of a failed bureaucratic enterprise or lack of will than it is a manifestation of the contradictory dynamics of Canadian society and the Canadian state.

2   A 'Featureless' Film Industry

Introduction

In the first three decades of the 1900s, the motion picture took shape as a significant new form of cultural practice.[1] The peepshows of the Kinetoscope and the more elaborate spectacle of Vitascope projections, which left audiences bemused by the sheer novelty of moving pictures, gave way to the creation of specially built theatres whose owners sought greater legitimacy by attracting a middle-class audience. Production houses discovered both the feature-length format and the narrative codes that would come to characterize the cinema's early aesthetic – genres were established, idioms were created, and stars were sold. The development of film exchanges and complex mechanisms of distribution ensured the fastest possible circulation of available films. Within 30 years, the motion picture went from a sideshow spectacle – a simple curio of the inventor's trade – to an integral part of contemporary cultural life.

While audiences may have regarded the cinema with a sense of wonder, there were many who looked upon this newest form of mass entertainment with a sense of dread. The cultural establishment – middle- and upper-class moralists and a wide range of intellectuals – came to regard the cinema, with its portrayals of violence, sex, and scandal, as a crude and potentially pernicious new form of social communication. In Canada, the Social and Moral Reform Association, the Society for the Suppression of Vice, and local chapters of the Legion of Decency, feared deeply the ill effects of motion pictures on the young, the uneducated, and immigrant populations. In 1915, the United States Supreme Court concluded that the motion picture was little more than an extension of the carnival sideshow and consequently did not deserve protection under the First Amendment; like other 'spectacles,' motion pictures were 'capable of evil.'[2] Similarly, a wide array of academics and cultural critics maintained that the newer forms of mass communication were establishing the conditions for moral, cultural, and political decay.[3]

There were others who regarded the perceived social power of the cinema with more optimism. As U.S. President Woodrow Wilson remarked: 'It is in my mind not only to bring the motion picture industry into its fullest and most efficient contact with the nation's needs, but to give some recognition to an increasingly important factor in the development of our national life. The film has come to rank as a very high medium for the dissemination of public information, and since it speaks a universal language, it lends itself importantly to the presentation of American plans and purposes.'[4] For those who would be on the receiving end of American plans and purposes there was something foreboding about Wilson's comment.

One thing is clear: by 1930 few people regarded the cinema as a passing fad or an inconsequential form of leisure. If anything, both its critics and supporters greatly exaggerated its powers of persuasion, in large part because they assumed that audiences received cinematic messages like so many well-trained Pavlovian dogs. Given this widespread belief in the cinema's persuasive powers, how would a state like Canada respond to the challenges posed by this new medium for public expression? How, in particular, would it react to the emergence of Hollywood as the celluloid capital of the world? Would the cinema be used, *pace* President Wilson, for the presentation of Canadian plans and purposes?

The Hollywood Nexus

In the early 1900s, three countries – the United States, France, and Britain – led the way in film production. Corporate manufacturers of cameras and projectors produced most of the world's motion pictures, while in each country there emerged a new type of cultural entrepreneur who established the venues for regular commercial exhibition. Given the relatively small investment necessary to establish a theatre – often just a rented store-front or converted amusement parlour – a number of enterprising Canadians tried their hand at the profitable business of film exhibition. Jules and Jay Allen, the most successful of English Canada's early exhibitors, opened the Theatorium in Brantford in 1906. The Allens later established their own film exchange and by 1920 controlled a chain of 50 theatres worth over $20 million in 21 cities.[5] The first financially successful Canadians in the film industry were thus exhibitors, whose economic well-being from the outset rested on a stable supply of popular films that could attract and sustain a regular audience. Apart from their ability to attract paying customers, the nationality of these films was irrelevant.

'Typical programs of the time suggest that Canadians were watching movies, sixty per cent of which were of American origin, forty per cent of British and French, with a scattering of films from other countries.'[6] The films and images of Canada and Canadians that did appear on the screen were, on the whole, gross caricatures of the Great White North produced on location in the back-lots of sunny California and the American Southwest. As David Clandfield explains:

By 1914 American film companies had discovered Canada and about 100 dramatic films had been made with Canadian content. From them was born a new genre, the 'northwoods melodrama' and its sub-genre the Mountie film. They were dramatized 'scenics,' borrowing stereotypes from the emerging American Western. Sheriffs donned Mountie uniforms; cowboys became lumberjacks and prospectors; Mexican villains and servants became French Canadian; the ingredients were those of the primitive melodrama – the 'race for life,' the Indian attack, the heroine saved from death or worse.[7]

Hollywood's early entry into Canada was not an isolated or unique occur-rence. In the interwar period, the American film industry established itself as the dominant cinematic force in the Western world. As Thomas Guback's detailed account shows, the economic stability of the European film industries was seriously disrupted by the First World War, while U.S. firms stabilized and expanded their production and distribution activities. Well on the way to solidifying a vertically integrated monopoly structure of exhibition, distribution, and production in their own domestic market (which all but guaranteed a stable and profitable operating environment), by the end of the war the American production and distribution companies were poised to expand their distribution activities into Europe and the world market generally. And so they did. 'By 1925, American films had captured 95 percent of the British market, and 70 percent of the French market. In Italy during this same period, American films accounted for 68 percent of screentime, a condition aggravated by dumping and underselling domestic producers.'[8] The promotion of the star system and the discovery of a viable sound system aided the initial expansion by driving up production costs and establishing promotional techniques that acted as barriers to entry for newer, unintegrated companies. Moreover, the large domestic market in the United States helped amortize the high production costs that became an integral part of Hollywood's narrative style. To be sure, the 'Big Five' (Warner Bros., Loew's Inc., Paramount, RKO, 20th Century–Fox) and the 'Little Three' (Universal, Columbia, and United Artists), as they came to be known, were not without their troubles within the United States. Intense domes-tic rivalry, a severe debt crisis during the Great Depression, labour disputes, attacks from the Legion of Decency, and a lengthy anti-combines investigation that ended in 1948 and forced the companies to divest their theatre holdings and curtail some of their more unsavoury 'trade' practices, plainly suggest that the industry was not bereft of turbulence and upheaval. But in the international marketplace, and despite numerous challenges, the American firms continued to dominate.

To assist its overseas expansion, the American film industry established and maintained an export trade association. The Foreign Department of the Motion Picture Producers and Distributors of America (MPPDA) was created in the mid-twenties as European governments began to take measures to protect their indigenous film industries from foreign competition. In 1945, the MPPDA was reborn as the Motion Picture Association of America (MPAA). On matters of international trade, the MPAA was represented by the Motion Picture Export Association (MPEA), the revamped Foreign Department of the MPPDA. According to Guback:

The MPEA was organized as a legal cartel under the provisions of the Webb-Pomerene Export Trade Act of 1918. This legislation was one of the earliest government efforts to stimulate exporting by small and medium-sized firms at a time when few companies were concerned with foreign markets. The act permitted domestic competitors to cooperate in foreign trade by forming export associations that might otherwise have been held illegal ... This exemption allowed companies supposedly in competition in the American market to combine, to fix prices, and to allocate customers in foreign markets ...

The MPEA facilitated the international activities of its members by expanding markets and keeping them open, expediting transfers of income to the United States, reducing restrictions on American films through direct negotiations and 'other appropriate means,' distributing information about market conditions to its members, and negotiating film import agreements and terms. As Jack Valenti, MPEA/MPAA president has remarked: 'To my knowledge the motion picture is the only U.S. enterprise that negotiates on its own with foreign governments.' It is not surprising that the MPEA is called 'the little State Department.'⁹

By the 1950s, foreign markets accounted for half of the revenues generated by the American majors. Jack Valenti's penchant for grandiloquence is not without foundation. Hollywood has been a constant pioneer in the globalization of contemporary culture.

Hollywood as Cause?

Though it would be difficult to overestimate Hollywood's grip on the international film industry, it was not the presence of Hollywood productions per se that prevented the production of Canadian feature films. As Janet Staiger and Douglas Gomery's discussion of the film industry in France and Germany in the twenties makes clear, even in the face of consolidated international production and distribution network, the structure of forces within discrete nation-states plays a crucial role in determining the dynamics of indigenous film industries and their relationship to Hollywood's global nexus. They pointedly ask: 'Are we to believe foreign capitalists and their governments sat by and let Hollywood do whatever it wished? Moreover, Germany and France, for example, were advanced capitalist countries in their own right, not easily exploitable underdeveloped areas. How did foreign capitalists and the governments of their companies react to U.S. firms "stealing" profits?'[10] As Staiger and Gomery show, in the interwar period both countries took measures to protect and develop their respective private film industries. In each case the policy interventions reflected the interests, indeed attempted to mediate the conflicting interests, that existed within the film industries.

In 1920, the French government imposed a tariff on imported films; however, the tariff rate was set too low to discourage exhibitors from importing American films. By 1925, American films accounted for 82 per cent of France's cinematic fare. In 1928, under pressure from the country's film producers, a government commission recommended a trade agreement whereby for every French film the United States imported four Hollywood films could be exported to France. With support from French exhibitors, the MPPDA threatened a boycott if the measures were introduced. An agreement was reached, after the government modified its proposal: import permits for seven foreign films would be issued for each indigenously produced French film. There was no longer any provision that tied the importation of American films to the exportation of French films to the United States.

During the same period, Germany was more successful in resisting the overseas expansion of Hollywood. In 1921, the Reich Film Act established a quota that restricted imports to 15 per cent of all films exhibited. Although the quota was consistently violated, German films occupied at least 40 per cent of the domestic market during the 1920s. In 1925, the Reichstag passed tougher legislation: for each German film shown domestically one foreign film could be imported. Opposition from the MPPDA was not sufficient to have the legislation rescinded. Indeed, government support allowed German producers to solidify their domestic operations and develop a viable export business. As Staiger and Gomery note: 'By 1929 Germany controlled 27 per cent of the total European market – second only to Hollywood's 60 per cent.'[11]

To explain the relative strength of the German film industry and its ability to find a comfortable niche within the international marketplace, Staiger and Gomery concentrate on the characteristics of its internal structure. At the end of the First World War, there were four major production companies in Germany that had received strong financial backing from both private and government sources. By 1921, a series of amalgamations had placed one company, Universum Film A.G. (Ufa), in a near monopoly position. Ufa was the country's major producer and distributor of films; it also controlled the largest theatre circuit in the country. Consequently, the German film industry, through Ufa, was able to present a relatively unified front in its negotiations with the German government (in fact, the German government had supported the consolidation of the industry under Ufa). Typically, the major source of competing interests in the film industry exists between exhibitors and producers: exhibitors want a stable supply of popular films regardless of their national origin, while producers need a venue to show their specific product. Because Ufa controlled the major theatre circuit within Germany, the tension between exhibitors and producers was drastically reduced; in the best tradition of vertically integrated firms, Ufa-owned theatres provided a ready outlet for films produced and distributed by the parent firm.

The economic structure of the French film industry was different in important respects. By 1925, the three major French production companies – Pathé-Cinéma, Gaumont, and Éclair – had suspended their production activities. Small, independent production companies mushroomed (as they did in Germany), but none was tied to a major theatre chain. As Staiger and Gomery argue: 'Since the French industry was not vertically integrated, a sharp separation of interests between segments of the industry existed with distributors and exhibitors quite willing to take the most profitable films whether or not they were French produced. As a result, no unified force appeared to lobby for state intervention when United States films continued to dominate the French market.'[12]

Staiger and Gomery's analysis demonstrates the need to examine the dynamics of each national industry if we are to understand the macro-trends of the international film industry. Although neither country was able (or indeed willing) to break completely from the activities and trends set by the American film industry, their varying experiences in dealing with American cinematic hegemony point to the need for a specific, case-by-case, analysis.

The Canadian State as Cause

Working with an analytical framework implicitly similar to Staiger and Gomery's, Peter Morris has argued that the stillbirth of Canadian feature film production can be explained with reference to two basic factors:

First, the fact that centralized studio production did not develop while regional production (often not using studios) persisted. And second, the fact that the federal and
provincial governments did not, in the Twenties, legislate effective protection and
support for the production, distribution, or exhibition branches of the industry. These
two factors (which may be related) fundamentally distinguish Canada's film history
from that of other countries. Certainly they distinguish it more fundamentally than
the factor of Hollywood's economic intervention – a problem faced equally in all
countries.[13]

Morris' argument provides us with a useful starting point for our analysis, but
in and of itself it contains some serious drawbacks. Morris is certainly correct
in pointing to the lack of 'a centralized, monopolistic, structure' as a principal
factor in explaining the inherent weakness of Canadian film production from
the early twenties onwards.[14] It is Morris' second point – that the Canadian
state failed to support the various branches of the film industry and facilitate
feature film production – that is more problematic. First, no branch of the
Canadian film industry – such as it was – made the case for legislative
protection and support for the production of Canadian feature films. There was
no producers' association, no organization of directors or film workers clam-
ouring for assistance from the state. Independent exhibitors in Canada, as we
shall see, were preoccupied with the emergence of theatrical chains and the
trend toward oligopolistic practices in exhibition and distribution. Like exhibitors elsewhere, theatre owners in Canada were primarily concerned about
ensuring a stable supply of popular films; the national origin or cultural
content of the films they exhibited was of little consequence from their perspective.

Second, to the extent that Canadians working within the exhibition and
distribution branches of the industry increasingly allied themselves with the
emerging Hollywood majors, a laissez-faire attitude on the part of the Canadian
state worked to their advantage. In one way or another, the introduction of
legislation to protect and support Canadian future films would have complicated
the cosy arrangements of Canadians working within the nascent Hollywood
nexus.

Finally, outside the industry, domestic production of feature films was
virtually a non-issue. When English-Canadian critics of Hollywood rallied a
voice, it was either to dismiss wholesale feature films as a cultural form, or to
argue for greater access to films from a more civilized source – Britain.

Simply put, in the period from which Canadian dependency in the feature
film industry dates, broad-based interest in the indigenous production of feature
films was non-existent. The lethargy exhibited by the Canadian state in chal-

lenging the emergence of Hollywood as the pre-eminent film force in Canada was not a function of a weakened state per se, but of broader social and economic dynamics that encouraged, condoned, or simply seemed to ignore the emerging relationship of dependency. The fact that the Canadian state itself demonstrated a somewhat enlightened interest in film as a medium of information and propaganda adds an ironic, and somewhat confusing, twist to this conjuncture. If the state could take the initiative in establishing its own film production unit, why could it not also move on its own to promote private, feature film production? The answer, as well shall see, stems not only from the limited perspective with which state officials advanced the project of state-supported film production, but from the fact that the private industry jealousy and effectively guarded its own autonomy as a 'featureless' film industry.

Truncated Production: Canada's Private Film Industry Takes Shape

Film production in Canada was minimal in the prewar period, most of it the result of industrial or government sponsorship. But the outbreak of the First World War and a growing sentiment of anti-Americanism (directed in particular at American newsreels and war films, which downplayed or completely ignored Canada's war effort) helped generate a small production boom in feature-length, narrative films.[15] Between 1914 and 1922, 36 production companies were established, yet less than half went on to produce any films. Many of these companies were little more than stock promotion swindles that used the allure of motion pictures to prey on the naïvety and anti-Americanism of would-be investors. Others were genuine attempts at Canadian film production that met with failure through a combination of inexperience and poor financing. Only one producer was able to sustain production and consistently turn a profit. Ernest Shipman made seven features between 1919 and 1922. Shipman parlayed heightened nationalism and a flair for enlisting community support into a formula that sought to depict Canada without Hollywood's grosser misrepresentations. *Back to God's Country*, his most successful film, earned over one-half million dollars and played throughout North America, Britain, Europe, Japan, and Australia.[16] But Shipman's success during this period was clearly an exception: Canadian feature productions remained marginal entities, and there was little basis upon which a more secure environment for production could be built.

The problems that beset the industry were manifold. The relatively small and highly scattered domestic market made financial success practically impossible without costly foreign distribution. As well, there emerged no large pool and readily available financial assistance, since private investors, including Canadian exhibitors and the large banks, were highly sceptical of the risks involved in the production process. Production activities were also hindered, as Morris argues, by 'the absence of an established theatrical tradition, the lack – or loss – of trained writers, actors, and technicians.'[17] Together these factors produced a situation in which no centralized or regularized studio-based production could emerge. Production companies sprang up helter-skelter across the country. The industry simply did not develop the necessary technical core, vertical integration, and sound financial backing necessary to offset the challenge of Hollywood's movement toward global control of the film marketplace. For Morris, it is precisely the lack of 'a centralized, monopolistic structure' – which had emerged in Hollywood and in those European countries that established their own, albeit limited, production sectors – that is the principal factor in explaining the inherent weakness of Canadian production from the early twenties onwards.

Industry representatives themselves were cool to the idea of full-length theatrical Canadian productions. Merrick Nutting, the first managing editor of the *Canadian Moving Picture Digest*, argued that long winters, a small market, the high cost of materials, and a lack of talent made it 'impossible' for Canadian productions to compete profitably against foreign productions.[18] Allan Dwan, a Toronto native who had become a well-respected Hollywood director, said that Canada had a 'movie future,' but only if 'it lowered import and export duties so that American firms could avail themselves of Canadian scenery.'[19] Canada's largest private production house at the time was equally uninterested in feature film production. Established in 1920 with backing from the Canadian Pacific Railway, Associated Screen News (ASN) produced newsreel footage, industrial films, and, in the 1930s, a rather successful series of theatrical shorts entitled the *Canadian Cameo*.[20] ASN also maintained a processing laboratory that prepared the positive release prints in Canada for all but one of the American companies. ASN was a profitable operation; feature film production would entail an unnecessary risk to its capital base. As Morris explains, this was certainly the view of ASN's director, Ben Norrish:

Norrish believed that Canada, with its limited population, 'had no more use for a large moving picture studio than Hollywood had for a pulp mill.' Noting that Florida had tried three times to establish a movie industry, 'and its principal business continues to be tourists and citrus fruits,' Norrish advised Canadians not to invest in feature production unless 'they had enough influence to move the centre of population as well.'[21]

In such an environment no organization of individuals involved in film production emerged to sell the state on the idea of public support mechanisms for the production of feature films. As it turned out, the Canadian state had its own, somewhat distinct, designs for the use of film.

The Canadian Government Motion Picture Bureau:
Selling Canada through Film

I have inaugurated what I consider is a very important adjunct towards the development of Canadian trade, and that is the advertising of Canada through film work ...
The idea is to have films prepared of the processes of production and of scenery,
which is a very large adjunct to the development of this country, and such produc-
tive facilities as lend themselves best to presentation on films ... The object of it is
to impress upon capitalists a realization of the magnitude of the water-power facilities and resources of Canada. It is an inducement to capital to come to this country,
and is an exhibition of the splendid facilities and waterpowers that Canada
possesses.[22]

By 1918, a number of federal government departments had experimented with
the film medium as a form of communication. The Department of Agriculture
was involved in a series of films intended to educate farmers on new agricultural techniques and other aspects of rural life, while the Parks Branch of the
Department of the Interior promoted conservation and the careful use of natural
resources through motion pictures. The war encouraged further forays into film
production: the Dominion Victory Loan Committee used films to promote the
purchase of war bonds; the Food Controller's Office commissioned *War Gardens*, which advised Canadians to use their backyards to alleviate possible food
shortages.[23] Given the lack of stable domestic production units and a reasonable
concern with quality, production was contracted out to private firms which, in
many cases, were of foreign origin. Ironically, the Department of Trade and
Commerce's interest in filmmaking seems to have been sparked by a request
from the U.S. Bureau of Commercial Economics (a non-profit, educational
institution) for films depicting industrial development and natural resources in
Canada. At the recommendation of the Canadian Pacific Railway, Trade and
Commerce commissioned eight films from the Essanay Film Manufacturing
Company of Chicago.[24] The films were a commercial success, and Essanay
made a tidy profit on their distribution. Not surprisingly, Trade and Commerce
officials wondered whether the same films could not be made by an in-house
government film unit with the financial returns accruing to the government
itself rather than some private, often foreign, production company.

Encouraged by senior officials within the Department of Trade and Commerce, Sir George Foster developed a plan by which his department would
centralize and regulate government film production. The Exhibits and Publicity
Bureau was established by an order-in-council in September 1918 (its name
was changed to the Canadian Government Motion Picture Bureau in 1923). The

Bureau was instructed to produce, acquire, and distribute motion pictures, while other departments were instructed to cooperate and consult with the Bureau as they carried out their own film publicity and propaganda.[25] By all accounts, the early work of the Bureau was a resounding success: by 1920, it could boast 'the largest and best equipped studio and laboratory in Canada' and theatrical and non-theatrical distribution encompassed all the Commonwealth countries, France, Belgium, the Netherlands, Argentina, Chile, Japan, China, and the United States.[26] The *Seeing Canada* series received considerable praise both at home and abroad, in terms of its technical quality and its 'softsell' approach. The *Canadian Moving Picture Digest*, the trade journal of the Canadian industry, offered these comments on the Bureau's early work: 'This is the purpose of the development of these films – to enable the people of the world to know the Canada that they have heard so much about in the last four years of war, to attract to Canada, as a result of showing a new and fertile field for industrial development, thousands of bona fide businessmen and millions of foreign capital. As flashes of lightning across the sky, so is Canada being flashed across the world on the motion picture screen.'[27]

Within the industry and the federal government, however, the Bureau was not without its critics. In a refrain that was to become even more commonly associated with the activities of the National Film Board, a number of private producers argued that the Bureau was taking work away from the private sector. For example, the Pathescope Company of Toronto, which had produced *War Gardens*, became increasingly incensed by the lack of private contracts. It eventually persuaded the federal government to subsidize its own newsreel, *Canadian National Pictorial*, which ran from 1919 to 1921, but it received little further work from federal government sources.[28]

A somewhat more interesting conflict emerged within the federal government when the Department of Agriculture refused to abide by the initial order-in-council.[29] The films being made for the Department of Agriculture were produced on safety stock. They could be shown in rural locations that had no licensed theatres, in schools, barns, and church halls. The Bureau's films were produced on nitrate-based, non-safety stock. Its films had to be exhibited in licensed establishments with approved equipment. After lodging a protest, the Department of Agriculture was granted an exemption from the original order-in-council and continued to produce its own films on safety stock. This was not a mere technical dispute. The use of safety stock was part of the Department of Agriculture's attempt to reach isolated rural communities with films of an 'educational' purpose. Its exhibition techniques were innovative: film programs were often accompanied by talks and discussions, and the evening's activities became an important community event (a practice continued later by the NFB).

Conversely, the Bureau's use of non-safety stock reflected its mandate of selling Canada to the world. Indeed, the *Seeing Canada* series was originally intended for foreign distribution only.

First and foremost, the Bureau's films were intended to attract foreign capital and labour to Canada. As the Minister of Trade and Commerce reiterated in 1924, the Bureau 'was established for the purpose of advertising aborad Canada's scenic attractions, agricultural resources and industrial development.'[30] The films were not necessarily designed with Canadian audiences in mind, and their distribution in Canada was very much a secondary consideration. In neither the domestic nor the foreign market were the films very profitable. Administered through the trade commissions in foreign countries, the films were often released free of charge or at cost for exhibition purposes. In 1926, at the height of its activity, the Bureau circulated 601 films with total revenues of $22,000 on expenditures of $45,000. Although the Bureau was proud of its widespread foreign distribution, as of 1926 over 98 per cent of the films in circulation were to be found in the United States.[31]

In this respect, the films produced by the Bureau in its early years of operation clearly fit into the reconstruction plans of the Canadian state.[32] Government officials and private businesspeople were particularly concerned over the prospect of a postwar depression. Moreover, an increase in labour strife and growing ethnic and regional tensions, including the rise of Canada's first 'protest' parties, suggested a very unstable postwar climate. If the films could attract new investment capital and hard-working immigrants, as well as nurture that illusive sense of 'national unity and pride' that the politicians of the centre so desperately sought, then they would be a worthwhile investment indeed.[33]

The rationale for the work of the Bureau confirms the limited perspective state officials had toward the motion picture. As an agent of government publicity and information the motion picture was valued highly, but there was little or no attempt to develop a strong Canadian presence in non-fiction theatrical releases. Government support could be rationalized in terms of previously articulated political objectives, yet there seems to have been little thought given to developing the distinct objective of fostering Canadian cultural activity.

These sentiments were clearly expressed by government officials, most notably by Ray Peck, who became director of the Motion Picture Bureau in 1920. Peck moved the Bureau more toward the production of travelogues and scenics, films that he felt were more attractive to foreign audiences. But Peck saw little or no role for the Bureau or private Canadian firms when it came to the production of indigenous feature-length narrative films. He was interested in supporting the production of feature films in Canada, but only if these would be films produced by American firms. To promote his vision of American feature film production in Canada, Peck more than once acted as a liaison between the Canadian government and Hollywood. In 1925, he announced that 'the Canadian government offers a warm welcome and all possible co-operation to legitimate American motion picture producers who care to take advantage of her great resources and beautiful scenic backgrounds.'[34] In March 1926, Peck wrote:

Personally, I think we have a great deal to learn from American producers. They have succeeded where British films have failed utterly. The American film, from a technical viewpoint, is practically perfect, and there is no question about the entertainment value that they can cram into the film ...

We are attempting at all times, as Canadians, to induce American capital and manufacturing interests to come into Canada and establish branch factories. *I look on the American film industry much as a branch factor idea in so far as it affects Canada. American motion picture producers should be encouraged to establish production branches in Canada and make films designed especially for British Empire consumption* ... We invite Americans to come over to Canada to make automobiles and a thousand and one other things, and why not invite them to come over to make pictures, but make them the way the British markets demand?

I believe that really worth-while American producers would be glad to make typically Canadian pictures if they can secure the right cooperation, assistance, and technical advice. I have just as much hope of the American film producers making box-office attractions in Canada, as British producers, should the British films become resuscitated to the point where they will amount to anything.[35]

What is so striking about Peck's remarks is not only his complete embrace of Hollywood productions as the norm – indeed the near-perfection – of cinematic work, but also the total lack of consideration given to Canadian production of feature films. It was an opinion shared by many Canadians: the prospect of feature film production in Canada was a choice between inviting British or American producers to do the work themselves. From this perspective, Peck's views made sense. He was not about to tie the possibility of a Canadian feature film industry to the marginalized activities of British producers. The British Empire was just a protected market that could be exploited to the advantage of both Canadian and American producers – if only a deal could be worked out.

Peck's assessment of the feature film industry and his desire to encourage the establishment of American branch-plant production units fit very neatly into what Glen Williams sees as the Canadian state's overall 'branch-plant export strategy of imperial import substitution' during this period.[36] According to

Williams, the 1920s and early 1930s were characterized by a broad alliance between U.S. and Canadian capital and the Canadian state designed to exploit the economic advantages of preferential tariffs within the British imperial market.

For a while this is exactly what happened in the feature film industry. In the ten-year period following the first British quota legislation of 1927, American firms produced 22 feature films in Canada that qualified as 'empire' productions.[37] Known as 'quota quickies,' most of the films were meagre, haphazard efforts that made a farce of the British legislation. In 1938, when the British changed the law to exclude Dominion productions (in part because of the abusive quality of the 'quota quickies'), the Americans closed shop in Canada. As befits a branch-plant industry, they left behind little basis upon which feature film production could continue. The 'quota quickies' were an early attempt at dependent development in the sphere of cultural production. They were a portent of things to come.

The Rise of Monopoly Practices in Exhibition and Distribution

The 1920s was a period of rapid concentration and vertical integration in the American film industry. Production companies, such as Adolph Zukor's Famous Players–Lasky Corporation, sought a secure market for their films through the acquisition of theatres, while exhibitors, most notably First National, attempted to alleviate their supply problems by contracting their own productions. Famous Players–Lasky, together with its distribution wing, Paramount Pictures, became a completely vertically integrated company by 1919; First National could claim a similar status by 1922; Fox and Loew's quickly followed suit. It was a period of fierce competition in which independents in both production and exhibition came under attack. But it was also a period in which the new vertically integrated companies developed a certain 'community of interest' and 'regularized' their competition through a series of tacit agreements and understandings held together by the Motion Picture Producers and Distributors of America (MPPDA).[38]

Exhibitors in Canada felt the repercussions of the merger movement almost immediately. The major American companies sold their films in seasonal packages, creating an environment in which theatre owners vied for the rights to exhibit a limited number of promising packages. The practice of block-booking, as it came to be known, gave the upper hand to the major distributors because independent exhibitors were confronted with a limited choice of seasonal programs. Failure to comply with the terms and conditions established by the distributors could easily spell the ruin of an independent theatre owner;

moreover, it soon became clear that the major distributors had a preference for long-term arrangements with large theatre chains, if they were not themselves already owners or partners in such a chain.

To represent their interests in negotiations with the distributors and act as a government lobby, theatre owners in Ontario formed the Motion Picture Exhibitors' Protection Association. In 1918, the Association successfully discouraged the provincial government from imposing a 150 per cent tax increase on the cost of imported films,[39] an early example that the first concern of Canadian exhibitors was a stable and cheap supply of foreign films. But the growing reliance on American films as the principal source of supply left the exhibitors relatively powerless to combat the practice of block-booking. As early as 1918, the secretary of the Association warned: 'There is only one safe investment for the future success of the Exhibitor, that is open-booking ... Therefore do not bind yourself to one exchange, keep them all open.'[40] Increasingly, this advice fell on deaf ears. In that same year the Allen theatre chain was approached by Adolph Zukor's Famous Players–Lasky Corporation with an offer to purchase its theatres. The Allens, who had built their success around its exclusive right to exhibit Paramount films (now owned by Zukor) in Canada, refused. In return, Paramount boycotted the Allen's chain. Soon after, the Allens succumbed to the market pressure of the major distributors by turning to First National as their major supplier.[41]

The Allens were not the only Canadians interested in developing large holdings in the 'bricks and mortar' branch of the industry. In January 1920, a group of Canadian investors led by N.L. Nathanson incorporated Famous Players Theatres with 13 locations across the country, including seven in Toronto.[42] As its name suggests, Famous Players Canadian Corporation was a subsidiary of Adolph Zukor's unfolding network; it was controlled in Canada through Paramount Pictures, which established an exclusive distribution contract with its theatres. Following Zukor's lead in the United States, Nathanson embarked on an aggressive campaign to establish control of the Canadian theatrical market, in particular to drive the Allens from their dominant position. For all intents and purposes, Nathanson's tactics were successful. In 1923, after the Allens were stretched thin by a fierce theatre building war, Nathanson bought out 35 of their 53 first-run theatres. By 1930, Famous Players controlled 207 theatres. It held an exclusive or dominant position in all but eight Canadian cities with a population over 10,000. There was no real opposition to its theatres in such centres as Calgary, Edmonton, Halifax, Ottawa, or Kingston and in Toronto only the Loew's Theatre presented a challenge to Famous Players' control of the downtown core.[43]

As evidence presented at a government investigation into monopoly practices in the film industry in the 1920s (known as the White Commission) reveals, Nathanson often employed ruthless tactics in expanding the Famous Players empire. For example, William James, an independent exhibitor who operated the Greenwood Theatre in Toronto, told the Commission of increasing problems in acquiring a stable supply of films in a zone controlled by Famous Players and its Toronto affiliates. James achieved a measure of success when he renovated his theatre and offered 'small films' in a quiet and comfortable atmosphere. The neighbouring Famous Players theatre started offering double bills and giving away candies in an effort to weaken James' business and eventually convince him to sell or affiliate. One evening the performance at the Greenwood Theatre was disrupted by the explosion of a stink-bomb. The perpetrator was the projectionist from a nearby Famous Players theatre. His fine was paid by the superintendent of equipment for Nathanson's company. Soon after, James sold his theatre to a Famous Players affiliate.[44]

In Vancouver, Joseph Langer owned six theatres that stood in the way of Famous Players' west-coast expansion. Telegrams disclosed at the White Commission show that, by 1926, Nathanson was incensed by Langer's unwillingness to sell or affiliate. 'We would have to stop him sooner or later,' wrote Nathanson in September, as he began to apply consistent pressure on Langer.[45] By January, continued harassment coupled with Nathanson's threat to build a major theatre opposite Langer's most profitable venue had weakened Langer to the point where he was prepared to enter into a rental agreement with Famous Players. On 19 January 1927, Nathanson wired his personal representative in Vancouver: 'This is a good job regardless of whether the theatres are profitable or not, as Langer situation was not a good one for us.' On 1 February, he wired further: 'If you think it advisable to buy pix on 15% basis for suburban circuit, do so. Use your judgment. What we want to do is to cut Langer film rental by one-third.'[46]

As one might expect, Langer and James were not alone in opposing the merger movement, though their eventual defeat was the common fate of many independent exhibitors. Organized under the Canadian Motion Picture Theatre Owners' Association, independent exhibitors started a campaign to stop the trend toward theatre concentration and the monopoly practices of distributors. 'Support every good movement for our industry's independence,' read an Association advertisement in 1926, 'do your bit by holding on to your theatre ... There is an inevitable breaking-point for Autocratic Power ... Just a little more time and they will destroy each other.'[47] The *Canadian Moving Picture Digest* itself campaigned for the rights of independent exhibitors, only to incur the wrath of the industry's major interests. Ray Lewis' editorials against monopolization (and the poor distribution of British pictures) provoked an advertising boycott led by Famous Players and the major American distributors. From the summer of 1925 to March 1926, only two exchanges, Vital and Film Booking Office, took out advertising space in the *Digest* and Lewis was almost forced out of business.

In 1928, under the leadership of Nat Taylor, 32 independents formed the Exhibitors Cooperative of Canada in an effort to improve their buying power. But it was too vulnerable and ineffective in the face of pressure from the major distributors and Famous Players.[48] Ultimately, independent theatre owners simply did not possess the necessary market strength to ward off the increasing collusion between Nathanson and the large American distributors. It is fair to say that by the late 1920s, Famous Players Canadian Corporation had cornered the exhibition market. As the general manager for Fox Film Corporation reported in 1928: 'Mr. Nathanson practically controls every key centre in Canada, and this business is closed in Toronto en bloc, and when you get through with them, there are only the "sticks" left.'[49]

Famous Players was not only the largest Canadian exhibitor, it was also, through its association with Paramount, the largest Canadian distributor. In the 1930–1 season, Paramount released 74 of the 462 feature films available for theatrical exhibition. Regal Films, which was controlled by Paramount and managed by Nathanson's brother (Paul), handled the release of films from MGM, Pathé, and British International, a total of 92 films in the 1930–1 season. From 1928 onwards, Columbia Pictures gave Famous Players first choice over the exhibition of its films, 20 in 1930–1. Thus, by the 1930–1 season, Famous Players either directly or indirectly controlled the distribution of just over 40 per cent of the films released in Canada. Most certainly, this represented an even higher percentage of the season's 'major' releases.

The other major American-based distributors were Fox and Tiffany, which released 48 films each in 1930–1, and Warner Bros. and RKO, which released 35 films in the same year.[50] For independent exhibitors, access to one of the major American distributors or affiliation with Famous Players was essential to their economic well-being. As Nat Taylor remarked: 'There was first run, and then no run.'[51]

To protect and promote their own interests, the Canadian subsidiaries of the American majors established the Motion Picture Distributors and Exhibitors of Canada (MPDEC) in 1924, with a loan of $2,500 from the MPPDA. Its loftily stated objective was 'to promote and conserve the common interests of those engaged in the motion picture industry in the Dominion of Canada by establishing the highest possible moral and artistic standards in motion picture production, by developing the educational as well as the entertainment value and the general usefulness of the motion picture by diffusing accurate and reliable information with reference to the industry, by reforming abuses relative to the industry, by securing freedom from unjust and unlawful exaction by other lawful and proper means.'[52] Although its name suggested that the MPDEC represented the interests of Canadian exhibitors, only Famous Players and its affiliates were admitted as members alongside the American distribution subsidiaries. Colonel John Cooper, a founder of the Canadian Club of Toronto and past president of the Canadian Press Association, became the MPDEC's first director. Cooper maintained that the organization was 'in substance and in fact a fully autonomous organization,' but the White Commission concluded that the MPDEC was 'a mere offshoot of a corresponding organisation in the United States, presided over by Mr. Will Hays [the MPPDA] ... the policies being dictated by, the finances controlled by, budgets subject to the approval of, and the activities generally subject to the control and direction of the Hays Organization ... [T]he New York office is consulted, not only on matters of importance such as censorship in Canada and amusement tax but also on matters which might be considered almost routine.'[53]

The MPDEC formulated and regulated the ground rules for the booking practices of the major distributors in their dealings with Canadian exhibitors. It established Film Boards of Trade in each major Canadian city to handle local issues and problems as they might arise. Major decisions were made by the central board, Col. Cooper, and ultimately the New York office of MPPDA. In establishing uniform prices on the rental of accessories, demanding cash in advance for shipments, opposing 'collective' booking by exhibitors, and regularizing 'block-booking,' the MPDEC made contract negotiations an exercise in futility for most exhibitors. An agreement known as 'protecting the contract' ensured that no distributor would sell to an exhibitor who had defaulted on a contract with another distributor. To codify its various practices, the MPDEC introduced the Standard Exhibition Contract on 1 July 1926.[54] While members of the Motion Picture Theatre Owners' Association opposed the Standard Contract, Famous Players fully endorsed it. When the Exhibitors Cooperative of Canada tried to change the terms of the Standard Contract and buy films as a collective, its efforts were strongly rebuked – the MPDEC distributors withheld contract negotiations to the point where the exhibitors ran the risk of losing an entire season's output unless they signed separately.[55]

The MPDEC operated on other fronts as well, lobbying effectively on a number of issues that 'infringed' upon the operation (and self-regulation) of the film industry. Legislative issues such as amusement taxes, import duties, and theatre regulations were central to the concerns of the Cooper organization. Together with its American counterpart, the MPDEC launched a particularly vigorous and somewhat clandestine campaign to offset emerging pressures of censorship against the film industry. Originally founded in large measure as a response to the growing public outcry against the salacious content of motion pictures, the MPPDA established its own list of objectionable film practices and regulated the industry accordingly.[56] Self-censorship was accompanied by vigilant 'cooperation' with the provincial censor boards and the various public organizations that had taken up the crusade against offensive motion pictures. The minutes of an MPDEC meeting in October 1930 suggest that 'cooperation' was sometimes aided by infiltration. Alice Fairweather, the MPDEC's secretary in New Brunswick, was a delegate at the annual meeting of the National Council of Women and played an instrumental role in watering down a resolution calling for stricter control over vaudeville and motion pictures.[57]

The MPDEC was certainly the most powerful private-sector representative of interests within the Canadian film industry, but it did not solely serve the interests of American subsidiaries operating in Canada. In the first place, Famous Players' prominence within the organization cannot be underestimated, and although the company itself was a subsidiary of Paramount Pictures, the exhibitors it represented were Canadians who had linked their own economic viability to the Hollywood nexus. Indeed, evidence from the White Report reveals that Famous Players often held the upper hand in contract negotiations and disputes with the Hollywood majors. In one documented case, the distributors within the MPDEC feared that legal action could ensue because of a Famous Players theatre owner's refusal to allow his competition to be supplied with all but the most second-rate product. In an attempt to drive his one competitor out of business in Trail, British Columbia, W.P. Dewees, who operated a Famous Players affiliate known as the Amalgamated Theatre Company, threatened to boycott any major distributor who supplied the other theatre with any first-run product. Dewees also insisted on contracts that gave him the rights to an entire season's program and the privilege of then refusing delivery on up to 50 per cent. His competitor was left with the films of only two exchanges, F.B.O. and Vitagraph. Nathanson vigorously defended Dewees' actions, and the distributors appear to have been powerless to change the situation.[58]

But it was not just Famous Players that benefited from a close working relationship with the American film industry. Independent exhibitors, although incensed at the monopoly practices of the major distributors, wanted little more than a stable supply of cheap American films for their theatres. Furthermore, the distribution companies themselves employed mostly Canadians. Of the ten American subsidiaries operating in Canada in 1928, 8 had Canadian general managers and 529 of their 563 employees were Canadians.[59] To be sure, the long-run interests of Hollywood in securing a global dominance in film were well served by the activities of the MPDEC, but we cannot ignore the fact that

Canadians themselves had become part and parcel of this unfolding world network, and that their interests too were advanced by the consolidation of American films in Canada. American interests were well served by their Canadian counterparts, but in a very strong sense the converse was also true.

British Films and Quotas: A Case of (Non)Intervention

The government of this country ought to have stricter and closer control over the moving picture showmen in this country. If we go into moving picture theatres, we see nothing but American pictures, nothing but the glorification of the American flag. And if there is an American feeling in this country, if there is a sentiment favorable to annexation, the government of this country is partly responsible for it, because proper control and supervision are not exercised by the government.[60]

In the period under consideration, governments in Canada took a few tentative measures designed to limit the influence of American films in Canada. At the height of anti-American sentiment during the First World War, various provincial censor boards demanded that American flags be banned from Canadian screens and that topical weeklies either be of British Empire origin or contain a minimum amount of British Empire content.[61] In Ontario, an amendment to the Theatres and Cinematographs Act also required that theatre owners, producers, and distributors be British subjects. No less important was the emergence in the late twenties of a movement to establish an exhibition quota for British Empire – or more precisely, British – feature films. As an instance in the history of film censorship and regulation in Canada, the question of legislative support for the production and exhibition of British Empire films is revealing, for it uncovers the ambiguity of the Canadian state's response to protectionist sentiment, the highbrow nature of the critique of American cinema, and the negative attitude of the major interests in the film industry to controls over production, distribution, and consumption. 'Proper control,' as Lucien Cannon put it, would have entailed a serious challenge to capital's vested interests in the film industry – as state intervention does in any sector of the economy – but there was little or no public support for such strident measures.

In Britain, where foreign films occupied fully 95 per cent of available screen time by 1926, the state began deliberations on a quota to protect and encourage indigenous production. The issue was raised at the Imperial Conference of 1926. A memorandum prepared for the Conference read in part: 'It is clearly undesirable that so very large a proportion of the films shown throughout the Empire should present modes of life and forms of conduct which are not typically British and, so far as setting is concerned, tend to leave on the mind of untutored spectators the impression that there are no British settings whether scenic or social which are worth presentation.'[62]

As Simon Hartog explains, the demand for legislative intervention to revive Britain's ailing film production came initially from the British Association of Film Directors; predictably, the Cinematograph Exhibitors' Association and Kinematograph Renters' Association did not support the director's position.[63] But Britain's film directors soon found a useful ally from outside the industry itself. The Federation of British Industries (FBI), Britain's most important national manufacturers association, supported the principle of state intervention to encourage British film production. The government handed the issue over to the Board of Trade, which was responsible for domestic, commercial, and industrial policy as well as foreign trade. The Board then asked the major interests within the film industry to formulate an acceptable compromise. The FBI, which had established its own film producers group, designed a draft bill that called for the introduction of an exhibition quota. Britain's exhibitors felt that restrictive trade practices (such as block-booking), had to be curtailed, but they were opposed to theatrical quotas. After nearly two years of brisk negotiations – both within the British industry and between it and the MPPDA – the British government passed the Cinematograph Films Act in 1927. Certain restrictive booking practices were banned and a quota was introduced: it was set at 5 per cent for the first year and was to rise to a maximum of 20 per cent in 1936. To qualify, a film had to be made by a registered British company, the author had to be a British subject, studio scenes had to be shot within the British Empire, and at least 70 per cent of the labour costs had to be paid to British subjects or residents. The term British was interpreted to mean a subject of the British Empire. The British government had set a precedent that the dominions of the Empire could follow. A vaguely worded resolution at the Imperial Conference suggested that member nations might be ready to support Britain's initiatives with similar legislation.

In the early 1900s pro-Empire sentiment was still a very powerful political and cultural force among English Canadians.[64] It was not only the 'sense of power' derived from aspirations of imperial unity that motivated Canada's twentieth-century Loyalists, but the sense of cultural civility and taste represented by the old imperial power, a culture that many believed was now under siege. In Canada the mass society critique was in large measure a critique of American culture, and vice versa. The major criticism levelled against American feature films (and American culture in general) was that they were too commercialized, too superficial, too base, too inclined to pander to the lowest levels of audience taste. As Dorothy Brown put it: 'American films which pour over our border in the thousands are bad, almost without exception – is this the best that can be done? The answer is of course in the affirmative – this *is* the best that money and the masses can do without the aid of brains.' On the other hand, British, or European films in general, were 'the result of sincerity plus brains and good taste.'[65] By the late 1920s a number of individuals and organizations, including the Film Committee of the Imperial Order of the Daughters of the Empire, had added their voice in protest against the lack of British films in Canadian theatres.[66] Certainly there was far more negative public reaction concerning the lack of British pictures than the lack of Canadian ones. A *Maclean's* survey of the motion picture industry in 1930 concluded: 'Chief general interest seems to centre around British films and the possibility of seeing them. This is a more widely discussed topic than the matter of purely Canadian ones.'[67] In English Canada, at least, there was public support for an exhibition quota that would promote British Empire films.

Ray Peck, director of the Canadian Government Motion Picture Bureau, held a different view. As an infringement against the 'free' market activities upon which the film industry was based, Peck was against protective legislation of any kind. Quotas, he argued, 'would tend to place a bonus on inefficiency.'[68] Yet when it became clear that the British government's quota law would go through, he remarked: 'I am not particularly interested in the quota plan for Canada at the present. What I am interested in, however, is the bringing of motion picture producers to Canada who desire to secure new locations, new scenic backgrounds for moving picture dramas and the gaining of having pictures made in the British Empire.'[69] Peck represented the emergence of Canada's new colonial loyalists; he had traded allegiance to the Empire for allegiance to America and continentalism. He travelled to New York in early 1926 and went to Hollywood for two months in the spring of 1927 in an effort to convince several American producers that they could establish production branches in Canada for the purposes of meeting British quota requirements. Some did. The 'quota quickies' met the bare minimum requirement for British classification. The Canadian representative of British International Pictures told the White Commission that the poor quality of these films served a covert purpose for the American producers: 'It was their object to kill British production, and by exhibiting pictures of weak and cheap quality, they were able to state that the quota had not been a success.'[70]

If a quota was to be introduced it would have to be established at the provincial level, because theatre legislation is a provincial responsibility in Canada.[71] Unlike Peck, certain officials within the government of Ontario were curious as to the possibility of establishing a quota to promote British and Canadian films. In 1924, the Provincial Treasurer of Ontario, Colonel W.H.

Price, sent two exploratory letters to the MPDEC to ask its advice. The first concerned the exhibition of more British films or, as Price called them, 'Old Country' pictures, to 'get away from American patriotic ideals, American historical reflections and antipathies.' The second letter asked: 'Would it be possible to start an industry in Canada providing Ontario insisted on a quota of Canadian pictures, say 25 per cent?'[72] Col. Cooper's reply, on behalf of the MPDEC, side-stepped the quota issue, saying only that the distributors were doing the best they could to introduce British films into Canadian theatres but that many were unsuccessful and that others could not get passed the government's own censor board. In 1927, after further inquiries, Cooper was more blunt and in a sense quite accurate: 'The profits of the Motion Picture industry in Canada are in the running of theatres and not in the making and distribution of Motion Pictures.'[73]

Not everyone was swayed by Cooper's argument. John Boylen, a member of the Ontario government's Board of Motion Picture Censors, lobbied aggressively for a British Empire film quota.[74] The government came under some external pressure as well. The Federated Women's Institute of Ontario sent a letter to Price's successor, J.D. Monteith, requesting that 'to furnish educative, wholesome films, and to eliminate everything of a degrading and useless character ... the use of British films be encouraged.'[75] In February 1930, Charles Roos of the Cinematographers and Motion Picture Craftsmen of Canada requested a quota of one reel of Canadian or Empire film to be shown once a month in each theatre, with letters of support signed by the mayors of eight Ontario cities including Kitchener, Kingston, Ottawa, and Chatham.[76] In 1931, Frederick Revell of British International Pictures sent a number of letters that warned government officials of Cooper's strong anti-British sentiment and attempted to demonstrate that British films could accommodate a quota of up to 15 per cent.[77]

For its part, the MPDEC worked hard to avert the introduction of quota legislation. In October 1927, it helped established the Canadian Council of Empire Films, which, through regular correspondence with the provincial treasurer, did all it could to explain why the lack of British films was the result of British producers' reluctance to distribute in Canada and not some ominous cartel of American-related interests.[78] In British Columbia, where a similar movement toward quota legislation was underway, Famous Players and the MPDEC performed some strong-armed last-minute lobbying to kill the bill's passage in 1929.[79] Even Regal Films and Canadian Universal Films, distribution agents for a number of British production companies in Canada, followed the MPDEC's course. In his investigation into the film industry, Peter White concluded: 'I can find no evidence that either of these distributors has made any serious effort to promote the exhibition of British pictures, and any utterance in the evidence has been more or less of a disparaging nature.'[80]

The government of Ontario decided to act in the spring of 1931. An amendment by order-in-council to the Theatres and Cinematographs Act gave the Ontario Censor Board the authority to require 'that a proportion of the films available for distribution, and the films exhibited in each theatre, shall be of British manufacture and origin, and fixing such proportions on a monthly or yearly basis.'[81] In a letter to the *Canadian Moving Picture Digest*, the provincial treasurer stressed that the government was still looking for 'cooperation' and that further study was necessary before an exact quota could be established.[82] In July, a timely increase in the exhibition of British pictures led the treasurer to report that 'the present supply already arranged for is of such an extent that the need for fixing a quota at present is unlikely.'[83] While the quota was never officially enforced, even its existence on paper rankled Canadian exhibitors. In June 1932, the Allied Exhibitors of Ontario sent a petition that read in part: 'We, as Canadian exhibitors owning Canadian theatres, and in no way associated with American or other interests, unanimously oppose the enactment of any law, which requires us to exhibit a fixed number of productions which may be of inferior quality and wholly unsuitable to our patrons.'[84] As one exhibitor put it a few days before the legislation received its final reading: 'You may censor what people want to see but you cannot force them to pay to see pictures they don't like.'[85]

The feeble manner in which the quota legislation was administered suggests that the Ontario government was not seriously interested in helping the cause of British Empire production at home or abroad. This was not surprising, for as we have seen, there was little or no support for Canadian production from within the film industry. Unlike the British Association of Film Directors, there was no core of Canadian directors or producers ready to mount a credible defence for protective legislation, and Canadian manufacturers and industrialists, unlike the Federation of British Industries, were uninterested in the economic potential of the film industry. Those Canadians who owned or operated theatres, like their British counterparts, argued that protective legislation was a threat to their profitability. With its close ties to American distributors, Famous Players was not about to support any state measures that altered prevailing distribution and exhibition practices. Generally speaking, distributors and exhibitors of all size found common cause on the quota issue. The public support that existed for quotas was scattered and tenuous; it stemmed more from a desire to see British pictures than from support for the production of Canadian ones. But for the most part, the motion picture's mass appeal was assailed as culturally degenerate, and while British pictures might have been considered more culturally responsible, the film industry was not something that preoccupied the minds of culturally concerned Canadians. In the end, the government of Ontario responded to these varied pressures with a legislative formula that was typically Canadian: 'quotas if necessary, but not necessarily quotas' was the gist of the legislation.

The Film Industry and the Combines Investigation Act: Monopoly-Made Canada

Relations within the film industry were far from harmonious in the first years of the Great Depression. Besides the push for some form of quota legislation in a number of provinces, the boom in theatre construction and the costly transformation to sound left many exhibitors, both large and small, in a weak financial position. The large American companies and their Canadian subsidiaries, debt-laden from a period of expansion, were also hurt by the decline in theatre attendance in the first two years of the Depression. A number of firms and individuals came close to bankruptcy. Some businesses eventually failed. Many others were sold or bought over.

Famous Players itself underwent a significant corporate reorganization. In May 1930, in a stock deal of byzantine complexity, Adolph Zukor and Paramount Publix bought out a number of Canadian shareholders and drove N.L. Nathanson from the company. A number of Canadians felt they had been 'hoodwinked,' as Ray Lewis put it, and a minority shareholders group was formed to protest the transaction.[86] The dispute came to the attention of the Conservative opposition, whose leader, R.B. Bennett, and one of its more prominent figures, Arthur Meighen, had some investments in Canadian film productions. When questions were raised in the House of Commons, Prime Minister William Lyon Mackenzie King suggested that the issue was really a private matter between the shareholders and Famous Players. Bennett, however, asked the government to consider an amendment to the Companies Act that would provide Canadian 'control of a medium, not only of amusement but of education of this type.'[87] 'We should consider,' Bennett continued, 'the national aspect of this question.'[88] Bennett made an investigation of the film industry a minor issue during the summer election of 1930. At the same time a group of independent exhibitors had renewed their complaints of restrictive monopoly practices within the industry. The Conservatives won the election, and Peter White began his investigation into restrictive trade practices and an alleged combine in the motion picture industry in September.

The prospects for an indictment were marginal from the outset. As Lloyd Reynolds argues in an early survey of Canadian anti-combines legislation, 'much more effort – public and private – has been spent in curbing competition than in preventing combination.'[89] The first Combines Investigation Act was introduced by King, as minister of Labour, in 1910. Like those that followed, it was an extremely weak piece of legislation. If criminal charges were substantiated, a penalty of up to $1,000 a day was set to begin only from the day following an indictment; there were no penalties provided for past actions and no machinery to ensure compliance with any court orders. During the first nine years of the Act's existence, only one case reached trial. The Act was amended in 1923 to ease the lodging of complaints and to provide a permanent investigating official, but it was still a comparatively lenient bill. Unlike the Sherman Anti-Trust Act in the United States, which was devised to discourage combines in principle, Canadian anti-combines legislation was designed only to discourage those combines that could be shown to operate against the public interest. The Liberal party felt that publicity and penalties would be enough to discourage harmful combinations, while the Conservative party was typically more concerned with 'price cutters' and 'unfair competition' than the forces of monopolization. As Reynolds concludes: 'Canadian legislators have tended to assume that amalgamation is beneficial and, though the danger of monopoly has been given verbal recognition, there have been no attempts at trust busting.'[90] In fact, the Act itself did nothing to discourage the merger boom that dominated the period from 1925 to 1929 – close to 40 per cent of all mergers between 1900 and 1948 occurred during this five-year interval.[91] The process underway in the film industry reflected the general trend toward capital concentration in other sectors of the Canadian economy, and there was no identifiable tradition of preventing such mergers or combinations, whether the capital in question was foreign- or Canadian-controlled.

It was against these odds that Peter White produced one of the most detailed studies of restrictive practices within the motion picture industry. His frank conclusion was that 'a combine exists and has existed at least since the year 1926.'[92] White's principal findings were directed against Famous Players, which in his own words 'had been able to acquire, particularly in the large cities and towns in Canada, where the most profitable business is, such substantial control as to reduce competition to a minimum, and to make it extremely difficult for the independent theatre to survive.'[93] Block-booking and blind-booking were the hallmarks of a 'system which effectively prevents the individual theatre operator from developing any individuality for his theatre.' While such practices indicated concerted action on the part of distributors to control the market, they did not hamper the operation of Famous Players. Indeed, the dominance of Famous Players was visible in its ability to negotiate lower rental prices and longer periods of protection or exclusive exhibition and to maintain first choice on most of the seasonal packages. 'Famous Players,' wrote White, 'is in a position to dictate to the exchanges in regard to the purchase, selection and booking of pictures, not only for its own theatres, but in large measure in regard to the booking of and contracting for the pictures in the theatres which are in opposition to them, and it remains to be considered ... whether the exerting of such influence is to the detriment of the public.'[94]

On this last – and in the light of Canadian anti-combines legislation – rather crucial question, the commissioner was rather vague. White argued that agreements entered into 'have or were designed to have the effect of preventing or lessening competition in the sale or supply of motion picture films to the exhibitors, and through them to the public.'[95] Yet with the exception of British pictures, White provided no firm evidence that there was no under-supply of films to the public. If White had one strong case to make, it seems to have been in the area of protection – the granting of exclusive exhibition contracts to first-run, usually Famous Players, theatres. White argued that the periods of protection were unnecessarily long and that they worked to the detriment of the public in terms of access and cost. But he made no general case with regard to the possibility that admission prices were higher as a result of the combine. His substantive conclusions referred exclusively to the injuries done to independent exhibitors; only implicit references were made concerning the broader public detriment of the combine.

There was clearly some public support for White's penetrating report, which was delivered only a month after the announcement of Ontario's quota legislation. Within the industry, Ray Lewis, still editor of the *Canadian Moving Picture Digest* and a stalwart defender of independent exhibitors and British pictures, wrote an open letter to Prime Minister Bennett citing the report as the 'first constructive move towards the liberation of the independent Film interests from monopoly control; and the freedom of our screens from foreign domination.'[96] Nat Taylor, representing the interests of independent exhibitors in Canada urged action as well. 'It is up to the Government' he wrote, 'to take steps by legislation and prosecution if the White Report is to benefit the independent exhibitors of Motion Pictures in Canada.'[97] The Toronto *Mail and Empire* used the report to editorialize on the deleterious effects of American culture: 'From coast to coast American picture shows have drilled American propaganda into the minds of the old and young.'[98] *Saturday Night* was equally incensed at the activities of the 'mushroom monopolists' and the 'monarchs of Paramount Public [who] are in themselves alien in sentiment and spirit to the finer elements of civilization in their own land ... Their interest lies exclusively in endeavouring to ascertain how far entertainment can be cheapened and vulgarized in order to yield a big turnover.'[99]

Prime Minister Bennett felt strongly that some action should be taken. In September, he wrote British Columbia's attorney general:

For years I have been convinced that the film situation is one of very great danger to this Dominion and have done my best to rouse public opinion, but you must realize that the Federal Government alone cannot deal with the situation, the provinces must do their part, and I regret to say that I find in many instances the film companies are so entrenched that it is difficult, if not well nigh impossible, to rouse public opinion to take action.'[100]

In fact, the attorneys general of four provinces – Ontario, British Columbia, Alberta, and Saskatchewan – decided on a course of action during the summer. On 26 September, it was announced that Ontario, with help from the other three provinces, would proceed with prosecution under the anti-combines legislation.

Famous Players had already stated publicly that it would 'welcome' prosecution since it did not expect a conviction.[101] By good planning or good fortune, a package of 24 British films (entitled the Victory Group and including such titles as *Blue Lagoon*, *Dreyfus*, *Flirting Wives*, and *Plunder*) were strong box-office performers over the summer months.[102] In September, it was reported that Famous Players had significantly lowered its demands for 'protection' (from an average of 90 to 28 days), and there were rumours that N.L. Nathanson was about to begin a chain of British-controlled theatres in Canada.[103] One cannot help but conclude that the industry was consciously working to forestall an upsurge in public support for prosecution and conviction.

The case was heard by Mr. Justice Garrow of the Ontario Supreme Court in January and February 1932. Fifteen corporations, and three individuals, including N.L. Nathanson, were charged with lessening or preventing competition in, or substantially controlling the sale of, motion pictures. According to Justice Garrow, the Crown's major argument was that 'Famous Players through its control of so many theatres was able to create and did create an unfair situation favorable to itself.'[104] It would not be an easy case to make, especially since many of the Crown's 'friendly' witnesses, those individuals who had exposed many of Famous Players' ruthless market practices during White's investigation, turned unfriendly during the proceedings; memory lapses – an inability to say for sure whether Famous Players had in fact carried out its many threats and innuendos – predominated. When Col. Cooper and Arthur Cohen, now managing director of Famous Players, took the stand, they referred to block-booking as 'preseason contracting,' explained that the long periods of protection were necessary because of the producer's need to recover investments, and argued that exhibitors as a whole were anxious to see a minimum admission fee maintained. A number of witnesses agreed that there was no real shortage of supply and that, if anything, distributors found it difficult to get all their films exhibited (with due disregard for the quality of such films).

Justice Garrow's summary of the evidence was more critical of the independent exhibitors than it was of the MPDEC members. He insinuated that the independents were simply poor businesspeople, too choosy in the pictures they bought and unwilling to pay a fair price for the best films available. The Crown had not convinced him that there was any public detriment as a result of the special arrangements between Famous Players and the major distributors; as far as Garrow was concerned, the arrangements were consistent with normal relations between suppliers and their best customer. Garrow found no evidence of price-fixing, of film shortages, or of unfair rental prices. He argued that the Standard Exhibition Contract merely helped regulate uncertainties within the industry; since play dates and prices were still negotiated, Garrow found no evidence of coercion or collusion. The defendants were acquitted.

'If Canadian stories are worthwhile making into films,' said Hollywood producer Lewis Selznick in 1922, 'companies will be sent into Canada to make them.'[105] With the exception of travelogues, the odd documentary, and sponsored industrial films, Selznick's remark is a fair assessment of the Canadian private production scene by the 1930s. If the Canadian state was to facilitate domestic production through protective quotas and discriminatory subsidies (as many European states began to do in the mid-twenties) the policy would have to garner support from within the Canadian industry itself. Yet by the mid-twenties the various interests within the Canadian film industry were almost unanimous in their disavowal, either tacit or explicit, of domestic feature film production. The production sector itself was weak, truncated, and under-financed. Canadian exhibitors were quite happy importing American films, and the subsidiaries of American distributors were more than happy to colonize the market. There was no real public support for the production of Canadian films, and only a very weak lobby existed for the exhibition of more British films. Even Peter White's exposé of the monopoly practices of the film industry failed to rouse a stronger nationalist voice. Undoubtedly the weakness of Canadian anti-combines legislation was a factor in entrenching the relationship between American distributors and Canadian exhibitors, but by then the basic dynamics were already well established: The Canadian feature film industry would develop along the commercial lines being established in the United States, with flanking support from Canadian capital in the sphere of exhibition. Neither the public nor the state was willing to fundamentally challenge the status quo.

Indeed, what emerged during this period was a trend toward monopolization within the sphere of exhibition and the consolidation of monopoly practices by

the major distributors and exhibitors. The rise of Famous Players as the dominant force in the Canadian film industry both reflected and reinforced the major
pattern for Canadian capital development within the feature film industry as a
whole. Canadians could find their niche in the sphere of exhibition and the
most important inter-industry dynamics revolved around the establishment of
large-scale exhibition chains tightly woven to the Hollywood nexus. As Mae
Huettig, a student of the film industry's early economic structure, wrote:
'Despite the glamour of Hollywood, the crux of the motion picture industry is
the theatre. It is in the brick-and-mortar branch of the industry that most of the
money is invested and made.'[106] Although Heuttig's observation was intended
to apply to the interwar structure of the American film industry, it was even
more applicable to the structure of the industry in Canada, especially after the
American majors were forced to divest themselves of their theatre holdings in
the United States and it became clear that the major source of Hollywood's
economic power was in distribution and not exhibition. Canadian interests in
the feature film industry focused around the ownership and control of motion
picture theatres, though here too foreign capital was integral to the development
of Canada's theatre chains. It was in the interaction between Canadians
involved in exhibition and the major American distributors that the structure of
dependency in the feature film industry was first institutionalized.

Most emphatically, it was not the case that this scenario was forced upon
Canada by the admittedly expansionist American film industry. It should be
recalled that in the sphere of radio broadcasting the Aird Commission of 1929
had flatly rejected the existing private, commercial system in favour of the
establishment of a publicly owned system that would use only indirect advertising. The Commission refused to consider broadcasting as mere entertainment;
it referred to radio's potential as 'education in the broad sense' and as 'fostering a national spirit and interpreting national citizenship.'[107] Only two months
after Justice Garrow had placed the stamp of legality on the practices of the
film industry, Bennett introduced Canada's first broadcasting legislation in the
House. 'This country,' he said, 'must be assured of complete Canadian control
of broadcasting from Canadian sources, free from foreign interference or
influence. Without such control radio broadcasting can never become a great
agency for communication of matters of national concern and for the diffusion
of national thought and ideals.'[108] In the eyes of many, film remained a licen-
tious form of entertainment, to be censored surely, but not to be encouraged.
In the hands of others it had become a source of great profit. By 1932, the
foundations of Canada's 'featureless' film industry were secure: Canadians
were selling American movies and watching American movies; they were not
making many of their own.

3   An Antidote to Hollywood?: The NFB and John Grierson

Introduction

When it comes to movies, Canada is a dependency of the United States ... We can shout as we like about this new nation we are building; we can be as proud as we please about the Canadian 'thing'; but when it comes to the movies, we have no emotional presentation of our own. It is another nation's effort and pride we see on our screen, not our own. We are on the outside looking in. Here is another problem you can argue among yourselves. Is it good or bad that this should be so? Is it necessary for a nation to have its own popular expression of its own loyalties, its own faith, its own pride? As we become more and more an important nation in the world, must we build our own film industry as an expression of our own life and a safeguard of our own national identity? Or is this just old-fashioned nationalistic nonsense? Is it not the curse of the nations that everyone of them should be so insistent on its own unique and special virtues?   – John Grierson[1]

The National Film Board's founder and first director, John Grierson, had a profound impact on the film policy and film culture of Canada. From 1938 until his departure after the Second World War, Grierson worked tirelessly to create a government film agency that would lead the world in the 'bright new field of national information and civic interest.'[2] Grierson was a crusader. The NFB became his broadsword. By 1945, the Board had 12 production units and close to 800 employees. While the links between Hollywood, Canadian exhibitors, and Canadian audiences continued to tighten, the NFB established itself as a considerable force in film production, both at home and abroad. In the immediate postwar period, the NFB could claim considerable public support, especially among the various film councils and film societies established, in part, to offer their members an alternative to Hollywood's omnipresent theatrical fare.

For many Canadians the Board came to symbolize and embody an alternative structure of production and distribution. That reputation has been sustained, and its work in various dimensions of documentary filmmaking has come to be defined as an essential – if not *the* essential – dimension of the Canadian film tradition. Grierson and the NFB have been canonized as symbols of Canada's cultural particularity and creative potential.

But what effect did the Board and Grierson have on the development of a feature film industry in Canada in the forties? Here their impact was far from positive or constructive. Government officials did not intend the NFB to be a challenge or antidote to Hollywood's screen dominance in Canada. Grierson made sure that it was not. As we shall see, while Grierson regarded almost all of the Hollywood's output as 'silly' and 'inconsequential,' he also had a more basic antipathy toward the feature film itself as a cultural form.[3] Like Ray Peck before him, Grierson saw no need to build an indigenous Canadian feature film industry. It would be, from his perspective, both an impractical and an unnecessary endeavour; it would be a form of 'nationalistic nonsense.' Instead, Grierson advocated cooperation with Hollywood and believed, naïvely to say the least, that Hollywood was ready to accommodate Canadian interests.

Origins of the National Film Board: Better Film Propaganda

The National Film Board, perhaps the most distinct symbol of Canadian cultural creativity, was the product of a unique conjuncture. Its seeds lay in prewar developments that reflected the same search for a new national policy as were the forces – social, political and intellectual – that resulted in the famed Rowell-Sirois Report. But it was the war, and the opportunities it afforded, that allowed the seeds to take root. The initial task of the NFB was the dissemination of wartime propaganda. To its credit, it would evolve into an organization that would offer Canadians, and people the world over, much more.

The NFB was a direct descendant of the Canadian Government Motion Picture Bureau.[4] By the mid-thirties, the Bureau had become a considerable liability: too many of its films were mediocre and unimaginative works with an ever-more-tiring emphasis on travelogues and scenics; much of its equipment was outdated; many of its prints were unusable; and its distribution network had come undone. At the onset of the Depression the Bureau's budget was frozen at $75,000. Two years later it was cut to $45,000. Money for sound equipment was granted in 1933 (four years after it had been first requested), but by then the Bureau was in a state of disrepair. Low salaries and poor equipment had encouraged the departure of many capable filmmakers. A number of government departments, including National Parks, Interior, and the

Royal Canadian Air Force had started to commission their own films. In 1937, the deputy minister of Trade and Commerce visited Great Britain (the Board's most important target market) and discovered that the distribution and exhibition of Canadian films was in complete disarray.

A similar conclusion had been reached by three influential Canadians stationed in London, England. Vincent Massey, Canada's high commissioner to England, and his secretary, Lester Pearson, became aware of the Bureau's flagging efforts through the advice of their staff secretary, Ross McLean. In 1937, Massey endorsed a memo, drafted by McLean, that read in part:

There is no sounder basis for the expansion of trade than a deeper and wider knowledge of differences in tastes and modes of life. These can be conveyed most effectively by interpreting in a wider sense the functions of the Motion Picture Bureau, by improving the quality and enlarging the quantity of Canadian films by adapting them more consciously to the demands of the British public.[5]

McLean wanted the government to review its policy of state-sponsored film production. He asked Trade and Commerce minister W.D. Euler to invite John Grierson to conduct an inquiry and make specific recommendations for the revitalization of Canadian government film production.

Grierson arrived in Ottawa in May 1938 and submitted his report a month and a half later. It was characteristic of Grierson to work at break-neck speed, to ignore the cautious customs of bureaucracy, to be terse and to the point; but it is also clear that he had a well-developed conception of his conclusions before he began his work. Grierson wanted to see the Canadian state establish a centralized film production unit, dedicated to the promotion of democratic ideals and ready to fight the impending war against fascism.[6] His report reiterated the complaints raised by McLean and others. Canadian government film production, the report concluded, was beset by three general problems: 'The absence of a considered directive policy with regard to propaganda for Canada as a whole; the lack of a strong, creative film unit which might carry out that policy and interpret it in imaginative terms; and the parochialism of the different departments.'[7] The Bureau itself was suffering from an 'inferiority complex to which departmental procedure and discipline had subjected it'; it had to be revitalized 'as a powerful instrument of government propaganda policy.[8] To this end, Grierson recommended the establishment of a central agency to coordinate all government film work. There would be no more duplication of production, no more ad hoc departmental decisions. The coordinating body would be overseen by a government film commissioner and a board of directors comprising at least two ministers, three civil servants, and three members from the general public. The Board's composition was designed to ensure that the new film unit would operate in unison with the state's broadest objectives. From Grierson's perspective, the new agency would not serve its proper function if it was either just an extension of Trade and Commerce or a more independent government agency.

Grierson was invited back in November to help implement his proposals. After insisting that the government introduce legislation rather than pass an order-in-council, Grierson helped draft the resolution to establish the National Film Board of Canada. In introducing the resolution to the House in March 1939, Trade and Commerce Minister W.D. Euler stressed that the Board would be responsible for the *coordination* of government film production and distribution. It would not engage in production itself. Aside from the government film commissioner, the only other new salaried position would be a stenographer.[9] Conservative MPs and commercial film producers (such as Associated Screen News, Crawley Films, the Vancouver Motion Picture Company, and Audio Pictures) were reassured by Euler that the Board would be responsible to Parliament, that it would not become a large new government department, and that his government had 'no intention through this medium of entering into competition with private business.'[10] Throughout most of the debate, Euler garbed the legislation in the cloth of administrative efficiency. Yet on more than one occasion he suggested that the Board might, in the future, encourage the production of 'national' or 'prestige-building films' – films that would 'in a dramatic and imaginative way ... show different aspects of a country's life.' 'Such films,' Euler explained, 'are designed to sell the idea of a country in terms of a national perspective, so as to build up an increased interest and a favourable sentiment towards a nation and its people, at home and abroad.'[11] The final wording of the National Film Act gave some legislative substance to Euler's latter remarks. The Board was given the authority 'to initiate and promote the production and distribution of films in the national interest and in particular to produce and distribute and to promote the production and distribution of films designed to interpret Canada to Canadians and to other nations.'[12]

At the outbreak of war in September the Board's directors had been selected, but the position of film commissioner was still vacant. The job was finally offered to E.A. Corbett. Corbett had been the director of the extension branch of the University of Alberta, which had developed an elaborate film network to service the needs of rural Albertans. An executive of the Canadian Radio League, Corbett was also director of the Canadian Association of Adult Education, a position he had held since its inception in 1936.[13] It was an intelligent choice, but Corbett refused the offer. The Board turned to Grierson, who was in Washington setting up a distribution centre for British films designed to build American support for the war effort. Grierson agreed to fill the position temporarily. The war had redoubled Grierson's sense of urgency; he was, no doubt, eager to ensure that at least one state-sponsored film unit would be effectively mobilized for the war effort. On his return to Ottawa, Grierson hired Ross McLean as his assistant commissioner and brought Stuart Legg from Britain to supervise production. As the old crew at the Bureau felt the full fury of Grierson's command, relations between them cooled quickly. The uneasy divide existed until June 1941, when, under Grierson's recommendation, the Bureau was dissolved and the National Film Board assumed full control of government film production.

John Grierson and Film: The Cinema as Pulpit

Through his work in the film units of the Empire Marketing Board and the General Post Office in Britain, Grierson had established his reputation as the 'father' of the documentary film movement and state-sponsored film production in Britain. His organization and zealous administration of the National Film Board of Canada during the war years has to be considered one of the most significant personal interventions on film policy and the nature of film production. As Gary Evans writes: 'Grierson, propagandist, educator, mastermind, and high priest of totalitarian information, was planning to build a brave new world based on the changes he could see coming as a result of the new age and new techniques of mass communication. The crusade was to change Canada's ideas about film, about propaganda, and perhaps even about the way it perceived itself as a nation.'[14] For Grierson, film was a medium suited to education and to the development of a more informed and democratic public opinion. His approach to filmmaking stood in stark contrast to Hollywood's preoccupation with the 'entertainment quotient.' 'I look on cinema as a pulpit, and use it as a propagandist,' he once wrote. Following in the tradition of conservative cultural criticism, he disdained current public tastes and attitudes and was horrified at how the new forms of mass media pandered to the lowest common denominator. But he also believed that the persuasive powers of the new media – in particular those of the cinema – could be used to mould a new consciousness. In classic Griersonian hyperbole, it was possible to be 'totalitarian for the good.'[15] The National Film Board was to become his most important experiment in a cinema of ideas and persuasion.

Grierson approached film as 'an instrument much more suited to the specific purposes of education than any other of the arts.' 'It is worth recalling,' he wrote, 'that the British documentary group began not so much in affection for film per se as in affection for national education. If I am to be counted as the founder and the leader of the movement, its origins certainly lay in sociological rather than aesthetic aims.'[16] Indeed, Grierson developed many of his core assumptions on twentieth-century democratic society and the role of mass communication while a postgraduate student under the supervision of Walter Lippmann at the University of Chicago. Lippmann shared in the then-growing pessimism toward traditional democratic theory. As Grierson noted, Lippmann 'drew the sad portrait of John Citizen, tired after the day's work, being asked to express his free and rational judgment on matters he could not possibly be equipped to judge. He charged that education was on the wrong lines if it thought to produce the all-knowing and rational John Citizen of the old-time liberal dream.'[17]

The increasing gulf between the specialist and John (or Joan) Citizen, whom Grierson later called 'the elect' and 'the average individual,' sapped democracy of its vitality and opened the way for the possibility of demagogues and totalitarian rule.[18] The problem, in part, was related to the role and nature of education. As long as educators held to the 'rational fallacy' – to the belief that the goal of education was 'the conveying of knowledge' – democratic societies would be brought to a 'state of disappointment, discouragement, impotence and frustration.'[19] 'What we are trying to arrive at is the point where we abandon that purely mystical concept of Democracy which encourages the illusion that ten million amateur thinkers talking themselves incompetently to death sounds like the music of the spheres. We want to arrive at the point where the democratic ideal can be brought down to the realm of practical consideration and achievement.'[20]

If film was to educate but could no longer use the discursive language of 'information' or 'rational explanation,' how then would it serve the interests of democracy and the development of active citizenship?[21] The new process of education, Grierson explained, would have to employ 'something more in the nature of a dramatic language'; it would have to be interpretive and evocative; it would have to 'give the citizen *a pattern of thought and feeling* which will enable him to approach [the] flood of material in some useful fashion.'[22] Education, in Grierson's view, should both simplify and inspire. It should provide answers and establish social bonds. It should not, necessarily, promote or condone debate. Documentary filmmaking could re-establish the bonds of citizenship; it could 'widen the horizons of the schoolroom and give to every individual, each in his place and work, a living conception of the community which he has the privilege to serve.'[23]

Ultimately this renewed sense of citizenship relied on an abiding commitment to the goals of the state. While Grierson maintained that his own partisanship was always 'an inch to the left of whatever party is in office,'[24] he remained committed to the state as the institutional embodiment of the goals that needed dissemination. He wrote:

The State is the machinery by which the best interests of the people are secured. Since the needs of the State come first, understanding of these needs comes first in education ... Since cooperative and active citizenship have become more important to the State than amateur judgements on matters beyond the general citizen's sphere of understanding, education must in part abandon the classroom and debating society and operate in terms of cooperative and active citizenship.[25]

To be sure, Grierson's rather unapologetic tone is related to the fact that he was writing against the backdrop of war, but his allegiance to the state as the ultimate embodiment of the good seems to have endured throughout his lifetime. In 1970, when the federal government declared the War Measures Act to deal with the supposed state of 'apprehended insurrection' by the Front de Libération du Québec, Grierson criticized the media for having become 'disputatious at a time when authority should be absolute. You must accept the word of your government, and it's a government with some power and with some authority and with some dignity.'[26]

Given Grierson's near-religious conviction that film was at the forefront of the battle to rejuvenate contemporary democratic societies, Hollywood itself often came in for harsh criticism. Like others, Grierson felt that the studio system of production absorbed the creative energies of some of the world's greatest directors. In its constant attempt to discover or fabricate 'popular stuff,' Hollywood successfully dramatized only 'the unreal ends' of citizenship.[27] In short, traditional Hollywood fare was 'lazy, weak, reactionary, vicarious, sentimental and essentially defeatist.'[28] 'Often they do not reflect a purposive society but a rather neurotic, meaningless society which is all dressed up and has nowhere to go. That is the really bad thing about the movies. When all the shouting is over and the excitement has died down, there is a distinct whiff of decadence and death.' Certainly a government film agency was not to waste time and money producing films that worked in 'a time killing way that makes no difference one way or another.'[29]

Undoubtedly, Grierson's sense of urgency and the speed and force with which he carried out his ideas, made Grierson the perfect foil to the cautious, lethargic, and derivative approach to film production taken in the Canadian private sector. He did create an impressive propaganda machine, and his plan to reach individuals with a cinema that emphasized community concerns and endorsed the principles of active citizenship was, to some extent, realized within the NFB. But Grierson's pessimism with respect to 'John Citizen' and his view of education as national propaganda warrant scrutiny and criticism.[30] Certainly, they did reflect an élitist, even authoritarian bias, a bias still shared by many Canadians who worry about the status of Canadian culture, and the culture of Canadians.

The NFB at War: Canadian Films Find an Audience

Soon after his return to Ottawa in the fall of 1939, Grierson sent a letter to Prime Minister King's personal secretary, A.D. Heeney, in which he outlined his intention of tying wartime propaganda to the development of Canadian unity. 'Whatever will educate public opinion in the assets, achievements and responsibilities of Canada as a nation and as a functioning constructive democracy,' read the letter in part, 'permits the use of the war situation for the emphasis of themes of long term importance to Canadian life.'[31] He also made it clear that he wanted to secure American distribution for many of the NFB's war-related pictures, since, as Evans explains, Grierson 'had taken on the task of initially coordinating the British wartime information effort in North America.'[32]

To reach as wide an audience as possible Grierson hoped to secure theatrical distribution for the NFB's pictures. Fortunately, the private film industry moved quickly to establish its loyalty to the war effort. Famous Players Canadian Corporation threw its weight behind a war support program and made good on its promise to ensure that the government's films were screened in almost 800 theatres. In 1940, representatives from all branches of the commercial film industry established the Canadian Motion Picture War Services Committee. Aside from offering screen time to government films, the Committee arranged for the production of its own Victory Loan shorts, directed the distribution of newsreel clips, provided publicity and advertising support to the war effort, and offered free Sunday shows to military personnel stationed in Canada.[33] The Canadian Committee worked in conjunction with Hollywood's War Activities Committee, which itself produced four shorts intended for Canadian audiences. Grierson's entreaties for theatrical distribution thus coincided with the industry's own perception of its wartime role. Such cooperation between business and the state was a unique feature of the wartime effort. It was not a situation that would be easily replicated after the war.

As a gesture of good faith toward the major distributors and exhibitors, Grierson recommended that while he was in Australia during the early months of 1940 Col. Cooper of the MPDEC be made acting film commissioner. In choosing Cooper as his temporary replacement, Grierson unknowingly involved himself in a domestic political squabble that did not endear him to Prime Minister King or his Liberal party cohort. In late fall of 1939, Grierson had started production of *Canada Carries On*, a joint project with the American screen-journal series *The March of Time*.[34] The film focused on Canada's war preparations and depicting King in a very favourable light. Ross McLean, whose Liberal party ties were well established, rushed to have the picture completed in time for the federal election in the spring of 1940. After seeing the pre-release print, Cooper, a staunch Tory supporter, tried to have the film's release delayed. He enlisted the support of both Famous Players and Ontario Liberal Premier Mitchell Hepburn, himself an open foe of the prime minister. But this time Cooper's contrivances incurred the full wrath of the Liberal party's federal machine. Walter Turnbull, King's personal secretary, threatened to stop Paramount Pictures' films from clearing customs. The threat seems to have been sufficient to change Cooper's mind on the issue. (Undaunted, Hepburn had the film banned in Ontario for the duration of the election campaign; even so, King's party captured 57 of the 82 seats in Ontario and handily won the election.) Smarting from his personal rebuke and looking to even the score, Cooper fired McLean while the election was still in progress. After the Liberal victory, McLean was promptly reinstated and Cooper himself was dismissed. As Turnbull put it: 'The question of a successor is not as important as getting rid of Colonel Cooper before he does any further damage.'[35] In a reorganization of the MPDEC later that year, which included a decision to drop exhibitors from the membership, Cooper was dumped as president. (The new organization was called the Canadian Motion Picture Distributors Association [CMPDA].) Cooper had run head-long into the federal Liberal party in a era when, as Reg Whitaker has detailed, party and state were being fused together as never before in Canada.[36] It was one thing to help establish a monopolized and dependent Canadian film industry; it was quite another to attack the Liberal party from inside the state: for once, Col. Cooper had met his match.

Although the incident cast some doubts on Grierson's political acumen, it did not hinder his mobilization of the NFB. Grierson initiated two major wartime series, both of which were major successes.[37] The *Canada Carries On* series began in April 1940. Films were produced at an average of one per month, with the annual total of 12 divided equally between domestic and international themes. Narrated by Lorne Greene, *Canada Carries On* resonated with the message that only collective energy, renewed productivity, and a new internationalism could secure victory for the forces of democracy. The *World in Action* series started a year later, with films designed to appeal more directly to an international audience and in particular to audiences in the United States. Gary Evans estimates that by 1943 the *World in Action* was seen by some 30 to 40 million people monthly in the United Kingdom and the United States.[38] Between theatrical and non-theatrical distribution in Canada, audiences for the *Canada Carries On* series reached two and a quarter million by 1944, while the world-wide audience for NFB newsreel material averaged between 40 and 50 million a week.[39]

The search for audiences led the NFB to develop an elaborate system of non-theatrical film distribution as well. In this respect, it built upon a tradition already well established in Canada. Aside from travelling projectionists, a number of rudimentary rural film circuits (usually connected with cooperative movements, farm machinery companies, or provincial departments of agriculture) had been set up in the twenties and thirties.[40] The most advanced program had been established at the University of Alberta, where the Department of Extension started a film distribution network in 1915. In the mid-thirties, urban film societies emerged in Toronto, Vancouver, and Ottawa in an attempt to gain access to foreign films not exhibited in mainstream theatres. In 1935, the National Film Society was established through a grant from the U.S.-based Carnegie Foundation, with a mandate 'to encourage and promote the study, appreciation and use of motion pictures as educational and cultural factors.'[41]

The NFB built upon these foundations. In 1941, Herb Lash, of the Wartime Information Bureau, helped Grierson establish an experimental travelling rural circuit under the direction of Donald Buchanan, the first secretary-treasurer of the National Film Society and a close friend of Ross McLean's. There were 30 circuits, each covering 20 adult communities a month. In the program's first year of operations NFB projectionists, or field representatives as they came to be known, would set up shop in community halls, churches, or schools and offer a 70- to 90-minute program that normally included one or two films on the war, an animated short (often from Disney productions, but also from the emerging talent of Norman McLaren), and a couple of films on topics of local interest. By 1945, there were 92 rural circuits, reaching a total audience close to a quarter of a million people a month.[42] The evenings became community events; the film program was often preceded by a town or county meeting and followed by more informal entertainment. As opposed to the passive reception of films in theatrical venues, the rural circuits were designed to encourage community discussion. The audience did not just watch the films, they talked about them in a collective setting. By all accounts, the NFB-led evenings became keenly anticipated monthly events where the interest, energy, and participation of the audience more than made up for the non-theatrical venue.

Alongside the rural circuits, NFB officials initiated three other non-theatrical networks in cooperation with interested groups. With the sponsorship of the Trades and Labour Congress and the Workers' Education Association, trade union film circuits were organized in 1942.[43] Members of 300 union locals in 84 districts attended screenings once a month by 1945. Topics included labour–management relations, postwar employment, and the state of international affairs. One year later, an industrial film circuit was organized in cooperation with Canadian chambers of commerce. Films shown to workers between shifts or at lunch time dealt with industrial development and safety – and often included an animated short. By 1944, this circuit reached over 385,000 workers a month.[44] Finally, the Board began to establish a series of film depositories in Canadian cities. The film libraries were to become the backbone of the NFB's postwar distribution system.

Propaganda for Peacetime?

As the war neared its end, Grierson began to speculate on the NFB's peacetime role.[45] In keeping with his firm opinions on the social importance of filmmaking, Grierson wanted the Board to turn its attention to the education and development of a more socially aware and responsible citizenship. Specifically, it seems that Grierson wanted the Board to endorse the concept of an advanced social-welfare state, such as the one being proposed in Britain by Lord Beveridge. The Board was also to continue to discuss themes of international importance and, if Grierson had his way, it would be aligned with External Affairs in an effort to promote a new spirit of international cooperation. Education, internationalism, citizenship: these were the Griersonian watch words.

At no time did Grierson propose that the NFB should begin to produce feature films, and he was dead set against the idea that the state should provide assistance to private producers who might come forward to take the risk. Grierson argued that the Canadian market was too small to sustain an independent feature film industry. At NFB Board meetings in the late summer and early fall of 1944, Grierson convinced the Board to reject the idea of exhibition quotas as a way of promoting the production of Canadian films. Instead, Grierson spoke of the need for cooperation with Hollywood. In an article entitled, 'A Film Policy for Canada,' Grierson argued that if Canadians wanted to produce feature films they would have to realize that 'the theatre film business is an international business, dependent when it comes to distribution on an alliance or understanding with American film interests.' 'If you can't fight them, join them,' said Grierson, who hoped that Hollywood might cooperate by establishing a 'production unit in Hollywood for the production of Canadian feature films.'[46] To this end, Grierson visited Hollywood in November 1944. Evidence uncovered by Peter Morris shows that the NFB already was sending scripts to Hollywood for consideration, and subsidizing the cost of Hollywood shorts to promote tourism in Canada.[47] Grierson's behind-the-scenes machinations and public statements would reappear a few years later in the form of the Canadian Co-operation Project.

Limited though they were, there was certain to be opposition to Grierson's plans with respect to the NFB. Within government ranks, Grierson had made too few trustworthy allies and had too many detractors. Some of the NFB's wartime films, most notably *Inside Fighting Russia* and *Balkan Powderkeg*, had unnerved government officials: the former for its seemingly wholehearted endorsement of the Russian Revolution, and the latter for its criticism of British policy in the Balkans.[48] Grierson's 'unbureaucratic' administration of the Board, particularly his penchant for hiring staff on three-month contracts in an effort to maintain a high degree of productivity, irritated Ottawa's civil servant core. To the Liberal party's central cohort, Grierson was seen as 'somewhat of a dreaming outsider,' in the words of Walter Turnbull.[49] As a government administrator, Grierson was a bit too frenzied for the postwar calm they hoped to create. His plans for a high-profile NFB were at odds with a government party all too willing to return to its preferred practice of politics as the 'art of muddling through.'

These obstacles may have proved sufficient to marginalize Grierson's plans for the NFB, but there was also a more insidious opposition coming to the fore. The NFB was to become a major casualty of the emerging cold war hysteria. The U.S. Federal Bureau of Investigation had been keeping a file on Grierson since 1942, on the assumption that the *World in Action* series was just a bit too leftist in its orientation. An unknown informant claimed that Grierson was a 'communistic sympathizer.' Leo Dolan, head of the Canadian Government Travel Bureau and a good friend of Mitchell Hepburn, had written that Grierson was 'an out and out C.C.F. supporter'; he was also 'convinced the little bastard was an English Jew.'[50] In 1944, Agar Adamson, a Conservative MP introduced a theme that was to repeatedly plague the NFB's postwar image. Adamson was convinced that the NFB was a 'propagandist for a type of socialist and foreign philosophy.' 'We have,' continued Adamson, 'a most sinister situation, because they get the adolescent mind in a receptive mood, in comfortable surroundings, and spray it with an anaesthesia of propaganda which in most cases it is not capable of resisting.'[51]

The paranoia was only intensified during the famous Gouzenko spy scandal. A cipher clerk at the Soviet Embassy in Ottawa, Igor Gouzenko defected in September 1945 and released the names of 'supposed' Soviet operatives in Canada. Freda Linton, who had been Grierson's secretary for six months in 1944, was implicated in the scandal and later fled the country. Grierson himself was named as a potential conspirator.[52] Grierson eventually cleared his name, but the event only served to advance speculations that the NFB was harbouring politically 'undesirable' elements.

In any case, Grierson had resigned as film commissioner in August with the intention of establishing a documentary film distribution company in the United States. In Canada, his plans for the NFB were quickly being pushed to the side.

With the war over, the government began a series of spending cuts that eliminated the Wartime Information Board and called for general government staff reductions, including the dismissal of 200 Board employees. Ross McLean was named temporary commissioner, but his position would not be made permanent for almost two more years.

At a Canadian government-sponsored banquet on 17 December 1945 at the Beverly Hills Hotel, Canada's ambassador to the United States, Lester Pearson, presented a plaque to the Hollywood Victory Committee to honour its assistance to the war effort. Pearson's speech lavished praise on the industry as an example of the unique Canadian–American relationship:

We have a common heritage in democratic ideals. We have a common language, common social customs, and in general a common culture. No better illustration of the general and constant commerce between our two countries can be found than that provided by our own domestic market. There is no quota for American films shown in Canada. Every theatre in Canada shows them and the documentaries of our government-sponsored NFB are widely shown in your country.[53]

Pearson's comments were accurate only insofar as they reflected the complex dependency that had emerged. If his remarks seem platitudinous it is only because they have come to be regarded by most Canadians (and Americans) as common sense – this alone speaks volumes about the embeddedness of dependency. To speak, as Pearson did, of a 'common culture' was to obscure the enormous imbalance in the flow of cultural products. Certainly, the balance that Pearson tried to describe with respect to films was a sham. After the war, NFB films would quickly disappear from American screens; they all but disappeared from Canadian theatrical screens as well. In the immediate future, the NFB would be far more preoccupied with survival than expansion, a product of the sometimes vicious prosecution of the cold war on both sides of the undefended border. Pearson's comments were accurate in one respect: there was no quota for American films shown in Canada. There was also nothing in Canada to match or counter Hollywood's popular stuff. And so it would remain. Among advanced Western nations, nowhere was the Pax Americana more tightly woven into the cultural, social, or political fabric than in Canada. Hollywood's celluloid threads helped ensure that the 'common culture' remained uncommonly American.

4 Cultural Conservatism and Canadian Cooperation

Introduction

The powerful influence of the modern cinema is not a new theme, nor need we here dwell upon its appeal to eye and ear, an appeal enhanced by the use of colour; we recognize, too, that its influences are all the more powerful because of the passivity with which they are received. We should, however, like to add that the cinema at present is not only the most potent but also the most alien of the influences shaping our Canadian life. Nearly all Canadians go to the movies; and most movies come from Hollywood. The urbane influences of Carnegie and Rockefeller have helped us to be ourselves; Hollywood refashions us in its own image.   – Massey Report[1]

Published in 1951, the first full-scale review of the Canadian state's cultural policy, the Massey Report, was a sombre, almost mournful, appraisal of the adverse effects of commercialized American culture on the Canadian psyche. Its critical tone echoed the views and expressed the sentiments of an increasing number of Canadians. As Harold Innis so succinctly put it in his last essay, Canada had 'moved from colony to nation to colony.'[2] For Innis, commercialized culture in both the media and advertising was a central attribute of the now firmly established, and rather brazen, American Empire. The feature film industry in Canada was one of the purest examples of 'American imperialism' at work.[3] Certainly for those engaged in the commercial film sector in Canada the relationship of dependency had become as natural as popcorn at the movies. From the White Commission onwards, the Canadian state accepted the fundamental status quo within the industry; on those few occasions when government attention turned to relations within the commercial film sector it led almost invariably to a strengthening of the imperial relation.

Still, the activities of the National Film Board and the Massey Report's endorsement of some form of 'cultural nationalism' implied a certain conflict with the prevailing dynamics of the commercial film sector – a conflict that raised the question not only of what the NFB's role would be in the postwar period but of whether measures might be taken to establish an indigenous private-sector feature film industry. Concern over the cultural and economic consequences of Hollywood's pervasive 'image-making' led many Western governments to take steps to protect and subsidize the development of an indigenous feature film industry in the immediate postwar period. But Canadian government officials followed a different tack. In 1948, they negotiated their own 'special' deal with the Hollywood majors, the foundation for which seems to have been prepared by John Grierson himself. The Canadian Co-operation Project, as it came to be known, was yet another attempt at branch-plant production; it could be termed a success only if its primary goal was to leave the commercial film sector unfettered and unchanged.

This meant that the Massey Report's resounding indictment of Hollywood's image-making had no immediate substantive impact on the commercial sector. The Commission's particular brand of 'highbrow' cultural conservatism led it to a dead end; it could not endorse the type of public steering mechanisms necessary to establish private feature film production. Popular culture was simply not the stuff upon which to build a proper national spirit. But the Massey Report's cultural bias was not the only problem. There was as yet no organized body or group that had made feature film production a primary goal, and many within the industry would have fought such a plan vigorously.

At the same time, even the NFB could not fulfil its promise. Arrayed against the NFB's supporters were an increasing number of detractors: private producers who felt that the NFB was cutting into their business with the Canadian government; politicians, private citizens, and state security forces increasingly convinced that the Board had become a hotbed of leftist radicalism in an era of cold war; and the governing Liberal cadre, their eyes firmly fixed on attracting American investment, who were in any case becoming uneasy over the Board's high profile and lack of discipline as an institution of the state. As we have seen, even without such external pressures, it is not altogether clear that the Board itself was interested in expanding its activities into feature film production during this period.

What is crucial to understand is that the Canadian state had not simply caved in to American pressure with respect to film policy. Nor did the problem lie in Hollywood itself, as though it stood alone as an ideological and commercial structure. In fact the continuing sorry state of Canadian cinema reflected the complex, much broader relations of dependency that deeply penetrated Canadian society.

The Postwar Industry: A Few More Actors

The war years were prosperous times for the feature film industry. Attendance levels soared. The saying was that 'every night was Saturday Night.' During the Second World War, the industry was regulated by the Wartime Prices and Trade Board, which froze ticket prices and guaranteed that exhibitors would share profits on a pro rata basis with distributors. In the interests of wartime solidarity, the industry grudgingly cooperated with the Board. But, while wartime restrictions would not permit the construction of new theatres, the Prices and Trade Board had no authority to prevent the establishment of a second major theatrical chain integrated into the Hollywood nexus.

Working from his position as president of Famous Players, N.L. Nathanson had begun acquiring theatres through an intermediary, Oscar Hanson, in the late thirties.[4] Disgruntled over his lack of control at Famous, Nathanson used his familial connections with Regal Films, which distributed MGM films in Canada, to lure independents into a new chain (apparently Nathanson expedited the process by leaning on affiliated exhibitors whose contracts with Famous Players were about to expire). Odeon Theatres was incorporated by N.L.'s brother, Henry, in April 1941. One month later, Nathanson resigned from Famous Players, assumed control of the new chain, and began negotiating a deal with Famous Players for an orderly share of Hollywood's films. At a meeting in New York, Odeon lost the MGM exhibition contract (though Regal Films maintained its distribution), but gained first call on all the pictures of Columbia, two-thirds of Universal's and one-third of Fox's. Famous Players maintained its first call on pictures from Paramount, Warner, United Artists, and MGM. The deal gave the two chains a stranglehold on first-run films in the Canadian market and all but guaranteed Canadian screen time for U.S. productions. By 1947, the two chains controlled just over 60 per cent of the total box-office gross in Canada.[5] The 'entente cordiale' between Odeon and Famous Players, as *Variety* put it, meant that the major distributors had little leeway in negotiations with the two companies. 'With Canadian rentals so satisfactory,' reported *Variety*, 'and apparently nothing to be gained by any public squawk against the alleged Odeon–FP entente [sic], major distribs are just swallowing their annoyance and keeping quiet.'[6] The 'entente' lasted until the early 1980s.

In the wake of these developments, Canadian independent exhibitors tried once again to raise the issue of monopoly practices. The Independent Motion Picture Theatres Association met in January 1942 and asked the Wartime Prices and Trade Board for assistance.[7] With theatre construction at a standstill, both Famous and Odeon were looking for takeovers and doing everything possible to keep the better pictures away from smaller exhibitors. Once again the independents encountered heavy opposition from within the industry. *Canadian Moving Picture Digest*, which had lent its support on earlier occasions, now criticized the 'indies' for tampering with the solidarity of the war effort. The movement fizzled quickly. Later the same year, a new exhibitors' organization was established. The Motion Picture Theatres Association of Ontario brought independents and chains together for the first time (Famous Players had left the MPDEC in 1940). The Association would focus its attention on items of common interest: censorship, taxes, and rental agreements were on the agenda; theatre divestiture and monopoly practices were not.

In 1945, Odeon entered a joint partnership with J. Arthur Rank, a leading figure in the British film industry, who was eager to establish a base in the North American market. Rank's postwar plans included an aggressive strategy of production-for-export to the United States. Odeon's 100 theatres would provide him with a beachhead for the exhibition of his product in North America. For Odeon, the deal meant access to more British pictures, at a time when British pictures were apparently rising in prominence on Canadian screens.[8] One year later, N.L.'s son Paul (who took control of Odeon after his father's death in 1943) sold his share of the company to Rank. J. Earl Lawson, who was minister of National Revenue in Prime Minister Bennett's cabinet, became company president. Both major theatre chains were now foreign-owned.

While private production in English Canada still centred around Associated Screen News' *Canadian Cameo* series and the production of industrial shorts and other sponsored material, a mini-boom in theatrical film production was underway in Quebec.[9] Between 1944 and 1953, 19 indigenously produced feature-length films were released in Quebec. Its catalyst was the wartime occupation of France, which caused a serious shortage of supply for exhibitors of French-language cinema. The principal figure behind the production boom was J.A. DeSève, who had set up a chain of theatres in the thirties and regularly imported close to 80 per cent of France's annual feature productions. In 1944, DeSève organized production of *Le Père Chopin*, which opened in 1945. For the first time cinema audiences in Quebec saw a story with characters and settings with which they could readily identify. In Quebec, *Le Père Chopin* was an enormous box-office hit. For his future ventures, DeSève had the good sense to obtain the public endorsement of the Catholic Church which, as a rule, regarded the cinema's secular bias with grave suspicion. Through Renaissance Films, DeSève set out to establish 'an international centre for the production of films of Christian inspiration.'[10] In 1946, a well-known French-Canadian radio producer, Paul L'Anglais, founded Quebec Productions Corporation and produced the moderately successful *La Forteresse*. Also sensitive to the pressures from the Catholic Church, L'Anglais took his future scenarios from popular Quebec radio dramas, including *Un Homme et son péché*, the most successful serial drama of its day. But, as Pierre Véronneau explains, both companies had difficulty sustaining production: neither firm was able to secure distribution in either the English-Canadian or international market; costs could not be amortized quickly enough in the small domestic market of Quebec; and the idea of government subsidies to production was anathema to the Union Nationale government of Maurice Duplessis. Even before the arrival of television put an end to the production boom, Renaissance Films and Quebec Productions had folded.

Hollywood Matures and Europe Intervenes

The major American film companies moved into the postwar period with their own concerns and anxieties. The war had provided the American majors with unrestricted access to most of the allied markets and had consolidated Hollywood's growth as an export industry; close to 50 per cent of its income now derived from export sales. In the immediate postwar period, most major western European nations were once again considering measures to facilitate and protect domestic production. The prevailing arguments for protectionist measures were further fuelled by a general shortage of American dollars and the need to repay enormous American loans. The Motion Picture Export Association (MPEA) would be kept busy over the next few years.

In the United States itself, the Hollywood majors encountered a different problem. In 1938 the Justice Department began an inquiry into the industry's trading and business practices, accusing the majors of conspiring to restrain trade in the production, distribution, and exhibition of films. Justice Department officials identified many of the same practices that the White Commission earlier had exposed in Canada. In 1948, the U.S. Supreme Court ruled that, among other things, 'two price-fixing conspiracies existed – a horizontal one between all the defendants [and] a vertical one between each distributor-defendant and its licencees.'[1] Block-booking was declared illegal and the major distributors were forced to divest their theatre holdings. Of course, these practices continued to be legal in Canada.

Perhaps the most significant long-term consequence of the antitrust decrees and the U.S. government's trade policy was that they left the distribution wing of the film industry in the strongest market position, both domestically and internationally. Only the major distributors, by buying feature films from both studio and independent producers, could spread their investment risk over a broad enough range of product to ensure profitable returns. As luck would have it, the major distributors were forced to sell their theatre holdings at almost precisely the moment that television's popularity began to weaken theatre attendance. In the next few years, the major Hollywood distributors cemented their position as the linchpin in the film industry's macro-economic structure. Around the world, support from a major American distributor was becoming more and more vital to the commercial success of almost every theatrical release.[12]

With the support of the U.S. State Department, the MPEA began a vigorous political and ideological campaign to maintain its foreign markers – a campaign it has continued, in varying forms, to this day. Increasingly, the MPEA and the State Department worked hand in hand to establish free trade and a free flow of ideas as fundamental conditions of Western alliance under American hegemony. As William Benton, assistant secretary of state, explained in 1946: 'The State Department plans to do everything within its power along political or diplomatic lines to help break down the artificial barriers to the expansion of private American news agencies, magazines, motion pictures, and other media of communication throughout the world ... Freedom of the Press – and freedom of exchange of information generally – is an integral part of our foreign policy.'[13] Though it operated as a cartel, the MPEA understood well the ideological value of free trade and freedom of expression. 'The free exchange of ideas,' MPEA president Eric Johnston said in his first address to the Motion Picture Association of America, 'is more important than the free exchange of goods. There must be no obstacle to the transit of the media of communications.'[14] Johnston argued that feature films were the 'people's art,' that their popular appeal could 'break down barriers of misunderstanding among nations.' Like all infringements on the 'free' market, protectionism promoted mediocrity, and state subsidies distorted the 'democratic' structure of demand and supply.[15] Of course, Johnston's rhetoric was based upon the assumption that an equal exchange of motion pictures actually existed in the market and that the monopolistic practices of the major distributors in no way distorted the dynamics of free competition. Behind the lofty rhetoric was no small measure of economic self-interest. Some people may have been fooled, but in a number of countries industry representatives not tied to the dominant distribution structure and government officials who realized the potential economic and cultural consequences of Hollywood's dominance, were not. On a number of fronts, the MPEA found itself the target of significant attempts to establish a more equitable exchange of films.[16]

Canadian industry and government officials watched with interest as such a scenario seemed set to unfold in the old imperial centre.[17] Before the Americans entered the war, the British government negotiated an agreement with the American majors that allowed them to repatriate about $17.5 million, or about a third of their total revenues. Once the Americans entered the war, the agreement was rescinded, but within the British industry discussions continued on the proper measures to protect the long-term structure of the industry. Two factions developed: the first, represented by Rank, promoted the principle of export-oriented production through the development of large vertically integrated British firms; the second, represented by Michael Balcon of Ealing Studios, the trade unions within the film industry, and the left-wing of the Labour party, argued that the development of indigenous production required aggressive legislation to end the monopoly structure of distribution and exhibition. (At one point, the Association of Cinematograph Technicians even suggested the partial nationalization of British theatres as a way of ensuring better access for independently produced pictures). In 1944, as Rank and his supporters gained strength, Balcon and his allies were dropped from the film committee of the Board of Trade. Contrary to what might have been expected, the electoral victory of the Labour party in 1945 did not lead to the immediate adoption of the more interventionist course. Indeed, Labour's new president of the Board of Trade, Sir Stafford Cripps, gave assurances that no new measures would be taken until the Cinematograph Film Act expired in 1948; however, a major currency crisis in the spring of 1947 prompted the British government to take more immediate and drastic measures.

In August, the government announced an ad valorum tax of 75 per cent on all remissible revenues paid to U.S. film companies. The Americans retaliated with a boycott of the British market. Rank, who had opposed the tax, took advantage of the opportunity to call for an increase in British production. British exhibitors, on the other hand, lined up in support of the Americans, now more determined than ever to shut Rank out of their own domestic market. British officials, who had not anticipated such a vicious reaction from the Americans, eventually negotiated an agreement resembling the compromise of 1939. The American firms could repatriate $17 million, and it was hoped that the blocked earnings would be invested in British productions. In 1949 the Labour government established the National Film Finance Corporation, which was given five million pounds to create a loan fund for private producers, while a box-office levy, known as the Eady Plan, created another fund that awarded British producers on the basis of their film's performance at the box office. The measures were not as interventionist as those employed elsewhere on the continent, but they did help to ensure a higher level of private production than otherwise would have obtained.

The Canadian Co-operation Project: Another Branch-Plant Industry?

As Britain, and other European countries, brought forth state policies designed to encourage feature film production, the NFB was fighting for it postwar life. From the floor of the House of Commons, Gordon Fraser, a Conservative MP from Peterborough, fulminated on the NFM's leftist leanings.[18] The *Financial Post*, which must be given full marks for developing an early and full-blown case of cold war paranoia, depicted the NFB as a 'publicly financed playground' for a 'coterie of young Canadians with interests in the glamorous field of the motion picture.'[19] But for young Canadian filmmakers the NFB was not, in the midst of the cold war, the place to be. A film made by Ross McLean's cousin, entitled *The People Between*, got the Board into further trouble with the Liberal cabinet.[20] *The People Between* focused on the civil war in China and it tacitly contradicted the government's foreign policy because it implied recognition of Mao's China. Lester Pearson, as minister of External Affairs, was particularly incensed at the Board's lack of diplomacy, and the film's release was delayed for some time. The experience only reaffirmed that the NFB would have to play it safe in the postwar period; aggressive, creative documentary filmmaking was out, cautious educational filmmaking fully in accord with government policy was in.

No less important, the NFB was also under attack from Canada's private producers, who took advantage of the anti-NFB sentiment to further their own interests. The producers wanted to see the NFB return to its prewar role as a non-producing agency whose sole purpose would now be to coordinate contracts between government departments and private producers. In June 1946, the major production companies, with the exception of Associated Screen News (ASN) founded the Film Producers Association of Canada to represent their interests.[21] It was the first producers' association in Canada, but unlike those that had surfaced in Britain it had little or no interest in developing a strategy for Canadian feature film production.

In an effort to stake out territory that was quite obviously under siege, McLean summarized the intentions of the NFB in *Canadian Business*, shortly after his official appointment as film commissioner. 'Our work is confined essentially to the field of information and adult education on all matters of public interest. We do not consider it part of our function to produce entertainment films. This is a field very properly left to private enterprise, particularly because of the substantial sums of money and risks entailed in feature production.'[22] McLean then noted that he was not aware of any requests for assistance by companies thinking of establishing feature film production, but said that if asked the NFB would be more than willing to rent out its equipment at very reasonable rates. He also noted, perhaps with a little irony given his English-Canadian audience, that *Le Père Chopin* had been a successful risk venture that had, aside from its box-office success, secured a favourable tax ruling with respect to depreciation allowances.

Events within the industry may have proceeded in their typical fashion had it not been for Canada's own serious balance-of-payments crisis. The federal government's plans for postwar reconstruction depended heavily on the revival of its trade surplus, but export levels remained low in the years immediately following the war.[23] Canada's poor trading performance was made worse by dramatic increases in both consumer and capital demand for goods produced in the United States and the net balance of payments skidded sharply into the red. In 1946, there was a net outflow of $266 million. In 1947 the figure rose to an alarming $668 million. As the government prepared its 1947 budget, most observers expected the government to impose temporary controls on a number of imports. By September, it was rumoured that the government was considering some form of restriction on the importation of film and related goods.[24] Trade figures, not a concern over culture, were spurring the government to action.

The film industry had had some previous success in dealing with federal duties. In 1936, when a general tax of five per cent was placed on all remittances sent out of Canada, the American majors were singled out as an exception and paid a tax of only two per cent.[25] In 1941, when the general withholding tax was increased to 15 per cent, the film industry was again singled out for special treatment and given a rate of 10 per cent.[26] Then minister of Finance James Ilsley explained the special treatment by saying that the distribution companies had convinced his department that they made no money in Canada (although in 1940 he himself had noted in the House of Commons that $3.1 million in royalties had been paid out between April and October alone!).[27] On both occasions, the MPDEC's powerful lobby had paid dividends to the major American distributors and helped sustain the tacit common market. It was a sign that any new measures to undermine the status quo were sure to meet with powerful resistance on the part of the major theatrical film interests.

As anticipated, the government's November budget included some significant import restrictions and a number of new import duties. Although American-made film projection and sound equipment were among the goods temporarily restricted, there was no mention of an increase in the withholding tax on royalties paid to American film distributors or of an import quota. One week later, at a press conference held by the minister of Finance, Douglas Abbott, and the minister of Reconstruction, C.D. Howe, the government's strategy emerged. Howe noted that at a conservative estimate $15 million in royalties were being paid out to American film companies; why was it, he wondered, that 'some of these films for which we pay a good many U.S. dollars could not be made and printed in Canada and distributed to other countries?'[28] At the same time, Abbott emphasized that the government was not considering measures to assist the establishment of an independent Canadian feature film industry. As Grierson had counselled, it seems that government officials were trying to induce American producers into establishing a quasi branch-plant feature film industry.

The Film Producers Association of Canada met one week later in Toronto to formulate their response. They praised the initiative and offered 'to pool personnel and equipment for services to those who may wish to start production.'[29] They did not, however, take the next step and outline a program by which, with government assistance, they themselves might begin production of feature films to offset the inflow of American products. Like ASN with its processing lab, these Canadian producers were hoping to tie their companies' futures to the dynamic of Hollywood-initiated productions. For its part, the CMPDA took the government's statement very seriously. After a meeting in Toronto, 'suggestions' were forwarded to New York, where they were to be taken up by the MPAA. Given the various attacks on the American film industry generally underway abroad, there is no doubt that Eric Johnston and his friends were concerned about a possible disruption of business as normal in Canada. Johnston immediately enlisted the support of J.J. Fitzgibbons, president of Famous Players, and struck a committee to look the issue over.

Ross McLean was not about to let this occasion slip by without making his own views known. On 1 December 1947, McLean sent a memo to the minister of National Revenue, J.J. McCann, that endorsed the government's stated intention of encouraging 'the investment of funds by United States owned companies in the production of films in Canada for international distribution.'[30] But McLean also wanted to see the Americans make a clear commitment to distribute more Canadian-made short films in the United States and elsewhere. McLean felt that friendly persuasion would not suffice to ensure compliance. Following events in Europe, McLean had come to the conclusion that a certain amount of legislative coercion was necessary if any arrangement with the American distributors was to bring significant benefit. He recommended that the American companies be 'induced or required to invest a proportion of their yearly Canadian revenues – say $4,000,000 to $5,000,000 – *primarily in producing films in Canada*.'[31] He also had some final words to say on the 'free flow of ideas' doctrine. 'Sooner or later,' McLean explained, 'they are simply going to have to discover the logic of international trading, that it is not and never can be for long a one way traffic. The process of learning has already proved to be a painful one for them.'[32]

The MPAA was developing its own ideas as to how the American film industry might help alleviate the dollar shortage in Canada. A letter from Johnston to Fitzgibbons on 29 January 1948, outlined the basic objectives of what was to become known as the Canadian Co-operation Project:

a) to make a short film explaining Canada's trade-dollar shortage to American and Canadian audiences; b) to increase coverage of Canadian subjects in American newsreels; c) to have short films made about Canada by U.S. film companies; d) to obtain distribution of some NFB films in America; e) to insert some Canadians sequences in U.S. feature films; f) to make a series of radio recordings by U.S. stars extolling the virtues of Canada as a vacation land; g) to distribute fewer 'low-toned' gangster films in Canada; and, h) to appoint a staff man for liaison of the Project.[33]

The letter made no mention of feature film production in Canada, but Johnston and his crew knew full well that some production activities would have to be promised and perhaps carried out. *Canadian Film Weekly* was convinced that an increase in Canadian production was a 'certainty,'[34] and in February Eagle-Lions announced plans for two full-length films to be shot in Calgary at a total cost of $2.5 million.[35] In the House of Commons, C.D. Howe boasted that 'negotiations are going on with the film industry which promise a substantial quid pro quo to offset the substantial drain of dollars.'[36] In response to repeated urgings from Co-operative Commonwealth Federation (CCF) members to take stronger action, Howe explained that the government was not considering 'quotas' or any other disruption of the present distribution system.[37] Finally, Howe made it clear that he expected to see an increase in production activities in Canada and then, for the first time, stated that an increase in tourism could be 'an important by-product' of the final arrangement.[38] M.J. Coldwell, leader of the CCF, was unimpressed. Coldwell noted that, among others, Britain, France, Sweden, and Norway had taken legislative steps to ensure domestic production. Coldwell did not want 'Hollywood producing our history.' Instead he suggested that 'a public authority similar to the radio corporation [CBC] do something in the way of presenting full-length films of Canadian life.'[39] Howe did not bother to respond, and the suggestion fell on deaf ears. Unlike the countries Coldwell mentioned, there was no organized group within the Canadian film industry that vigorously supported this option.

The MPAA's lobbyists moved quickly to consolidate the deal. Over lunch at Ottawa's Château Laurier Hotel, Fitzgibbons, Francis Harmon (vice-president of the MPAA), Taylor Mills (the MPAA's New York coordinator), and Blake Owensmith (who was to oversee the insertion of Canadian sequences in Hollywood-produced films) met with Abbott, Pearson, Howe, McCann, and representatives of the Bank of Canada. The Americans effectively presented Canadian officials with a fait accompli. Harmon informed the gathering that more Canadian shorts, newsreel footage, and scenic backgrounds were already being used by the major American companies. He also announced plans for possible production in Canada. One of the projects, 20th Century–Fox' *Canadian Pacific*, had been in the works for quite some time, but it was now being touted as 'a cornerstone of the Canadian Co-operation Project.'[40]

While most government officials expressed satisfaction with the Project's development, Ross McLean still had his reservations. In May, McLean wrote to Harmon in New York, complaining 'that while there is a great deal of good will evident, this good will has not so far been translated into concrete results or plans.'[41] McLean aired his contempt for Hollywood's tendency to focus on the 'cops and robbers motif' when it depicted Canada. He also pointed out that the distribution of Canadian shorts so far achieved has been 'anything but encouraging.'[42] McLean was the only thorn left to contend with, but he was already in a weakened position because of the NFB's postwar fall from grace. Although he was the government's film commissioner, he was not involved first hand in the negotiations. J.J. McCann, the minister to whom he was responsible, seemed to hold all of Grierson's old friends in contempt.

The deal was given its final vote of confidence after the MPAA held a special luncheon for Donald Gordon, deputy governor of the Bank of Canada and the man who presided over the country's currency flows. Gordon came away with no reservations. He felt that through the project the government of Canada was to receive 'service beyond valuation by any conceivable commercial criteria and one which any government or country would consider itself fortunate to obtain.'[43] In a letter to Howe, Gordon outlined the plan's objectives and tried to establish a priority sequence for the government. First, there was the possibility of production in Canada and the distribution of more Canadian material in the United States. Gordon felt that these activities might bring in between three to six million dollars over the next 18 months. More important was the promotion of tourist traffic in Canada and the presentation of general information about Canada to the American public. Together these latter objectives could 'produce immediate cash result considerably in excess of those possible through new production in Canada, purchase of Canadian film product, etc.'[44] Aside from McLean, government officials were becoming convinced that a possible increase in tourism from the United States was enough to justify acceptance of the project. The MPAA had succeeded in downplaying the need to begin large-scale production activities in Canada. Gordon had given the MPAA's figures the Bank of Canada's stamp of approval. Finally, Gordon pointed out that there still 'appears to be a divergence of views among agencies of government as to the aims that should be pursued.'[45] McLean and the NFB were singled out as having 'reservations' – they would have to be whipped into line.

Gordon praised the Project as an example of 'imaginative spirit, rather than legal restriction, as well as an outstanding example of good neighbourliness.'[46] In the House, Howe used the example of the Project to put a positive face on the Liberal government's Emergency Exchange Conservation Act, the umbrella bill designed to deal with the currency crisis. Howe, however, still harboured the assumption that there would be a significant increase in production activities in Canada. The notion seems to have been genuinely held by Howe, and it was certainly in line with the government's macro-economic policy direction.

As David Wolfe has cogently argued, the Liberal government (and Howe in particular) was eager to encourage direct American investment in Canadian manufacturing. Indeed, Wolfe suggests that the Exchange Conservation Act made the building of branch plants the 'government's explicit goal.'[47] Seen from a broader perspective, the Canadian Co-operation Project can be quite conveniently situated within the overall effort to attract direct American investment to Canada in the immediate postwar period. Moreover, the Canadian government strongly supported the principle of tariff reduction at the first round of the GATT negotiations. Thus, coercive or discriminatory measures, such as quotas or subsidies for private Canadian film production, would have been anathema to the overall macro-economic strategy of the Canadian state. Hollywood had, in a sense, made an offer that Canadian officials, *given their own economic policy preferences*, could not refuse. What was perhaps even more important is that no one within the private Canadian film industry had proposed a better scheme to increase production activities.

Although a number of commentators have described the Project as a clear case of Hollywood imperialism and Canadian government sell-out, the facts suggest a more tempered explanation. Hollywood, not surprisingly, responded to the Canadian state's economic discomfort in 1947 with a program that involved as little commitment as possible. The Canadian state, in consideration of its own macro-economic policy concerns, and not unaware of the absence of any independent initiative from the Canadian film industry, took what it could get. Protective legislation and subsidies to private production toward nationalist-inspired ends do not spring *ex nihilo* from the minds of bureaucrats or politicians; rather, they emerge from a political conjuncture that places these policy options squarely on the political agenda. In this respect, the Canadian Co-operation Project was a product of its time.

The Project was administered by Archibald Newman, with the help of Don Henshaw of the MacLaren Advertising Agency, which would later become one of the Liberal party's chief publicity firms. Newman's reports, of which only a few remain, were masterstrokes of public relations: he made a point of listing every reference to Canada made in Hollywood films, and always listed the films that were scheduled or planned for production in Canada in the upcoming season. As Pierre Berton chronicles, the films and the references remained as inane as ever – it was a very unreal Canada that found its way onto the theatrical screen.[48] Tourism figures do show an increase in American visitors to Canada, but the figures are far lower than the increase in Canadian tourists to the United States.[49] American films were still doing what they did best – selling the United States to the world. The MPAA continued the project until 1957, when it was quietly put to rest.

As the project was getting off the ground, there was a brief flurry of activity around the possibility of activating Ontario's dormant exhibition quota. The impetus came from a somewhat surprising source, Odeon Theatres. Odeon's president, J. Earl Lawson, wanted the Ontario government to institute a quota of at least 10 per cent to support the exhibition of British Empire films. It was clear, however, that Odeon was acting as a representative of Rank's production interests; its actions had nothing to do with support for indigenous feature film production.[50] In January 1951, the MPAA's liaison officer for the Co-operation Project, Archibald Newman, presumptuously spoke for the federal government, stating flatly that 'no steps will be taken to discriminate against the films of any nation.'[51] O.J. Silverthorne, head of the Ontario Censor Board, who had initially supported the idea of a British quota, reversed his position in mid-February. Silverthorne felt that the scheme was bound to fail if the quota was fixed in only one province, and he saw no possibility of nation-wide agreement on protective measures.[52]

Hollywood had managed to come through the postwar conjuncture with Canada still firmly entrenched as part of its 'domestic market.' Indeed, with theatre divestiture and the end of block-booking in the United States, Canada had come to represent the one last bastion of Hollywood's halcyon days. The MPAA's annual report of 1952 noted that Canada's percentage of Hollywood's domestic market had gone from 4 per cent in 1948 to 10 per cent in 1951. With $18.5 million in remittances, Eric Johnston was able to report that 'outside the U.S. itself, Canada ranks as the second largest market in the world for Hollywood films.'[53] Seventy-five per cent of the films shown in Canada were of American origin, films of British origin comprised 20 per cent, while the paltry remainder were made up of films from western Europe. As Hye Bossin of *Canadian Film Weekly* wryly remarked: 'Canadian film folk will be happy to hear how helpful they have been to Hollywood in such troublesome times.'[54]

Making the Massey Report

As the leadership of the Liberal party passed from King to St. Laurent in 1948, a number of related issues demanded urgent attention. In the field of radio broadcasting, the regulatory structure was under attack from both private broadcasters and Conservative MPs, who considered it inappropriate that the CBC should have regulatory control over the activities of private stations; moreover, the licence fee of $2.50 on radios no longer provided sufficient funds for the operation of the public broadcasting system. There was also the newer problem of the introduction of television: would the system replicate the structure of radio broadcasting, or were different measures necessary? The government also faced a crisis over university funding. In the face of opposition from Quebec Premier Maurice Duplessis, the federal Liberals wanted an authoritative answer to the question of whether its government could help finance postsecondary education.

The idea for a Royal Commission to deal both with these issues and the question of government support to the arts and letters more generally, was first proposed by the Canadian University Liberal Foundation at the party's convention in August.[55] Brooke Claxton supported the proposal and, with the help of Lester Pearson, convinced St. Laurent that a Royal Commission would greatly assist the Liberal party's policy considerations. Claxton had a specific chairperson in mind for the Commission: Vincent Massey, who was still High Commissioner for Canada in London. Massey accepted the position in early January and the government announced the appointment of the Royal Commission on National Development in the Arts, Letters and Sciences in early April. Massey's co-chair was to be the Most Reverend Georges-Henri Lévesque, dean of the Faculty of Social Sciences at Laval University.[56]

The Commission's work was to proceed from the assumption that the state had an important role to play in the development of a national culture. '[It] is in the national interest to give encouragement to institutions which express national feeling, promote common understanding and add to the variety and richness of Canadian life, rural as well as urban,' read its terms of reference.[57] The commissioners were instructed to examine the full range of state agencies and activities that contributed to these ends, and make recommendations for 'their most effective conduct in the national interest.'[58] It was to be the first full-scale review of Canadian cultural policy undertaken by a Royal Commission, and in that sense alone it represented something of a watershed in the history of Canadian cultural policy. As Vincent Massey later wrote: 'We had to ask ourselves how the State can promote the welfare of our cultural resources without creating an artificial, hot-house atmosphere.'[59] This was one of the central dilemmas the Commission faced: how to provide state support for cultural activities, without unduly hampering the operation of the market. The other was how to ensure that Canadians were exposed to the right kind of culture – refined, enlightened, and uplifting.

Both the commercial film industry and the NFB and its supporters were immediately aware that the Commission represented a new institutional forum for the representation of their interests. Its conclusions would obviously bear on the future structure of the film industry in Canada. In May, the private industry established the Canadian Motion Picture Industry Council to promote the industry's interests and enhance its public image. By October, the Council had set up a committee to monitor the progress of the Commission and consider the drafting of its own brief. Chaired by Jack Chisholm of Associated Screen News, the committee was instructed to study the briefs of the NFB, CBC, and their supporters 'as they may affect free enterprise in general, and in particular the Canadian production, distribution, and exhibition of motion pictures and television.'[60]

The NFB itself was in an unenviable position. Suspicion of subversive activities at the Film Board had reached new levels by the spring of 1949. At a board of directors meeting in April, it was revealed that the government had declared the NFB to be a 'vulnerable agency' and McLean was told to assist the Royal Canadian Mounted Police in a screening process of NFB personnel.[61] Not surprisingly, morale at the Board was at an all-time low. Adding insult to injury, the Department of National Defence had decided to contract its films from private producers, whose own workers had received security clearance.

Against this background of suspicion and uncertainty, the NFB submitted its brief to the Royal Commission in July. The brief opened with a Grierson-like description of its perceived role. 'The prime duty of a government information agency in a democracy,' it read, 'is to explain and illuminate, under parliament, the common objective of the people. Its function is to stimulate and strengthen the process of representative government, to reinforce a sense of commonality, and to emphasize not only the privileges but the responsibilities of a free society.'[62] In order that the NFB could continue to carry out its mandate in a responsible and efficient manner, the brief requested that the Film Board be granted a budgetary increase to improve production activities and to increase its own distribution network. The Board also recommended the construction of a centralized building to replace the motley array of ten buildings on John Street that still served as its home. It was also time, the brief argued, to grant the Board corporate status, to make it a Crown corporation with greater independence from day-to-day ministerial control.[63] Close affiliation with government officials may have served the purposes of wartime propaganda, but it was now more appropriate to recognize the arm's-length principle as the proper basis for the relationship between the Board and the state. Finally, the NFB signalled its desire to be an integral part of Canadian television broadcasting. The Board was 'ready to go'; it wanted the mandate to become a major producer of Canadian television programs for distribution both at home and abroad.[64]

The NFB may have been under considerable strain, but McLean and his officials were not about to miss this opportunity to push their case. When asked by one of the commissioners whether the NFB was looking for entertainment value or educational value in its productions, McLean was not timid in his response: 'We feel we are not in a position to impose our interpretation of things particularly on people. Nevertheless, we are bound in making a film to have a point of view, and if it happens sometimes that we get a considerable number of people in the country who disagree with that point of view, we do not necessarily feel that it endangers the harmony among groups if they argue that point and we then give a production of a film on a similar thesis at a later date. I think we are primarily interested in the educational aspect and not primarily in the entertainment aspect.'[65]

The NFB's brief was supported, its work praised and defended, by a number of representations received by the Commission. Although NFB field staff had been cut by 40 per cent following the war, non-theatrical distribution of NFB films had grown steadily.[66] Thanks mostly to the growth of film councils and NFB libraries, over one million Canadians a month were watching NFB films in non-theatrical venues. There were now over 250 film councils nation-wide, with links to over 6,000 local organizations. As a report on the structure of non-theatrical film distribution concluded: 'The provision of film service and the development of film use has been a cooperative effort to a greater extent than is the case of any other medium or service to the public.'[67] The Trades and Labour Congress, the Canadian Federation of Agriculture, the Canadian Association for Adult Education, the Canadian Council for Reconstruction through UNESCO, the Community Planning Association of Canada, the Public Affairs Institute, and 55 other organizations that appeared before the Massey Commission commended the NFB on its work and argued for an increase in production.[68] Briefs from various film councils and the National Film Society also wholeheartedly endorsed the activities of the NFB. The Film Board now had a healthy number of public allies. Massey himself was already on record as saying that the Board's work had helped 'to promote national unity' through films of 'recognized excellence.'[69] Still the briefs all maintained a clear distinction between films for the purpose of education and films for the purpose of entertainment. Not one of them went on to suggest the need for domestic production of feature-length 'entertainment' films. Each, in its own way, implicitly accepted what Massey himself had earlier concluded: 'The production of films – that is, films for the purpose of entertainment – prospers best in the field of free enterprise. In Canada we are largely dependent in the commercial cinema on films from the United States or Great Britain, and for the most part we must take what is sent us.'[70]

The groundswell of support for the NFB worried private Canadian production companies and film laboratories. In terms of government contracts, Canadian producers had the most to lose, or rather would gain the least, from a continuation and extension of the Board's activities. Within the Motion Picture Industry Council they were most vocal in calling for an aggressive, united opposition to the mounting NFB support. At first, the producers wanted the Council to present a brief representing the industry as a whole, but major exhibitors and distributors, sensing the possibility of a public backlash, decided against such a show of strength. Canadian producers, whose organization had been renamed the Association of Motion Picture Producers and Laboratories of Canada (AMPPLC), were left to present a brief on their own.

The AMPPLC went before the Commission in April 1950. It offered, in its own words, a 'practical Canadian standpoint' on the question of the 'propriety of the engagement of government in the field of dissemination of information, news and culture'[71] The AMPPLC raised the spectre of a 'government monopoly' in the production of information and culture that worked against the creation of a vibrant private film production sector. Because it paid no taxes, and was exempt from import duties on film equipment and supplies, the NFB represented unfair competition. The AMPPLC took the NFB's own request for corporate status as a sign of its 'expansionist, monopolistic psychology.'[72] The brief claimed that the cultural integrity of the nation could only be maintained through the development of a private sector committed to cultural production, and that unless members of the AMPPLC received a far greater share of government contracts they would be unable to develop into major forces of cultural production. Accordingly, the NFB should be 'limited to the production of cultural, informational and educational films of a non-departmental and non-commercial character'; private producers would take up the bulk of government-sponsored productions as a base from which to expand.[73]

The AMPPLC also submitted a short supplementary brief on the possibilities of feature film production in Canada. It pointed out that this was a 'pioneer-like activity,' made especially difficult by the risk-averse nature of the country's financial community and the high import duties on film equipment.[74] The brief did mention that a government-sponsored loan fund would be of considerable assistance to private producers, but the request was not strongly defended or explored in any detail. At the hearings on the AMPPLC brief, Guy Roberge, who was later to head the NFB and to provide in the late 1950s much of the initiative for a loan fund, asked the Association to expand on this request. Did they want to see a tax of between 15 to 20 per cent imposed on theatres with the funds redirected to Canadian producers, asked Roberge? No comment, was the producers reply: they had not envisioned or considered this question. When asked further whether they wanted to see an exhibition quota, the producers replied that quotas had not been very successful elsewhere and were not therefore desirable.[75] It seems clear that the AMPPLC was not fully committed to the idea of a state-initiated program to assist private-sector feature film production (similar, say, to the National Film Finance Corporation recently established in Britain). The producers did want government funds, but they wanted them in the form of contracts for government productions. Their main goal was still to curtail the production activities of the NFB.

A Reprieve for the NFB

As the AMPPLC was developing its brief to the Royal Commission, the *Financial Post* renewed its attack on the Film Board. On 19 November 1949, a feature article disclosed the fact that the Film Board had been named a vulnerable agency, that the Department of National Defence was no longer using its services, and that a security investigation was already under way. 'Is the Film Board a leftist propaganda machine?', the article asked.[76] It also accused the NFB of 'Hollywood ambitions,' making the absurd and unsubstantiated argument that its request for corporate status was a veiled attempt to take over the lion's share of film production within the country as a whole.

Brooke Claxton, then minister of National Defence, admitted in the House that his department was no longer using the services of the Film Board and that a security screening was under way.[77] In fact McLean had already been furnished with a list of 'suspects' and had been asked by the RCMP to dismiss the 'undesirables.' To his credit, McLean refused to fire anyone until a clear case of disloyalty could be proved. McLean's contract was up for renewal in December, and the government took the opportunity to rid itself of this rather uncooperative character. W. Arthur Irwin, who was editor of *Maclean's*, was appointed the new film commissioner in January 1950. He took the job with the assurance that, one way or another, the government was going to maintain the Film Board.[78] But, for many at the Board, Irwin's replacement of McLean was another set-back – the last of Grierson's original allies was gone.

The St. Laurent government was not about to let the Film Board become an issue it could not control. In December 1949, Robert Winters, the minister in charge of the Film Board stated that the NFB's brief to the Royal Commission did not reflect government policy and that the management consultant firm of Woods Gordon had been retained to re-evaluate the functions of the Board.[79] As the report was being prepared, Irwin successfully minimized the effects of the purge at the NFB. In the end, 3 of the 36 suspects were discharged, and the matter began to die down.[80]

Presented to Winters in March 1950, the Woods Gordon Report probably surprised many people. On the whole, the Report commended the Film Board's activities and suggested that its major administrative problems were the result of limitations in its initial legislation, which did not anticipate the Board's growth. Woods Gordon recommended that the Film Board be expanded, that its organization be streamlined, and that both a new building and corporate status would help facilitate these ends. Winters, who had never been a strong supporter of the Film Board, may not have liked the conclusions reached, but the recommendations become the substance for new legislation introduced in the House in the June.[81]

The Film Board became a full-fledged Crown corporation and Irwin set about the task of pushing the government to make good on its promise of new, centralized facilities. Irwin also tried to bring the Film Board closer in line with cold war sentiment. In late 1950 he announced a new series of films, entitled the *Freedom Speaks* Programme, to 'counter communist propaganda with a positive statement in effective dramatic form of the values which we as a free people believe to be basic to democratic society.'[82] In 1952, an all-party committee of the House announced that it was 'impressed' and 'gratified' by the Film Board's work.[83] The Committee had been treated to a screening of the Film Board's *Royal Journey*, a patriotic feature-length documentary about Queen Elizabeth's recent visit to Canada. *Royal Journey* was a hit with audiences as well. It played in over 1,200 theatres and was seen by over two million Canadians.[84] In 1952, the NFB also collected its first Academy Award for Norman McLaren's live-action animation entitled *Neighbours*, which was, and remains, a brilliant piece of anti-war and anti–cold war sentiment. *Neighbours* and *Royal Journey* had helped to save the NFB from its political foes. Plans for a new building were finalized with the approval of the all-party committee. Construction began in Montreal on Côte de Liesse Road in 1953.

The Massey Report: Cultural Conservatism Confronts the American Menace

The Massey Report released its findings in June 1951 and immediately became the benchmark for discussions on Canadian cultural policy. The Commission's general justification for state-sponsored cultural development was that the integrity and vitality of Canada as a nation depended heavily on its cultural development. 'Physical links are essential to the unifying process but true unity belongs to the realm of ideas. It is a matter for men's minds and hearts.' In the context of the Korean War and general escalation of the cold war, the Commission questioned whether a military strategy alone would suffice: 'If we as a nation are concerned with the problem of defence, what, we may ask ourselves, are we defending? We are defending civilization, our share of it, our contribution to it,' came the response.[85] In order to flourish as a nation, Canadians would have to restore the 'balance between the attention we pay to material achievements and to the other less tangible but more enduring parts of our civilization.'[86]

From the Commission's perspective, the development of a national culture faced three basic obstacles. The first two were internal: 'Canada has a small and scattered population in a vast area,' wrote the Commission.[87] Geography itself made the problem of unity a daunting task. Building a railway across the country to provide the physical link of nationhood was difficult enough; how much harder would it be to establish cultural bonds of similar fortitude? These two obstacles alone were quite sufficient, but the Commission recognized a third problem that came, in the first instance, from an external source: Canadians had developed what it termed an 'easy dependence on a huge and generous neighbour.'[88] In the various sectors of 'mass' culture the United States enveloped Canada like a cloud. The American invasion by film, radio and periodical is formidable,' wrote the Commission.[89] The Massey Report graciously noted the contributions of the Carnegie and Rockefeller Foundations to the arts in Canada, but it was far more concerned with the negative consequences of imported American mass culture. The Commission quoted favourably a background study done by George Grant, one of Canada's leading conservative critics of modern culture. According to Grant: 'Our society is being challenged to defend itself against a barbaric empire which puts its faith in salvation by the machine.'[90] In the Commission's own words, 'a vast and disproportionate amount of material coming from a single alien source may stifle rather than stimulate our own creative effort ... We are now spending millions to maintain a national independence which would be nothing but an empty shell without a vigorous and distinctive cultural life ... We must not be blind ... to the very present danger of permanent dependence.'[91]

But what exactly did the Report mean by the term 'culture'? 'Culture,' it concluded, 'is that part of education which enriches the mind and refines the taste. It is the development of the intelligence through the arts, letters and sciences.'[92] This view of culture served more as a model for development than a definition of the field. 'Culture' was to be equated with an enlightened state of personal and national development; in the context of the new 'mass' media, 'culture' was something that had to be preserved and protected from the ravages of commercialization. Again and again, the Report spoke of the pernicious effects that 'mass' commercialized culture had on the process of national development. It is in this respect particularly that the influences of American culture, which in both radio and television had succumbed totally to the rule of the marketplace, had to be checked. The Massey Report thus worked with a classic distinction between 'high' culture, which was valued highly in terms of its educational and metaphysical dimensions, and 'low' culture, which was at best mere entertainment and at worst the debilitating instrument of an emerging 'mass' society.

It is with such a distinction in place that the Royal Commission turned to the question of films in Canada and indicted the omnipresence of American movies. 'Hollywood refashions us in its own image,' the Report read. 'For general film entertainment, Canadians want commercial features; and in this field there is practically nothing produced in Canada. Promising developments in feature films Canadian in character are taking place in Quebec; but English-speaking audiences are still exposed to strange Hollywood versions of a Canada they never thought or wished to see.'[93] The Commission made a passing reference to the Canadian Co-operation Project. It hoped that if films were made in Canada they would 'not grossly falsify Canadian life or Canadian history' – the Commissioners were either not regular movie-goers or were trying not to offend.[94] In any case, they chose to ignore the criticism levelled against the Project by one of their special studies.[95] Similarly, the Report offered no discussion of monopoly practices within the feature film industry, and no analysis of its daily economic practices. These were questions obviously too mechanical for a Commission that was more concerned with the intangible or spiritual aspects of civilization. On the other hand, the NFB was highly praised for its documentary tradition. Because its productions were 'intended to reproduce "real" rather than synthetic situations and to evoke an awareness of life, rather than to provide an escape from it,' the Film Board's activities served to promote the goals of national education and cultural enrichment.[96] The Report could not agree with the private producers who wanted the Film Board's work curtailed; rather, it endorsed the position of those organizations who 'greatly fear the effects of commercialization and are convinced that the truly and typically Canadian films they want can be given them only by the Film Board.'[97]

The Commission recommended that funding to the NFB be increased, so that both production and distribution could be improved. It also expressed a desire to see the Film Board act as coordinator, with the CBC, in the production of films for television. 'Only a national organization,' it concluded, 'protects the nation from excessive commercialization and Americanization.'[98] But in the terms of the commercial sector, the Report faced a conundrum from which it could not escape. Hollywood films were clearly antithetical to Canadian cultural development, yet no protective measures were considered. Private producers had, however meekly, suggested a loan fund to produce feature films, yet the Report contained no mention of such a scheme. Instead, the Report expressed a desire to see more private production of documentaries, more films that fell in line with its conception of proper cultural pursuits. Canadian documentaries alone would have to stem the Hollywood menace.

The immediate limitations of the Report should now be apparent. The Massey Report wanted to see the state develop mechanisms to facilitate cultural production that would be based on non-commercial criteria. 'Low' culture had to be countered with 'high' culture; the effects of the market had to be countered by state policies designed to promote traditional and élite forms of cultural practice. The commercialization of cultural production was deleterious but it was also inevitable. While the state could be used to facilitate non-market production, it could not interfere directly with the marketplace for commercialized culture. Quotas or discriminatory levies to assist private production were steering mechanisms the Commission could simply not endorse. Canada's private industry was on its own. The Massey Report had aimed a sharp critique at Hollywood's pervasive presence in Canada, but it could offer no substantive measures to change the status quo.

In 1953, the Motion Picture Association of America's report on the Canadian Co-operation Project declared that Canada 'has been one of the bright spots in the world for American motion pictures.'[99] Given Hollywood's penchant for hyperbole, this was something of an understatement. Neither the establishment of the NFB nor the recommendations of the Massey Report effectively challenged Hollywood's presence on Canadian screens. The private film industry in Canada generally favoured, even benefited, from the status quo. The major complaint of Canada's production companies and laboratories was not directed toward the prevalence of American films in Canada (in fact the laboratories were more than happy with the work they received making prints of American films), but toward the NFB and its near monopoly on films sponsored by the federal government. The NFB survived this challenge, but at the outset of the cold war the Board had been seriously weakened when it was declared a 'vulnerable agency.' Even without these pressures, it is not altogether clear that the NFB would have become a threat to Hollywood's position in Canada; as we have seen, John Grierson's own approach to filmmaking led the Film Board away from theatrical feature film production. Concerned interest groups either implicitly or explicitly shared Grierson's and Massey's perspective. The dynamics of Canada's feature film industry both reflected and helped shape

Canada's postwar commitment to continentalism and American-led Atlanticism. As Leo Panitch has written, Canada had 'exchanged the "shadowy and unreal" independence offered within the British Empire for the "shadowy and unreal" independence tolerated by the Americans.'[100] Hollywood's presence in Canada had become a fine example of American economic and cultural hegemony in the postwar period.

5   A Change of Heart

Introduction

We shall have a production industry in Canada, a good and thriving one, if our government ever gets around to extending a helping hand. We shall make good and marketable films.
— Nat Taylor[1]

In March of Canada's centennial year, the federal government passed the Canadian Film Development Corporation Act. With a 'miserable ten million dollars,' as Secretary of State Judy LaMarsh put it at the time, the CFDC was given a mandate 'to foster and promote the development of a feature film industry in Canada' through the provision of loans, advice, and awards to private producers and filmmakers. In the history of the Canadian film industry the formation of the CFDC was quite obviously a watershed event. After more than 40 years of toiling in the margins, Canadians finally entered the business of feature film production. Sporadic production of feature films, in both the private sector and the NFB, had been in evidence since the early 1960s, but both industry representatives and government officials hoped that state intervention would provide a more conducive environment for the regular production of private-sector Canadian feature films. How had it come to pass? What had changed within the contours of the industry itself to make feature film production both desirable and apparently viable? Why did the position of the state change from one of neglect to one of support? What forms of intervention would be considered? How far-reaching would be the measures finally introduced?

Until now the focus of our attention has been on Canada's truncated, or 'feature-less,' film industry. I have argued that the major explanatory factors for the lack of feature film production in Canada lie within the interactive dynamics of the Canadian film industry, Canadian state, and Canadian society as a whole. Hollywood's influence cannot be, and has not been, underestimated, but earlier chapters have shown that the structure of cultural dependency is ultimately mediated and shaped by forces indigenous to Canada. A general lack of interest in feature filmmaking on the part of Canadians working within the film industry – whether exhibitors, producers, or government film commissioners – and a pervasive cultural conservatism that regarded feature films as at best frivolous and at worst culturally deleterious ensured that the development of an indigenous feature film industry would be kept off the political agenda. Moreover, the willing embrace of continentalism by Canadian capital and the Canadian state throughout this period meant that *if* a coherent challenge to Hollywood's dominance had arisen it would have come up against serious opposition from the dominant political and economic forces in Canada. The Hollywood majors and their Canadian allies took what they could get and worked to keep it. They were allowed to take a lot.

Through the late fifties and early sixties a number of changes within Canada created a climate more conducive to the emergence of government support for a feature film industry. Within the industry, various individuals and organizations began to argue more concretely for measures to promote feature film production. From within the NFB, Guy Roberge, who became government film commissioner in 1957, started the research that led to the government's acceptance in principle of a fund to assist private production of feature films in 1964. In part a personal crusade, Roberge's initiatives were also a response to the growing sense of frustration being expressed by many of the Board's filmmakers. Criticism over the administrative and financial constraints imposed by the government agency went hand in hand with the argument that the opportunities for filmmaking, and especially feature filmmaking, had to be expanded. It was maintained that the demand could only be met through an expanded private production sector, developed and stabilized through state support mechanisms. In 1963, French-Canadian filmmakers within the Board joined forces with those already working outside its structure to form the Association professionnelle des cinéastes (APC). One of its fundamental goals was state support for private feature film production. In English Canada, the AMPPLC moved hesitantly toward a similar position. Other industry organizations, most notably the Directors' Guild of Canada (DGC), also began to prod the state into action. Most important, the principle of state-supported feature film production also came to be endorsed by Nat Taylor, whose long-proved acumen in the film business and solid connections with the major interests in both exhibition and distribution made him the dominant sage of Canada's private film industry. Taylor's carefully reasoned endorsement of feature film production in Canada

– his oft-quoted phrase that 'Canada must export the fruits of its talent, not its talent' – lent credibility to the aspirations of the filmmakers themselves, a credibility they might otherwise have lacked. Yet it would be wrong to suggest that pressure from the industry had grown to the point where the state had little choice but to act. There was still much dissension within the industry, and little agreement on specifics. In fact, the most vocal proponents of the plan, the APC and DGC, did not emerge as effective lobby groups until after the state had begun to explore its options.

The emergence within the film industry of a broadly based, if still rather disorganized, movement for state support to private production was complemented by more general changes in Canada's political climate. The tightly knit, almost cosy, bonds of continentalism were beginning to show signs of wear by the 1960s. Although the 'nationalist movement' in English Canada did not emerge as even a semi-organized political entity until the late 1960s, the penetration of American culture and American capital had become issues of some concern by the early part of the decade. Fissures began to appear as early as 1957 with the publication of Walter Gordon's Royal Commission on Canada's Economic Prospects, which warned of the potential loss of sovereignty, both economic and political, entailed by high levels of direct foreign investment in Canada's high-technology and resource industries. To be sure, it would be a gross exaggeration to speak of an open break with continentalism during the 1960s. The practice of 'quiet diplomacy,' of airing bilateral differences calmy and privately, was still a prominent feature of this decade.[2] But differences there were, and as the decade progressed it became increasingly clear that the Canadian state was trying to renegotiate the terms of the postwar arrangement with the United States. At another level, the 1960s was also characterized by the federal government's growing commitment to the image of a 'positive state,' of a state that would assume greater responsibilities in both economic and social management. The Liberal governments of Lester Pearson introduced significant changes to the welfare state, with important implications for the administration of Canadian cultural policy.

The commitment to an expanded state and the emergence of a still very unrefined English-Canadian nationalism were both accompanied and, in part, fostered by a much more focused set of socio-political events: the emergence of the Quiet Revolution in Quebec, an era characterized by vast social and institutional changes in which the secularization of education, the extension of social services, the nationalization of electric power utilities, and an emphasis on French as the proper language of social interaction, were bound up with a desire to protect and rejuvenate the culture of Quebec as a province with national aspirations. Early on, the provincial Liberal government served notice that the cultural component of the Quiet Revolution was to be of prime symbolic importance. The first plank in the Quebec Liberal party's election platform of 1960 was the establishment of a Department of Cultural Affairs. As William Coleman so cogently argues, while the economic thrust of the Quiet Revolution was to 'opt in,' to bring Quebec closer in line with the structures of North America's advanced capitalist economy, the political and cultural emphasis of the Quiet Revolution was to 'opt out,' to establish Quebec as a distinct nation with a provincial government, which in one way or another would possess greater autonomy either inside or outside of Canada's federal system.[3]

For our purposes, this dramatic alteration of Canada's political matrix had two basic effects: on the one hand, more and more French Canadians became sensitive to the need for a state-directed process of cultural development (and while some began to look exclusively to the Quebec government as the only legitimate source of assistance, others continued to focus their now heightened sense of urgency on both levels of the Canadian state); on the other hand, the events taking place within Quebec influenced the political agenda of English Canada, and most especially the federal government, in the sense that cultural issues were brought to the centre of those policies deemed vital to the 'national interest.' The very political survival of the nation came to be identified with the search for a more highly developed sense of Canadian cultural identity. For representatives of the federal government the issue was partly one of survival as the pre-eminent institutional force in the Canadian state system. The federal government itself, qua institution, had an interest in expanding the symbols of nationhood. Support for a feature film industry would be just one facet of a renewed and more urgent attempt to maintain and secure the cohesion of the Canadian state and Canadian society.

None of this is meant to suggest that in establishing the CFDC the state was acting on its own. At the most general level, the higher priority accorded cultural issues in the late 1960s was a function of a broadening political consensus that the cultural industries deserved greater public support. Even if it can be rightly said that the federal government had its *own* interest in expanding its presence in the cultural field, it would be as a general response to events in Quebec and involve an attempt to build national institutions and cultural agencies designed to promote integration and maintain the federal government's pre-eminence in issues deemed vital to the nation as a whole. But discrete public policies deal in specifics, and here the government was not operating on its own. Once the decision had been made to intervene and support Canadian feature film production, the various options and private interests had to be weighed and measured in an effort to develop a 'credible' and 'appropriate' course of action. Would there be a box-office quota? A levy? Restrictions on the outflow of capital to the American majors? Whether visible or not, the various forces within the film industry bore heavily on the policy-making process.

Signs of Life: Growth in Canada's Private Film Industry

On 27 April 1949, at the Little Elgin Theatre in Ottawa, 400 guests attended the first annual Canadian Film Awards.[4] *The Loon's Necklace*, Crawley Films' innovative and haunting theatrical short based on a West Coast native legend, was named film of the year. The only full-length feature film produced in Canada that year, Paul L'Anglais' melodramatic *Un Homme et son péché*, was given a special jury award for its artistic and technical qualities. Norman McLaren was presented with a similar award for his pathbreaking work in the field of animation. Organized under the auspices of the Canadian Association for Adult Education, the awards ceremonies certainly displayed little evidence of the glamour and glitz characteristic of Hollywood's annual Academy Awards bash. The emphasis on non-theatrical documentary and theatrical-short award categories clearly reflected the limits (and strengths) of Canada's film production.

Throughout the fifties the awards were dominated by NFB productions, with Crawley Films of Ottawa being the only consistent winner of major awards among private producers. In 1952, the NFB's *Royal Journey* won the award for best theatrical feature, and in 1955, *The Stratford Adventure* was accorded the same honour. While both of these films were given wide theatrical distribution, they were both documentaries with running times of less than one hour each. *Tit-Coq*, a L'Anglais production of Gratien Gélinas' stage play, won the award for best feature film in 1953 – the last award given to a full-length feature film until 1964.

Hollywood's Dorothy Lamour graced the ceremony at which *Tit-Coq* received its award. Two years earlier, Mary Pickford, Canadian-born 'sweetheart' of the silent screen, had been the honoured guest of the evening. Even as Canadian filmmakers honoured themselves, Hollywood's presence was never far removed. Indeed throughout the fifties, the Motion Picture Association of America continued to wax eloquent over the success of the Canadian Co-operation Project. In 1956, the MPAA's annual report concluded: 'Now beginning its ninth year, the Canadian Co-operation Project is a dramatic example of the mutual cooperation and understanding as opposed to restrictions and retaliatory measures in international trade.' In the same year *Film Daily Year Book* reported that remittances from Canada to the United States had topped $24 million, the highest total foreign earnings for the Hollywood majors

(British receipts totalled \$50 million, but \$28 million was blocked for reinvestment).[5] Hollywood was at home in Canada.

Elsewhere the American film industry was undergoing a period of instability and declining profits. In Europe especially, protective measures and currency restrictions had taken their toll on an industry that relied heavily on receipts from exports. In response the American majors adjusted their corporate strategies. Blocked currency was used to shoot 'exotic' location films. The U.S. majors also learned to take advantage of European subsidies designed to promote national production. By 1965, for example, American subsidiaries in Great Britain were estimated to have received nearly 80 per cent of the British production fund, leading one British producer to conclude: 'We have a thriving film production industry in this country which is virtually owned lock, stock, and barrel by Hollywood.' Between 1967 and 1968, American funds constituted close to 90 per cent of the total investment in 'British' productions.[6]

In the United States, where the antitrust decrees had led to divestment and corporate reorganization, the introduction of television sharply reduced theatrical attendance and forced a reappraisal of production strategies. The studio system of production began to break down, and many theatres were closed for good. By the end of the fifties, the major production interests in Hollywood learned to use their facilities to make television programs and discovered that their vast stock of old films was a ready-made source of television profit. For the cinema, production strategies were reoriented to emphasize the release of fewer, bigger pictures utilizing innovations in colour and cinematography to attract audiences back to the theatre.[7]

Theatrical production was on firm footing again by 1960, but there had been one significant change that would have a direct bearing on attitudes toward a feature film industry in Canada. The decline of the studio system of production, the experience of joint productions in Europe that made use of blocked earnings and local subsidies, and the risk-averse strategies of the distribution companies each reinforced the trend toward a more decentralized structure of production. By 1960, productions in the United States hovered around 200 films a year, nearly half the total in the immediate postwar period. In that same year, production totals in France, Italy, and Great Britain respectively reached levels slightly over one-half of the U.S. total.[8] American distributors remained firmly in control of the world-wide film trade, but they were no longer marketing an exclusively American product, and no longer interested in making everything that they sold. Increasingly there was a viable global market for independently produced films, though there was also a growing trend toward films that had a 'Hollywood' look.

There had already emerged in Canada a cautious optimism, often tinged with a sense of frustration, that the film industry was reaching the mature state at which feature film production could begin. In 1952, the chairperson of the Canadian Film Awards described the industry as 'a mere infant in comparison with the colossus that is Hollywood' but added assertively that the child was 'healthy, good looking, and growing normally.'[9] Three years later, CBC television ran a 'Newsmagazine' program that supported the idea of feature film production; it ended with a remark from Ralph Foster, a former deputy film commissioner who had moved to Batten Films in Toronto, that 'conditions have never been better for the birth of a genuine Canadian feature film industry.'[10] The *Toronto Star* had given editorial support to the idea, while Hugh MacLennan had presented 'the case for a real Canadian film' in a 1955 issue of *Saturday Night*.[11] Writing in the *Canadian Forum* in 1957, E.S. Coatsworth felt that proponents of a feature film industry in Canada had become 'caught up in the heady currents of new Canadian nationalism ... Whereas twenty years ago few people beyond a handful of professionals could see any reason for a specifically Canadian feature film industry [he mentions no names], today, it seems, few people care to suggest that we should not have our own production industry.'[12]

These optimistic assessments of the private production industry's growth and potential stemmed in large measure from the boom in Canadian television production. By 1957, there were close to 60 production companies – nearly double the total in 1952 – and television productions had added close to $5 million to a total production volume near $15 million.[13] Much of the activity centred around American-sponsored productions, many of which were targeted for the British market. As was the case with the 'quota quickies' of the 1930s, a number of American firms located productions in Canada to satisfy the provisions of British content quotas. Such was the case with 'Last of the Mohicans,' produced by Normandie Productions, the Canadian subsidiary of Television Programs of America (TPA). Together with 'Tugboat Annie,' another TPA-sponsored television series, 'Last of the Mohicans' set the pattern for cooperation between Canadian and American interests.[14] The CBC had also become a major purchaser of private productions, since, unlike the NFB, it did not yet have the technical facilities to initiate or complete many of its own projects. In 1959, the CBC spent $3.5 million on film productions and of this amount $2.75 million was contracted out to some 30 private companies.[15] No less important to private producers was the boom in television advertising. *Canadian Business* estimated that in 1958, 'TV advertisements alone now account for 50 per cent of the film companies' total dollar volume.'[16] Like the production of sponsored theatrical shorts, television advertising was a safe and lucrative venture. Historically risk-averse, most private producers remained wary of initiating large-scale entertainment-oriented productions on their own, but the experience of producing such programs in conjunction with U.S. firms or the CBC undoubtedly made the option of doing so appear more viable than ever before.

Despite its growth, private film production was still far from being anything but a minor industry. The total dollar volume of production was relatively small, and many new companies expired in the course of a few years – victims of the ever-illusive search for that one successful, and stable, production contract. Yet a few firms did reach positions of relative strength. Certainly none was more successful over the long run than Crawley Films of Ottawa.

Started in the same year as the NFB, Crawley Films quickly established its place in the industry by becoming the leading private producer of industrial-sponsored short subjects. Its sponsors, as *Canadian Film Weekly* noted, read like 'a parade of the country's top enterprises'[17] (Imperial Oil of Canada, for example, had sponsored *The Loon's Necklace*). Television productions added to the company's growth. In 1958, the production schedule of Crawley Films included 60 films with an average running time of 19 minutes, and 150 shorter assignments. With the cooperation of the CBC, Crawley Films started production on a TV series entitled 'Royal Canadian Mounted Police'; it was later followed by the series 'St. Lawrence North.'[18] By 1961, the company had produced over 1,000 pictures. They had been seen in 21 countries and had won 119 national and international awards.

In that same year, F.R. (Budge) Crawley, the company's president, announced plans to produce two feature films. Crawley, who had earlier argued that a feature film industry in Canada 'has never made economic sense' and that production companies should stick to television if they want to make 'entertainment' films, had himself caught the feature film bug.[19] Although the originally announced projects were never made, in 1963 Crawley produced *Ville jolie*, a French-Canadian musical satire. The film was not particularly well received, and did not recoup its production costs of $200,000. Crawley took one more shot at the feature film business as associate producer on *The Luck of Ginger Coffey*, a film that presented a hard and uncompromising look at the life of Irish immigrants in Canada.[20] But the actual production of the film was not as 'Canadian' as its story line might imply: the director, major actors, director of photography, and editor were all non-Canadian. Released in 1964, to better reviews than its predecessor, *Ginger Coffey* was still not a money-making venture, and Crawley Films bid a hasty retreat to the friendlier fields of television and short-subject production.

Crawley's ill-fated venture into feature filmmaking only serves to highlight the problems to be faced by would-be Canadian producers. If a well-capitalized and able producer such as Crawley could not sustain feature film production, how much greater would be the obstacles encountered by a less established producer? While the technical core of the industry was sound, there were, given the particular history of the industry, few Canadians experienced in the more creative functions of feature film screenwriting and directing. Moreover, the financial community – the banks and investment houses – remained leery of investing in such high-risk ventures. As *Canadian Film Weekly* showed in a survey of Canadian private feature film production in the early 1960s, while many projects were announced, few were actually made, and of those most were failures. The survey concluded: 'Some films, then, do get made. But the dreamers and schemers are still there and the ones that don't get made seem to outnumber the ones that do. And the ones that do get made are more often than not losers.'[21]

Perhaps Crawley showed a lack of business acumen in his venture into the production of feature films. Still, his error could be considered noble from the standpoint of producing Canadian culture. For his feature films, Crawley chose themes that centred around Canada and Canadian life. *Ville jolie* and *Ginger Coffey* more closely resembled the tone and content of NFB films than those of other English producers. Crawley had clearly played it safe until the early 1960s, but he then took a risk that his English-Canadian colleagues in the private sector were to avoid steadfastly: he made films with the Canadian market principally in mind. 'If Canadians want to develop a domestic feature industry,' said Crawley in 1963, 'we just have to take some gambles ourselves. Right now we have to do something distinct that has sales appeal because it's a production unique to Canada. Otherwise there is very little future for Canadian producers.'[22]

It was not a sentiment shared by many of his colleagues, especially those in English Canada. Most of them had cut their teeth working within the circuit of Hollywood's dominance; most believed that only distribution in the United States would assure a film's profitability. To avoid Crawley's misfortunes, the solution seemed simple: make films in Canada but make them the way American distributors would want them. English-Canadian producers were particularly susceptible to the argument that Canadian features would have to be oriented around themes deemed 'appropriate' for the U.S. market; quite often it would mean importing American talent to do the job. For companies with heavy fixed capital investments in labs and studios, the best arrangement might be one in which American-backed projects would utilize their technical infrastructure (admittedly the formula applied to *Ginger Coffey* as well). For years, Canadians, insofar as they viewed anything at all to do with Canada when they went to the movies, had been treated to Hollywood's vision of Canada: it now seemed that they might be treated to Canada's vision of Hollywood.

If in the early 1960s Crawley symbolized that small assembly of Canadian producers who had not completely internalized the ethos of Hollywood, Nat Taylor represented that larger group of Canadians who had tried to use Hollywood's network as the basis for personal and corporate success. Taylor's life-long involvement in the film industry began in the sphere of exhibition. In the 1930s, he organized Twentieth Century Theatres, and after turning down an offer to become Odeon's first general manager in 1941, Taylor aligned his 17-theatre circuit with Famous Players.[23] By the early 1960s, there were 65 theatres in the Twentieth Century chain. But unlike those individuals who operated entirely as compradors for American companies in Canada, Taylor maintained a certain independence, working with, but not necessarily for, the American film industry. As an exhibitor, Taylor was innovative: in 1946, he opened the first Canadian theatre devoted to the exhibition of 'art' films (the International Theatre in Toronto); he was also a pioneer in the conception and introduction of multiplex theatres. By the 1950s, Taylor had become a prominent and respected figure in the film industry as a whole, and his regular column in *Canadian Film Weekly* became the oracle of the Canadian industry. Still, success did not breed complacency. By the early sixties, Taylor had built a small corporate empire under N.A. Taylor Associates through which he held controlling interests in Toronto International Film Studios (the largest private film studio in the country), International Film Distributors and Allied Artists Pictures (both film distribution companies), Beaver Film Production (which held international theatrical and television film rights), and NTA Canada Ltd. (a television program distribution company).[24] Like many other interests in the film industry, such as Famous Players and Paul L'Anglais, Taylor also moved into the field of television broadcasting; in 1960, he became a major shareholder in CJOH, Ottawa's new private station.[25] Taylor had established the first vertically integrated corporate network in the Canadian film industry. He knew the business. He would certainly be a force to reckon with in any discussion over the nature and extent of state support to the film industry.

Taylor was well aware that one could make a very good living in the film industry without actually producing films, especially feature films. As we have seen, feature film production is the riskiest facet of the industry's cycle – a few unsuccessful ventures can deplete even a large capital pool. It is in the exhibition, distribution, and leasing of technical facilities (such as studios and labs) that the 'safe' money can be made. Nonetheless, Taylor joined rank with the adventurous when he teamed with Julian Roffman to produce *The Mask* in 1960.[26] It was emblematic of the kind of film Taylor thought Canadians should be making. *The Mask* (also known as *Eyes of Hell*) was a 'gimmick' picture, a low-budget shocker about a psychiatrist who discovers an ancient Aztec voodoo mask with hallucinatory and murderous powers. When the doctor in the film uses the mask, audiences donned 3-D glasses to partake in the experience. The film was given wide publicity in the United States by its distributor, Warner Bros., and although the critical reviews were rather negative, the film was moderately successful. Clyde Gilmour, movie critic for the Toronto *Telegram*, saw the film at its première in New York and called it 'a professional hunk of horror-movie fiction.'[27] For Nat Taylor the remark was probably much better than faint praise. *The Mask* was the kind of film many people within the industry felt should be made. There was certainly going to be an uneasy tension between those who wanted a feature film industry that could 'interpret Canada to Canadians' and those who saw it as a business with an almost ineluctable continental orientation.[28]

One other English-Canadian film company is worth noting at this point. With Hollywood's studio system in decline, Seven Arts Productions became a major force in the industry by the early 1960s. The company was listed on the Toronto Stock Exchange, the majority of its shareholders were Canadian, and its chairperson, Louis Chesler, resided in Toronto. But as *Canadian Film Weekly* explained, this was a case where 'the tail wags the dog.'[29] The American subsidiary of Seven Arts carried out all of its productions, and its films were released through the major American distributors. In 1962, Seven Arts announced that it would spend $25 million on 10 Hollywood projects, including *Dr Strangelove, What Ever Happened to Baby Jane?*, and *Of Human Bondage*.[30] Seven Arts never joined the growing legion of support for a feature film loan fund in Canada. It was already well established in the heartland of the industry.

It would be all too easy to ignore the existence of Seven Arts – to say that it was not really a Canadian company – but it would be far more valuable to recognize this apparent anomaly for what it was. Seven Arts was the ironic result of the triumph of cultural and economic continentalism. The structure of dependency was not so unyielding that it would prevent Canadian capital from engaging in film production at the centre. Apparently, there was money in Canada for feature films. What there was not was money for feature films that had a specifically 'Canadian' look.

The NFB and French-Canadian Filmmakers

The move to Montreal in 1956, into a building one source called a 'filmmakers dream,' was symbolic of the turnaround in the Film Board's postwar status.[31] Productions grew steadily in the new headquarters, and there was ample evidence of polish and creativity in much of the Board's work. Norman McLaren had become recognized as an international leader in the field of film animation, and the work of the English-language Unit B, led by Tom Daly and Colin Low, displayed a new technical maturity in the production of documentaries.[32] Although the Film Board had not been accorded a major role in the planning and development of television, television provided it with a new market. In 1955, two large-scale series of films specifically designed for television were initiated: the *Perspective* series for English audiences, and the *Passe-partout* series for French audiences. Television productions proved to be particularly important to the development of the Board's French-Canadian filmmakers. Through the *Passe-partout* (and later the *Panoramique*) series, a number of Quebec filmmakers (among them Claude Jutra, Gilles Groulx, and Michel Brault) learned the craft of filmmaking and began to stretch the boundaries of the NFB's traditional conception of form and structure.

While the Film Board had successfully weathered the cold war–inspired attacks, there was a new tension surfacing within the organization itself. French-Canadian filmmakers, still a minority within the Board, had grown incensed at the lack of opportunity for planning, writing, and producing films that reflected their own creative priorities.[33] Much of their time was spent producing French-language versions of English-Canadian films, in an environment dominated by Anglo-Canadian concerns. As one filmmaker put it: 'Dans une atmosphère restreinte de conformisme et d'objectivité anglo-saxonne très fortement implantée, les sujets que les cinéastes proposaient étaient ceux que la maison aurait proposé ... *L'autocensure* jouait toujours énormément.'[34] In 1953, a memo drafted by producer Roger Blais brought the issue into the open for the first time. Criticizing the ethnic inequalities that pervaded the Board's management and organizational priorities, Blais argued that a separate French unit should be established and that it should be made responsible for the conception and direction of its own program. The suggestion did not find favour with the Board's chief administrators, and Blais himself was soon marginalized from major administrative decisions taken with respect to French-Canadian production.[35]

The issue was left to brew until early in 1957, when the Quebec press, led by *Le Devoir*, launched a full-scale exposé of the administrative subjugation of French-Canadian filmmakers and producers.[36] 'L'Office du film,' wrote *Le Devoir* editor Pierre Vigeant, 'n'a jamais voulu voir dans la groupe française qu'un élément inférieur auquel il suffit d'accorder quelques concessions.'[37] The invective was sharp: in describing the activities of the NFB's Anglo triumvirate of Albert Trueman, Don Mulholland, and Grant McLean, *Le Devoir* spoke of 'brainwashing' and 'le supplice moral.'

The allegations were neatly timed to coincide with an upcoming spring federal election. As part of its attempt to crack the Liberal's stronghold in Quebec, the Progressive Conservative party, under John Diefenbaker, took up the cause for a separate French section within the NFB. The Liberal party responded to the charges and the challenge by reshuffling the NFB's leadership. In mid-April, Guy Roberge became the first French-Canadian government film commissioner (Trueman was moved to the newly established Canada Council). Roberge quickly installed Pierre Juneau as the first French-Canadian executive director of production. Such changes would hardly suffice to save the Liberal party from electoral defeat, but they certainly signalled the growing importance of French Canadians within the National Film Board.

According to Robert Boissonnault, not all French-Canadian filmmakers at the Board were in favour of establishing separate and autonomous sections divided on the basis of language.[38] Those working in television production saw the recommendation as an attempt by French-Canadian producers within the Board's more traditional documentary division to shift decision-making power to themselves. Like Juneau himself, many also felt that a division along ethnic lines smacked of the old-style isolationism they were trying to overcome. The French-language television units had developed a certain de facto autonomy, strongly supported by Juneau. Juneau was not the 'béni oui oui' *Le Devoir* had suggested he might be, and the television productions of the French unit testified to the increasing strength within the Board of a large group of French-Canadian filmmakers. In fact, the debate over organizational structure would soon be overshadowed by significant breakthroughs in production.

In the late 1950s, a number of filmmakers at the Board became interested in a new form of documentary filmmaking. Advances in the development of lightweight cameras with synchronized sound – 'cinéma direct' as it came to be known – encouraged filmmakers to abandon carefully planned scripts and meticulously arranged scenes to concentrate on real, often spontaneous, events in which normal people in normal places provided the foundation for the filmic event.[39] English-Canadian filmmakers, especially those associated with Unit B, explored the potentials of this new cinematic form through the *Candid Eye* series. In their hands, as David Clandfield argues, cinéma direct took the form of 'dispassionate empiricism,' which encountered its subject matter as an objective reality to be chronicled by the filmmaker, whose status was that of a neutral observer.[40]

But, as Clandfield and others have argued, the Board's French-Canadian filmmakers pushed cinéma direct in a different direction. In their hands, it became a technique to develop 'impassioned' collective portraits of the social milieu with which the filmmakers themselves identified.[41] For Gilles Groulx and Michel Brault, who co-directed *Les Raquetteurs* in 1958, cinéma direct was the form through which they could develop a self-reflexive and subjective study of the ideological and cultural changes under way in Quebec. *Les Raquetteurs*, a 15-minute film about a snowshoe meet in Sherbrooke, won the French unit international acclaim among filmmakers interested in the new cinematic movement. It was followed by films such as *Normétal* (1959), *La Lutte* (1961), and *Québec-USA, ou l'Invasion pacifique* (1962). Together these films represented a sharp departure from the traditions of earlier NFB productions, not least because of their clearly critical political tone. They also marked the beginning of a new collegiality among the Board's French-Canadian filmmakers. As one filmmaker put it: 'Le corridor de la production française était physiquement un lieu d'ebullition extraordinaire. On était toujours en train de parler, de faire des projets. On installait des tableaux pour mettre des affiches, des notes, des idées, pour communiquer. Il y a eu une espèce de réseau interne de communication fantastique.'[42] While none of these films was a full-length feature (*Les Raquetteurs* itself ran only 15 minutes), the experience of producing films that took contemporary Quebec as its focal point lead almost inexorably to the desire to produce feature-length films. The social transformations occurring in Quebec and the creative impulse of its filmmakers could neither be contained nor summarized in a theatrical or television short.

The NFB and Feature Films

It was perhaps inevitable that filmmakers at the Board, ever more self-assured and refined in their craft, would become interested in the feature film format. While European filmmakers (the French New Wave and the neorealist movement in Italian filmmaking, for example) had begun to use documentary techniques to develop socially relevant, almost didactic, feature-length fictional films, the Board's filmmakers would move in the opposite direction, stretching their documentary techniques to accommodate fictional narratives. In many cases, the first feature films at the Board surfaced by accident; in others they were the product of clandestine machinations.[43] The first feature-length films of this period – Pierre Perrault and Michel Brault's *Pour la suite du monde* (1963) and Don Haldane's *Drylanders* (1963) – were conceived originally as one-hour television films. *Pour la suite du monde*'s mystical treatment of villagers on a remote island in the St. Lawrence and their re-enactment of a traditional whale hunt is regarded by many as the finest example of the cinéma direct movement in Canada. The final cut ran 105 minutes, and the NFB decided to try a limited theatrical release after the film was highly praised at the Cannes film festival. Somewhat shorter in length, *Drylanders* was originally planned as part of a documentary series on Canadian frontiers. The film portrays both the hardships and the endurance of Canada's Prairie settlers in what was supposed to be a film about a dam in Saskatchewan. (Unlike *Pour la suite du monde*, *Drylanders* was scripted and used professional actors). The CBC turned it down on the basis that it ran over one hour, but the film was picked up by Columbia Pictures for theatrical distribution, and the company later reported that it was 'thrilled' by its box-office performance.[44]

The following year, two feature films were shot without the knowledge or the approval of the Board's management. They have come to be regarded by many as 'the classics,' marking Canada's entry into the world of contemporary feature filmmaking. Working within Unit B, Don Owen set off for Toronto to shoot a half-hour dramatic film about a probationary officer and a juvenile delinquent, entitled *Nobody Waved Goodbye* (1964). He was given an initial budget of $30,000. Working without a script, Owen and his crew kept on shooting. As Owen recalls: 'I kept on ordering more film. It so happened that all the people were away so that in fact there was nobody at the NFB to say don't send any more film ... the story kept on getting more and more elaborate, and I added some scenes ... And when I came back to Montreal four weeks later, I was then something like $10,000 over budget, and I shot 50,000 feet instead of 25,000 feet, and I said: I shot a feature.'[45] That same year, Gilles Groulx converted what was planned as a half-hour documentary into a critical, politically informed feature film about an alienated Québécois youth struggling through the questions of his cultural identity – it was called *Le chat dans le sac*.[46] One year later, Gilles Carle went off and made *La vie heureuse de Léopold Z*. It was another feature film made without Pierre Juneau's approval, despite the fact that he was now, supposedly, the executive director of all French productions. After considerable hesitation, Juneau decided to allow completion of the film. In essence he had been presented with a fait accompli, but the experience led him to establish a much tighter reign over production plans, schedules, and budgets.[47]

It would be wrong to suggest that Juneau and the NFB's management did not feel they had the budgetary leeway or the mandate to produce feature films. By the mid-sixties, they seemed prepared to sanction a few full-length productions each year. But they were not prepared to leave production plans for such ventures to the discretion of the filmmakers themselves. When asked for his criteria in accepting a feature-length proposal, Juneau responded that budgets, distribution potential, and the competence of the filmmakers themselves were all important, and then added: 'Il faut qu'un film réalisé ici soit significatif par rapport à la réalité canadienne collective (et non individuelle).'[48] In effect, there were two types of scenarios Juneau and the NFB's officialdom would not support: those that challenge 'les institutions canadiennes d'une manière trop directe,' and those that 'relève de la psychologie individuelle.'[49] As Juneau candidly remarked, the Film Board was no place for a Godard or an Antonioni (or it seemed for anyone with a vision not in accordance with the national priorities of the Board).

Given the predilections of the French-Canadian filmmakers in particular, Juneau's statement of priorities underscored an increasing divide. In April 1964 Jacques Godbout, Gilles Groulx, Clément Perron, Gilles Carle, and Denys Arcand published articles in the leftist Québécois journal *Parti pris* condemning the NFB's priorities. As the editor concluded: 'The Film Board is an instrument of colonization. It is a gigantic propaganda machine whose role it is to put the public to sleep and to exhaust the creative drive of the filmmakers.'[50] It was an assault that paralleled what was increasingly being heard in Quebec regarding the federal state as a whole.

Serious political calculations were undoubtedly behind much of the new tension at the Board, but even without such a conflict it is unlikely that the Board would have been able to accommodate the filmmaker's aspirations. As Peter Harcourt notes in an article aptly titled 'Years of Hope':

There was a time in the early sixties when there was a lot of talent at the board.
From the war years through to the dominance of television, these filmmakers had
built up their own way of examining the personal and political realities of the world
we live in. When the time came, however, for them to extend themselves into features, the film board couldn't really manage to support this extension. So within six
years, most of the real talent left the board.[51]

In 1962, Claude Jutra took a leave of absence from the Board to produce, write, direct and star in *À tout prendre*, which won Best Feature Film at the 1964 Canadian Film Awards. In 1963, Pierre Patry left the Board and established Coopératio, which, as its name implies, involved a cooperative method of filmmaking and financing. Between 1963 and 1967, the company made seven films, its most notable production being Michel Brault's *Entre la mer et l'eau douce*.[52]

But the transition to the private sector was far from smooth. In interview after interview the filmmakers revealed a clear understanding of the pressures and uncertainties that attended private sector production. 'Chaque film tourné dans le secteur privé en ce moment est une folle aventure,' said Claude Jutra after his experience with *À tout prendre*.[53] Others agreed. As would-be producers they spent more time making financial arrangements than making films, a situation made only worse by the dearth of feature filmmaking that had typified Canada's past. Making feature films is always a risky venture, but for these intrepid filmmakers it must have felt like sheer folly. Increasingly, they were conscious of the double bind within which they were caught: the limits imposed by the NFB were unacceptable, but so too was the instability, the uncertainty, and the near chaos that characterized production in the private sector.

More and more, these filmmakers, like many others in Quebec, looked to the state for support in establishing a more viable private sector. In 1963, 104 French-Canadian filmmakers from both inside and outside the Film Board, established the Association professionnelle des cinéastes (APC). With Claude Jutra as its first president, the APC began to barrage both the provincial and federal governments with requests for support. It made its first presentation in November 1963 to the Conseil d'orientation économique du Québec, which, in conjunction with the Office du film du Québec had begun an inquiry into issues related to the development of the Quebec film industry. Jutra told the inquiry:

Such an industry cannot flower within the framework of government production. To give this industry the dynamism it needs, feature films must be made under conditions which ensure both liberty and healthy competition ... The NFB's proud display of international trophies only serves as a thin camouflage behind which lurks the poverty of our native cinema. Our movie houses have never shown anything to the Canadian public except the sights of other lands and the cultures of other peoples.[54]

Positions on State Support: Disparate Voices from the Industry

The APC had become the most vocal and insistent proponent of state support for the development of a private feature film industry, but it was certainly not alone. Although it never developed the same unity of purpose, by the late 1950s the Association of Motion Picture Producers and Laboratories of Canada (AMPPLC) had also come to see the wisdom of lobby efforts that extended beyond protracted attacks against the NFB. In English Canada it was joined by the newly formed Directors' Guild of Canada (DGC) and by the personal campaign of Nat Taylor, in an attempt to prod the state into action. Not surprisingly, the industry was not of one voice on the issue. Radical measures, including the possibility of levies or quotas, were proposed by the APC and the DGC, while Nat Taylor, who in a sense represented the interests of private Canadian capital in the industry, criticized such proposals as unworkable and undesirable. The AMPPLC, which struggled throughout this period to develop a firm position, fell in line behind Taylor. If the Canadian state decided to move on the issue, it would be faced with a range of policy options, reflecting the range of interests and demands within the film industry itself.

Throughout this period the major exhibitors and distributors remained public-ly silent on the issue. Given their comfortable position within the Hollywood nexus, they had little to gain from expanded Canadian productions but much to lose if the state decided upon quotas or levies as a way of bolstering feature film production in Canada. Undoubtedly, they would be heard from if the state decided to use measures that would disrupt their normal market operations, but any complaints in advance of such measures might backfire and serve the interests of those who sought a more radical solution to the problem. Still, their silence was ominous. As the momentum for state support built there loomed the knowledge that theatrical exhibitors and their American suppliers would not take kindly to measures that altered their customary business practices.

The AMPPLC: Cautious Interventionism

To the country's private production interests, the recommendations of the Massey Report, the restatement of state support for the NFB embodied in the New Film Act of 1951, and the large infusion of new public money for the NFB's Montreal headquarters had all become symbols of their continuing status as second-class citizens. It was not that the private production community wanted the state to establish a complex structure of subsidies and supports to aid their enterprise. Throughout most of the fifties, their position remained rather simple. As Budge Crawley had argued two months following the release of the Massey Report, private producers would be satisfied if the NFB were 'required to give each year to outside film producers or to outside photog-raphers, work equal to the value of one half its production of films or of photographs.'[55] In 1951, annual film production had totalled $2 million, of which $1.25 million was accounted for by federal government production – less than ten per cent of the latter was contracted out to private producers. Accord-ingly, Crawley and the AMPPLC were looking for an increase in annual revenue of about $500,000. While that figure obviously increased throughout the 1950s, as we have seen, the new market for television productions placed the private producers on much firmer financial footing and made access to government-sponsored productions a much less obsessive concern.

In fact, by the late 1950s the AMPPLC became interested in the possibility of general state intervention to consolidate its growth and facilitate its expansion. In 1958, the Association struck an Industry Development Committee, chaired by Ralph Foster of Meridian Films, to examine the applicability of British support mechanisms – such as the Eady Plan – to the Canadian film industry.[56] In an address to the Annual Convention of the Canadian Council of Authors and Artists in St. Adèle, Quebec, Arthur Chetwynd, president of the AMPPLC, displayed a new tone of confidence: 'Films can be planned, produced, and sold economically and efficiently in Canada, and most importantly, in all other countries with television networks.'[57] Crawley echoed these sentiments, explaining that the 'time is right to attempt the establishment of a Canadian television entertainment film production industry.'[58] The key term in both these statements was television. The AMPPLC was primarily interested in the stable production environment that television could provide: television projects were less expensive to initiate than feature films, costs could be amortized much more quickly, and the market was not as tightly controlled by a few major companies. For an industry still characterized by risk aversion, feature films were seen as adjuncts to the production of television programs – special projects that could generate super profits and might be worth the risk if a stable production environment were first secured.

Economics makes strange bedfellows. Until how, the AMPPLC had stood firmly on the side of private interests when questions of state intervention into the cultural sphere had surfaced. Its consistent attacks on the NFB apparently made it the natural ally of private broadcasters and business interests, which wanted to keep state intervention in the sphere of cultural production to a minimum. But in the late 1950s, tensions surfaced over the issue of Canadian-content legislation in television broadcasting. The Canadian Association of Broadcasters and the Association of Canadian Advertisers soundly denounced the Board of Broadcast Governors' decision to adopt Canadian-content regulations in 1959.[59] Given its stake in made-in-Canada television, the AMPPLC joined forces on the other side of the debate, strongly endorsing the principle of a 55 per cent minimum for Canadian content.[60] The private producers and laboratories found themselves in the novel position of endorsing a significant new form of state intervention and regulation that would very likely improve their overall production activities. They had, in fact, discovered the 'benevolent' side of the leviathan they had hitherto despised.

Although the content regulations were watered down and then poorly enforced by the Board of Broadcast Governors, they had reaffirmed an important principle of Canadian public policy: that Canadian consumers must have access to more Canadian cultural products than the private market would otherwise bear. Because it was less expensive to buy American shows than produce Canadian ones and because advertising revenues for the former were usually much higher, television broadcasters, both public and private, minimized their commitment to Canadian programming. Through the Canadian-content provisions, the state undertook a dramatic new form of intervention into the sphere of cultural production. Unlike the establishment of the CBC, or the Canada Council in 1957, the 'Cancon' principle had a direct bearing on the everyday business practices of the private sector. It was a discrete, targeted form of intervention that gave special privileges to a specific practice within the industry as a whole. Its counterpart in the film industry would be an exhibition quota ensuring a minimum number of Canadian films on Canadian screens.

At about the same time as the content regulations were being developed, the AMPPLC presented a brief to Ottawa entitled 'A Report and Recommendations Concerning the Development of the Film Industry in Canada.'[61] While reiterating the AMPPLC's complaints with respect to the NFB's monopoly over government productions, the brief no longer suggested that the contracting-out of government productions would be enough to satisfy its interests. Instead, the AMPPLC proposed that a joint government–industry committee be established to consider different strategies for the development of a feature film industry. Not surprisingly, the brief emphasized the need for a large state-sponsored capital pool that could be used for television productions. Even so, it was the first time that the issue of state support to feature film production had been placed on the federal government's agenda by industry representatives.

In retrospect, it is not altogether clear that the AMPPLC was strongly committed to its proposal. According to a former MP in the Diefenbaker government who supported the AMPPLC's position, the organization itself did not pursue the matter as aggressively as possible. 'I had the PM hot on the subject two years ago,' John Pratt told *Canadian Film Weekly*, 'but I never followed it up because of lack of interest on the part of people in the industry itself, who had originally raised the question with me, but who had failed utterly to show any continuing interest.'[62] Although the committee that drafted the brief was told to investigate the applicability of measures used in Britain, the final draft recommended neither a box-office quota nor a box-office levy as ways of facilitating Canadian production. Perhaps the 'Cancon' television provisions had satisfied the immediate desire for an expanded market; yet it is also hard to imagine how firms that drew a considerable portion of their business from American sources, whether as laboratories that produced the positive prints for the Canadian market or as production companies involved in location shoots and television co-productions, could suggest legislation that would draw the ire of the dominant interests in the film industry. AMPPLC members would take what they could get – without damaging their position within the industry as a whole. It wanted the issue dealt with quietly and without fuss. Given the competitive nature of the sector and the different priorities of the various firms, it is not altogether surprising that the AMPPLC could not develop a solid and effective lobby.

Nat Taylor: An Independent Film Industry and Indistinguishable Films

One member of the AMPPLC, however, did present a solid case for state support to feature film production. Through his regular weekly column in *Canadian Film Weekly*, Nat Taylor persistently pushed the issue. When Maurice Lamontagne formally announced the government's intention to establish support mechanisms at the 25th anniversary celebration of the NFB, Guy Roberge singled out Nat Taylor as the one individual in the private sector whose efforts over the past four years had been most responsible for the government's initiative. Roberge had sought his advice; so too, had the interdepartmental committee that laid the basis for the government's plan. Both formally and informally, Taylor was a prominent figure in the events that led to the feature film loan fund. His position was influenced more by business acumen than cultural romanticism.

As early as 1954, Taylor surveyed some of the trends within both the film industry and the Canadian economy and wrote: 'The day is coming when there will be feature film production in Canada.'[63] Recognizing the trend toward the use of independent producers by the major Hollywood distributors, Taylor felt it would become easier for Canadian productions to access and compete in the world market. The technical and acting skills in Canada had now been developed to the point where feature film production could be legitimately undertaken. In fact, Taylor argued that Canadian-based productions might have a distinct advantage over their European counterparts in one fundamental respect: because of its proximity both geographically and culturally to the United States, Canada could make films that were 'practically indistinguishable' from American ones.[64] While Taylor was not opposed to films that could 'interpret Canadians to the world' (he always had kind words for the work of the NFB), he emphasized that 'the box-office must be our goal at the outset.'[65] Most important, Taylor maintained that a Canadian feature film industry would have to be run as an export industry. As he frequently argued, Canada was a 'trading nation' and, in the case of feature film production, where a small domestic market would make it all but impossible to recoup the high costs of production, the industry would live and die on the basis of its ability to produce a product worthy of export. Speaking of would-be producers who had approached him for advice, he wrote: 'I found that primarily they didn't know what to make or what would be acceptable to the box-offices of the world. This I consider to be the greatest drawback to potential Canadian film production today.'[66]

Sound business practices in a global market now open to new producers – that was the core of Taylor's argument. But like those film industries in countries other than the United States – those that could not rely on an imperial state to guarantee a global film market – public assistance was a necessary component of private growth. In late 1959, Taylor wrote: 'Only one spark is necessary to set ablaze a whole new industry: Government subsidy.'[67] Taylor offered a strategy for intervention that would maximize individual initiative and guarantee export-oriented production. Exhibition quotas were ruled out for the simple reason that they would establish a bias for production oriented to the home market, which in Canada's case represents approximately three per cent of the world box-office total. (Of course, as an exhibitor Taylor would have found such a scheme unacceptable in almost any circumstances.) Instead, Taylor offered a novel innovation on Britain's Eady Plan: aside from loans, producers should be given a subsidy based on their film's performance in foreign markets to be applied to future productions.[68] Since it was based on exports, the subsidy would indirectly pay for itself through increases in the state's current accounts balance. Taylor felt that such a strategy would boost the government's overall objective of increasing exports and improving the balance of trade. It would also, of course, encourage producers to make films that were 'practically indistinguishable' from American ones. 'We shall have a production industry in Canada, a good and thriving one, if our government ever gets around to extending a helping hand. We shall make good and marketable films. However, such an industry will not be activated by pseudo-professionals, no matter how enthusiastic ... The climate is right. World markets are wide open and theatre owners everywhere are glad to play anything that will sell to the public.'[69] Taylor did not want 'arty' films. He wanted films that would sell. Films that would attract a large audience in the global marketplace. Films like *The Mask*.

No Consensus on a Plan of Action

In the fall of 1961, the AMPPLC came together with four industry organizations to form the Motion Picture Production Council. AMPPLC members, including Nat Taylor, were joined by representatives from the Canadian Society of Cinematographers (CSC), the International Alliance of Theatrical and Stage Employees (IATSE), and the nascent Directors' Guild of Canada.[70] The meeting was held to build support for government assistance to production, but from it there emerged no firm statement of intent and no commitment to coordinated representation. Interests were simply too divided or too unclear for a broad consensus to be reached.

The AMPPLC itself was showing signs of political 'split personality.' On the one hand, NFB bashing was back in style. A report to the 1961 Motion Picture Industry Council emphasized the problem of maintaining a private industry in the face of 'the creeping claustrophobia of more and more government production of films.'[71] But one year later, after the Board of Broadcast Governors had given the producers another potential bonanza by imposing a 20 per cent tax on foreign-produced television advertisements, the AMPPLC ask the Motion Picture Industry Council to consider a similar tax on feature films.[72] The AMPPLC had the audacity to ask the major exhibitors and distributors for their cooperation; needless to say, it was not forthcoming.

The Canadian Society of Cinematographers had been formally established in the fall of 1961, with Herbert Alpert of Meridian Films as its first president. A reading of its own trade journal, *Canadian Cinematography*, shows that the CSC was at best only lukewarm to proposals for government support to feature filmmaking. As late as 1964, an editorial entitled 'Do We Expect Too Much Too Soon from the Film Industry?' cautioned that 'the industry is being forced into a position (without ever being consulted) where it is expected, eventually, to produce films.'[73] The editorial suggested that the industry should concentrate on television productions and documentary filmmaking as more solid industry foundations. The argument was roundly denounced by Guy Coté, president of the APC, in the following issue, and later by Robert Barclay of the Directors' Guild, who characterized it as a timid, narrow, and utterly self-conscious response to an issue of major importance to the film industry.[74] Once announced by Lamontagne, the CSC carefully endorsed the plans for a feature film fund, but like the AMPPLC it remained studiously cautious in its public pronouncements on the issue.

At least initially, IATSE Local 873 took a much firmer position in support of state intervention. IATSE is an international union, with its headquarters in New York, whose membership includes projectionists, camera operators, and theatrical and stage employees (including film technicians and electricians). In 1961, Bob Milligan, president of IATSE's Toronto Local 873, which covers theatrical and stage employees, called for an exhibition quota to support the production of more Canadian films.[75] Milligan sent a forceful letter to federal MPs. It noted that in Finland film production alone outstripped the Canadian total for both film and television. While other countries had moved to protect the drain on balance of payments, Milligan noted that Canada was losing close to $100 million annually in the film rentals. (The actual figure was much closer to $30 million). 'Canada is a rapidly growing country,' the letter said, 'but as far as the film industry was concerned, we are being left behind.'[76] The initiative for the letter and the proposal of an exhibition quota seems to have come from the Toronto local itself. In general, IATSE stayed away from formal pronouncements on the issue. Fearing lower attendance and therefore the possibility of less work, Canadian projectionists would probably have sided with exhibitors in rejecting the notion of a box-office quota. More specifically, this was a union dominated by its New York office and one in which American jobs came first.

Following the pattern of conservative unionism in the United States, IATSE officials had developed a close working relationship with the dominant interests in the American film industry; it would have been extremely surprising if it had endorsed radical measures in Canada that might upset its major employers. After Milligan's intervention in 1961, IATSE seems to have taken a vow of silence on the issue.

Film workers, whether technicians or camera operators, could for the most part be satisfied as long as there existed a stable production environment. As was the case for Canada's production companies and laboratories, television projects, advertisements, industrial-sponsored shorts, and American-controlled 'shoots' constituted their bread and butter and satisfied the demand for employment. Whether a production was 'Canadian' or 'American' made little difference, since in both cases the division of labour meant that 'control' was not in their hands. It is not that the concerns of film workers are necessarily economistic; they may very well come to link stable employment with the need to support productions that promote certain themes, issues, or identities. But such a connection has to be made at a political level, and it may entail economic sacrifices, whether through the rejection of employment offers on particular projects or through demands that the whole production environment undergo changes that will disrupt, at least temporarily, normal activities. It is a conundrum faced by many cultural workers, particularly as their once creative ambitions are routed into functionary tasks.

But for some individuals in the film industry the dilemma is more immediate. Those who perform the creative tasks, such as directors or screenwriters, whose jobs entail positions of considerable 'control,' cannot as easily satisfy their employment needs if the production industry remains derivative. To Canadian directors, established or emerging, the issue of employment was intimately bound up with the existence of a full-scale domestic industry in which creative positions were reserved for Canadians. American-backed productions may well have produced employment for Canadian film workers and profits for Canadian production companies, but they typically shunned the use of Canadians in the creative roles.

It is not surprising then that the Directors' Guild of Canada, like the APC, took a much harder line on the issue. The Guild was established in late 1961, as a fully autonomous affiliate of the Screen Directors' International Guild. In March 1964, it presented a full-scale brief to the federal government committee charged with developing a feature film policy. While the brief stressed the economic importance of a feature film industry (in terms of trade, tourism, and employment), it also linked the production of feature films to the promotion of national identity. Indeed, the brief argued that the two concerns were enmeshed: 'to correct the situation culturally would also be to correct the situation economically.'[77] The DGC felt that support was necessary in three areas. First, given the hyper-conservative nature of the financial community, a government-backed loan fund was needed to establish the basic preconditions for production. Unlike the AMPPLC, it suggested that funds should in part be derived from a tax on the rental receipts of foreign companies. Second, the brief pointed to the problem of distribution and argued that distributors based in Canada should be persuaded to handle a certain number of Canadian films a year. While the DGC rejected a screen quota, in the interest of emphasizing quality productions, they nonetheless proposed that the CBC should be required to buy the television rights of an average of 12 features a year, at $50,000 a year. Given the low budgets of Canadian films at the time, such a scheme would represent an important source of capital. Finally, the brief argued that Canada Council grants to writers should be extended to include the writing of screenplays, which was typically the most important component of a producer's pre-production costs.

In recommending a levy on foreign film receipts and in focusing on the need to address the question of distribution generally, the DGC's brief called for a significant restructuring of the feature film industry's current structure. In this respect, it shared much in common with the various briefs presented by the APC in the fall of 1963 and early 1964.[78] In terms of endorsing a break with the status quo, the APC's position was clearly the most far-reaching. It wanted a loan fund, paid for through a box-office levy and a tax on foreign-film rental receipts. It wanted a screen quota, similar to those in place in most European countries. And it wanted majority ownership of Canadian theatre chains transferred to Canadian hands. The APC took its case to both levels of government, presenting it on grounds that stressed equally the dimensions of culture and economics. In rhetorical terms, the APC's briefs were the only ones that recaptured the tone of the Massey Report. Nothing less than the survival of the nation was at stake: 'Des peuples ont disparu à partir du moment où ils ont vécu par procuration, où ils ont vécu les rêves des autres, à partir du moment où ils ont été incapables de récréer l'image de leur univers, où ils sont allés chercher ailleurs toute leur mythologie.'[79] At the same time, however, there was none of the earlier cultural conservatism that saw all 'mass' culture as debilitating and pernicious. Instead, the APC twisted the constructs of the Massey Report and extolled the cinema as 'l'art le plus proche des foules.'[80] It was in the fleeting images of popular culture, not the rarified air of the 'arts' or didactic documentaries, that the foundations of national identity lay.

In its own slow manner the Canadian state had also come to recognize that the cultural industries had become, for better or worse, the most important source of daily cultural expression and consumption. A program to support the development of a Canadian feature film industry was in the works. Would there be quotas, a box-office levy, a tax on foreign receipts, or a demand for greater Canadian ownership in the fields of exhibition or distribution? Different forces within the industry held different views on these questions. Where would the Canadian state come down?

6   The Helping Hand

Comme forme de création artistique, comme témoignage global de l'homme, le film de long métrage est un mode d'expression fort séduisant et sans nul doute très efficace. C'est au cinéma aujourd'hui que, dans une très large mesure, nous retrouvons toutes les grandes interrogations contemporaines, toutes les angoisses, tous les problèmes, mais aussi toutes les réussites de l'homme. Un pays qui n'a pas de cinéma de long métrage se prive d'un des plus importants moyens de s'exprimer ...

Dans le passé, nous avons confié notre vie culturelle presque exclusivement à l'initiative des individus et des organismes privés. L'épanouissement très relatif de notre culture montre que cela n'est pas suffisant. Il m'apparaît que le concours de l'État est aujourd'hui indispensable pour favoriser les progrès culturels d'un peuple. Dans l'ordre du cinéma, le Gouvernement doit soutenir l'Office national du Film et je crois que, parallèlement, il doit apporter un appui nécessaire à la réalisation de longs métrages par des producteurs indépendants.   – Maurice Lamontagne[1]

Introduction

Maurice Lamontagne's speech at the NFB's 25th anniversary celebration, announcing the government's intention to support private-sector feature film production, reflected a clear break with the cultural conservatism of the Massey Report. It was also made amidst important changes to the general policy thrust of the Canadian state. Although there was no open break with continentalism, a number of events pointed to increasing tensions between the United States and Canada, and a willingness on the part of the Canadian state to be more assertive in its defence of declared national interests. In 1963, the Canadian government imposed retroactive legislation to prevent an American takeover of a Canadian bank; the two countries had also discovered that they were involved in a balance-of-payments pas de deux, in which Canadian toes were being badly bruised. In 1965, just as it seemed that the doctrine of 'quiet diplomacy' had been fully reconfirmed, Prime Minister Pearson took the rather uncharacteristic step of openly denouncing the American bombings of North Vietnam. One year later, Canada's endorsement of United Nations membership for the People's Republic of China went against U.S. foreign policy interests.[2]

In 1964, Walter Gordon had introduced a budget that became infamous for its 'nationalist' predilections. Among other things it included a provision to help Canada's ailing periodical press by disallowing the tax write-off for Canadian advertising in foreign-based periodicals. The budget was sternly denounced by representatives of Canadian capital – the business community was still firmly committed to the general contours of continentalism – and Walter Gordon began a long slide into political oblivion. The new legislation concerning periodicals was symbolic of the contradictions that were emerging as Ottawa sought to renegotiate the terms of the postwar settlement with the United States. *Time* and *Reader's Digest*, the two largest-selling foreign periodicals in Canada, were made exempt from the new tax provisions.[3] Nationalist sentiment may have been on the rise, but it would not be easily welded onto a political economy and political strategy that were still, at root, resolutely continentalist. Indeed, if there was a general strategy to the Canadian state's strained attempt to restructure the relationships of dependency, it was the following: advance Canadian interests without seriously damaging or disrupting prevailing American interests and their Canadian allies. It was a rule to be invoked when it came time to establish the Canadian Film Development Corporation (CFDC).

While federal governments of the sixties remained cautious in their attempt to renegotiate the pattern of continentalism, they were far more aggressive in terms of expanding the parameters of the welfare state. In particular, the Pearson government, much more than its predecessors, accepted the logic of Keynesianism and state planning. State expenditures were to be used to generate private investment and economic growth, while at the same time providing an expanded network of public goods and services, aimed at improving the 'quality of life' under advanced capitalism. Borrowing from the rhetoric of the New Deal, Pearson's 1963 election campaign promised 'sixty days of decision'; he talked about improved regional development programs, a 40-hour work week, portable old age pensions, a national health plan, and a department of industry.[4] The reforms took shape over the next four years, a period one might justifiably call the second wave of the Canadian welfare state. In the context of economic growth and budgetary surpluses that prevailed, new state programs and expenditures met with far less political resistance. A relatively small loan fund for the development of a private film industry would not be difficult to justify.

Perhaps the most important social base for the new thrust in state intervention came from the growing ranks of postsecondary graduates, the first generation of a vastly expanded and far more accessible university system. Imbued with a mild reformism, the 'baby-boom' generation had internalized the broadly social-democratic norms of the postwar consensus. As the war in Vietnam intensified, and as domestic racial violence tarnished America's golden hues, the prospect of becoming part of the 'brain drain' to the United States became less and less attractive. The postwar generation increasingly looked to Canada itself as a source of opportunity and, perhaps, as a haven from the turmoil ever more apparent in the new imperial centre. In what might be called a latent 'defensive nationalism,' many of these new middle-class aspirants began to look to the state as an instrument through which better jobs and opportunities could be created. In general, there was increasing unease with both the symbol and the reality of Canada's 'undefended border.'

At the same time, a new orientation toward the cultural industries and the importance of popular culture was emerging. To the postwar generation in particular, film, television, radio, and the new media in general did not pose an affront to aesthetic and cultural values; in fact, they were seen as promising avenues where viable employment did not foreclose the possibility of creative expression. We have already seen such views expressed in the briefs of the APC. The cultural conservatism of Canada's old guard was in decline (perhaps this itself reflected the triumph of American cultural hegemony over the legacy of British colonialism). Of course there were still those, like George Grant, who sought salvation in a return to the old values of an élite culture, but romanticism for the past was no longer regarded by most as the solution to the problem of foreign cultural penetration. It was now much more a question of developing Canada's own cultural industries, of dealing with such influences as American movies and American television through the establishment of Canadian alternatives within those same media. Given the structure and dynamics of these industries, already well documented by earlier government reports, the Canadian state would have to take a lead role in establishing the basis for a greater, more independent presence in the field of popular culture. It was a question of economics *and* culture – it had become impossible to consider the latter without due regard for the former.

While the establishment of the CFDC was one of the clearest examples of the Canadian state's decision to promote the Canadianization of popular culture in Canada, it was not an isolated event in the history of Canadian cultural policy during the 1960s. The Royal Commission on Bilingualism and Biculturalism, the significant budgetary increases to the Canada Council, the National Museums Act of 1964, the *Time* and *Reader's Digest* débâcle, the enormous expenditures for the Centennial celebrations, and the new Broadcasting Act of 1968, together attest to a decade in which cultural issues moved to the forefront of the state's agenda.[5] These various policy initiatives reflected a wide range of immediate concerns, but they were driven by two particularly prominent objectives. In the first place, the Canadian state had increased its responsibility for the expansion of privately produced Canadian cultural products in an effort to reduce dependence on foreign, mostly American, cultural products. In the second place, federal officials and politicians recognized the need to respond to events taking place within Quebec by asserting, more clearly than before, the federal government's role in establishing and maintaining a *national* cultural identity. Neither objective was realized fully or unproblematically, and much of the history of Canadian cultural policy from this point onward is precisely about the contradictions and limitations these policies encountered and displayed.

Cultural Policy in Quebec

As we have noted, the transition to a more focused concerned on cultural issues was not something unique to the federal government. In fact, it was in Quebec where a new political strategy first brought the interaction between state and culture to the top of the public agenda. On 2 March 1961, the new Liberal government in Quebec announced the establishment of the Department of Cultural Affairs. 'Par l'établissement d'un ministère des Affaires culturelles,' explained Jean Lesage, 'le gouvernement de la Province jouera le rôle qui lui incombe dans la vie culturelle du Québec et de la nation.'[6] The department, with Georges-Émile Lapalme as its first minister and Guy Frégault, a noted historian, as its deputy minister, consisted of four branches: the Office de la langue française, le Département du Canada français d'outre-frontières, the Conseil provincial des arts, and the Commission des monuments historiques. Lesage moved quickly to dispel any fears that the Quebec government was establishing a cultural czar. His comments nicely capture the general manner in which Canadian governments have both approached and rationalized the question of state intervention into the cultural sphere.

Entendons-nous biens. Le gouvernement ne crée pas la culture et le gouvernement ne la dirige pas non plus. Le gouvernement cherche tout simplement à créer le climat qui facilite l'épanouissement des arts. Ni socialiste, ni conservateur, le gouvernement libéral veut agir envers les arts comme envers l'entreprise privée: sans paternalisme et sans laissez-faire.[7]

Those who feared a dirigiste approach fashioned along the lines of France's

Ministry of Culture could relax, less because of what government officials said about the new department than because of what the department actually did and did not do. The initial budget of the department was less than $3 million, and it grew slowly throughout the 1960s.[8] The most significant new expenditures were reserved for the construction of performing arts centres: Place des Arts in Montreal and the Grand Théâtre de Québec were both completed in 1968 (perhaps a response to the federal government's own emphasis on new buildings for the performing arts as the basis of its Centennial expenditures). More important, in the long run, the Office de la langue française was laying the groundwork for the language laws of the 1970s, as it concerned itself with the arduous task of 'codifying and stabilizing language usage and bringing technical and economic lexicons into the language.'[9] In the short run, however, these changes had little effect on the production or consumption of Quebec-based popular culture. In fact, the department did not administer any significant new programs of monetary support to individual artists, and although lengthy position papers on the publishing and film industries recommended radical new forms of state intervention, the Liberal government left Quebec's cultural industries relatively unchanged.

Quebec filmmakers could be excused for showing a degree of optimism in 1963, when the government's newly established Office du film du Québec was told to prepare a new film law. Presided over by André Guérin, a five-volume study was prepared by the Office in collaboration with the Conseil d'orientation économique du Québec, the government's own policy think-tank. The final report, *Cinéma et Culture*, reflected the priorities of the Association professionelle des cinéastes. It presented a strong case for a loan fund, a box-office levy, an exhibition quota, and the improvement of educational opportunities in filmmaking as the mechanisms by which a Quebec-based film industry could be developed. In its conclusion, *Cinéma et Culture* echoed the sentiments expressed before it by Claude Jutra: 'Il est urgent que l'État Québec abaisse les murailles qu'affronte l'entrepreneur de longs métrages afin que ce dernier puisse n'avoir qu'un défi normal à relever et que puisse naître, au soleil, dans le secteur privé, un production national de longs métrages. Il n'y a de grand cinéma, que dans la liberté, la clarité, la compétition.'[10] For all intents and purposes, the report was shelved. In fact, the only significant change in Quebec film policy during this period was the revision of its censorship provisions. In keeping with the trend toward secularization, Quebec established a censorship code that followed North American standards, rescinding the old law, which kept children under the age of 12 out of Quebec's theatres – the legacy of the paternalism of the Catholic Church.

The decision, or more appropriately non-decision, maddened Quebec filmmakers. APC president Jacques Godbout thought that the Quebec government was suffering from 'une myopie dangereuse'; Lamontagne, on the other hand, was described as 'un visionnaire.'[11] André Guérin wrote his own report in 1966 which examined Quebec's position in light of the federal government's plans to support feature film production. Guérin could barely contain his frustration and anger. He ridiculed the Quebec government for its 'caractère plutôt négatif et passif.' Lamontagne's announcement 'n'a suscité ni commentaire ni réaction de la part de Québec! Aveuglement. Ignorance, ou naïveté?' Guérin asked.[12] Guérin argued that the federal law was unconstitutional, that it would lead to federal control of the Quebec cinema, and that there was every chance it would only profit English-Canadian, or even American, filmmaking. He wanted the impending law declared *ultra vires*, and he wanted the Quebec government to declare immediately its intention to legislate in this domain. At the very least, Guérin thought the government should try to 'opt out' of the plan and receive in return a grant from the federal government to administer its own program of loans and subsidies.

Guérin's proposals were ignored, and the electoral victory of Daniel Johnston's Union Nationale government in June 1966 made it even less likely that Quebec would be the sight of state intervention to support the cultural industries. But why had the Liberal government, which had quite clearly placed the preservation and development of Quebec culture at the forefront of its political agenda, been so lax in its substantive implementation? In the first place, the rhetorical appeals to Quebec culture were strategically important to the establishment of an ideological consensus around the vast economic and social reforms put in train by the Liberal government. If French Canadians could come to identify themselves as Québécois – and see their culture as something forward-looking and dynamic – they would be much more willing to accept the Quebec government as their 'state,' as the principal institution responsible for the 'modernization' of Quebec society. As William Coleman maintains, the Quiet Revolution itself was mainly an attempt to integrate Quebec society more fully into the advanced industrial economy of North America. As his analysis shows, economic policies were accorded a much higher priority than those that involved the cultural field. Coleman suggests that stripped of its rhetoric the program for cultural development was principally geared toward the establishment of French as the acceptable language of business in Quebec. There was indeed an explosion of new cultural forms and practices in Quebec in the 1960s, but very little of it was the result of government-sponsored programs. As Coleman concludes: 'In cultural policy, then, the Quiet Revolution itself was a revolution of symbols.'[13] They were symbols, however, the federal government could not afford to ignore.

Lamontagne and the Secretary of State: Planning and Assistance

The federal government had continued its incremental development of cultural policy throughout the 1950s. Aside from the presiding over the introduction of television, the St. Laurent government gave substance to the major recommendation of the Massey Report when, in 1957, it established the Canada Council. There were also more Royal Commissions, each one more stridently committed to increasing state support in the various cultural fields. In 1961, the Royal Commission on Publications (O'Leary Commission) observed that 'communications are the thread which binds together the fibres of a nation ... The communications of a nation are as vital to its life as its defences, and should receive at least as great a measure of national protection.'[14] The O'Leary Commission, like the Fowler Commission on Broadcasting before it, seemed much less obsessed with the problem of mass culture as the basis upon which national identity could be built. The cultural industries had been deemed worthy of public support. Increasingly the major issue was cast along nationalist lines. 'Can we resist the tidal wave of American cultural activity? Can we retain a Canadian identity, art, and culture – a Canadian nationhood?' asked the Fowler Committee.[15] Of course there was a certain irony in the O'Leary Commission's reference to culture as another form of national defence (a metaphor used previously by the Massey Report). The NORAD Treaty of 1958 made it abundantly clear that the United States would control the future of continental defence. In one sense then everything was in order. Canadian culture was receiving the same treatment as was the nation's defence.

As part of its 'New Deal' tone, the Pearson Liberal government committed itself to addressing the problem of state support for Canadian culture. The decision was part not only the party's emphasis on a more interventionist state, but also of its recognition that forces within Quebec were working, perhaps still unwittingly, to undermine the national interest as defined by Ottawa. In December 1962, three months before the Liberals toppled the minority Conservative government, Pearson called for an inquiry to examine 'the means of developing the bicultural character of Canada.' Pearson rejected the isolationism that had characterized relations between the two founding cultures, saying that he would not condone a situation in which 'what is called the "French fact" was to be provincial only.'[16] Instead, French Canadians had to be given 'equal and full opportunity to participate in all federal government services,' while at the same time there had to be 'the greatest possible constitutional decentralization ... to strengthen, indeed to establish and maintain, unity.'[17] Only a few months after obtaining office, the Liberal party announced the formation of the Royal Commission on Bilingualism and Biculturalism. (It would deliberate on the problem for most of the rest of the decade.) Pearson's speech made it clear that the Quebec problem, as it came to be known, had opened up a second front in the attack on Canadian cultural unity. The first front had by now become well known: 'We are becoming more and more dependent upon the United States, culturally, economically, and even politically.'[18] Somehow both issues would have to be addressed.

The author of Pearson's speech was Maurice Lamontagne, a francophone economist with a Harvard PHD who had moved to the forefront of the Liberal party. An economic adviser to the Privy Council in the 1950s, Lamontagne became one of Pearson's personal advisers during the Liberal party's stint in opposition. He was first elected to the House in the 1963 election. Although Lamontagne preceded Jean Marchand, Gérard Pelletier, and Pierre Elliot Trudeau – the Liberal party's 'three wise men' from Quebec – into the upper echelons of the party's leadership by two years, his role in establishing the party's early strategy toward Quebec's Quiet Revolution has probably been underestimated. In fact, the Royal Commission on Bilingualism and Biculturalism was only a part of his strategy to integrate French and English Canada and refurbish the bonds of national identity.

Lamontagne became secretary of state in February 1964. *Le Devoir*, in a reference to France's illustrous Minister of Culture, referred to Lamontagne as 'un Malraux Canadien,' while the *Toronto Star* claimed that Canada had its first 'cultural czar.'[19] Lamontagne himself suggested that 'my post would be better called 'Minister of culture and education,' but the provinces are sensitive about culture being part of education and thus a provincial matter.'[20]

Whatever he was called, or called himself, Lamontagne's notability derived in large measure from the bureaucratic transformation of his portfolio.[21] Although the Secretary of State had existed since Confederation, its principal responsibilities – the Registrar General of Canada, the government's Translation Bureau, a small protocol section, the Companies Branch, and the Patent Office – had hitherto been far from onerous. But it was this department that became the focal point of the Liberal government's attempt to establish a more coordinated approach to cultural policy. By 1965, the Secretary of State had taken on administration of the following cultural agencies: The Canada Council, the CBC, the Board of Broadcast Governors, the NFB, the National Gallery, the National Museum, the National Library and Public Archives, the Centennial Commission, and the Queen's Printer. The revamped department was well suited to Lamontagne's attitude toward cultural development and his perception of the important steering role to be played by the state.

In speech after speech during his tenure as secretary of state, Lamontagne returned to certain basic themes. 'Since 1867, we have left our cultural life almost exclusively to personal initiative and private organizations. As a result, the body of our national culture has remained relatively anaemic; and to the extent of their development, our principal cultures, French and English speaking, and even our other cultures, had grown up in isolation. This cultural poverty and isolation are two of the main sources of tension in our country today.'[22] Although Lamountagne understood the ill effects that attended the massive inflow of foreign cultural products, he refused to depict this as a problem that stemmed from sources outside of Canadian control, from a rapacious American culture exercising its own version of manifest destiny. Rather, the problem lay in the fact that Canadians had 'adhered much to closely to the American tradition of non-intervention by government. As a result, our cultural life is relatively weak and dangerously exposed to the dominating influences of the United States.'[23] In his own variation of welfare state rhetoric, Lamontagne declared war on 'cultural poverty': the goal was not isolation from American culture but more and better Canadian culture, including, *pace* the Massey Report, 'better Canadian ''escapist entertainment''.'[24]

The principal vehicle for this cultural expansion was to be the state, working with and through private cultural producers in all sectors of cultural endeavour. In making the promotion of 'popular' culture a priority for the state, Lamontagne had broken through the practical and ideological limits of the Massey Report. In a speech to the Canadian Conference of the Arts entitled 'Planning and the Arts,' Lamontagne outlined his perspective on the nature and importance of state intervention:

How are we going to overcome the crisis? There are, in my view, two complementary ways: planning and assistance. Planning without assistance is not enough; but assistance without planning leads to a waste of human resources.

In recent years the need for economic planning has been recognized by the leaders of the private sector ... The kind of economic planning that we are trying to develop in Canada can be described as a conscious and organized attempt by governments and other collective bodies to co-ordinate public and private policies more rationally in order to reach desirable objectives or goals more effectively. This is indicative planning which provides knowledge of prospects and targets as well as incentives but excludes compulsion and controls. This is co-ordination by consultation and assistance.

I believe that the same kind of indicative planning is also necessary for the arts ... We should try to improve administration and organization, but we must preserve at all costs creative independence. Planning would simply mean that the private artistic community would be organized more effectively, that it would be more closely integrated to the social environment, and that it would be in a better position to meet its local, regional and national purposes.[25]

Given state officials' predilection toward incremental policy formation, Lamontagne's faith in planning was a somewhat radical departure from the norm of Canadian bureaucratic practice. 'Un Malraux Canadien' appeared to be an appropriate and prescient label. In fact, Lamontagne did take steps to improve the planning process for cultural policy within his own department and within the state apparatus as a whole. He instructed many of the cultural agencies, such as the NFB, to conduct internal reviews of their own operations, and he took steps to establish a departmental inter-agency committee to discuss common problems and improve coordination. A Cabinet Committee on Cultural Affairs was also established, and Lamontagne spearheaded a movement to form a permanent parliamentary committee in the same field.[26] To complement this internal rationalization, Lamontagne prodded the country's various private cultural organizations to tailor their own administrations toward greater coordination both with the state and with each other, in some cases giving them public grants to do so.

Although he ardently defended the extension of state support to cultural development, Lamontagne also endorsed the principle that, first and foremost, the state's role was to facilitate greater cultural production by the private sector. In a speech to the House of Commons, Lamontagne explained that the fundamental goal of cultural policy was to provide 'assistance to individuals and private groups to enable them to improve themselves ... This is an essential element in a society like ours which relies primarily on private initiative.'[27] The state could improve the investment climate for cultural productions by offering financial incentives for certain types of production and providing a certain amount of protection from foreign competition; it could also help build the infrastructure that would be necessary for expanded cultural activities. The state, to use the rhetoric of the 'New Deal,' could 'prime the pump' of Canada's private cultural sector.

Inside the State: Making Policy for a Feature Film Industry

On 9 December 1963, Lamontagne's predecessor as secretary of state, J.W. Pickersgill, issued a Cabinet memorandum establishing the Interdepartmental Committee on the Possible Development of Feature Film Production in Canada.[28] The Committee included representatives from the Department of Finance, the Department of Industry, the Department of Trade and Commerce, External Affairs, the Bank of Canada, and the National Film Board. It was chaired by the government film commissioner, Guy Roberge. The NFB was also represented by its director of planning, Michael Spencer, who, along with Roberge, would carry out the burden on the Committee's work. Although Lamontagne would soon speak of a new spirit of cooperation between the cultural community and the state, the work of the Committee was done *in camera* and without the formal participation of interested groups or individuals within the industry. The various briefs submitted to the Committee certainly played a part in the deliberations, but ultimately the policy was constructed by state officials acting in rather typical bureaucratic fashion.

The board of the NFB asked Roberge to pursue the question of state support for feature filmmaking after a meeting with Nat Taylor in late 1962. Received by Pickersgill in September 1963, the memo was drafted by Michael Spencer and signed by Roberge.[29] Spencer and Roberge recommended the establishment of a loan fund of $3 million to be dispensed over the course of three to four years, with not more than $50,000 going to any single production. Although the numbers were moderate, they felt that such a fund 'would provide adequate assistance to launch a feature film industry in Canada.'[30] Given its role as the coordinating body of government film activities, Roberge and Spencer assumed that the fund would be administered by the NFB. Undoubtedly, this assumption would draw the ire of private producers, many of whom still harboured a certain paranoia at the mere mention of the words 'National Film Board.' Pickersgill accepted the main points of the memo, but in the tradition of Liberal politicians well schooled in the practice of avoiding potential conflicts, and as one who could recall earlier public roastings of the NFB, he directed the Inter-departmental Committee to develop plans for a new agency to administer whatever programs were decided upon.[31]

At the same time, federal officials were moving on a second front to support the development of a feature film industry. In 1963, in conjunction with the Department of External Affairs, Roberge and Spencer began negotiations on co-production treaties with a number of European countries. They were assisted in their efforts by Budge Crawley and Julian Roffman.[32] Co-operation treaties facilitate film productions by allowing producers to take advantage of whatever subsidies and protective legislation exist in the signatory countries involved in a given project.[33] They had become all the rage in Europe; in Italy and France especially, co-production established the economic basis for the boom in film production in the early 1960s. Canada's first treaty was signed with France in the fall of 1963. Films made by citizens of France and Canada, in which the artistic, technical, and financial involvement of the minority partner was not lower than 30 per cent could qualify as co-productions and take advantage of the support mechanisms in place in each country.[34] Roberge felt that the treaty would give Canada's young film industry 'a shot in the arm.'[35] Of course, it was highly unlikely that French producers would be interested in any deals until the Canadian state developed its own package of supports.

The Interdepartmental Committee held its first meeting in January 1964 and by late July Lamontagne was able to go to Cabinet with its first proposal. The main recommendation, the establishment of a loan fund, had already cleared its most important bureaucratic hurdle – the Department of Finance had agreed to supply the funds.[36] Even so, Lamontagne had trouble getting the Cabinet Committee on Cultural Affairs to consider the report, and the NFB's 25th anniversary, the perfect occasion on which to announce the new policy, was less than a week away. After considerable bureaucratic manoeuvring, a summary of the report was tabled in Cabinet and quickly approved. Aside from agreeing to the loan fund, Cabinet asked the Committee to work out details of the program and include in its next report an examination of the 'distribution problems faced by Canadian films,' and of 'other practical measures that could help the production of Canadian films.'[37]

Five days later, Lamontagne made the decision public at the NFB's anniversary celebration:

We have come to the conclusion that the establishment of a feature film industry in Canada is highly desirable and that technical facilities and talent are available in our country to make such a development practicable. We are also conscious of the fact that some form of public assistance is required to foster the Canadian feature film industry. Therefore it is the intention of the government to ask Parliament for the necessary authority to establish a loan fund for the production of feature films of high quality in Canada ... Ce sera là un signe de notre progrès et peut-être aussi de notre maturité culturels.[38]

Not surprisingly, Canadian producers and filmmakers met the annoucement with considerable elation. Guy Coté, president of the APC, felt that it was a momentous occasion 'aussi importante pour les cinéastes et tout le public canadien que celle, il y a 25 ans, qui donna naissance à l'ONF.'[39] Not everyone displayed the same enthusiasm. The *Globe and Mail*, in an editorial entitled 'Money to Burn,' called it 'a most expensive, and most uncertain business.' If Canada was to have a feature film industry then it should come about through 'private citizens risking their own money, in the belief that their venture can succeed. Government assistance, whether in loans or subsidies – or loans that turn into subsidies – is the wrong way to go about it.'[40] The Tories were equally circumspect. 'What cultural development, to which lip service is given in the statement of the minister, can be achieved in this way?' asked

Diefenbaker in the House.[41] Opposition to the proposal probably reflected both a cultural conservatism with respect to 'mass' culture, and a general distrust of state intervention in the economy, but it was not strong enough to deter the Liberal party's initiative.

The Committee resumed its work in the fall and commissioned three detailed studies on the structure of the film industry: one by Fernand Cadieux on the private production sector in Quebec, a second by Michael Spencer on the private production sector in English Canada, and a third by O.J. Firestone on the question of distribution.[42] Spencer's study was by far the more detailed of the first two. After interviewing 16 of the country's producers and reviewing the briefs of the APC, DGC, and Society of Film Makers (a new organization representing both English and French NFB filmmakers), Spencer concluded once again that a feature film industry could get off the ground on the basis of a loan fund alone.[43] Such a fund was necessary, Spencer argued, because the Canadian financial community had shown itself to be extremely conservative in its support to private producers. 'Referring to banks in general, the experience of producers has been uniformly discouraging,' wrote Spencer. As one producer told him, 'they require far tighter control and excessive collateral compared to U.S. bankers,'[44] Spencer argued that a state-sponsored loan fund would encourage the private financial community to loosen its investment criteria.

The loan fund had been agreed upon, but where would the Committee fall on the question of other types of support to the industry? There is little evidence that an exhibition quota or box-office levy were ever considered to be serious options. It is hard to know whether this was simply because theatre legislation is a matter of provincial jurisdiction, or if it was because federal officials could not condone such interventionist measures. More than likely it was a combination of the two – the intricacies of federalism allowed the Committee to avoid a recommendation that would have angered both the major exhibitors and distributors, and, no doubt, a major portion of the Canadian public.[45] In an interview, Spencer commented that an exhibition quota would have been a grave mistake at this point: there were simply not enough Canadian feature films being produced to fill even the most minimal of quota formulas.[46] This was true insofar as one considered the various European schemes for reserving 20 per cent or more of national screen time for domestic productions, but the committee could have recommended that, at the very least, Canadian films that had won national or international awards be guaranteed proper exhibition in major theatres.

The Committee also decided to leave the distribution system the way it was. While Spencer's report noted that four private producers supported the position of the DGC and APC and their proposal of a special tax on foreign distributors, both Spencer and Roberge held serious reservations about interfering with the market practices of the major distributors. They were of the opinion that American distributors would accept good Canadian feature films into their distribution system when the time came. There seemed no point in creating a hostile environment before it was absolutely clear that Canadian films would find distribution hard to obtain.[47] After conducting his own study, Firestone was less than enthusiastic about the prospect of cooperation from American distributors. He noted that the subsidiaries in Canada 'were not in a position to make any important decisions at all,' and told the Committee that when he met with representatives in New York and suggested that they agree to reinvest ten per cent of their film rentals in Canadian productions the reaction was 'leave us alone we're doing a great job providing first-class entertainment.'[48] Firestone likewise concluded that it would be unwise to take discriminatory action in advance. Indeed the Committee seems to have shared the view expressed by Nat Taylor that, given the costs of feature filmmaking and the small size of the Canadian market, Canadian productions would have to gain significant export revenues to be profitable. In this respect, distribution through one of the major American companies was considered crucial to the long-term commercial success of the Canadian feature film industry. It would be best, therefore, if relations with the American majors remained amiable.

After a weekend meeting at the Seigniory Club in Quebec, where Committee members were joined by John Terry, of Britain's National Film Finance Corporation, and Jean-Claude Batz, who had been instrumental in drafting Belgium's new film laws, the details were finalized.[49] Terry's contribution was particularly important. He recommended that the fund be set at $10 million to be spent over five years, and that the definition of what constituted a 'Canadian' film be left rather vague so that it could be 'interpreted' by the new agency as circumstances changed. The final report emphasized 'continuity of production' and 'international distribution' as essential attributes of a stable and successful Canadian feature film industry. The focus was clearly on films that would sell in the international marketplace, and although the Committee felt that sufficient technical and creative personnel already existed in Canada, it noted that 'in some instances' it would be advantageous to employ 'foreign creative talent' and 'foreign stars.'[50] What then would constitute a 'Canadian film'? Here, the Committee followed John Terry's advice on a general definition and concluded that a Canadian film would be one in which 'the copyright is the property either of a Canadian citizen or of a company incorporated in Canada,' and in which 'the creative, artistic, and technical contribution by Canadian collaborators is of obvious importance.'[51] This definition did not undergo any significant modifications in the final Act.

The Committee's final report was submitted for Cabinet approval on 12 August 1965, slightly more than a year and a half after its deliberations had begun.[52] Cabinet agreed to a total fund of $10 million, to be dispensed over five years. Of this amount, $8.5 million would be used for investment loans to producers, and the remaining $1.5 million would be used for awards and assistance to producers, scriptwriters, filmmakers, technicians, and film administrators for the improvement of their craft. On the question of distribution, Cabinet followed the Committee's recommendation to work through the 'established channels'; however, it also noted that 'other measures may be necessary if such distribution cannot be obtained on an equitable basis.'[53] It was a phrase that both reflected and sought to ameliorate concern that the major American distributors might not do all they could to support Canadian productions. For the time being, however, the majors and their allies in exhibition had been spared any inconvenience. A $10 million loan fund to production would certainly not create a major upheaval in the day-to-day operations of the major interests in the Canadian film industry. And, if the loan fund would help create a few Canadian features deemed worthy of international distribution, then Nat Taylor was probably right to argue that the Hollywood majors would pick them up. Cabinet also recommended that the new agency, the Canadian Film Development Corporation, should establish an 'advisory group' made up of 'professional producers' and filmmakers' associations, exhibitors, distributors, and unions in the Canadian film industry' that would advise the Corporation on matters referred to it.[54] The CFDC and its activities would be subject to an internal review at the end of five years.

Soon after Cabinet approved the plan, Secretary of State and Department of Justice officials began drafting the legislation. Guy Roberge tried to play a prominent role in this process, but his dedication to the task did not find favour with the undersecretary of state or other federal officials. In a memo to Lamontagne, G.G.E. Steele wrote: 'I think you might wish to consider whether the lead on this legislation should be given to Guy Roberge. You noticed from the Cabinet Committee meeting some suspicion of how the NFB will be involved in the new program and I think it is important from the point of view of policy to create a clear distinction in the public mind.'[55] In terms of policy making it is not altogether clear how Roberge's involvement could be so detrimental, but for 'political' reasons the NFB's involvement was clearly deleterious: it conjured up images of government monopoly and state control at a time when it was trying to give a new importance to private production and market forces.

Neither Lamontagne nor Roberge would be around for the Bill's passage through Parliament. After close to eight years as government film commissioner, Roberge was appointed to the Quebec House in London in April 1966. Grant McLean became the acting commissioner until a full-time replacement could be found. Lamontagne's career as secretary of state came to a more ignominious end. In December 1965, his name was added to the growing list of Liberal party scandals after it was revealed that he had received free furniture from a Montreal company. Lamontagne resigned and was later appointed to the Senate. Judy LaMarsh became the new secretary of state.

Before his departure Lamontagne had suggested that the CFDC Act would be passed by April 1966, but as LaMarsh told the *Globe and Mail*, Bill C-204 did not receive the highest priority from Cabinet.[56] That was a bit of an understatement. If cultural affairs had moved closer to the top of the political agenda, it was the drafting of the new Broadcasting Act and the preparations of the Centennial Commission that most preoccupied the Liberal government. In comparison with the CFDC's allotment of $10 million to be spent over five years, the Centennial Commission had a budget of about $100 million (though it is quite probable that much more was finally spent).[57] The Centennial celebrations had been conceived as a way of boosting national unity, of breaking down the barriers of isolation that Lamontagne had described, and, of course, of promoting the political fortunes of the Liberal party itself. Much of the money went to the construction of large centres for the performing arts, testament to the fact that state support to 'high culture' was still accorded a high priority, perhaps because there was still no better way of promoting the image of a strong, but 'civilized' state.[58]

Bill C-204, an Act to provide for the establishment of the Canadian Film Development Corporation, was introduced in the House in June 1966. It received final reading in March of the following year. Opposition members, while critical of the lengthy delays in bringing the legislation before Parliament, generally supported the government's initiative. There were, however, some important objections to the details of the legislation. Most of them were raised not by the NDP, but by David MacDonald, a 'red Tory' and United Church minister from Prince Edward Island. Macdonald was upset that the ownership and copyright clause of Bill C-204 left the door open for American production companies to establish subsidiaries and take advantage of the proposed funds. 'I think there is a loophole in this legislation big enough to push a whole movie studio through,' MacDonald told the House.[59] LaMarsh would not accept an amendment that called for '51% ownership' or even for 'significant Canadian ownership' in the corporation that held the copyright to an eligible film. From her point of view, the major studios were not going to rush northwards for 'a miserable $10 million.'[60] She was probably right, and there was no way the government was going to entertain more restrictive clauses that would undoubtedly draw fire from the United States.

MacDonald also aired the APC's and DGC's concern that Canadian productions would be marginalized by the dominant interests in distribution and exhibition.[61] LaMarsh again stood her ground. As she told the *Globe and Mail*: 'This isn't an anti-poverty program. It's to get an industry going which we expect will be able to stand on its own feet.'[62] In the House, LaMarsh explained the government's position further: 'We should ... be under no illusions about the difficulties which Canadian producers will face in building up a commercially viable industry in this country. They will have to make it commercially viable by exporting their work, which will have to be done by profitable distribution arrangements. Canadian films must prove good enough to win their own place on world screens.'[63] The marketplace would determine the ultimate success of the Canadian feature film industry. Distribution through the majors would have to be 'deserved.' As LaMarsh told the House: 'If we try to pass off a lot of second-rate films, or art films, and wave a nationalist flag and say, "You fellows who show films in this country are going to have to show ours," we may find some resistance.'[64] That too was a bit of an understatement.

Bill C-204 had just gone through first reading when the Secretary of State received a request for funds. It came from David Griesdorf, vice-president of International Film Distributors.[65] Nat Taylor and Griesdorf were interested in co-producing a film to be called *Ski Bum*, with Embassy Studio, an American production company. Norman Jewison, a Canadian citizen who was beginning to make it big in Hollywood, was touted as the 'possible' director. The 'ski bum' in question would be either Peter O'Toole, Paul Newman, or Steve McQueen. Production was budgeted at $4 million (a hefty sum even by then-current Hollywood standards), and Taylor and Griesdorf wanted a loan of $1 million from the CFDC (ten per cent of the entire five-year budget). As if history actually repeats itself (recall Nelson Eddy and the Canadian Co-operation Project), the proposal was rationalized as 'a good Centennial ploy for tourists in spotlighting the Rockies,' where most of the 'action' would take place. The request was turned down, on the basis that the money could not be advanced before the CFDC was established.

Taylor still believed that Canada might hold an advantage over European film industries because of its potential ability to 'produce, what or practical purposes, might be adjudged an American film'[66] He for one seemed ready to give it a try. Others would follow. But at the same time, there were filmmakers – especially those in Quebec – who seemed genuinely excited about the prospect of constructing a specific, national cinema that would establish its own aesthetic and narrative codes. Two very different perceptions of what a Canadian feature film industry should look like confronted the CFDC as it began the business of establishing the industry's foundations – albeit on the basis of 'a miserable $10 million,' the total cost of about five major Hollywood pictures at the time.

7 The CFDC and 'A Miserable Ten Million Dollars'

We have failed to answer the historic question: Is film an art or a business? Government policy has been trying to serve both masters simultaneously, rather than identify the dichotomy between them and deal with each separately. This is the prime contradiction, and the failure to resolve it, has led to the present paralysis of policy. The result has been confusion, and finally crisis, in film production. – Kirwan Cox[1]

Introduction

There had been no immediate sense of urgency in getting the CFDC Act through Parliament. Nor was there any apparent rush to make the Corporation operational once its legislative existence had been proclaimed. The chairperson, Georges-Émile Lapalme, and board of directors were not appointed until February 1968; one year later, Michael Spencer was named executive director (having served as acting secretary in the interim). It was late fall before the Corporation made its first investments.[2] Since it had taken the federal government over 40 years to initiate some form of public support for private-sector feature film production, this latest procrastination may seem neither consequential nor surprising; yet it is hard not to conclude that the delays themselves reflected the provisional nature of the CFDC's status with respect to the government's overall policy objectives in the cultural sphere.

Because of the very weak structure of Canada's feature film (and television) production industry, the CFDC would be an enterprise fraught with difficulties and prone to failure. Certainly, other facets of the federal government's forays into the cultural sphere at this time offered better prospects for success. Aside from the Centennial celebrations (which had consumed a considerable amount of state capital and political energy but paid handsome and immediate political dividends), in 1968, after numerous studies and commissions, Parliament passed a new Broadcasting Act. The legislation 'declared that all broadcasting under-takings, public and private, constituted a single system,' and that 'the Canadian broadcasting system should be effectively owned and controlled by Canadians so as to safeguard, enrich and strengthen the cultural, political, social and economic fabric of Canada.' It stated also that 'programming provided by each broadcaster should be of high standard, using predominantly Canadian creative and other resources.'[3] The Canadian Radio-Television Commission (CRTC) was entrusted with the task of interpreting and enforcing the new Act. Its first chairperson was Pierre Juneau, who by now had a reputation as an effective public administrator with strong nationalist tendencies. Given its mandate, and the fact that television had superseded the cinema as the pre-eminent form of popular culture, the CRTC quickly occupied centre stage in the conflict over the extent to which the state would redress the inflow of foreign cultural products and support the development of Canadian cultural industries.

If the CRTC represented the 'stick' approach to the issue of Canadian content – by regulating broadcasters to deliver more domestic programming than they would have under normal market conditions, the CFDC approached the issue of Canadian content with a 'carrot' – by offering subsidies to defray or underwrite the costs of production. Certainly, for the growing ranks of Canadian national-ists the CFDC was to be a key institution in the drive to 'Canadianize' popular culture. So it was, but the one-time grant of $10 million, and the decision to forgo legislative measures with respect to distribution and exhibition, also suggest that the state was taking a minimalist approach to the problem. Remarkably, government officials also believed that the CFDC would have a finite existence: it was to establish the foundations for a feature film industry that over time would become self-financing and self-generating. The CFDC reflected both the rhythm and the limitations of state policy; it would be diffi-cult for it to set a tempo of its own.

Moreover, although conceived during a period of relative fiscal abundance, the CFDC began operations precisely at the point when the state came under increasing pressure to impose a new regime of fiscal restraint. By the late 1960s, the boom period of the postwar economy had played itself out, and inflation had become a serious economic and political issue.[4] In 1969, the federal government announced austerity measures intended to cut the budgets of all government agencies by between 10 and 20 per cent (with inflation in the private sector to be regulated by the newly established Prices and Incomes Commission). Conceived in a period of budgetary surpluses, the CFDC would have to operate in a period of growing fiscal restraint. It was critical that the CFDC make sound investment decisions, particularly if it was to sustain the support of the Department of Finance and the Treasury Board in the context of an ever-increasing concern with inflation and the emerging 'fiscal crisis of the state.'

Given that private risk capital for feature filmmaking in Canada had always been hard to come by, there was no doubt that the CFDC would be a crucial variable in establishing the direction of the feature film industry. As a loan agency, the Corporation was not to engage in production itself, but it was equally clear that the feature film fund was not designed as a ready pool of capital to be tapped at will by private producers. The CFDC was to operate first as a banker with a solid interest in securing a return on its own investment. As undersecretary of state, G.G.E. Steele told the first meeting of the board: 'The challenge to the Corporation is to use the $10 million to establish the base – within the fairly near future – of a successful feature film industry.'[5] The underlying policy objective of the CFDC was to achieve sizeable monetary returns on investment in feature films with 'significant Canadian creative, artistic and technical content.'[6] Success was to be measured by two criteria simultaneously: CFDC-backed films would have to show a profit and they would have to contribute to the articulation of a Canadian cultural identity. It would become quickly apparent that these two objectives were not necessarily mutually compatible.

The problems to be faced by the CFDC would not be confined to the sphere of production. CFDC-backed films would have to achieve adequate distribution and exhibition, yet even the Interdepartmental Committee had noted that the major distributors and exhibitors might display a prejudice against Canadian feature films and continue to promote the traditional fare of the Hollywood majors. While hopeful that the dominant interests in exhibition and distribution would cooperate and promote a significant number of Canadian films, federal officials were also aware that these corporations operated according to strict market criteria, a market in which monopoly practices such as block-booking were common. The bottom line was commercial success. During debate on the CFDC Act, Secretary of State LaMarsh had served notice that 'other measures might be necessary' if support for Canadian films was not forthcoming. The CFDC itself was not empowered to regulate the circuit of distribution and exhibition; it was only to advise and assist producers in their search for a viable distribution deal. But the CFDC was entrusted with a watchdog function. As the undersecretary of state said at the first meeting of the CFDC, its annual report 'was considered the means by which the Corporation could bring pressure to bear on distributors and exhibitors.'[7]

Ultimately, the CFDC's success would depend as much upon its own investment decisions as upon the development of a broader political commitment to the 'Canadianization' of the various cultural industries. The new Broadcasting

Act, and the tough-sounding rhetoric of Pierre Juneau and the newly formed CRTC, suggested that the effort to Canadianize the cultural sector was underway. While *Time* and *Reader's Digest* managed to forestall the effort to limit their dominance of the periodical press market, Juneau and the CRTC were much more successful in establishing Canadian ownership in the broadcasting sector.[8] 'What has Famous Players done in past years to contribute to the social and political development of Canada?' asked Juneau at the hearings where the Corporation's attempt to Canadianize its operations was rejected.[9] In 1969, Famous Players was forced to divest itself of its broadcast holdings, and its effort to expand into cable television was rebuked. Finally, although discriminatory measures (such as a quota) were not introduced, the dynamics of cultural dependency were also altered by the decision to establish the CFDC, if only because it put the promotion and protection of Canadian cultural products more firmly on the public agenda. The American majors would have been better off without the CFDC, better off if the Canadian state had continued to accept the status quo.

The NFB to the CFDC: From Interpreting Canada to Investing Money

Can financial support for Canadian feature film producers in the private sector enable them to launch themselves upon the world market or are other measures required to achieve this objective? The main task of the Government's special agency in feature film production – the CFDC – is to find the answer to this question.[10]

The CFDC had been in the movie business for less than a year when, in November 1968, it was called to make its first presentation before the Parliamentary Standing Committee on Broadcasting, Films and Assistance to the Arts. The NFB, with Hugo McPherson as the new government film commissioner, was also before the Committee. It was the first and last time that the two government film agencies would appear together before the Standing Committee, and it was as if they were speaking a different language. In representing the CFDC, Spencer and Lapalme were particularly careful to distance themselves from the old traditions of government film activity. At the same time, they seemed eager to offer Committee members a rather frank statement of the unfolding rationale behind the Corporation's activities.

In his defence and promotion of the NFB, McPherson marshalled the now well-tested arguments in its favour, referring to its international record of achievement and innovation and its ability to produce films that 'educated' Canadians (with particular emphasis on its success in reaching the young). Once more, the NFB was fighting to maintain, not expand, its position within the film industry. Although its annual appropriation in 1968–9 was $9.45 million, budget cuts in line with the federal government's austerity measures had forced it to tighten its adminstration and programs. And once again, its legislated monopoly over government film contracts was under attack from the private sector.

Two years earlier, the NFB had signed an agreement with the CBC to produce four English features at a total cost of $1.5 million. Only two were made: Don Owen's *The Ernie Game* (1969) and Ron Kelly's *Waiting for Caroline* (1969). Both films went over budget (by a total of $250,000), and neither film was favourably received. The CBC concluded that the deal was a failure and cancelled the other two projects to cut its losses.[11] The agreement also incurred the wrath of Bill Cole and IATSE Local 644. IATSE had lost its bid to unionize the NFB to the Quebec-based Syndicat général du cinéma et de la télévision and threatened to have its projectionists boycott NFB theatrical films across North America. Cole sought support from the Association of Motion Picture Producers and Laboratories and sent a memo to Prime Minister Pearson, arguing that the NFB did not have a mandate to produce feature films. Cole's memo was sharply rebuked by Secretary of State LaMarsh. The AMPPLC, while undoubtedly sympathetic to the gist of Cole's argument, refused to partake in such high-handed tactics.[12] The whole affair suggested that the NFB would not find it easy to move more fully into the sphere of feature film production.

Of course, the Board still had its supporters. After it became clear that the government's austerity measures would be meted out through immediate cuts in the Board's production staff, as opposed to a process of natural attrition, the Canadian Society of Film Makers (SFM) issued the following statement: 'The values of the marketplace, good as they might be in some respects, are not the only values. There are things that cannot be bought there, and one of the most important of these is independence – intellectual, spiritual, and even national.'[13]

The SFM, like the NFB, was talking about 'films for culture'; the CFDC would talk about 'films for profit.' Spencer and Lapalme displayed a remarkable confidence and frankness before the Committee. To distinguish themselves from the NFB, they spoke the language of 'industry,' of 'banking' and 'commercial success.' When asked whether the CFDC's activities would 'supplement or supplant' the activities of the NFB, Michael Spencer replied: 'I think the answer is of course that we may well do both. As Mr. McPherson has already said, the Film Board has every right to produce, and under its Act can produce feature films, but it seems to me that it is limited in respect to the fact that every film it produces has to be "in the national interest," and particularly interpretive of Canada to Canadians. I think our feeling is that any film that has a chance of developing the Canadian film industry, *even if that film is not particularly interpretive of Canada to Canadians*, would still be considered and possibly invested in by us.'[14] Lapalme described the CFDC as a 'specialized bank established to provide financial assistance on the basis of which a Canadian feature film industry can be launched.' 'We are not filmmakers,' he explained, 'we are just investing money and making loans ... If we were to judge our scripts from an intellectual and cultural point of view we would not be a bank anymore.'[15]

In keeping with the 'industry' theme, the onus for success was placed squarely on the establishment of a stable core of producers and production firms. When a Committee member asked if part of the problem to date had been a lack of private entrepreneurs, Lapalme wholeheartedly agreed, while Spencer, as if to distance himself even further from his old employer, added that this was an unfortunate 'effect of government domination of the industry.'[16] The second annual report of the CFDC made the point bluntly: 'The evolution of a cadre of experienced producers remains the most important need of the feature film industry at this time. It is the producers who will achieve the union of ideas, talents, and skills that promise to provide a steady output of good quality films.'[17]

CFDC officials also tried to clarify their position with respect to the plethora of 'other measures' (an exhibition quota, a box-office levy, higher remittance taxes, or direct government assistance and involvement in the spheres of distribution and exhibition) that had been suggested as ways of ensuring that Canadian films would have access to Canadian screens. For the moment, they considered such measures unnecessary. Lapalme argued that Canadians 'seem to be satisfied' with the array of films available, and that 'the onus is on the feature film producer in Canada to try to create a demand for his product.'[18] Consumer sovereignty and a competitive market: these were assumptions that militated against discriminatory or protective measures, assumptions that Nat Taylor and the major players in the industry had worked hard to maintain. At the same time, Lapalme referred to television as a 'growing and significant market' for Canadian films, a hint that the CRTC's Canadian-content quotas could serve a useful purpose, especially if the theatrical distribution of Canadian films became a problem that the CFDC and government did not want to confront head-on.[19] Even so, Lapalme could not completely avoid the importance of theatrical distribution to the success of the CFDC's program. 'Is this distribution problem going to be licked?' one of the Committee members asked Lapalme. 'That is the $64,000 question,' he replied.[20]

The First Ten Million

To ensure that the production fund was not depleted too quickly, the CFDC's board decided that it would invest a maximum of $300,000, and not more than 50 per cent of the production costs, in any one feature film. Eligible projects would have to have a distribution contract already in hand, giving the distributor a significant voice in the process of production. The emphasis on a solid, market-oriented production base, coupled with the view that Canadians were still quite inexperienced in the business of feature film production, led the CFDC to consider joint productions with American interests.[21] As Spencer told the committee: 'If a Canadian producer can work with an American producer – which is the kind of film we would like to see – and if it is going to get international distribution through a foreign distribution company then, I think, on balance we would be wise to invest in that rather than to reject it.'[22]

By the summer of 1968, it was also clear that the CFDC would consider involvement in projects where foreigners occupied many of the key creative positions. The CFDC's debut was a film called *Explosion* (1969), produced by Nat Taylor and Julian Roffman of Meridian Films. In the words of film critic Martin Knelman, *Explosion* was 'an inept piece of action trash' about a young man who, troubled by the death of his brother in Vietnam and harassed by an over-bearing father, flees to Vancouver and drifts into a life of crime. *Explosion*'s Canadian content was satisfied by virtue of its location and the use of Canadian technical crews. American interests were also involved in another early CFDC-backed film. Paul Almond's *Act of the Heart* (1970), with Geneviève Bujold and Donald Sutherland, received generous backing from Universal Pictures. But *Act of the Heart* was a very different kind of film, a psychological drama about a young woman's love for an Augustinian monk.[23]

As one might expect, the CFDC's choice of films elicited controversy from the start. Roy Krost of Toronto had worked out a co-production deal with Sagittarius Productions of New York to shoot a film entitled *Kashmiri Run* in the Canadian Rockies. Krost guaranteed that two-thirds of the film's $800,000 budget would be spent in Canada, and he wanted the CFDC to back the project. The CFDC turned down *Kashmiri Run* because the director, screenwriter, director of photography, and lead actors were all non-Canadians.[24] Krost argued that the film had at least as much significant Canadian content as did *Explosion*, but the CFDC responded that *Explosion* was a bit of a mistake, something it had hurried into in order to get started. By trial and error, the Corporation was developing some conception of what significant Canadian content should look like.

In 1969, Denis Héroux and Cinépix released *Valérie*, a $70,000 black and white film that earned over a million dollars in the Quebec market. Héroux had discovered an emerging formula for commercial success in the film business: sex. 'Il faut déshabiller la petite québécoise,' was how he explained *Valérie* to *Maclean's*.[25] Although *Valérie* was made without the CFDC's assistance, the

Corporation quickly became a partner in the new trend. Between 1969 and 1971, it financed *L'Initiation, Love in a Four-Letter World, L'Amour humain, Pile ou face*, and *Deux femmes en or*. Of the bunch, Claude Fournier's *Deux femmes en or* (1970) was the most commercially successful, grossing over $2.5 million in Quebec (one out of three Quebeckers are said to have seen it). The dozen or so films of what *Variety* called 'maple syrup porno' played an important role in establishing the commercial base of the Quebec film industry.[26]

Not everyone was enthusiastic about the CFDC's decision to support such carnality. One member of the House of Commons complained of 'film obscenities,' and 'words that vilely sully the beliefs of the majority of Canadians.'[27] A critic for the *Toronto Star* described *Love in a Four-Letter World* as 'crummy sexploitation' and a 'pornographic movie with pretensions.'[28] The Secretary of State and the CFDC itself received a significant number of complaints from private citizens, mostly from southwestern Ontario, furious that their tax money was being spent on such ventures.[29] In its annual report for 1969–70, the CFDC responded to the criticisms in the following manner:

Some concern has been expressed by the public generally about the increasing number of 'sexploitation' films now appearing in Canadian cinemas. It is clear that these films are popular and that film industries in other countries receive state aid for pictures designed particularly for this market. In the opinion of the Corporation, this wave of films based on the commercial exploitation of sex is a world-wide phenomenon and Canada cannot possibly be an exception ... In its selection of proposals, based on a review of the scenario, the Corporation tries to avoid the worst aspects of this market, but it feels that, in the final analysis, it cannot take a moral position vis-à-vis its applicants.[30]

The CFDC argued further that it would leave it to provincial censor boards to decide on the morality or obscenity of the films in question. Since all of the films were passed by the Ontario Censor Board, albeit some with a few cuts, the CFDC felt that its decisions had been vindicated.

After 1971, the issue died down, partly because of a decline in the popularity of the genre, partly because the CFDC became a bit more cautious in its selection of projects, and partly because the trend to greater sexual explicitness in the movies came to be accepted as a cultural norm. Be that as it may, the episode highlights the troubles that can face public officials once they become responsible for the content of popular cultural products. In terms of their creative personnel and distribution contracts, these films were very 'Canadian' (more so than many others in fact), but were they 'Canadian' in terms of their content?

CFDC officials quickly realized that there was no easy formula for deciding what was 'Canadian' on the basis of what appeared on the screen; moreover, they wanted to stay away from such decisions. As an investment agency entrusted with developing a viable private industry, the CFDC wanted, as far as possible, to leave the major decisions on content to the private sector. The solution seemed simple enough: to fulfil its mandate that it invest in films with 'significant Canadian creative, artistic, technical content,' the CFDC decided to base its principal calculations for support on the level of employment in the creative positions. By 1970, with few exceptions, the CFDC required that at least two of a film's three principal creators (producer, director, and screenwriter) be Canadian, while a maximum of two of the other major creative contributors (cinematographer, designer, editor, composer) could be non-Canadians.[31] While the 'creative-role test' was far easier to manage than any conception of what a Canadian film should look like, the criteria themselves became a source of continued controversy. As many Canadian filmmakers noted, for those who wanted to circumvent the intent of the criteria there was still considerable room in which to manoeuvre. Consider the following: since it is not uncommon for films to have more than one producer or screenwriter, and since it is relatively easy to hide the actual contribution that each individual makes on a given production, a film could qualify as 'Canadian' even though foreigners controlled each of the creative roles. On more than one occasion, this is precisely what occurred.

By October 1971, the CFDC had exhausted its $10 million fund. According to its annual report for 1971–2, the Corporation had invested in 64 films with a total budget of $17.7 million.[32] The CFDC's share of this total was $6.7 million; private Canadian investors had contributed $7.3 million; while the remaining $3.7 million had come from foreign investors, mainly the U.S. majors. The statistics revealed that the CFDC had not become a self-financing agency. It had recovered only $600,000, or roughly nine per cent on its investments to this point. Of the 64 films, only 3 were in a profit position. At the same time, the CFDC had been involved in the production of some critically, if not financially, successful films. In 1970, CFDC money was behind the production of Don Shebib's *Goin' Down the Road* and Gilles Carle's *Les mâles*, while in 1971 the Corporation was a principal investor in Claude Jutra's *Kamouraska* (1973), Peter Carter's *The Rowdyman* (1972), and Gilles Carle's *La vraie nature de Bernadette* (1972).

Although the CFDC did not release detailed figures on each film, we can establish from the gross figures available that the average cost of the 64 feature films was slightly more than $250,000. This figure concealed the actual range of budgets however, since the CFDC had a special program for financing low-budget (between $25,000 and $75,000) films. Until 1971, the largest budget on a CFDC-financed film had been that for *Kamouraska*: it cost somewhere in the neighbourhood of $750,000, still a relatively low figure by Hollywood standards. In fact, from 1970 onwards the CFDC had consciously avoided more expensive films. As its annual report for 1969–70 explained:

The Corporation may well continue to invest up to an official ceiling of $300,000 in big productions, but it sees the future of the industry more in the direction of films costing between $200,000 and $300,000 which can be financed in Canada and recover almost all of this amount through TV sales as well as theatrical distribution. The Corporation believes that only in this way can a Canadian film industry *uncontrolled from abroad* be established on a firm basis.[33]

There are a number of hidden messages in this statement. In the late sixties, over-investment in a number of high-priced, poor-quality 'blockbusters' precipitated a financial and managerial crisis in the American film industry that brought a number of Hollywood studios close to bankruptcy. In 1969, the American majors had a backlog of unreleased films worth $1.2 billion.[34] The success of inexpensive, independently produced films, such as *Easy Rider* (1969), and the failure of many big-budget musicals that followed in the wake of *The Sound of Music* (1965) had thrown the industry into confusion. It appeared that Hollywood's basic formula for success, which had always been related to large budgets and high production values, was in the midst of being overthrown. Like many others, the CFDC believed that Hollywood's crisis had created a window for low-budget independent films.

Undoubtedly, the emphasis on low budgets also reflected the growing awareness that French-Canadian films were doing much better at the box-office, and in the television market, than their English-Canadian counterparts. Here, the CFDC was in a bit of a quandary: Nat Taylor would have told them that low-budget films stood little chance of success in the English market, but could the Corporation really take the risk of producing more expensive films that would then require distribution in both North American markets to recover their costs? Matters were only made worse by the fact that Hollywood rebounded quickly from its crisis. By 1973, the profits of the eight major companies had reached $168 million. One year later, rentals from Canada alone totalled $54.4 million, making it the biggest foreign market for the Hollywood majors, while Canadian films still occupied less than five per cent of available screen time in Canada.

The CFDC had also learned the hard way that production and distribution deals with American firms were no guarantee of healthy commercial returns. On the contrary, the participation of the major American distributors in such films as *Fortune and Men's Eyes* (1971), *Act of the Heart* (1970), and *Face-Off* (1971) left the CFDC with the feeling that it had been 'used.' Although Spencer tried hard to develop cooperative relations with the major U.S. distributors, he would eventually become a rather staunch critic of their practices in Canada and with the CFDC. As he told *Trade News North*:

We've been in bed with the major companies from the very beginning. There was *Fortune and Men's Eyes*; we never got any money back on that. You know *Act of the Heart, Fan's Note* and even *Eliza's Horoscope* was originally financed by us and Warner Bros. We never got any money back on any of these pictures. We gave up on the majors some time around *Duddy Kravitz* because we made that with totally Canadian financing and then we sold it to Paramount afterwards.[35]

The CFDC discovered what many others had already known: first, that the American majors were generally uninterested in distributing Canadian films; second, that when they did, they were expert at hiding any profits from Canadian producers or the CFDC; and third, that in a market dominated by monopoly practices, independent Canadian distributors did not have the necessary clout to secure adequate release dates or times for Canadian films.[36] By late 1971, the Corporation had decided that it could no longer afford to involve American distributors as production partners. The low-budget films the CFDC spoke of were pictures that did not need American financial support or American distribution to recoup their profits. Television was touted as a market in which inexpensive productions could recoup much of their cost.

Adequate theatrical distribution for Canadian films was still the exception rather than the rule. The CFDC had been told to monitor the problem through its annual reports, but initially its appraisal of the situation, like Spencer and Lapalme's presentation before the Standing Committee, was very low-key. The reports offered no detailed data on the distribution or exhibition of Canadian films in Canada or abroad. In general, they emphasized the few success stories and downplayed the disasters. In 1972, the CFDC offered this heavily guarded comment on the problem: 'How are Canadian films going to reach the small but important groups of potential viewers which would seem to have not had much of an opportunity to see them to date?'[37] But the report made no concrete recommendations; instead it passed the buck to the Secretary of State, which had initiated its own study of the problem. The following year's report was even more of an affront to those who believed that some form of protectionist legislation was necessary. In noting that English-Canadian films in particular were having 'great difficulty in finding their audience,' the CFDC offered the following advice to those now frustrated by the lack of adequate distribution:

For English-Canadian filmmakers, and perhaps eventually for French-Canadian film-makers also, there are solutions to be considered: firstly, they should begin to look more in the direction of television which is where the mass audience can be reached ... secondly, they might perhaps reflect on the words of the late Noel Coward as quoted in *Variety*: 'Consider the public, treat it with tact and courtesy. It will accept much more from you if you are clever enough to win it to your side. Never fear or despise it. Coax it, charm it, interest it, stimulate it. Shock it now and then if you must. Make it laugh, make it cry. But above all, dear pioneers, never, never, bore the living hell out of it.[38]

Charming. But what of the monopoly in distribution and exhibition? And what about a Canadian cinema as an alternative to the mainstream? And what about some sign of the CFDC's sensitivity to the interests and problems of Canadian filmmakers. Among others, the $64,000 question had been raised. To this point the CFDC had merely blinked.

The First Phase of a Comprehensive Federal Film Policy?

As the CFDC worked through its first $10 million appropriation, the administrative apparatus of the Canadian state underwent some significant structural changes. In the first years of the Trudeau regime, the Cabinet committee system was formalized, an internal network of planning committees and agencies was established, and new budgetary procedures were introduced, each with the intention of developing a more rational approach to long-term policy planning.[39] But the optimism with which the new mechanisms were initiated was soon dampened by the many problems they engendered; certainly, by the mid-seventies, it was clear that the Canadian state had not been transformed into a coherent planning apparatus. Nonetheless, the effort to establish indicative planning had its effect in the cultural sphere. Under the guidance of Gérard Pelletier, secretary of state from 1968 to 1972, the federal government tried to develop a more comprehensive approach to cultural policy, including a federal film policy. Like Trudeau, Pelletier was firmly committed to the new planning logic.

Pelletier partook of suggestive and promising code words for his policy initiative. Canadian culture was to undergo a process of 'democratization and decentralization.'[40] Pelletier wanted to expand the opportunities for the production and the consumption of Canadian culture with a strategy that would encompass both the traditional arts and the cultural industries, from 'Bach to the Beatles,' as Pelletier put it.[41] (From Glenn Gould to the Guess Who would have been more to the point.) While his public speeches on the themes of 'democratization and decentralization' remained consistently vague, within the bowels of the Canadian state Pelletier tried to give the idea some substance.

In June 1969, Cabinet gave Pelletier the go-ahead to establish 'les grandes lignes d'une politique culturelle.'[42] In line with the new planning mechanisms, he was asked to devise a five-year blueprint for the development of all the cultural activities under the purview of his department. In a memo to the new chairperson of the CFDC, Gratien Gélinas, Pelletier outlined his rather classic position on the question of culture, nationalism, and the state. 'La politique culturelle, en reflétant la personalité canadienne dans son originalité, dans sa diversité, doit provoquer une prise de conscience nationale. À défaut d'une telle démarche, les grands courants d'autres cultures transmis par les moyens modernes de communication et en particulier ceux qui nous viennent des États-Unis nous pousseront inevitablement vers une désintégration de notre propre personalité et, entre autres, de notre dualité culturelle.' Pelletier rightly suggested that 'la culture de l'élite' was, in and of itself, insufficient to secure national unity and establish a sense of identity among the majority of Canadians.[43] Like Lamontagne, Pelletier hoped that state support for indigenously produced popular culture, without any measures to actually limit the flow of foreign products, would be sufficient to redress 'la désintégration de notre propre personalité.' Given Pelletier's emphasis on the development of popular culture, the CFDC would play a particularly important role in the implementation of a new cultural policy. Gélinas was asked to begin a process of re-evaluation within the CFDC in preparation for meetings in the spring of 1970 with the Secretary of State and the other cultural agencies.

Gélinas' formal response to Pelletier's memo is indicative of the problems that would be encountered by the secretary of state as he tried to coordinate the various cultural agencies and institutions. Delighted that the government had said it would accord cultural policy the same priority as economic policy, Gélinas was at the same time concerned about the prospect of coordinating the CFDC's priorities with those of the other agencies. While he agreed that the CFDC was well placed to redress 'la culture de l'élite,' Gélinas was not convinced that it would be able to help establish a strong sense of Canadian identity. 'Nous croyons que le rôle qui nous a été dévolu nous oblige à appliquer au monde des arts *la rude philosophie des affaires*.'[44] Given the commercial imperatives under which the CFDC was to operate (especially the pull of world markets), Gélinas was not optimistic about the prospect of developing 'Canadian' films. He argued that as an industry, 'Canadian cinema must strive to please the American public'; if Pelletier wanted films that would promote 'Canadian identity,' then Gélinas proposed that the CFDC produce low-budget films for the Canadian market.[45] Gélinas balked at the suggestion that the budget of the CFDC be pooled with those of the other cultural agencies (a suggestion in line with the Treasury Board's desire to establish a more efficient process of government expenditures). He argued that because the pace of the CFDC's investments was set by demands emanating from the private sector, the CFDC's expenditures were not amenable to such a budgetary process.

Gélinas' remarks reflected the conflicting policy objectives under which the CFDC was operating and an awareness that this conflict had become entrenched within the Canadian state. On the one hand, Finance and Treasury Board officials expected the CFDC to make a profit or, at least, to operate in a businesslike manner, while Secretary of State officials were more inclined to privilege the more vaguely conceived cultural objectives. A review of the CFDC's operations would not occur without a considerable degree of bureaucratic manœuvring and struggle. Obviously, Gélinas was moving to protect his turf. Officials at the other cultural agencies would do likewise.[46]

By 1971, it was clear that a major component of Pelletier's initiative would be the development of a new federal film policy. Extensive meetings were held between officials at the NFB, CBC, and CFDC, and a committee was established under the guidance of Wendy Porteus to examine the question of film distribution. The CFDC itself was eager to re-examine its activities. When Cabinet approved its second $10 million appropriation in November 1971, it asked the CFDC to clarify its investment criteria and establish a review committee to develop a careful five-year plan. Spencer and Gélinas were more than willing to cooperate. In April 1972, they issued a 'General Statement on CFDC Policies' that read in part:

In considering its position for the next five years, the Corporation could either: (1) support films exclusively designed to meet commercial criteria, which would certainly cause further criticism from the public and most of the film industry; (2) support projects of a kind which in its experience generally receive good reviews but only manage to reach a small audience with corresponding small rates of return; or (3) try to strike a balance by selecting properties which it is felt have an entertainment potential, guaranteed to some extent by distributor involvement, as well as good film quality confirmed by an effective group of readers. Since many of the films which it supported largely on the ground of commercial promise have been disappointing from the point of view of audience response, commercial success appears to be unpredictable. Thus, after much discussion, the Corporation has decided to select the third option.[47]

The CFDC was trying to fashion its own compromise between the commercial and cultural objectives of the program. Two principal categories of support would be established. First, the Corporation would make available 'special high risk investments' for low-budget feature films designed to develop new talent. The CFDC would invest a total of $600,000 a year in films with an average budget of $100,000 and in which all the creative and technical crew were Canadian. A second category of investment would be targeted for 'producers aiming for major release.'[48] The CFDC was prepared to spend approximately $3 million a year on films that had a distribution guarantee, the potential for television release and in which the director and writer and all other creative personnel were Canadian. The Corporation would, however, consider exceptions to the personnel requirements; in particular, foreign stars could be used 'to enhance the possibility of international distribution.'[49] The policy paper conspicuously avoided the questions of distribution and exhibition, presumably because they were being taken up by the Secretary of State's own committee under the guidance of Wendy Porteus.

The film policy review was primarily an internal bureaucratic exercise.. No formal mechanism for consultation with the private sector was established, and in turn the private sector undertook no full-scale mobilization to effect the policy review process. The new emphasis on indicative planning did not include the adoption of mechanisms that would have extended the practice of democracy (if only as formal interest-group representation) into the bureaucratic exercise – the Canadian state still functioned internally on the basis of bureaucratic expertise. But even if Secretary of State officials had wanted to establish formal contact with industry representatives, the rather large list of groups within the private sector was a significant disincentive. Two months before the new policy was announced, Pelletier told the Standing Committee that his department had informal conversations with almost all of the industry's organizations. 'It was not always easy,' he explained. 'because you could say that the film industry in Canada, according to your personal judgement, is either under-organized or over-organized because there is such a multiplicity of organizations and sometimes you get lost in all these areas.'[50] Federal officials themselves may have had a bias toward internal, bureaucratic policy formation, but the industry itself, through its multiplicity of organizations, and through its apparent unwillingness to confront government officials or establish its own unified position, did little to curb this tendency.

Of course, most of the industry's views were already well known. In 1969, for example, the Standing Committee on Broadcasting, Films and Assistance to the Arts had heard submissions from the Canadian Society of Cinematographers, the Association of Motion Picture Producers and Laboratories, and the Association des producteurs de films du Québec.[51] On one point they were unanimous: the NFB had to get out of feature film production and at least 50 per cent of its government contracts should be awarded to the private sector. Beyond this, the top producer associations were noncommittal – with respect to the CFDC and the operation of the loan fund, they had adopted a wait-and-see attitude. The CSC, however, was already convinced that without an exhibition quota, a significant levy on the receipts of American distributors, and the establishment of some form of government-sponsored distribution company, the decision to assist private-sector feature film production would meet with failure. The submissions showed once again the divisions we have previously noticed within the various sectors of the Canadian film industry. For Richard Stanbury, parliamentary secretary to the secretary of state, these early meetings made it clear how difficult it would be to establish a 'comprehensive and cohesive national film policy.'[52]

Before the policy was announced, Pelletier received an important and lengthy brief from the Toronto Filmmakers' Coop, a non-profit organization comprising 150 independent filmmakers. The brief had been circulated to over 400 film-makers across the country and had received more than 200 endorsements. From the Coop's perspective, the fundamental policy issue that now had to be addressed was the inadequate distribution and exhibition of Canadian films.

Films are made to be shown: if they are not, their production becomes an exercise in futility. As long as Canadian films are being denied access to their natural forum, all other questions of their development remain academic. Until there is a break-through in the distribution and exhibition of Canadian films paralleling the one which the CFDC made in production, that agency will merely be working at cross purposes with itself, and the Canadian film industry will be racing its engines without going anywhere.[53]

Not surprisingly, the major recommendation of the brief was the establishment of a Canadian-content quota for all commercial exhibitors. An initial quota of 15 per cent for features, instituted on an equal percentage basis (i.e., block-booking a certain number of weeks a year to prevent exhibitors from covering the quota through Sunday morning or matinée showings), would immediately rewrite the basic rules of the game within the industry. According to the brief, 'once Canadian films were allowed as serious contenders for a box-office audience, a commercial advantage would be attendant on finding good Canadian films.'[54] A quota, the Coop believed, would force the major exhibitors and distributors to become more involved in the development and promotion of Canadian films. The brief also recommended the following: the establishment of an independent network of government-subsidized theatres to exhibit non-commercial Canadian films, art films, NFB films and some foreign films; the development of a National Film School; better access to the NFB's facilities for private filmmakers; better exhibition of Canadian films on both the CBC and private television networks; and a re-evaluation of film financing, including discontinuation of the CFDC's distribution prerequisite, a new system of pre-production grants, and 'a federal tax on revenues of non-Canadian films which exceed a set gross, the profit from which could be invested in the production of Canadian films.'[55] Finally, in the process of defining Canadian content, the Coop wanted the CFDC to 'place emphasis on a film's cultural and artistic determinants, as well as its cast, crew and creators. This [did] not mean limiting scripts to those dealing with hockey and beavers, but rather to those which indicate artistic integrity, and make some reference at root to the Canadian situation.'[56]

The Coop's position on Canadian content came close to what the CFDC's 'third option' would have to entail to be successful, but in general the brief itself symbolized the continuing conflict between different interests within the private film industry. While the Coop represented the interests of filmmakers who had become leery about 'la rude philosophie des affaires' and who believed that Canadian cinema would require new and aggressive forms of state support in order to flourish, it certainly did not articulate the general interest of most Canadian producers, the majority of whom treated film as a business first and foremost. It was either with naïvety or coy evasion that the Coop suggested that the introduction of exhibition quotas would not entail a 'conflict of interest, as there is neither benefit nor profit in any part of the present process for anyone or anything Canadian.'[57] Canadian exhibitors, for one, simply did not share this sentiment. A year earlier, Nat Taylor had once again denounced the idea, arguing that 'quota' films are always 'notoriously cheap' and that given Canada's small market 'the production of feature films becomes primarily an export product.'[58] When asked at a public forum whether he would ever support exhibition quotas, Taylor purportedly replied: 'The answer is a big yes, provided, at the same time, the government will legislate that people will have to go and see them.'[59] Furthermore the Coop's recommendation of a special levy on the super-profits of foreign films would certainly have angered both the Hollywood majors and their Canadian subsidiaries. A conflict of interests *did* exist within the film industry, and policy makers were keenly aware that the divisions were deep, complex, and internal to the groups that composed the Canadian film industry. Like the CFDC itself, Secretary of State officials would try to fashion a compromise.

On 4 July 1972, Pelletier announced the government's new position in a speech entitled 'The First Phase of a Federal Film Policy.' After reviewing the state's general commitment to developing the cultural industries in Canada, Pelletier offered the following thoughts:

If films are also looked upon as cultural tools of the utmost importance, it is clear that Canadians must play the leading role at home in this medium, and that ways will soon have to be found and used to reach this essential goal ... [We] must be able to ensure that Canadians may not only express themselves in films but may also expect their films to be given their rightful place in their own country. As things now stand, it does not appear that foreign interests can be counted upon to achieve this dual objective.'[60]

The intent seemed clear enough. Pelletier appeared to be establishing the rationale for protective legislation and more discriminatory forms of state intervention. But it was still just words and Pelletier was not yet prepared to announce any detailed proposals along these lines. Instead, the secretary of state called for further study. Over time it became clear that the statement was more a threat than a promise. This really was only the 'first phase' of the film policy and it was rather thin on substance.

Pelletier announced that one theatre dedicated to showing Canadian films would be established in the National Capital Region and that the CBC had agreed to increase the number of Canadian films it broadcast. He had instructed the CFDC to explore the possibility of establishing a government-subsidized distribution network and to consider the idea of offering loans to television movies. To assist the development of the film policy's 'second phase,' Pelletier also announced the establishment of a film advisory committee consisting of five representatives each from the government and the private sector. Finally, the NFB was to undergo a process of regional decentralization and it would 'now have to compete with private producers for all film contracts awarded by the federal government or agency.'[61] This was perhaps the most significant change in government policy, and it was firmly in line with the government's desire to promote more private-sector cultural production. It was also the one point on which most of the interests within the private film industry agreed. After many attempts, private producers had finally captured their share of the public trough. Pelletier tried to put a brave face on the announcement, saying that these new priorities and policies had 'taken over two years to develop.' 'I hope,' he continued, 'that we have not laboured and brought forth a mouse, and that the long period of reflection and waiting has not been spent in vain.'[62]

It was a false hope. Aside from the 'decentralization' of the Film Board, the policy lacked any real substance. It was a 'non-policy,' significant primarily for its silences. It certainly did not affect the basic conditions of production and distribution for Canadian feature films. To this point, the attempt at rational planning in the cultural sphere had produced few tangible results. Notwithstanding Pelletier's prominent stature within the Liberal party and his commitment to establishing 'les grands lignes d'une politique culturelle,' policy making within his department, as within the government as a whole, could still be typified as the 'art of muddling through.' Through the course of the 1970s, the production of Canadian cultural policy would not get any easier. Within the film industry itself there was no sign that the disputes and conflicts over the nature of state support would abate. Furthermore, by the middle of the decade, the federal government's policy agenda was increasingly dominated by concerns over inflation and the declining health of the Canadian economy as a whole. As in the past, the development of Canada's cultural policy would very much reflect the economic priorities of the Canadian state, which now included an increase in the use of tax breaks as a way of reflating the economy and new limitations on direct government spending as a way of relieving the 'fiscal crisis of the state.' Both within and outside the state, it was to be a period characterized more by indecision and conflict than rational planning.

In its first few years, the CFDC spent public money on 'maple-syrup porn,' and loaned funds to many of the early classics of the Canadian cinema. It tried to define a Canadian film via employment criteria, made deals with the American majors, and lost most of its money. It was not an overnight success. At a very basic level, the CFDC floundered between the opposing options of a film industry for profit, and a film industry for culture. Gélinas had spoken of 'la rude philosophie des affaires' and of 'pleasing the American public,' Pelletier of 'une conscience nationale.' To be sure, there were no films yet that seemed able to do both, and lots of good examples of films that did one but not the other. Were these objectives irreconcilable? Could they be pursued separately? Should one be dropped? As it turned out, these were questions that would continue to dog policy makers and analysts for a long time to come.

In the short run, the CFDC's halo faded quickly, primarily because its films were not having the desired effects: neither making money nor raising a national (and nationalist) consciousness. As a counter-force to cultural dependence the CFDC was very lightweight. This should have come as no surprise, for the establishment of the CFDC was effected within the logic of compromise: Canadian filmmakers and cultural nationalists had gained a policy that might significantly increase the production of Canadian cultural goods, but the state had stopped short of taking measures that would seriously disrupt established market practices.

This was not a compromise struck exclusively between cultural nationalists and foreign corporations. As we have already realized, relations of dependency and the structure of continentalism are not principally maintained by outside force. Continentalism is not a function of external repression or force; its strength and resilience derive from the extent to which the dynamics of dependency are maintained and reproduced internally. In the first place, a large segment of Canadians have come to rely on the existence of American capital in Canada as the source of their livelihood. The relation can be direct, as in the case of a comprador bourgeoisie who direct and manage American subsidiaries in Canada (such as Famous Players and the major distributors), or indirect, as in the case of Canadian independent exhibitors, producers, and film workers, who, with some justification, have come to situate their own economic well-being within the circuit of dependent capitalist relations. Together these forces form the economic and political base for the reproduction of dependency within the feature film sector. But there is a second dimension to the reproduction of dependency that in many ways is far more significant precisely because it is far more amorphous. In a manner no better illustrated than by the history of the cinema itself, Canadians have come to enjoy and identify with much of what passes for American culture. There has never been sustained and broad-based opposition to the fact that Hollywood, in the words of the Massey Report, 'refashions us in its own image.' This is not to suggest that Canadian culture has somehow become indistinguishable from American culture, but at the very least the existence of American culture in Canada is a crucial component of Canadian cultural consumption. By the early seventies (if not much earlier), Canadians had by and large come to regard Hollywood's fare as the normal and natural form the cinema (and television) should take. Any radical attempt to challenge seriously this relationship would surely be met with public displeasure, puzzlement, and resistance.

8   From Voluntary Quotas to *Jaws*

Not making the films you should be making is awful, but making them and not having them shown is worse.   — Claude Jutra[1]

Introduction

By the early 1970s, the equitable distribution and exhibition of Canadian films had become a major issue. The entrenched distribution and exhibition network did not significantly alter its longstanding monopoly practices. Not only was it difficult for Canadian films to get adequate screen access, but the revenues generated by Canadian ticket sales were being repatriated to support the production of more U.S.-backed films. Pressure mounted to consider 'other measures' designed to break the de facto quota of Hollywood films in Canada. The CFDC would have an important role to play in deciding how the issue should be dealt with, but ultimately – because of the fractious nature of the problem – this would be a decision made at the highest reaches of the Canadian state.

There are two related policy measures that governments have adopted to improve the exhibition of national films and ensure a stable supply of capital for film production: exhibition quotas and a box-office levy. Exhibition quotas set aside a minimum number of dates for designated films in order to ensure market access. At the time the CFDC was established, Britain had a screen quota of 30 per cent for British first-run films. France, Italy, and Spain also had exhibition quotas of one form or another. There was also a Canadian precedent for such a measure in the form of Canadian-content provisions for Canadian radio and television broadcasters. A box-office levy is a tax on ticket sales that goes toward financing film production. All of the European countries mentioned above had adopted a levy of one form or another as a means of ensuring a stable flow of capital for state-supported film production and of rewarding domestic films that did well at the box-office. Canada did have a levy of sorts. Amusement taxes were applied in most provinces (theatre legislation being a provincial responsibility in Canada), but the revenues generated did not go directly to support film (or cultural) production.

Support for some form of exhibition quota or box-office levy would come not only from certain segments of the filmmaking community but from a wider collection of public interests now more focused than ever on the issues of cultural and economic nationalism. But the forces of opposition were equally numerous and undoubtedly more powerful. The Hollywood majors would fight tooth and nail any measure that hampered their cosy and lucrative business practices. Likewise, almost all theatre exhibitors regarded quotas and levies as an outrageous attack on their livelihood.

From 1972 onward, the issue of quotas and levies would be a primary preoccupation of policy planners and industry representatives alike. It is fair to say that the government would do all it could to avoid a major, highly public, battle over the issue. In the end, it sought a way around the problem. Slowly, but surely, the federal government came to believe that it had found a solution in the never-never land of the capital cost tax allowance.

Shaky Foundations

In the early seventies, the most important new development in the sphere of production came not from any fundamental reorientation of the CFDC's activities, but from the discovery that significant tax savings could be realized through private investment in feature films.[2] In simplified terms it worked this way. Since 1954, film investments had been eligible for a basic capital cost allowance (CCA) of 60 per cent (meaning that 60 per cent of a given investment could be written off against taxable income). The CCA applied to any film, regardless of national origin. The high-risk nature of Canadian film production meant that it was not a particularly attractive tax investment. The investment climate changed somewhat when producers and their ilk decided that film investments were eligible for leverage – that is, a given investor could claim as a tax write-off other monies borrowed to produce and distribute the film. A typical deal might look like this. An investor places $30,000 in a film whose total cost is $100,000. The capital cost allowance is then calculated on the total cost of the film; thus if the investor is in the 50 per cent tax bracket, he or she would enjoy a $30,000 tax reduction in the first year, a $12,000 reduction in the second year, and so on. In this case the leverage, at 3.3 to 1, is relatively small, but by 1972, some deals were based on leverages of 10 to 1 or more. It was not the most stable way to finance a new industry, let alone a new form of cultural expression. As Michael Spencer remarked: 'There is no way to create an industry based on investors' expectations that films will be losers.'[3]

The leveraged capital cost allowance was probably behind one of the early attempts to establish a stable and large-scale Canadian production company. In March 1972, Harold Greenberg, president of Bellevue-Pathé, announced a multimillion dollar fund to 'augment' the CFDC's loans.[4] By the fall, the fund had been put to use on six films, the most notable being *The Neptune Factor* (1973), directed by Canadian-born Daniel Petrie (who had worked in Hollywood for over ten years) and starring Ben Gazzara, Ernest Borgnine, Walter Pidgeon, and Yvette Mimieux. 20th Century–Fox guaranteed world-wide distribution and invested $700,000 in this $1.5 million underwater version of *Marooned* in which a deep-sea mini-submarine races to the rescue of three men trapped in an ocean floor laboratory. The CFDC invested $200,000, and the project also received private funding from Quadrant Films. By February 1973, Bellevue-Pathé had joined forces with Astral Films in Toronto and Gendon Films in Montreal. Greenberg explained his strategy in the following terms: 'All the films will have international distribution. And Astral ... will be expanding its distribution of Canadian and international productions. But the key to the success of the industry here is better product. There is no way you can get people to see movies just because they're Canadian. Some of my films have had CFDC help; others haven't. But my philosophy about building an industry here is somewhat different from theirs. You've got to get pictures into the theatres and for that you've got to make good movies.'[5] *The Neptune Factor* had its gala première in Toronto in the summer of 1973. It was one of those 'special' evenings, full of enthusiasm and promotional hype. Among producers there was even talk of establishing a mutual-fund–type investment pool to take advantage of the upbeat investment climate. But the excitement and publicity generated around *The Neptune Factor* only served to draw attention away from the more sombre reality of Canada's production sector.

According to a report done for the Secretary of State, in 1973 there were approximately 150 companies engaged in film production.[6] This rather large number, however, was more a sign of instability than healthy growth. Two-thirds of the companies reported that their total output was less than $100,000 a year, a half of the companies had fewer than five permanent employees, and three-quarters of the companies had fewer than ten. In general, the production sector had very poor links with the major distributors, and most companies faced severe difficulties in maintaining a profit position. The report concluded that the sector was operating at only 50 per cent of its present possible capacity. As for feature filmmaking, the industry was simply not characterized by the stable private production companies that had been deemed crucial to long-term economic and cultural self-sufficiency.

Already on precarious footing, the feature film industry was dealt a serious setback when Revenue Canada and Finance Department officials began to question the legality and integrity of the leveraged investments. Early in 1973, producers were warned by federal officials that the current rash of leveraged capital cost allowance investment deals was unacceptable. A flurry of meetings between private producers, Revenue Canada, Finance, and the Secretary of State did nothing to solve the problem.[7] In May, a Secretary of State official, who accused producers of using leverages as high as 50 to 1, told them that the loophole would be closed in six months. It was. English-language feature film production was almost completely paralysed. Most of the films intended for the CFDC 'major release' program were put on hold, and while the CFDC's low-budget fund was still in demand, the films it helped produce were never intended to be more than pilot projects and a training ground for young film-makers. By 1974, most everyone agreed that the industry was in crisis.

The only bright spot was the release of the film version of Mordecai Richler's *The Apprenticeship of Duddy Kravitz* (1974), which became the most commercially successful English-language film to that date. The film was produced by John Kemeny (a Hungarian émigré who had worked at the NFB) and directed by Ted Kotcheff, who had cut his teeth in British television and had been a friend of Richler's since the two shared a flat in London in the late fifties. With a budget of $800,000, *Duddy Kravitz* was a considerable gamble for all the players. In search of a hit, the CFDC went over its self-declared maximum investment of $300,000; the rest of the capital came from Greenberg, Famous Players, Global TV (a new private network in southern Ontario), and Gerald Schneider (a real-estate developer from Montreal). The gamble paid off: critically and commercially *Duddy Kravitz* was a hit. Paramount Pictures bought the U.S. distribution rights and most everyone went away happy from the deal. But while the success of *Duddy Kravitz* may have fooled a number of outsiders into believing that the industry had come of age, informed observers realized that the feature film industry was on the verge of collapse.

In the spring of 1974, the Standing Committee on Broadcasting, Films and Assistance to the Arts was given a rude shock when a newly established English-Canadian lobby group, the Council of Canadian Filmmakers (CCFM), appeared before it. Formed one year earlier, the CCFM included representatives from ACTRA, NABET, IATSE, the CSC, the Canadian Film Editors Guild, the Directors' Guild of Canada, the Toronto Filmmakers' Coop, and almost 300 individual filmmakers.[8] Frustrated and angry by a government and an industry that – by their actions if not always by their words – apparently held the production of Canadian films, films 'written, produced, directed, acted, made by, and majority owned by Canadians,' in high disregard, the CCFM launched a political offensive.[9] The future of Canada's feature film industry, much like its past, resided in the decisions that would be made by policy makers. Push had come to shove. On 25 April 1974, with CFDC officials in attendance, the first chairperson of the CCFM, director Peter Pearson, read the following statement to a slightly startled group of parliamentarians:

Mr. Chairman,
We commend the government for its bold concept in establishing the first steps toward a feature film industry in Canada.

We realize the taxpayers have committed $20 million in expectation of seeing Canadian films for the first time in their neighbourhood theatres. These films have seldom appeared.

In six years we've learned that the system doesn't work for Canadians.

The film financing system doesn't work. Thirteen major films were produced in English Canada in 1972. Six in 1973, only one so far in 1974.

The film distribution system doesn't work. In 1972, less than 2 per cent of the movies shown in Ontario were Canadian, less than 5 per cent in Quebec, the supposed bedrock of Canadian cinema.

The film exhibition system doesn't work. The foreign-dominated theatre industry grossed over $140,000,000 at the box office and is recycling only nickles and dimes into future domestic production.

Clearly something is wrong.

It is no wonder then that the Canadian Film Development Corporation can't possibly work.

And neither can we.[10]

Muddled Responses and Voluntary Quotas

The CCFM's statement before the Standing Committee did not catch government officials completely by surprise. In the two years since Pelletier's announcement of the first phase of a federal film policy, considerable discussions had been undertaken to establish a credible and feasible position on the questions of distribution and exhibition. With the establishment of the CFDC, federal officials had hoped to develop the framework for a healthy Canadian feature film industry, *without* instituting measures that would anger the major interests in exhibition and distribution. There was also concern that the Canadian public would not wholeheartedly endorse protective measures: while opinion polls showed that a majority of Canadians would support measures to increase the exhibition of Canadian films, the support itself was soft, since a majority also said they would be disinclined to go and see them.[11] If a box-office quota could be depicted as limiting access to American films (and there is little doubt that this is how the majors would characterize them), the federal government ran the risk of considerable public backlash. Certainly, quotas were not an automatic vote-getter. Discussions were further strained by the different positions that had emerged within the state itself. By 1974, the CFDC was on record as supporting both quotas and levies.[12] But officials within the Department of Finance and the Treasury Board were steadfast in their opinion that Canadian films had to make it on their own.

Matters were made only more complicated by the fact that theatre legislation was a provincial responsibility; the establishment of quotas or a box-office levy would therefore require the cooperation of the various provincial governments – not a very likely scenario given the increasing antagonistic air of federal–provincial relations. Within the film community, the proponents of theatre legislation often downplayed the seriousness of this jurisdictional hurdle, but there can be no doubt that it further frustrated the possibility that quotas or levies would be established. While some provinces, most notably Quebec and Manitoba, moved some distance toward adopting the requisite legislation, they were more than willing to leave the final initiative in the hands of the federal government. Negotiations would also be hampered by the fact that the provinces had adopted different approaches to theatre legislation: British Columbia and Alberta had abolished theatrical amusement taxes altogether, while in Saskatchewan and Quebec they were administered by the municipalities.

Discussions within the federal government concerning quotas and levies began in earnest in the fall of 1972 (with the release of the Porteus Committee's *Working Paper on Film Distribution*), but some earlier events are worth noting. In January of the same year representatives of the CFDC and the Secretary of State held a meeting in Montreal with five independent Canadian distributors: Georges Arpin of France Film, André Link of Cinépix, Bennett Fode of Phoenix Films, John Bassett of Glen Warren Productions, and Pierre David of Les Productions Mutuelles.[13] Federal officials wanted to know if the five companies could establish a cooperative venture to improve the distribution of Canadian films. Alone, the companies were too small to compete with the Hollywood majors, but combined they might be able to secure a more substantial position within the marketplace. While some of the distributors felt the idea had merit, the meeting's conclusion was that, given their different business styles and the intense rivalry between them, it was simply not a feasible suggestion. The episode reveals further evidence that federal officials wanted to see some large-scale Canadian corporations established in the hitherto fragments and unintegrated industry.

A few months after Pelletier's speech, the CFDC received an unsolicited offer from Martin Bockner of Astral Films to start a third theatre chain that would show a significant proportion of Canadian films.[14] Bockner would establish the chain if the government provided him with a preferred loan of $2.5 million with the provision that a considerable portion of any profits be reinvested in Canadian productions. The proposal 'aroused interest' among CFDC board members, and they decided to discuss it 'seriously' with other state officials.[15] Ultimately, Secretary of State officials deemed the proposal unfeasible. As Michael Spencer explained, the idea of establishing a state-sponsored theatre chain was considered a non-starter; it was simply not in line with the overall intention of establishing a private feature film industry. To be sure, the proposal would have met serious resistance from Canada's existing exhibitors.

The Porteus Committee's *Working Paper on Film Distribution* reflected the government's apprehension at taking aggressive measures to deal with the problem. Curiously, after outlining the now well-known evidence on the sorry state of theatrical exhibition for Canadian films, the Committee argued that the most important area for concern was in fact the lack of Canadian-made films in Canadian schools and other non-theatrical venues. Its major conclusion was that 'non-theatrical production and distribution in Canada deserves more government attention than theatrical.'[16] Be that as it may (and it is a very moot point), the Committee did suggest that government officials try to negotiate a voluntary quota for the theatrical exhibition of Canadian films. If these negotiations failed, the Committee cautiously suggested that a non-voluntary quota be established for a period of not more than five years. The Committee also thought that the federal government should begin talks with the provinces to establish a box-office levy. Calculated at 1972 attendance rates, a levy of five cents would have brought in close to $4.5 million a year, more than the CFDC had invested in any one year to date.

Secretary of State officials quickly seized the idea of a voluntary quota as a novel way of avoiding a serious conflict with the major chains and distributors. It would give federal officials time to negotiate a more substantial position with the provinces; it would diffuse some of the criticism that surrounded the issue; and it seemed like the logical next step in the process of moral suasion that had begun in the late sixties. Aware of an ever more hostile political climate, Famous Players and Odeon seemed prepared to go along with the scheme.

In July 1973, Secretary of State Hugh Faulkner announced that a voluntary quota had been successfully negotiated with the major exhibition chains.[17] The terms of the agreement were hardly onerous. Feature films produced or dubbed in English were to be guaranteed two weeks screen time in either Toronto, Vancouver, or Montreal. If successful, the films were to be given wider release.

The CFDC would share the cost of promotion and publicity, and Canadian-owned distributors agreed to provide a special publicity program. Famous Players would be responsible for two-thirds of the films, Odeon for the other third. Faulkner described the voluntary quotas as yet another first step in the elaboration of the federal government's feature film policy.

By the time the voluntary quotas were announced, the film advisory committee established by Pelletier had been meeting on and off for almost a year. The five private-sector members were: George Destounis, president of Famous Players Canada; Joan Fox, a film critic; Roche Demers of Faroun Films; Jacques Godbout, ex-president of the Association professionelle des cinéastes; and Thomas Shandel, a free-lance filmmaker.[18] At its first meeting, Undersecretary of State Jules Léger told committee members that the government was 'going through an era of decentralization,' and that they must 'recognize the new function of the private sector of the film industry in making recommendations concerning measures designed to assist it in discharging its functions.'[19] Needless to say, the composition of the committee did not bode well for a consensus. Destounis and government film commissioner Sidney Newman were adamantly opposed to the idea of mandatory quotas; Spencer favoured a box-office levy; while Shandel presented a position paper that concluded that 'anything less than a quota system continues this blatant cultural bigotry.'[20] After the release of the Porteus Committee's report, the advisory committee reached modest agreement that a voluntary quota might be worthwhile, and with Destounis in attendance the details of the formula were worked out. Further than this the committee would not go. After two years of meetings, the committee offered this strange assessment of Canada's cultural dilemma, which in its own way captures the contradictory nature of Canadian cultural development:

Having failed to assume its cultural destiny at other times, Canada has seen its territory occupied culturally and economically by foreign interests and capital. This situation, which has lasted a long time, has inevitably created, behind foreign distribution and exhibition networks, habits and behaviours which risk, and this has already been started, being contested by the creation of an autochthonous culture which is imposing itself more and more on its own market and on outside markets.[21]

Only in Canada could an autochthonous culture begin to impose itself on itself. Of course, what the quotation implies is that if there was a 'Canadian' culture it did not have adequate market access. It had been marginalized, excluded from the dominant pathways for cultural exchange and expression. The voluntary quotas were going to be part of the effort to contest the habits and behaviours that had worked against Canadian culture for such a long time. But they were not going to be much of an imposition.

The CCFM and a Radical Solution

The Council of Canadian Filmmakers had decided that the time had passed for such cryptic evaluations of Canada's cultural dilemma. Its first major policy statement, released in late 1973, had a significant new recommendation to go beyond the old demands of a mandatory quota and a box-office levy. Because current practices in the private sector placed more emphasis on commercial success than cultural relevance, and because that sector was now in a state of near total paralysis, the CCFM wanted the federal government to 'undertake some form of fully publicly supported production.'[22] The CCFM envisioned production of approximately 15 films a year, with budgets that ranged between $250,000 and $700,000, with a maximum annual government investment of $10 million. The films would be made by independent producers. Cast, crew, and all creative personnel would be Canadian. The statement was followed by a declaration in Winnipeg the following spring that read in part: 'We insist that the various governments of Canada implement the necessary policies to provide for an alternative and a complement to the private production capacity in the Canadian feature film industry by providing a public mechanism and the resources to fully finance Canadian features.'[23] As Kirwan Cox explained in *Cinema Canada*: 'The problems of film as art and film as commerce are separate and distinct and require separate policies ... Government must make two clearly defined sections of this unruly jumble – public and private – and stop this schizophrenic requirement that both fit into the same mould.'[24]

Curiously, an evaluation of the CFDC's activities done by the government's Bureau of Management Consulting appeared to reach a similar conclusion.[25] Recognizing the contradictory pulls of a film industry for culture and a film industry for profit, the study came to the conclusion that if the 'cultural objectives are paramount' then the only 'viable option' would be a 'Conseil des Arts for the CFDC' wherein the Corporation would make outright grants to producers of Canadian films.[26] If it was decided that the cultural objectives were less important than the establishment of a self-sustaining commercial industry, then the study concluded that the CFDC should concentrate on the development of a few 'established Canadian film companies.'[27] The report also noted that 'there is no consensus within the CFDC or the industry itself on the policies that should be followed by the CFDC.'[28] This was the one thing that everyone agreed upon.

There is little evidence that state officials took seriously the idea of establishing a production sector that would not be based upon commercial criteria.

Léger's remark to the advisory committee made it clear that the government wanted the feature film industry to be driven by private-sector forces, and an atmosphere of increasing budgetary restraint made it very unlikely that a system of grants or awards would be approved. Michael Spencer wrote a rather terse response to the CCFM's proposal, which read in part: 'We have considerable reservations about your new category of funding to provide investments amounting to 100 per cent of the budget under certain specific conditions. Since we have always understood that our mandate was to create a film industry in the private sector, we find it hard to grasp how such a proposal would be helpful.'[29] Spencer put the point more forcefully in the *Toronto Star*: 'If some people want government support all the way through let them go and work for the NFB or the CBC. [The federal government] should give investors a 100 per cent tax write-off the first year they put their money in. I'd rather see that than the government manœuvered into giving more CFDC investment in each picture.'[30] The CFDC may have come to endorse the principle of protectionist measures, but it was also still a staunch defender of the principle that Canadian feature film production had to be developed along the lines of private capitalist accumulation.

Talking to the Provinces: Theatre Legislation

It would not be easy to manufacture an agreement among the provinces for a quota or a levy, but there did appear to be some provincial support for the idea. In January 1973, a report commissioned by the Ontario government recommended the adoption of a quota whereby every theatre in the province would be required to show eight weeks of Canadian features over a two-year period.[31] The report also recommended that the provincial tax on admissions be used as an incentive for the exhibition and production of Canadian films, preferably Canadian films made in Ontario. If the film was made in Ontario then the exhibitor and producer would share the receipts from the 10 per cent tax; if the film was not made in Ontario (but still Canadian) then the producers' share would revert to the Ontario film office to help further productions in the province. The quota recommendation was modest, but for some observers it was an important breakthrough. More significant was the recommendation with respect to the provincial admissions tax. The Bassett Report, as it came to be known, had fashioned a recommendation that would give exhibitors a small financial incentive for showing Canadian films. At the same time, the tax rebate would not in any way affect the financial receipts of the Hollywood majors; indeed, its major effect might have been to discriminate against films made in other parts of Canada! Nonetheless, the Ontario government did not make any moves to introduce the recommendations. In the typically cautious fashion of its Progressive Conservative regime, the government adopted a wait-and-see attitude.

As Michael Spencer and Secretary of State officials began their negotiations with the provinces, Leonard Evans, minister of Trade and Commerce in Manitoba's New Democratic government, came out in full support of the CCFM's recommendations. 'Canada has become a dumping ground for the films of American distribution companies,' Evans explained. 'Unless Canadian filmmakers have access to the medium that shows their films, we might as well stop fooling ourselves into thinking we are going to produce feature films in this country.' Evans strongly endorsed the need for the quotas and he wanted the federal government to purchase and operate 'one of the film distribution systems in Canada.'[32]

It was the most radical position taken by any of the provinces, but Manitoba certainly did not possess the weight to carry the negotiations. Indeed, Evans' remarks were in stark contrast to the position taken a year earlier by Tom Vant, the Alberta government's officer for film development, who told a panel of producers: 'Film is a business, like making and selling shoes. It must stand on its own economically first ... Film must be entertainment. Otherwise it is of no use.'[33]

While there was some speculation that Quebec might support a system of quotas, filmmakers there had become accustomed to an endless series of false promises. As filmmaker Robin Spry remarked, 'since 1962 there had been sixteen reports, one white paper, four draft laws, Bill 52 dealing primarily with censorship, research trips to study foreign film industries ... and numerous interventions, meetings, lunches, telegrams, and articles.'[34] But there was still only meagre support for the production and exhibition of Quebec-based feature films. Frustrated by the lack of public support in the context of high-sounding rhetoric, the Association des réalisateurs de films du Québec (ARFQ) took direct action on 22 November 1974 and occupied the Bureau de surveillance du cinéma, the Quebec Censorship Office. The filmmakers would not leave until a 'loi cadre' on the cinema was tabled in the National Assembly and a public, parliamentary commission on film was called. The government stalled for time, while public support for the action grew.[35] The occupation lasted 11 days, but as the Christmas season approached distributors and exhibitors became increasingly anxious that there would not be time to classify their new films for the most important box-office period of the year. On 3 December, the Quebec government decided that the offices had to be cleared. In the midst of a heavy snowstorm the police were called in and the filmmakers were carried out and dumped on the sidewalk. In April of the following year, the Quebec government introduced yet another draft film law, ominously entitled Bill 1. It offered more financial support for the production of Quebec feature films and contained a carefully worded suggestion that quotas might have to be considered if Quebec films continued to receive inadequate exhibition.[36] At almost the same time, Premier William Davis of Ontario announced that he was personally opposed to mandatory quotas. It is hard to imagine how an agreement could be struck without the support of the country's largest province.

The Second Phase of the Federal Film Policy

Discussion over Bill 1 was soon overshadowed by news that the federal government was close to announcing its own new film policy. In May, Secretary of State Faulkner appeared before the Standing Committee on Broadcasting, Films and Assistance to the Arts and stated flatly that 'one of the major problems which has faced Canadian filmmakers for many years is the difficulty of securing adequate distribution for their films.' Faulkner continued: 'In July, 1973, I negotiated a voluntary quota with Famous Players and Odeon ... I am not satisfied with the results of this agreement since adequate exposure for Canadian films, particularly in theatres with favourable locations has not been achieved. It has been evident for some time that a more effective system must be found.'[37] Once again the rhetoric seemed to favour a radical solution to the problem. Once again the secretary of state would bring forth a mouse.

Faulkner announced the federal government's new policy on 5 August 1975. There were two principal measures. First, a new income tax regulation would allow investors in an eligible Canadian feature film to deduct 100 per cent of their investment in the first year. An eligible film would be one that was over 75 minutes long, in which the producer and two-thirds of the creative personnel were Canadian, and in which at least 75 per cent of the technical services were performed in Canada (formal co-productions were automatically eligible). Faulkner also announced that after 'extensive negotiations' Famous Players and Odeon had agreed to a voluntary quota of four weeks per theatre a year (the theatre chains also agreed to an investment program of at least $1.7 million to aid Canadian production).[38]

Most of the industry's representatives were pleased that the government had improved the tax write-off for Canadian films, but beyond that, unless one was an exhibitor or a major distributor, there was little to be thankful for. Although Faulkner insisted that this time the CFDC would take an active role in monitoring the quota, the CCFM was furious that the scheme was still voluntary.[39] Furthermore, the agreement applied to theatres not screens – at a time when exhibitors were transforming many of their venues into multiscreen sites.

Informed observers also realized that an eligible film could still be made without Canadians in many of the principal creative roles. There was a flurry of other criticisms. Why was there no levy that would affect the distributors' receipts? Why were the provinces, or anyone else for that matter, not informed that a voluntary quota was being negotiated?

As it turned out, there was an even more significant question. The day after Faulkner's announcement, the *Vancouver Sun* revealed that the Treasury Board had decided to refuse the funds necessary for the CFDC to continue its operations.[40] Was phase two of the federal film policy to proceed without the CFDC? If so, why had the secretary of state failed to mention the Treasury Board's decision during his announcement? The Canadian Association of Motion Picture Producers (the revamped AMPPLC) rightly questioned the sincerity of the federal government's whole initiative and wondered 'how a programme so haphazardly conceived can restore the confidence of the financial community.'[41] It was certainly another sign that the government's planning mechanisms had become terribly disorganized.

It seems that the Treasury Board's decision was based upon the continuing poor financial returns on the CFDC's investments, but it is not altogether clear whether the action was really just a strategic ploy to get the CFDC to think more along the lines of commercial success. Whatever the cause, the Treasury Board released the necessary funds in November, after extensive lobbying by industry representatives and the Secretary of State, and after yet another report on the film industry by the Bureau of Management Consulting had been commissioned. The Treasury Board's actions had the effect of putting Canadian filmmakers and their allies on the defensive. Instead of concentrating on the repercussions of Faulkner's policy statement, they found themselves mobilizing to defend an institution many still considered inadequate but certainly better than nothing.

The Tompkins Report

The Secretary of State's study of the film industry prepared by the Bureau of Management Consulting (commonly referred to as the Tompkins Report) was released in March 1976. It encapsulated what was quickly becoming the prevailing rationale among both government officials and many of the industry's leading producers. The Report tapped a sentiment that had always existed in Canada, namely, that the film industry should be first and foremost a business and that feature film production in particular had to be structured as a business for export. This was the Report's basic argument:

In the feature film industry it is recognized that there is a world-wide shortage of 'good' feature films. A good feature film is understood here as one that has a mass audience appeal beyond the boundaries of any one country, and subsequently returns a gross revenue well above the production costs ... With the costs of production rising (including substantial fees to performers) producers and investors have to be concerned with a breakthrough into the international market and subsequent large audiences. A film such as *Jaws* is a classic example of this trend ...

It is our considered opinion that the Canadian feature film industry has to aim for a world-wide market, and that any actions taken by the various governments in Canada should lead to this end.[42]

According to the Report's calculations, an exhibition quota was completely unworkable and undesirable because even a 50 per cent quota would bring in less revenue than a 5 per cent increase in foreign sales; it would also have the effect of angering the major distributors and thereby jeopardizing the possibility of foreign sales under their auspices.[43] Since commercial viability, not cultural development, was the principal concern, quotas were not the answer. Canada simply had to develop a feature film industry that could 'hold its own in the export market; it must be able to compete with the products of the film industries of other countries ... The leaders of the Canadian film industry must become sufficiently knowledgable and skilful to face this competition with marketable standards.'[44] Moreover, the Report made no mention of the need to support Canadian distributors as either domestic or foreign agents for Canadian films. It thus ignored evidence of the CFDC's difficulties in dealing with the Hollywood majors and the extent to which profits from distribution in Canada were going to support the production of films elsewhere.

If there was one single factor external to the decision-making abilities of producers that so far had hampered the industry, it was not foreign penetration or a monopolized distribution and exhibition network, but rather the existing practices of public agencies, such as the CBC and NFB, which had 'impeded the market mechanism, disregarded all yardsticks of competition and reduced the private sector to a marginal existence.'[45] The report was particularly harsh on the NFB. Although it now contracted out 50 per cent of government productions, the Film Board was accused of holding a 'messianic view' of its film-making role 'without the constraints of commercialism.'[46] Wherever possible the state had to get out of direct production and curtail its role as a price-setter; public agencies had to learn to operate in a 'spirit of market complementarity.'[47] The report wanted the NFB to become both a centre for creative and technical experimentation and a training ground for filmmakers who would eventually move to the private sector.

On the other hand, the CFDC's efforts to support private production were generally praised. The Tompkins Report was optimistic that, together with the new tax regulations, CFDC loans could be used to make Canadian feature films internationally competitive. To this end, the Report also suggested that the CFDC and Canadian producers more actively pursue co-productions 'as one way of getting Canadian films and talent into a wider market than Canada alone.'[48] Finally, the Report contained an explicit bias toward the production of English-language feature films, arguing that films made for the Quebec market, while modestly successful, were limited in their 'international appeal.'[49] It was a rather odd conclusion given that the success of the Swedish film industry demonstrated 'the universal appeal of high quality and a distinctive national ambience.'[50] The remarks were made just one page apart, but the Report did not dwell on the possibility that they were contradictory statements.

The Tompkins Report had made its point: Canada's feature film industry had to be driven by big-budget, internationally oriented, mostly English-language films produced by a private sector geared toward commercial success. 'Other measures' were not necessary. Although it was not accompanied by an immediate ministerial announcement, this was to be the second phase of Canada's feature film policy. As Secretary of State Faulkner told the Standing Committee on Broadcasting, Films and Assistance to the Arts in April 1976, 'we must recognize the growing capacity of the private sector and encourage its further development.'[51]

The new tax legislation was beginning to have the desired effect: private capital was moving back into the feature film business. The trend was already noticeable in the CFDC's year-end reports. In 1975, the Corporation invested $3.8 million in 18 features, whose total cost was $5.9 million.[52] Reflecting the uncertainty in the market, private investment accounted for only 35 per cent of the total funds. In the following year, the CFDC invested $2.7 million in 16 features, whose total cost was $12 million.[53] The CFDC's share was down to 23 per cent, average budgets had gone to $750,000 from $327,000, and foreign investment in CFDC-backed films went from 8 per cent to 39 per cent. The increase in foreign investment reflected the fact that 'to create bigger budget films ... for international acceptance, the Corporation was actively involved in a number of co-productions (four with Britain and one with France).[54] As the CFDC also noted, 1976 was the 'first time a significant number of major feature films were made without the financial assistance of the Corporation. At least thirteen such films (five of them co-productions) were produced during the past twelve months.'[55] A few of the CFDC-backed films – such as *Outrageous!* (1977), *Who Has Seen the Wind* (1977), and *Why Shoot the Teacher?* (1977) – were critically praised and also commercially respectable. These films stood as evidence that some filmmakers (English-language filmmakers at that) were still interested in producing films that did not abandon cultural considerations to the dictates of commercial success. But within the industry and within the state this was definitely the viewpoint of a minority.

Twenty million dollars later, the CFDC had still not been able to establish a stable environment for the production of Canadian feature films. While industry and government representatives groped and clashed over further policy initiatives and refinements, Canada became the number one revenue-generating foreign market for Hollywood films. In 1974, the American majors recouped $54.4 million from the Canadian market; from France and Great Britain (each with roughly twice the population of Canada) the majors recouped $35.0 and $36.5 million respectively (see Table 1).

The voluntary quota program was a sham. More than anything else, it symbolized the government's discomfort and unwillingness to deal concretely with the issue of adequate distribution and exhibition of Canadian films, its desperate hope that the problem would go away on its own. It didn't. And in the quagmire of proposals and counter-proposals two dramatically opposed options surfaced. The first option was carried forward by the Council of Canadian Filmmakers. The CCFM argued that, given the market structure for feature filmmaking, Canadian feature film production would be, with few exceptions, unprofitable. Instead of trying to make commercially viable films (and failing), the government should begin to treat Canadian filmmaking as an art that merited funding along the lines of Canada Council grants. A theatre levy and quotas would provide the money and the venue for production and exhibition of fully subsidized Canadian films. In time, Canadians might even grow accustomed to the oddity of seeing Canadian films. The second option was embodied in the Tompkins Report and supported by the exhibition chains and most of the larger production houses. It was to develop a Hollywood North, to make films that would be attractive to the American majors and that would sell in the mainstream international market. This was how Nat Taylor had envisioned the Canadian film industry; it had also been the view of Ray Peck and John Grierson.

For state officials the second option was obviously the path of least resistance. Aside from the jurisdictional difficulties in establishing a box-office quota and levy, and the obvious furore that would have resulted over their implementation, the state was moving into a period of protracted deficit financing; the prospect of an unprofitable industry dependent upon government grants was a non-starter. It must be said that this was as much a question of appearances as it was a question of economic and political priorities. The capital cost allowance is a form of state expenditure; it represents revenue forgone, taxes

TABLE 1

Gross Rentals from Top Foreign Markets for American Distributors, 1974–86
($ millions, U.S.)

	1974	1975	1976	1977	1978	1979	1980	1981	1982	1983	1984	1985	1986
Canada	54.4	63.2	60.8	64.3	77.6	75.0	91.5	88.7	99.8	91.0	111.0	75.5	86.8
France	35.0	54.6	51.9	46.5	95.6	80.8	88.9	83.0	71.6	81.3	69.5	50.2	98.5
U.K.	36.5	37.8	37.1	36.1	72.2	79.4	86.3	76.6	51.9	49.7	35.0	41.2	49.1
Italy	47.7	56.4	45.0	39.6	55.8	58.9	55.1	41.0	43.6	48.4	40.0	31.0	64.6
W. Germany	35.0	45.7	41.3	51.7	70.0	97.1	88.5	77.6	60.2	66.2	48.0	48.5	64.7
Australia	38.1	37.5	38.7	26.1	40.2	40.1	42.4	51.3	44.7	44.8	33.0	28.8	27.4
Japan	37.1	56.7	52.2	48.9	95.4	80.8	76.6	68.5	54.5	102.4	77.0	74.9	102.6

Source: Manjunath Pendakur, *Canadian Dreams and American Control* (1990), Table 7, 121

not collected. The state, as we shall see, would actually spend an enormous amount of money on the film industry with the CCA, but because these were tax expenditures the costs were difficult to calculate, and, for all intents and purposes, hidden from public scrutiny. Relatedly, tax expenditures go to investors, entrepreneurs, producers; they can be rationalized as attempts to improve the business climate, while Canada Council–type grants have the annoying tendency of being regarded as 'handouts' to ungrateful artists. And so, the industry and the government geared themselves toward the fabrication of a Hollywood North. If luck would have it, there might still be room at the margins for films that were critically praiseworthy but unlikely to meet the box-office success of a film like *Jaws*.

9   The Ten Per Cent Solution and the Tax-Shelter Boom

Artists cannot survive on art alone. Schlock – to use an inelegant word – is necessary as a solid base for creativity; it provides employment for talents which would otherwise not be able to survive, nor thus be available for projects of a higher artistic value.
The success of our policies will be in whether we go beyond an industry of commercial profits to an industry which also creates films which are a lasting contribution to Canada's cultural heritage.
– John Roberts[1]

Introduction

After years of meetings, countless background studies and briefs, the 1978 film policy statement by John Roberts, Hugh Faulkner's successor as secretary of state, was a significantly inauspicious occasion for those who still hoped that the federal government might fashion a film policy that could accommodate both culture and commerce. On the other hand, Millard Roth, executive director of the Canadian Motion Picture Distributors Association (CMPDA) was 'pleased.' As he put it, the announcement was 'rather consistent with a lot of the views which we presented.'[2]

What Roth did not say was that the CMPDA and its allies could now breathe a collective sigh of relief, for it was well known that six months earlier the Secretary of State had prepared a document that called for a ten per cent tax on the gross receipts of distributors. The money raised (estimated roughly at $6 million in 1977) would have gone directly to the CFDC, thereby doubling its annual funds and eliminating the need for the government subsidy. In other words, the gross receipts of the major American distributors would have become the principal financial source for the Canadian government's support to private domestic feature filmmaking. John Roberts' ten per cent solution was an aggressive and creative proposal. But in November 1977 it was scuttled by

TABLE 2
Certified Canadian Film Productions, 1974–85
(Applications for Certification) ($ millions, Cdn)

Year	Features		Shorts		Total	
	Num.	Budget	Num.	Budget	Num.	Budget
1974	3	1.58	0	.0	3	1.59
1975	18	6.67	1	.006	19	6.68
1976	33	19.19	34	6.2	67	25.39
1977	37	35.28	72	14.11	109	49.33
1978	37	48.66	93	15.67	130	64.32
1979	66	171.78	156	39.03	222	210.81
1980	53	147.38	179	62.90	232	210.29
1981	43	64.08	156	69.13	199	133.22
1982	30	34.55	103	31.93	133	66.49
1983	29	19.96	90	23.87	119	43.84
1984	40	36.85	87	42.93	127	79.32
1985	38	56.85	89	78.93	127	135.78

Source: Canadian Film and Video Certification Office, adapted from
Manjunath Pendakur, *Canadian Dreams and American Control* (1990),
Table 12, 172.

the Liberal Cabinet. As we shall see, from within the state the main opposition
came from the Department of Finance. And as we should now expect, the
feature film industry itself was clearly divided on the issue: the Council of
Canadian Filmmakers, and the French and English directors' associations
endorsed Roberts' proposal; but it was explicitly rejected by the CMPDA and
more tactfully opposed by most of Canada's independent distributors and major
private producers.

In retrospect, Roberts' spring-time announcement to the Standing Committee
on Broadcasting, Films and Assistance to the Arts, was an admission of defeat.
Of course, he did not say so explicitly. Instead, he lauded the 'recent success'
and 'continued progress' of the film industry and said that this meant there was
no need for a 'radical renovation of our structure for government support.' All
that was now needed was 'a jigging of the present institutions to provide an
even more effective context for growth.'[3] The members of the Committee may
have had a premonition that Roberts' policy had been emaciated – they failed
to muster a quorum for his appearance.

To be sure, Roberts' assessment of the film industry's recent 'success' was
not entirely without substance. From a commercial standpoint the Canadian
feature film industry had embarked on a new and apparently healthy phase.
From 1978 to the fall of 1980, Canadian feature filmmaking entered what has
been described as its 'boom' period. Although accurate figures are difficult to
come by, at the height of the 'boom' in 1979 approximately 66 feature films

with a total budget of $172 million were produced (see Table 2).[4] This new phase was not to be one of quotas, levies, or other measures designed to directly or significantly alter the distribution or exhibition sectors of the industry, nor one in which the paramount concern was the production of self-consciously 'Canadian' films. Rather, it was to be the era of tax-sheltered productions designed for distribution through the American majors.

The enormous increase in both productions and budgets was the result of three main factors. Most important was the incentive provided by the capital cost allowance and the development of the 'public offer' by which producers raised capital by offering small-scale investors a share in the production (and an immediate tax write-off). Second, Canadian producers had learned to make greater use of the co-production treaties that now existed with France, Italy, the United Kingdom, the Federal Republic of Germany, and Israel. Third, and not least important, was the fact that the CFDC itself, under the new leadership of Michael McCabe and Michel Vennat, made support of big-budget 'international' films its own top priority.

As we have seen, the major interests within the industry had always considered Canadian feature films to be an export commodity. Now, the code word for success was 'international appeal.' In plainer terms, this meant sales to the United States. Of course the American majors had always said that they would be more than willing to distribute Canadian pictures that could hold their own in international markets, while many of the major producers in Canada had always been rather unapologetic in their desire to obtain distribution through American firms. The tax-shelter boom was the culmination of this logic. Canada's feature film industry had finally succumbed to that old adage: If you can't beat 'em, join 'em. *Meatballs* (1979), *Murder by Decree* (1979), and *The Changeling* (1980) were some of the more notable and successful emanations from Hollywood North. Even the CFDC dropped the assumption that it was as important to assist productions that made a lasting contribution to Canada's cultural heritage as it was to sustain an industry for profit. As Michael McCabe explained:

The CFDC decided film was essentially an export product and, since it was not normally possible to recoup the budget in the Canadian market, producers should make films that were capable of recouping budgets in other markets ...

Too often, we hid behind our nationalism to protect mediocrity. Too often, all it really means is we are afraid to get out there and compete.[5]

One person's definition of art is another person's definition of mediocrity. While it is certainly true that private feature filmmaking in advanced capitalist countries is at root a commercial activity, it is no less true that the tax-sheltered commercial boom in Canadian films produced far more 'shlock,' to use Roberts' phrase, than art. The production of film as art was both limited and marginalized during this period, as efforts were geared almost entirely toward success in the mainstream international marketplace. Inevitably this revealed some notable contradictions for Canadian cultural policy, above all the fact that the orientation to the international market heavily favoured English-language productions, which far outnumbered their French-language counterparts in absolute terms and respective budgets. Furthermore, the notion that shlock was to provide 'the foundation for art,' as Roberts bravely put it, was itself rather questionable. Many of the Canadian directors who had made a start at developing their cinematic craft in the early 1970s found themselves out of work during the boom or, perhaps worse, at work on projects for which their particular talents were ill-suited. On the other hand, many of Canada's producers made a healthy living for themselves, particularly those who learned the art of structuring deals that paid a hefty producer's fee regardless of a given film's commercial success.

In any case, the increase in production in the late seventies did not create a stable or balanced industry; with few exceptions most of the films were not commercial successes – many were never even shown. Ultimately, the tax-sheltered boom did not lead to the establishment of stable production houses that could produce films without tax-shelter financing. This had been a longstanding goal of the feature film policy and it was perhaps the basis upon which the shlock-begets-art assumption was supposed to work. It didn't. When the boom ended in 1980, the industry was once again in the throes of a crisis, the victim of over-production (a new phenomenon in Canadian film production to be sure), the loss of investor confidence, and uncertainty over the future of the capital cost allowance provisions.

1977–8: An Industry in Transition

Ironically, 1977 (the year before the start of the tax-shelter boom) was a watershed year in the history of Canada's feature film industry. For the CFDC the fiscal year 1977 marked the completion of its first ten years of operation. Fresh from the challenge to its existence that came from the Treasury Board and Department of Finance, the Corporation proudly pointed to its tenth anniversary as a 'vintage year.'[6] From a fiscal standpoint, a frame of reference that Treasury Board and Finance officials could more easily appreciate, the box-office success of certain CFDC-backed films was heartening. Richard Benner's *Outrageous!*, which starred Craig Russell in a virtuoso performance of gay camp, Allan King's film version of W.O. Mitchell's *Who Has Seen the Wind*, and Silvio Narizzano's *Why Shoot the Teacher?* suggested that commercial and cultural considerations were compatible; these films were critical as well as financial success stories. The CFDC recovered $1 million from its investments in one year (it had taken the CFDC five years to recover its first $1 million). Other films released in 1977 were equally noteworthy for their contribution to a Canadian cinema. Jean Beaudin's NFB production, *J.A. Martin, photographe*, swept the Canadian Film Awards, and garnered considerable praise at Cannes (along with *Outrageous!*). Equally noteworthy was Jean-Pierre Lefebvre's *Le vieux pays où Rimbaud est mort*. 'Suddenly and in spite of everything,' wrote Martin Knelman in October 1977, 'projects that seemed to have the usual ingredients of failure were alchemized, one by one, into stunning hits.'[7] Yet, rather than being a sign of things to come, these films were a sign of things that were to pass. With few exceptions, the tax-shelter boom would channel resources into high-budget, American-oriented pictures. 1977 was indeed a 'vintage year,' for vintage years are, by definition, rare.

The CFDC's report on its investments for 1977–8 showed that of $1.6 million invested in 20 films, $1 million went to five English-language productions, whose total cost was $4.3 million. The films included: *Power Play* (with Peter O'Toole and a budget of $2.1 million); *Disappearance* (a Canada–U.K. co-production with Donald Sutherland); and Robert Lantos' production of *In Praise of Older Women*.[8] As the annual report noted, the trend toward higher budgets and English-language productions had taken its toll on the French-language industry. In the same year, the Corporation invested $580,000 in the production of 15 French-language films, whose total budget was $1.3 million. Eleven of these films were documentaries, which helps to explain why their average cost was $85,000 as opposed to an average cost of $840,000 for the CFDC-backed English-language films. The French-language industry was still in a state of crisis. In 1977 none of the French-language films produced with the help of the CFDC received investment from private sources outside the industry.[9] Where such money surfaced was in Franco-Canadian co-productions such as *Violette Nozière* and *Blood Relatives* (both directed by France's Claude Chabrol).[10] While such films paid handsome dividends to producers and created employment for Quebec-based technicians, they did precious little to advance the talents of Canadian directors, screenwriters, or cinematographers. Directors such as Claude Jutra turned to television and English Canada to find a place to work.

Not surprisingly, the trend toward co-productions had sparked a new conflict within the industry. As the Council of Canadian Filmmakers (CCFM) remarked:

The credit list for eleven coproductions made in Canada since August of last year reads like the European Common Market and Canadian writers, directors and lead actors are conspicuous by their absence ... Coproductions offer the easy way to qualify for the 100% capital cost allowance tax break now in effect for Canadian films ... to the extent that Canada has become a Bahamas-style tax shelter.[11]

Even within the Canadian Association of Motion Picture Producers (CAMPP) there was some dispute over the propriety of the current co-production arrangements. While most producers argued that production, any production, was good for the health of the industry, at a heated meeting in the summer of 1977 some dissension emerged. As one producer colourfully remarked:

The commercial is necessary, but that's all co-productions are now, and that's not enough. You need a commitment to the industry and the country. What happens with co-productions depends on the CFDC and the Secretary of State ... We've kissed American asses and look what we've got. Now we are going through the British, Italians and French. Now, it's just a gallery of asses to kiss.[12]

Expressing similar reservations, Michael Spencer had already hinted that the CFDC was considering the option of investing in co-productions, if and only if either the main star, the director, or the screenwriter was a Canadian citizen. But such a decision, if and when it came, would not affect the growing number of films being produced without the CFDC's assistance.

Distribution and the Ten Per Cent Solution

When John Roberts became secretary of state in September 1976 he signalled his intention to complete the task of developing a comprehensive film policy begun by his predecessors, Faulkner and Pelletier. Hugh Faulkner had left Roberts with a draft film policy ready for Cabinet discussion. In both tone and substance it followed the main assumptions and recommendations of the Tompkins Report and reflected the Trudeau government's economic priorities: it was thought to be far easier to legitimate the privatization of state activities than new forms of state intervention in the economy, such as a quota or box-office levy. As Faulkner told *Cinema Canada*:

The principal element, I think, that characterizes our approach to film policy is our attempt to create an economic climate with some form of government assistance that will enable the film industry itself to develop ... We're trying to move away from a cultural sector dependent entirely on government handouts to create a combination of economic forces which make it possible for the private sector to develop along with parallel government activity.[13]

To this end, Faulkner's draft film policy placed far more emphasis on limiting the amount of public-sector filmmaking than on breaking up the monopoly structure within the private sector. Its most forceful conclusion concerned the non-theatrical film market (i.e., television and educational films): 'The domination of this significant informational and cultural medium by publicly owned enterprises is probably no longer a situation that best serves the national interest or allows for the kind of environment best suited to the creative and professional development of the film industry.'[14] In an effort to stimulate private production, Faulkner wanted in-house production at the NFB and the CBC to be drastically reduced over the next few years. Faulkner also felt that the CFDC should be able to invest in all manner of film production, including television and industrial films, and that these investments should be geared toward the establishment of a more integrated sector of film companies.

In general, Faulkner's discussion of the major problems facing the private film sector coincided with the basic concerns expressed by Canadian major producers. On the one hand, the private production sector was set against an 'entrenched, publicly financed industry, and, on the other, a strong competitive force in the form of lower-cost imported films and other audio-visual products.'[15] From the private industry's point of view, the CBC – far and away the largest producer of film and television programming – was as much a barrier to expansion as was the exhibition and distribution monopoly in feature films. Faulkner was not oblivious to the structural problems within the feature film industry, but it was obviously far easier for the state to tackle the problem of under-production and instability in the private sector by amending the practices of its own institutions. This position was only reinforced by the increasing tendency to treat all manner of film production (including television production) as a single policy unit. In the long run (the introduction of pay TV was now being debated) and in the short run, television had come to be seen as the most important medium for the exhibition of Canadian visual productions. While the exhibition of Canadian feature films in the more glamorous theatrical market retained its appeal, for many industry representatives and public officials the theatrical market was simply too risky and too unstable a base on which to build a healthy private production sector.

While Roberts may have concurred with the main premises of Faulkner's argument, he was not about to abandon attempts to restructure the theatrical market and could not put his signature to the draft film policy. In his opinion, the proposed policy statement failed to deal substantively with one of the oldest and most important of issues: film distribution in Canada and the near-monopoly position of the Hollywood majors and their Canadian allies. Faulkner's draft had called for more 'negotiations' with the CMPDA, and an extension of the voluntary quota agreements. Roberts wanted those negotiations completed, and he wanted the new policy statement to take a firm position on the issue of distribution. Roberts himself met with both the CMPDA and the Motion Picture Association of America. As he told *Cinema Canada*: 'I was a little tough on them when I met them, but they must understand that we don't have much time left, that the file has been around a long time and that we must make decisions now.'[16]

There was a recent precedent for a more aggressive policy with respect to the major American distributors, which fit directly with the Trudeau government's extensive use of the tax system as a conduit for public policy in the seventies. In 1976, the Trudeau government enacted Bill C-58, which amended the Income Tax Act in a bid to improve the economic viability of Canadian magazine publishers and television broadcasters.[17] In the publishing sector, Bill C-58 withdrew the privileged tax status of *Time* magazine's Canadian edition, finally implementing one of the principal recommendations of the 1961 O'Leary Commission. In an effort to solidify the commercial base for Canadian television, Bill C-58 also made Canadian advertising on American television stations non-deductible. American border television stations denounced the bill and sought retaliation from Washington. They got it. The U.S. Administration was quick to impose punitive counter-measures and unwilling to let the matter rest.[18] The federal government withstood the pressure to abandon Bill C-58, making it clear that on some issues at least it was prepared to support the Canadian cultural industry by discriminating against American firms.

But while Bill C-58 was hailed as a triumph for cultural nationalists, it was not without its limitations. The other principal target of the O'Leary Commission, *Reader's Digest*, managed to retain its privileged tax status, and Canadian magazine racks continued to display a predominance of foreign material. Undoubtedly, Bill C-58 was a benefit to Canada's largest newsmagazine, *Maclean's*, which began to produce a weekly shortly after the Bill's introduction, but it did little to help the industry as a whole. Similarly, while Canadian television stations did receive a sizeable increase in advertising revenue (estimated in 1984 to be worth between $36 and $42 million annually), Bill C-58 said nothing about how this money was to be spent. Ideally, the increase in revenue was to go toward the production of more Canadian television programs, but there is nothing to indicate that this in fact occurred. Of course, an amendment to the Income Tax Act does not in and of itself constitute a comprehensive cultural policy. Bill C-58 was a limited measure, and has to be evaluated as such. It is not without significance that the Bill had the effect of supporting already well-entrenched interests within the cultural sector, *Maclean's* and Canadian broadcasters.

Bill C-58 may have provided Roberts with a rough model for dealing with the question of distribution, but the U.S. reaction was also a warning: any measure that significantly altered the current business practices of the American majors would be strenuously resisted, both by the distributors themselves and by the U.S. administration (bear in mind that the American border television stations were minor interests next to the combined clout of the Motion Picture Association of America). In fact, the very existence of Bill C-58 militated against the introduction of further protectionist measures in the cultural sphere in the near future. As Stephen Clarkson so cogently argues, Canadian–American relations are typified by an elaborate, and very often implicit, quid pro quo bargaining process. The introduction of Bill C-58 made it very unlikely that the Canadian state would soon risk another protectionist measure, especially one in the same general sphere.

Roberts presented his first proposal to Cabinet in November 1977.[19] It represented a significant departure from Faulkner's draft of the previous year. The document dealt almost exclusively with the question of distribution and the privileged position of the American majors, then receiving about $60 million a year in film rentals, almost all of it returning to the United States. Roberts felt that some mechanism had to be found to keep a larger portion of this money in Canada for the purpose of financing Canadian films. He proposed a ten per cent tax on the gross rental receipts that distributors collect, with a rebate equivalent to the total amount they return to Canadian producers from Canadian films distributed in Canada and abroad. The revenue generated, estimated at between $5 and $7 million for 1977, would go directly to the CFDC. In keeping with Faulkner's desire to begin treating the film production sector as a single unit, Roberts also recommended that the CFDC be able to invest in television productions. The document also described co-productions as one way to meet the 'permanent American domination of the world film market.'[20] Finally, with Odeon Theatres up for sale, Roberts wanted Cabinet to consider financial assistance for prospective Canadian buyers.[21]

Although limited in scope, and certainly not a comprehensive policy statement, the document was significant for its attempt to address the issue of distribution. Roberts well understood at least some of its implications. As the Cabinet brief explained: 'The foreign distributors will rise up violently against the fiscal measures and will use their influence in Washington. The American government will probably take measures of reprisal, notably, to exclude Canadian films from the American market.'[22] Such a boycott would not last very long in Roberts' opinion, because the American majors would not want to risk any further measures with respect to their largest foreign market.

But like Bill C-58, Roberts' ten per cent solution would be a limited and perhaps contradictory measure. In the first place, the proposal did not distinguish between Canadian and American distributors; roughly 20 Canadian distribution firms, with combined earnings of approximately $10 million a year, would also be subject to the tax. Many of these firms were already in a weak financial position, and the tax may well have seriously eroded their already unstable market position. Relatedly, the proposal would do nothing to make Canadian distribution firms more attractive to Canadian producers; in fact, the provision of a rebate for the distribution of Canadian films probably would have made it even more likely that the major American distributors would handle the most potentially profitable Canadian films, since there would be a small financial incentive to do so. With respect to financing the production of films in Canada the proposal was inventive, but it would not diminish the privileged position of the American majors within the Canadian film industry. At best the proposal would serve to integrate the major distributors into the production cycle of Canadian films. The record of such collaborations in the past suggested that this would do very little to improve the quality of Canadian films.

We cannot know for sure what effect the policy might have had because it never received Cabinet approval. The major opposition from within the state came from the Department of Finance. Finance officials were clearly unimpressed by the CFDC's track record. Though they had shown themselves to be far from opposed to the use of tax expenditures intended to stimulate private investment, they had a particular aversion to a tax scheme so discretionary in its application. As the self-appointed representative of GATT within the Canadian state, Finance held in disfavour all economic proposals that discriminated, or appeared to discriminate, on the basis of nationality. Moreover, American reprisals with respect to Bill C-58 probably made Finance in particular, and the Cabinet in general, leery of introducing another controversial trade measure. In the ensuing discussions, the Department of Finance apparently exercised its de facto veto over the introduction of new fiscal measures. As Roberts told the Standing Committee in late November, 'the area of taxation, as you known, is a peculiarly sensitive one in federal government terms and is the responsibility of the Minister of Finance.'[23] By December, Roberts had back-tracked even further, explaining that the policy announcement, now expected in mid-January, would not include fiscal measures, as these could only be introduced in a federal budget.

The conflict between Finance and the Secretary of State reminds us again of the unequal structure of representation within the state and the disunity that often typifies state activity. It reflected the different policy designs and priorities of the two departments and different assumptions as to the correct course of action with respect to the film industry. While it may appear to some that Finance had simply succumbed to the actual and potential pressure of American capital and the U.S. state, and that the Secretary of State had become a haven for cultural nationalists, the dispute was not all that simple. While discretionary spending is the norm for departments such as the Secretary of State, the tradition of macro-economic planning within the Department of Finance made its officials bureaucratically hostile to the ten per cent tax. The Department of Finance was simply not accustomed to tax measures that explicitly shifted money from one specific group of private citizens to another.[24] Still, this was not simply an intra-state dispute. The Department of Finance had received representations from industry groups opposed to the proposal. The American majors were obviously the most important oppositional force, but they found a number of allies who properly enough called themselves Canadian.

One Industry, Many Voices

In the mid-seventies, the Canadian film industry continued to be characterized by a plethora of associations and organizations. The distribution sector itself contained three such groups. As of 1977, the longest-standing trade association in the Canadian film industry, the CMPDA, included representatives from the subsidiaries of the seven major American distributors operating in Canada as well as three Canadian firms: Astral, Ambassador, and Bellevue. The Canadian members not only marketed their own acquisitions but also handled Canadian distribution for some films from American distributors. Their own business practices were intimately connected to current distribution arrangements, and although they were minor partners within the CMPDA, these three firms were among the giants of Canada's distributors. More than 20 private Canadian distributors, including Astral, Bellevue, and Ambassador, were grouped into two separate and autonomous associations. In English Canada, approximately ten firms were represented by the Association of Independent and Canadian-Owned Motion Picture Distributors (AICOMPD). In Quebec, the same number of firms were grouped within the Association québécoise des distributeurs de films. It was these three associations and their member companies that would be most directly affected by Roberts' intention to deal with the question of distribution. None of them liked the proposal. While the CMPDA had historically maintained a low profile in preserving and promoting its interests, persistent rumours that the largest foreign market for the American majors might be tampered with, coupled with attacks from organizations such as the CCFM and the introduction of Bill C-58, put it on the offensive.

As befits an industry that has cherished – and very nearly perfected – the art of publicity and hype, the CMPDA announced the inauguration of the Golden Reel Award in the fall of 1976 to be presented to the Canadian film achieving the highest box-office gross during the past year. It was a simple gesture, but one that served to reaffirm the CMPDA's unwavering contention that the feature film industry 'is primarily a commercial enterprise geared to the "leisure time market".'[25] This view was the basis for a brief prepared by the CMPDA in 1976, and it was carried over in various submissions made to the Secretary of State and Department of Finance in the following two years. The CMPDA maintained that because of a 'world-wide shortage of motion pictures that have a high degree of public appeal,' the major distributors 'have a particular interest in supporting an internationally competitive Canadian production industry.'[26] The brief emphasized that it was 'impossible to make money on a Canadian film where distribution is restricted to Canada,' but went on to argue that the feature film 'industry in Canada was now in a position to build an export-oriented activity that could eventually serve to reinforce Canadian identity and culture.'[27] Government support for the feature film industry was acceptable, so long as it took the form of incentives (such as the 100 per cent capital cost allowance) that encouraged private production for the international marketplace. As the executive director of the CMPDA explained: 'We must find ways of encouraging the development of the entrepreneurial spirit in a larger proportion of film-makers and technicians. This would serve to direct their skills and knowledge to worthwhile commercial projects. Such development is an essential main-spring for the future evolution of a viable feature film production industry with a strong position in the Canadian and international marketplace.'[28]

The CMPDA emphasized that it was presenting 'an economic argument in place of nationalistic or anti-American rhetoric.'[29] There was some truth to this. The submissions are all rather blunt in outlining the commercial imperatives and macro-economic dynamics of the industry, but not surprisingly they nowhere discuss the important process by which the major distributors decide which films will receive the most thorough marketing and publicity campaigns, a process that has much to do with the creation of consumer interest and demand. Even so, the pith and substance of the discussion papers were not far removed from the general opinions on the economics of the industry held by many of Canada's filmmakers, producers, distributors, and exhibitors. As we have seen, the scenario of an export-oriented feature film industry was widely supported by Canadians working within the industry.

The CMPDA was wise enough not to rest its entire case on economic rational-ity. Along with the establishment of the Golden Reel Award, it reactivated the Motion Picture Institute of Canada in conjunction with the Motion Picture Theatres Association of Canada. Its stated goal was 'to further quality films and their presentation,' but as *Cinema Canada* reported, it was implicitly established to fight the possibility of quotas or a box-office levy.[30] And once Roberts' tax proposal became known, the CMPDA did not shy away from more direct confrontations. As Millard Roth explains, the CMPDA held detailed meetings with officials within the Secretary of State and Department of Finance, enlisting its own number crunchers to emphasize the dangers of a designated tax.[31] The CMPDA told officials in both the Department of Finance and the Secretary of State that the tax may very well violate the terms of the GATT, that the burden of the tax would eventually fall on movie-goers themselves, and that no real benefits would accrue to Canadian distributors as a result of its implementation. Finally, the CMPDA was not above invoking the bugaboo of U.S. retaliation. 'The U.S. are [sic] likely to regard any significantly discriminatory tax ... as being capable of being regarded in the international community as a precedent. There would appear to us, therefore, to be a real risk of a serious U.S. reaction that would not necessarily be limited to the taxation of film royalties or, indeed, to the field of taxation.'[32]

While the CMPDA was clearly the most incessant critic, Roberts' proposal received very little support from those Canadian interests in the industry who may have been expected to be sympathetic. It appears that Roberts drafted the proposal without formally seeking the advice and support of the factions within the film industry who believed in protectionist measures (the details of the scheme were kept under wraps until the fall).[33] It was a tactical error that gave potential supporters of the measure, such as the CCFM, little time to mobilize public support. In fact, the CCFM itself was showing signs of weakness. Sandra Gathercole, who had tirelessly spearheaded much of the Council's activities, resigned as chairperson in the summer of 1977, and in December, at a meeting that failed to produce a quorum, Jack Gray and Kirwan Cox also announced their resignations from the executive.[34] The CCFM was at low ebb, weakened by a lack of funds and by a membership evermore resigned to just making a living under the terms of the status quo. The production companies and laboratories that comprised the Canadian Film and Television Association (the closest organization to the now defunct AMPPLC) hinted that they would welcome certain protectionist measures, but as usual the CFTA was far more vocal about a reduction in the size of the public production sector than anything else that might appear in Roberts' policy statement.

Given the specifics of Roberts' proposal, the reaction of Canada's private distributors would be crucial. For reasons we have already discussed, they were almost unanimously opposed to the ten per cent solution. In November, the Association of Independent and Canadian-Owned Motion Picture Distributors sent a letter to the minister of Finance, Jean Chrétien, asking him to reject the tax in its current form. Chrétien quickly informed them that the decision to implement such a tax had been delayed indefinitely.[35] Quebec-based distributors undoubtedly shared the same basic concern, but like their colleagues in French-language production the focus of their attention was now shifting to the provincial scene, where the newly elected Parti Québécois was trying to put some substance into the 1975 film law.[36]

The 1978 Policy: More of the Same

Unlike Bill C-58, there was no significant sector within the industry itself that saw immediate benefit in Roberts' proposal; there was certainly no groundswell of support. The support that did exist for protectionist measures was still more focused on some form of quota or box-office levy, but Roberts had devised the tax proposal as a way of getting around the provincial cooperation that such measures required. Roberts had backed himself into a corner. He had committed himself to a policy announcement. Once the tax proposal was shelved, it was only too clear that the new policy would be little more than an exercise in fine-tuning. And so it was.

Roberts bravely tried to make his announcement seem significant. Following the line developed by the Tompkins Report and Faulkner, the NFB was to continue the process of contracting out government-sponsored films, while the CBC was told to increase the amount of programming made in cooperation with private producers (although no specific targets were set).[37] Perhaps because of the critical success of *J.A. Martin, photographe*, the NFB would still be allowed to produce the odd feature film. With respect to the CFDC, Roberts suggested that 'the Corporation should not be asked to determine whether a film is "cultural" or "commercial," but simply ask what contribution the proposed film, program, or production company can make to the development of the industry.'[38] The Corporation's investment portfolio was broadened slightly to include feature films that were to have their first release on television. The announcement did not touch on the inequities apparent in current co-productions, and Roberts side-stepped the critical question concerning the definition of a Canadian film by asking for more advice from the industry. Roberts did not shy away from critizing the current exhibition and distribution structure, but substantively he offered only a continuation of the voluntary quota arrangement together with the prospect that, if current practices were not altered to improve the imbalance between Canadian and foreign films, other measures might be taken in a year's time. Roberts now insisted that because Canadian films needed international distribution, it would not be altogether wise to upset the American firms by trying to 'threaten your way into that market.'[39] 'If we apply drastic measures in Canada,' Roberts later remarked, 'we may risk not having the means necessary to create a stable profitable basis for Canadian films outside the country.'[40] The 12-month review period was intended to keep the American distributors 'in as great a state of uncertainty as possible,' and the CMPDA cooperated by displaying suitable (if only slight) annoyance at the prospect of a year-end review.[41] As Peter Pearson quipped shortly after the announcement was made: Roberts 'went into Cabinet with a lion of a film policy and came out with kitty litter.'[42]

The Tax-Shelter Boom: Big Budgets, Little Success

With hindsight it appears that the most important decision Roberts made in the spring of 1978 was not revealed in his policy announcement. Early in March, press reports suggested that Michael Spencer was about to be replaced as executive director of the CFDC.[43] Roberts initially denied the rumour, but as the month wore on it became clear that Spencer's ten-year term was coming to an end. On 9 March, Michel Vennat was appointed the new chairperson of the Corporation, and at a board meeting on 20 March Spencer was dumped. On 2 May, it was announced that Michael McCabe would take over as executive director. The industry was furious at the way Spencer's dismissal had been handled; over the years, he had earned the (sometimes grudging) respect of almost everyone associated with Canadian feature films.[44] Spencer may have wanted to be relieved of his duties (he was certainly not completely pleased with the direction of Canada's film policy, especially the lack of a box-office levy); regardless, it appears that Roberts was under some internal pressure to have him replaced.

Given the penchant for patronage appointments in Canadian politics, Vennat and McCabe were obvious candidates. Assistant deputy minister of Consumer and Corporate Affairs at the time of his appointment, McCabe was a long-time friend of Roberts. He had also spent time writing the English speeches for Finance Minister Jean Chrétien. Earlier, McCabe had worked as executive assistant to Mitchell Sharp, at the same time as Michael Vennat was Sharp's special assistant.[45] Vennat himself was a corporate lawyer from Montreal with strong connections to the Liberal Party; it was later revealed that many of the film deals concluded during the next few years were handled by the firm with which he was associated.

Vennat and McCabe shared the same basic approach to the job at hand. As McCabe told *Maclean's* shortly after his appointment: 'Roberts suggested to me that the industry had reached the point where it could take off, but we're short in the entrepreneurial area. The government and the economy dictate a results oriented approach, so I propose to be not a filmmaker but a banker and a marketer.'[46] As Vennat told *La Presse*: 'Notre mandat est assez précis: il consiste à développer l'industrie privée. Il y a d'autres institutions dans la domaine fédéral qui favorisent un mandat culturel, notamment l'Office national du film.'[47] Shortly after his appointment, McCabe was asked by *Trade News North* to draw a distinction between American-style films and Canadian cultural priorities. McCabe responded: 'You know these questions can't be answered.'[48] All pretence was gone. The feature film boom was on.

No one better articulated the rationale behind the tax-shelter boom than McCabe and Vennat, and the CFDC, which had come under their control. According to its annual report for 1978-9, the CFDC had embarked upon a 'new strategy' whose basic assumptions were as follows:

Unless the industry was commercially successful, the cultural objective would not be achieved. It would not be acceptable to produce films only for a small elite nor could such a small elite provide the revenues needed to allow our creators to continue to create ... At the base of a feature film industry must be a group of entrepreneurs who raise money, assemble the creative team, get the film made and sell it. Hence the focus on developing and supporting producers.[49]

Without the benefit of protective measures, which McCabe himself was most assuredly against, Canadian producers would have to gear production toward the global film market. The report itself neatly summarized the shift toward an emphasis on commercially successful, export-oriented films.

In most instances, if we are to have the stars and the production values that will bring Canadians to see our films, the budgets will be too high to recoup our costs in our relatively small market.

We must therefore earn revenue in the rest of the world and to do this we must have the themes, stars and production values to meet our competition.[50]

In accordance with the new strategy, the CFDC restructured its investment program. Instead of providing equity loans, the Corporation shifted its focus to the provision of interim or bridge financing. Interim loans functioned as 'seed money,' extended to producers whose projects would later be financed through private investments, utilizing the provisions of the capital cost allowance. Once private money was secured, these pre-production loans would be repaid. Loans advanced in this manner operated as a revolving fund, allowing the CFDC to initiate more projects at far less risk to its capital pool. In the first year of the plan's operation, the CFDC forwarded $3.3 million in the form of interim loans, of which $3 million was repaid by the end of the fiscal year.[51] The main purpose behind the program was to allow the private sector to take an even greater lead in establishing the production priorities for the industry.

Although the basic provisions of the 100 per cent capital cost allowance had been in effect since 1975, repeated confrontations between Revenue Canada and film investors over its interpretation had restricted its use. In general, the disputes centred not around the point system devised to establish the certification of a film as 'Canadian,' but around the portion of a film investment that was 'at risk' and therefore eligible for tax deduction. The federal government attempted to clarify the existing uncertainties in December 1978, and an interpretive bulletin from Revenue Canada 11 months later helped ease confusion even further.[52] By 1979, private investment deals were being structured in two basic forms. Producers could finance a feature film by issuing a private placement offer that involves a limited number of usually large-scale investors (the number varies from province to province).[53] Private placement offers were attractive to producers because they did not require public disclosures, involved fewer legal costs, and typically required less interim financing. Increasingly, feature films were also being financed through public offers in which smaller shares are offered to a much larger number of investors. Such deals required a public prospectus, involved higher legal and brokerage cost, and typically required more interim financing because most of the investment capital is raised near the end of the year. *Agency*, produced by Robert Lantos and Stephen Roth in 1978 at a cost of $4 million and starring Lee Majors and Robert Mitchum, holds the distinction of being the first film to be financed through a public offer. Although both types of deals were initially structured on a film-by-film basis, would-be film investors soon had the opportunity of investing in a package of projects, thus allowing them to reduce the risk they faced from investing in only one film (although it also tended to reduce the possibility of super-profits).

The public-offer film investment very quickly became one of the most popular forms of investment and tax deferral for Canadians in the top income bracket: few were deterred by the often skimpy details provided in many of the prospectuses; many were undoubtedly attracted by the allure of movies that boasted major American stars.[54] A number of investment firms and brokerage houses handled the transactions and advised clients on the suitability of particular projects. One such firm, CFI Investments, was chaired by John Turner, who had been minister of Finance when the expanded tax allowance was first introduced. CFI's prospectus made it clear that it was looking to secure equity in films with safe 'family' plots and with one or more 'immediately recognizable stars.' The prospectus went on to say that it was not going to support 'self-indulgent producers' or 'personal statements.'[55] Return on the dollar was the modus operandi.

Statistics issued by the Canadian Film and Video Certification Office, which oversaw the administration of the point system and established the eligibility of projects for the capital cost allowance, provide clear justification for the argument that the industry was undergoing a production 'boom.' In 1978, there were 37 certified feature films with production budgets totalling $48.6 million. In 1979, the apex of the 'boom,' 66 feature films with budgets totalling $171.8 million were certified. And in 1980, the last year of the 'boom,' there were 53 certified feature films with budgets totalling $147.4 million.[56]

As the CFDC had intended, most of the capital for production was now being generated from within the private sector. In 1979–80, the Corporation invested $10.8 million in 34 films with budgets totalling $107 million.[57] Close to 80 per cent of the CFDC's investment was in the form of development or interim loans, most of which had been repaid by year's end. The CFDC's equity involvement in the biggest year yet for feature film production in Canada was only $2 million, or a little more than one per cent of the total production value. More than a third of the productions proceeded without any involvement whatsoever from the CFDC.

Gross production figures indicate a very high level of activity, but they tell us very little about the nature of the films produced, their commercial success, and their impact upon the structure of the industry itself. Perhaps the most important fact hidden by the general figures is that there was no significant increase in French-language productions as a result of the tax-shelter boom. In 1980, the CCFM estimated that nearly two-thirds of French-language feature films made between 1978 and 1979 were 'produced without the benefits of the CCA.'[58] According to one estimate, of the certified films between 1978 and 1981, 'only three per cent, or less than $10 million went into French-language films. The average budget of these French-language films remained below $500,000, while the average budget for English-language films increased to over $3 million.'[59] CFDC figures indicate a similar discrepancy between French- and English-language productions. Between 1978 and 1980, the CFDC invested $3.7 million in 27 French-language films with combined budgets of $25.3 million. Of the CFDC's investments only $800,000 was in the form of interim loans. In contrast, between 1978 and 1981, the CFDC invested $17.8 million in 62 English-language films with budgets totalling $217 million. Of these investments, $15.1 million were in the form of interim financing.[60]

It was patently obvious to even the most casual observers of the industry that the dominant trend was toward the production of big-budget, English-language productions geared for international distribution. The logic was seemingly indisputable: Canada had to produce films for export, the major external market was the United States, and Americans speak English (and display near paranoia at the prospect of subtitles). McCabe and Vennat certainly embodied this line of reasoning. In early 1979, they found themselves with Secretary of State Roberts in Hollywood trying to convince the American majors that the new Canadian films were worthy of distribution by the "Big Six." As McCabe told *Variety*: 'Our image is still one of parochial and provincial films. We feel we're changing that.'[61] McCabe later told the Standing Committee on Broadcasting, Films and Assistance to the Arts: 'I think the chief impediment over a great many years to Canadian films being distributed more widely in Canada was that we were not making films good enough to warrant distribution in many of the houses where they expect as businessmen to make a profit.'[62]

The Association des réalisateurs de films du Québec (ARFQ) had its own opinion on the Hollywood meetings and the production boom underway. In February it called for the resignation of Vennat and McCabe, denouncing 'the use of public funds to orient Québécois and Canadian production towards a unique American model.'[63] French-Canadian directors were furious that the CFDC 'maintenant favoriser la production de films dits "internationaux" avec vedettes "internationals" et ce, pour que les majors américains consentent à les distribuer en territoire canadien.'[64] The Council of Canadian Filmmakers shared the same concern. It had held a meeting with McCabe in December to protest 'the direction the industry is taking towards an American branch-plant operation.'[65] Two years later, the CCFM made the following observation: 'What had been encouraged in the past year are not even good films in any nationality. We seem not to have learned that Americans can make American films better than we can.'[66] In the aftermath of the tax-shelter boom many more industry representatives would come to share this attitude of scepticism and derision, but for the moment such a view had few supporters. The Quebec producers association dismissed the ARFQ's remarks as partisan and uninformed. Denis Héroux, president of APFQ and one of the country's most prominent producers explained that his association was happy with the new money and financing.[67]

Denis Héroux' activities during this period highlight the shift in production priorities. Arguably one of the most successful participants in the tax-shelter boom, Héroux channelled his efforts toward international co-productions. The undisputed Canadian master of the Canada–France co-production treaty, Héroux produced *Atlantic City* in 1980 and *Quest for Fire* in 1981. Both films used French directors, Louis Malle and Jean-Jacques Annaud respectively. *Atlantic City* was shot in English, while *Quest for Fire* used a prehistoric language all its own. Both films were distributed by American majors, the former by Paramount and the latter by 20th Century–Fox. Héroux himself is quite proud of his solid co-production record. As he tried to explain it: 'For my last three films I spent between $27 and $30 million. That money, 80%, came from elsewhere. I brought it back to Canada and spent 60% on Canadians ... I work with Québécois, with Québécois first, the technicians are Québécois, then for the actors I take English-Canadians ... I'm somebody who can build a bridge between Europe and America. What I do, what's marvellous about being Québécois, is that we're American but we so completely understand Europe.'[68]

The CFDC did not totally disregard the problem of French-language production, which by the summer of 1979 had reached such crisis proportions that the only films being made were co-productions with France. To encourage private investment, the CFDC announced that until further notice it would allow private investors to recoup all of their money in French-Canadian productions before it began to collect its own share.[69] It was not, however, a sign that the CFDC believed it had committed a fundamental error. For instance, the CFDC could have insisted that French-language productions with which it was involved would require at least a French-Canadian director or screenwriter. No such guidelines were issued. Asked somewhat later about the CFDC's support for French-Canadian films and French-Canadian filmmakers in general, McCabe produced one of his many candid, if not altogether sensitive, remarks: 'Unfortunately, a great many of them are narrow and self-indulgent, but we will continue to be with the better French filmmakers.'[70]

McCabe was probably not thinking of Claude Jutra when he referred to those narrow and self-indulgent French-Canadian filmmakers, but all the same Jutra had been unable to sustain himself as a director in Quebec. After years of frustration in his native province, Jutra moved to Toronto to direct television dramas for the CBC, including the award-winning *Ada* (1976) and *Dreamspeaker* (1976). During the tax-shelter boom, Jutra directed *Surfacing* (1978), produced by Beryl Fox. The story behind the production of *Surfacing* was typical of many of the films made during the tax-shelter boom. 20th Century–Fox hired an American screenwriter to adapt Margaret Atwood's novel, and cast American actors in the leading roles. Jutra intimated that he did not like the screenplay, later commenting: 'I fear what I'm getting into. I should. The ground starts moving under my feet. I do not recognize the film I thought I made. I am ostracized for it.'[71] As Jay Scott remarked: 'When *Surfacing* finally emerged, an intransigently Canadian, intransigently anti-American novel had become an astonishing thing: a film almost for Americans – a film in which anything that might offend Americans was carefully excised.'[72] Jutra did not produce another French-language feature until 1984, when he completed *La Dame en couleurs*. Soon afterwards, he became a tragic victim of Alzheimer's disease. Jutra disappeared in November 1986; his body was found the following spring on the shore of the St Lawrence River.

The transformation of *Surfacing* into a pseudo-American film was, however, atypical of the trend in English-language productions made during the tax-shelter boom. *Surfacing* at least began with a Canadian theme, while most of the 'major' films of this period eschewed Canadian themes from the start. The Canadian cinema was overcome by a wave of mid-Atlantic mediocrity. Most Canadians who remember the tax-shelter boom will recall first hand the publicity and hype that characterized those years; most would also be hard-pressed to recall even a few of the films produced. Very few are worth remembering, even though they boasted big budgets and 'foreign' stars. Numerous examples abound: *Bear Island* (1980), a $9 million adventure film starring Vanessa Redgrave; *Nothing Personal* (1980), a $5 million comedy starring Suzanne Sommers and Donald Sutherland; *Circle of Two* (1980) with Richard Burton and Tatum O'Neal; *The Last Chase* (1981), with Lee Majors and Burgess Meredith; *Murder By Decree* (1979), with Christopher Plummer as Sherlock Holmes, James Mason, Donald Sutherland, and Geneviève Bujold; and *Running* (1979), a $3.6 million drama about jogging with Michael Douglas and Susan Anspach.[73] All of these films qualified as 'Canadian' under the provisions of the point system or the co-production treaties. Many of the projects made liberal use of the term 'executive producer,' ensuring that an American was never far behind the Canadian producer necessary for qualification under the terms of the capital cost allowance. Fewer than half of the scripts were written by Canadians, and rumour has it that in a number of cases American screenwriters were busy scribbling behind the scenes. Film critic Martin Knelman offered one of the most acerbic comments on the whole episode: 'What could have better filled the Canadian need for self-denigration than the flowering of a shlock movie industry? The insults Canada has endured from Hollywood begin to look like petty mischief compared with the abusive treatment Canada had been getting from its own moviemakers.'[74]

Given that the films were intended for the international (or more precisely the American) market, the commentary of a few American observers is worth noting. Many were thrilled at the direction the Canadian industry had finally taken. Writing in *American Film*, Keith Burr hailed the new atmosphere that had 'lawyers, accountants, investors and filmmakers buzzing on both sides of the border.' 'For film lovers ... [the tax-shelter legislation] meant a new flow of production from a hitherto dormant production centre.' The Canadian government now had 'a chance to hold its head high in international film circles.' According to Burr, the old NFB-style films were 'literary, verbal, unredeemably artsy and elitist in ... tone and assumptions, and, in the long run, exceedingly dull. On the other hand, the new Canadian films are, or at least try to be, visual, fast-paced, and strictly commercial in their aim and appeal.'[75] Other Americans however were more circumspect about the new 'Canadian' cinema.

Producer Hillard Elkin remarked: 'If you can't get it on in the States, you look for somewhere else to do your film. Canada's close and comfortable. Right now Canada is a dumping ground for inferior products.' Arthur Knight argued that the Canadian industry was on a 'suicide course.' 'Unfortunately,' he said, 'all the current efforts are bent on making these films look as "Hollywood" as possible. The search is on for locations that will suggest middle America, or California, without the palms and eucalyptus.'[76]

A new style of Canadian cinema seemed to demand a new style of awards presentation. In 1979, the Canadian Association of Motion Picture Producers (CAMPP) threatened to boycott the Canadian Film Awards unless they were given a bigger say in its proceedings. What CAMPP really wanted was an awards show that reflected the shift toward the production of internationally styled feature films, something that bore a closer resemblance to the glitz of the Academy Awards. Not surprisingly, the CFDC supported the producers' position, and with a grant from the Corporation the Academy of Canadian Cinema was created. The first Genie Awards were held in 1980. The big winners that year were some of the more commercially successful tax-shelter films.[77] *The Changeling*, a horror film starring George C. Scott and Trish Van Devere and produced by Garth Drabinsky, took eight of the ten awards for which it was nominated, including best picture. *Murder by Decree* won five awards, while *Meatballs* took two awards, including best original screenplay.

Produced by Dal, *Meatballs* turned out to be the most commercially success-ful picture during the tax-shelter boom. The film cost a relatively modest $1.6 million, and starred Bill Murray. Paramount Pictures bought the U.S. distribu-tion rights for the film for $3.3 million (and paid $300,000 more for the Cana-dian rights). In 1979 alone the film grossed $40 million, placing 16th on *Variety*'s list of 1979 money-makers. As Rick Salutin noted, *Meatballs* was in some respects the most 'Canadian' picture of the bunch; it, at least, took place at a summer camp where the kids woke up to the singing of 'O Canada.'[78] For director Ivan Reitman, *Meatballs* was his last Canadian hurrah. Already a bankable Hollywood producer on the strength of *Animal House* (1978), Reitman settled in Hollywood, where he has applied the Midas touch as direc-tor to such films as *Ghostbusters* (1984) and *Kindergarten Cop* (1990).

Meatballs' distribution in both Canada and the United States by Paramount was typical of the deals being sought by Canadian producers. With the undis-guised blessing of the CFDC, Canadian producers were looking for distribution through the American majors. With few exceptions, independent Canadian distributors found themselves picking up the scraps; the production boom was doing very little to establish a stable, independent Canadian distribution sector. The issue came to a head early in 1979, when it was announced that Universal offered roughly $2.5 million and a percentage of box-office revenues for the world distribution rights for Ronald Cohen and Robert Cooper's production of *Running*.[79] Cohen was reportedly 'delighted' by the deal. Independent Canadian distributors were furious; they simply could not outbid the U.S. majors on films that had good box-office potential.

Less than a year earlier, in a rare display of solidarity, the major Canadian producers and distributors associations had met with Roberts to complain that the American majors had taken complete control of the Canadian box-office. Now, however, it appeared that the distributors were on their own, as Canadian producers were bending over backwards to secure American distribution. Roberts' promise to entertain further negotiations with the majors had come to nought. As André Link, one of *Meatballs'* producers explained: 'Either the Americans could voluntarily decide to leave the Canadian distributors a little space, or the government could legislate. Off hand, I don't see signs that either of these things are going to happen.'[80]

Once the row over *Running* surfaced, Roberts was quick to say that Canadian distribution was (again?) the top policy priority and that the Secretary of State was considering a proposal to restrict foreign distributors to films they had produced themselves.[81] This was also the position being advanced by most Canadian distributors themselves, and as we shall see, it was an option being pursued with increasing vigour by Quebec.[82] But in a speech just three months later (the follow-up to his policy announcement of a year earlier), Roberts made no mention of the exhibition or distribution problem; indeed he provided an uncritical list of the Canadian films being considered for distribution by the American majors, delighting in the prospect that '1979 will really be the first year that Canadians will produce a significant number of films of international commercial standard.'[83] That 'vintage year' was but a vague memory. For his part, Michael McCabe staunchly defended Universal's distribution of *Running*: 'That's good from the industry's point of view; and the more Majors we can convince to distribute Canadian films, the more money our producers will make and the better capacity they will have to make more films ... Frankly, we're not very interested in a fortress culture because all you end up doing when you build walls is, in fact, protect mediocrity.'[84] The production community thus continued to develop close ties with the American majors.

While McCabe's enthusiasm continued unabated, many industry observers began to question the wisdom of the policies that had initiated the boom. No one put it better than a study for the University of Toronto's Institute for Policy Analysis:

If one is to judge on the basis of what politicians and officials have said are the objectives, the principal reasons for public concern with the state of the film industry are *cultural*, in the sense, for example, that films can (or should) provide a means by which Canadians can explain themselves to themselves and to the rest of the world. On the other hand, if one determines the intended objectives in terms of what the policies actually *do*, the tax incentive approach seems primarily to expand the total amount invested in 'Canadian' films, defined in terms of the nationality of the individuals involved in production ... In fact, it seems likely that the very existence of the film incentive has in some ways had a perverse effect on Canadian film culture ... Increased production budgets require large foreign sales (which essentially means U.S. sales) in order to have the slightest chance to recoup their costs ... It may therefore be argued that one result of the expanded investment fostered by the tax shelter has been a reduction in 'truly Canadian' films.[85]

According to a study for the Ontario Economic Council, analysis of the tax incentives revealed 'that a relatively small number of high-income taxpayers are being allowed to allocate public revenues as they see fit.'[86] Both studies also raised serious questions about the economics of the tax-shelter boom. They pointed out that higher budgets did not necessarily translate directly into higher on-screen production values. Much of the money was being eaten up by such 'soft costs' as interest on interim financing, brokerage commissions, lawyer and accountant fees, non-productive fees, executive producer fees, and the exorbitant salaries paid to foreign 'stars.' The CCFM's 1980 study noted that the film boom was not only encouraging higher budgets, but also the production of too many films. The total output for 1979 exceeded 50 per cent of Hollywood's output during the same period in a country one-tenth the size of the United States.[87] It was the heyday of Canada's Hollywood.

The Boom Goes Bust

Too many expensive films, too many mediocre films, and too few outlets for successful distribution and exhibition was a recipe for financial disaster. It came. According to the Ontario Economic Council report, as of 1981 close to 40 per cent of the films produced in 1979 had not received distribution; by 1981, less than 10 per cent had any measurable commercial success.[88] Private investors soon discovered that the short-term benefits of the capital cost allowance did not offset the losses incurred from box-office duds. They had begun to realize that 'you don't spend a dollar to save 60 cents!'[89] By the end of 1980, nearly $40 million worth of public units had been left unsold. The 'boom' was over. The industry was about to undergo what insiders tactfully called a 'shakedown.'

Even before the boom went officially bust, the CFDC came to reconsider its investment priorities. In light of criticism from many quarters that the increase in production was having a negligible if not negative effect on the production of films with Canadian themes in identifiable Canadian settings, the CFDC announced a new set of guidelines at the end of March 1980 (that is, before it made its investment decisions for the new fiscal year). From this point on, the CFDC: would only invest in projects where all producer functions were carried out by Canadians (except co-productions); would prefer that both the director and the screenwriter were Canadian (and would not invest in films where both functions were performed by foreigners); would only invest in films that had at least one Canadian lead actor; would not participate in films that unnecessarily disguised their Canadian locations; would normally only participate in co-productions that had majority Canadian participation.[90] As its annual report for 1979–80 explained, the CFDC was now prepared to 'do its part to strengthen the Canadian character of the production in which it is involved.'[91] It was a decision the Corporation believed it could afford to take. The private production community as a whole no longer lived and died on the basis of loans from the Corporation; in fact, as the annual report noted, 'a number of producers, particularly in the English sector, now operate successfully without requiring or desiring help from the CFDC.'[92]

The new guidelines seemed to signal the demise of McCabe and Vennat's vision of the CFDC's role. Rumour had it that McCabe was not getting along with the staff or the board of the Corporation. He announced his resignation in early May. Buoyant to the end, McCabe told *Variety*: 'I was the right guy from the start, the flash and razzle dazzle of the marketing drive.'[93] His replacement was André Lamy. Lamy had been the government film commissioner and chairperson of the NFB in the mid-seventies, had served as a vice-president of the CBC, and had been a founding member of Onyx Films in the mid-sixties. Once again the CFDC would at least be run by someone with concrete experience in the film industry.

By refusing to act upon the problems of exhibition and distribution, the Canadian government chose the path of least resistance. A tax on the distributors' gross would have generated a reasonable sum from which to support Canadian productions, while a law that restricted the activities of foreign distributors to films that they themselves had produced would have helped establish a stable base of Canadian distributors more likely to invest in domestic productions. Neither proposal was perfect but they had the advantage of addressing the problem at the core of the industry's economic structure. Certainly the possibility of American retaliation weighed heavily on the government's decision, as did the increasing fiscal and political conservatism of the Department of Finance. But it should also be recognized that the Canadian industry as a whole would not be behind such interventionist measures. American-inspired tax-shelter films meant steady employment for an increasing number of film workers, and many English-Canadian producers in particular positively drooled at the prospect of a U.S. hit. Weaned on a diet of Hollywood films and television from day one, most Canadians viewed domestic productions with a mixture of prejudice and suspicion.

The tax-shelter boom did nothing to resolve the tensions inherent in the Canadian government's film policy; rather it served to place them into bold relief. To most observers, the experiment was at best comical, at worst a failure. But it did serve a purpose. For one thing, the production boom helped develop a large pool of better trained technicians and crews. It had also helped establish the careers of a few Canadian producers (such as Dénis Heroux, Roch Demers, Robert Lantos, Robert Cooper, and Ron Cohen) who, in one way or another, were committed to the industry and the business of production. Finally, it had led many people to believe that the government had to deal with the question of distribution, even if this meant annoying the neighbours to the south. As the eighties began, the government of Canada would have a few more kicks at the can.

10 The Third Phase of a Federal Film Policy: Toward Telefilm Canada

Introduction

The last year of the tax-shelter boom coincided with that brief interlude during which the Trudeau Liberals were deposed by the Progressive Conservatives under Joe Clark. From the spring of 1979 to early 1980, David MacDonald assumed the positions of secretary of state and minister of communications in Clark's government. For over a decade MacDonald had distinguished himself as one of the most informed cultural critics in the parliamentary opposition; his comments in both the House of Commons and committee hearings displayed a keen sensitivity to the ambiguities of the Canadian state's feature film policy. In his only appearance before the Standing Committee as a minister, Mac-Donald was highly critical of the policy drift that had occurred over the last few years, serving notice that he would 'try to encourage a greater development of the Canadianization, if you like, of the film industry.'[1] MacDonald planned to tighten the definition of 'Canadian' for qualification under the capital cost allowance by insisting that the production company, the copyright, the director, the domestic distributor, and all but two actors be Canadian. Furthermore, he planned to extend the 100 per cent tax write-off to exhibitors for receipts from the screening of Canadian films, and to raise the duty on remittances from foreign film rentals from 15 to 25 per cent.[2]

Precisely what type of support these measures had within Cabinet or the Tory party in general is unclear. MacDonald was a 'red Tory,' a member of the government's 'left wing.' His policy proposals would have meant an even stronger and more visible federal presence in the operation of Canada's cultural industries; as such, he had staked out a position plainly at odds with Clark's vision of a more decentralized federalism and with the Tory party's general distrust of dirigiste state planning. In any case the legislation was never introduced, as the short-lived minority government fell in early 1980. The Canadian state had undergone a brief interregnum; by spring, the Liberal party had reassumed control of the federal government.

The Liberals' 1980 election victory was noteworthy for the strong nationalist intonations that emanated from the party's leaders. Once in office, the introduction of the National Energy Program confirmed the party's decision to resurrect its left-of-centre image and suggested that it might be more willing to challenge other American interests and their allies in Canada. Once again, the Trudeau Liberals were employing the rhetoric of planning as a way of rationalizing state functions and developing a coherent, centralized strategy to pull Canada out of the world-wide recession.

The post-election atmosphere had a direct impact on the government's approach to the development and administration of cultural policy. Driven by the same administrative concerns that led the Tories to bring the Department of Communications and the Secretary of State under one minister, the Liberals transferred the responsibilities for arts and culture from the Secretary of State to the Department of Communications in an effort to revamp the process of cultural policy making. On the surface, it appeared that David MacDonald's emphasis on 'Canadianization' would be carried forward by the new Liberal government. Less clear were the precise policy initiatives that would emerge for the film industry. Was the public sector to be expanded? Would tax expenditures continue to be the principal form of intervention? Would the government finally decide to address the question of distribution and introduce measures that would help establish a fully integrated Canadian film industry in the face of certain opposition from the Hollywood majors?

While old issues continued to dog Canada's policy makers, the development of new technologies and new distribution systems in the film and television marketplace were raising new concerns. Innovations such as videocassettes and pay television, for example, would rapidly change many of the business practices within the film industry. Videocassette rentals became a major source of revenue in the early 1980s and outstripped cinema revenues by 1984.[3] Pay television also became a significant source for investment and revenue. Certainly, the new technologies made some old policy options, such as theatrical exhibition quotas, seem obsolete. They also suggested that the fortunes of Canada's film industry increasingly would be affected by the structure and operation of Canadian television and that a feature film policy could no longer be designed or implemented in isolation.

The Department of Communications would play a pivotal role in addressing the challenges and opportunities facing Canadian culture in the 1980s, and Trudeau's appointment of Pierre Juneau as its deputy minister only served to highlight the Department's rising prominence. Established in 1969, when it assumed responsibility for the telecommunications sections of the departments of Transportation and Defence, the Department of Communications was devised as one of the Trudeau government's new 'think-tanks.' Officials spent much of their time during the early seventies trying to establish a comprehensive strategy for the coming information and computer revolution (including publication of the internationally acclaimed *Instant World* in 1971). A Department publication explained the 1980 addition of the arts and culture branch of the Secretary of State in the following manner: 'This realignment of responsibilities recognized the close link between culture and communications. It was intended to ensure that communications policy would be conducted with the highest concern for cultural content and the cultural implications of communications technologies, and that the cultural milieu would benefit from the advances in communications.'[4] In plainer terms, it was clear that the emphasis would be placed squarely on the development of Canada's cultural industries, as much for economic as cultural concerns. In the context of a world-wide recession, the ever-expanding global market for cultural products and information technology had been targeted as important growth areas for the Canadian economy. Almost immediately the Department initiated a series of internal policy reviews, and in August 1980 the government announced the establishment of the Federal Cultural Policy Review Committee – the first full-scale government-sponsored review of cultural policy since the Massey Report of 1951.

But as in the sixties, the Liberal rhetoric of planning, promising a comprehensive and coordinated approach to the wide range of public policy issues that encompassed the cultural sector, would again not be translated into political reality. The Canadian state seemed destined to continue its incremental, piecemeal, ad hoc, and often contradictory approach to public administration. This was nowhere more apparent than in the administration of the Canadian state's cultural policy and, more specifically, its film policy. Even before the government announced its National Film and Video Policy in 1984, policy decisions with a major impact on the feature film industry were made with respect to the capital cost allowance, the introduction of pay TV, the operation of the CBC and NFB, the funding priorities of the CFDC, and the exhibition and distribution system. In policy terms at least, 1980 to 1984 was a very busy period. The sheer number of initiatives taken in the early 1980s might have given the impression that a process of comprehensive change was underway, but the process could hardly be said to have been coordinated in a manner consistent with the basic premises of rational planning. In terms of a direct challenge to American interests and their allies operating in Canada, the National Energy Program turned out to be the exception that proved the rule.

The Industry Restructures: A Fork in the Road

As the federal government prepared its new policy forays, the feature film industry itself was undergoing a significant restructuring process. The collapse of investor confidence and the box-office failure of many of the tax-shelter films threw the industry into a period of flux in the early 1980s. In terms of production, two separate – almost diametrically opposed – trends soon emerged. The first trend involved the usual concentration and 'rationalization' that follows a period of over-production in any industry. Among those who had used the tax-shelter boom as a way of moving Canada's film industry closer to the form and substance of a Hollywood North, the neophytes – those fly-by-night producers with little or no long-term experience in the film industry – bid a hasty retreat, while the more successful producers bravely depicted the production downturn as a necessary, and useful, consequence of market adjustment. As the *Financial Post* noted in 1981: 'The winners of last year ... like to call it a shakedown, putting themselves clearly on the side of the good guys. And they herald the beginning of a new era for the film industry, with major producers forming bigger companies with solid in-house financial resources and strong connections with distribution channels in the U.S., the most important market.'[5]

In April 1981, nine of the ten largest feature film production companies gave this trend an organizational dimension. Increasingly upset by the loose membership criteria and organizational framework of CAMPP, the country's major producers established the Association of Canadian Movie Production Companies (ACMPC). As André Link said at the time: 'We wanted to regroup those companies which have permanent staff, who are open for business everyday and carry an overhead, who are seriously engaged in the business of producing feature films. We're less interested in the producer who comes up with a project once every three years.'[6] Dues were set at a hefty $10,000 per company – individual producers were not welcome to join. The ACMPC grouped producers eager to exploit the entente cordiale that had been established between themselves and the American distributors during the tax-shelter boom. As Ronald Cohen put it, the major goal of the ACMPC was 'the strengthening of relationships on the development, production and distribution levels with American "Major" and "mini-Major" distributors.'[7]

And so they did. While the industry as a whole was mired in the post-boom blues, the 'Gang of Nine' (as some called them) were hard at work fashioning products with the American market in mind. Garth Drabinsky's Tiberius Productions made *The Amateur* (1981) as part of a deal with 20th Century–Fox; Stephen Roth and Robert Lantos' RSL Productions had gone to Israel to make

Paradise (1982) with advance support from its distributor Avco-Embassy; Denis Héroux and John Kemeny's International Cinema Corporation was still working on *Quest for Fire* (1981) with the help of 20th Century–Fox; and Harold Greenberg's Astral Films was in Florida shooting *Porky's* (1981) with a budget of $6 million. Each of these films achieved a decent measure of commercial success, attributable in part to the support provided by the American majors (and mini-major in the case of Avco-Embassy). *Porky's* would in fact become a box-office smash; distributed by 20th Century–Fox, the film grossed $11 million in Canada and $152 million world-wide in 1982, more than doubling the box-office take of *Meatballs*.[8]

But a second, very different, trend in film production emerged (or re-emerged) in this same period. Smaller-budget films, taking Canada and Canadians as their thematic source made a comeback. Although it is true that some films of this sort had been produced throughout the tax-shelter years, there was a noteworthy increase in both their number and quality in the early 1980s. It was as if filmmakers in Canada had rediscovered the formulas that had led to the critical success of films such as *Mon oncle Antoine* and *Why Shoot the Teacher?* The trend could be said to have started with Francis Mankiewicz' *Les bons débarras*, winner of the Genie Award for best picture in 1981. Produced for little more than $600,000, *Les bons débarras* captured life in the Quebec Laurentians, where a single mother battled poverty, loneliness, and the sagacity of her 13-year-old daughter. *The Hounds of Notre Dame*, based on the exploits of Père Athol Murray and the young schoolboys whom he disciplined with equal doses of religion, hockey, and anti-communism in northern Saskatchewan in the 1940s, was also representative of the trend. The return to indigenous themes, to films that worked against the homogeneity of Hollywood was confirmed in the next few years by the production of *Les Plouffe* (1981), *The Wars* (1983), *Une journée en taxi* (1982), and *The Grey Fox* (1982). These films were designed to find an international audience based upon their use of national particularities, their rootedness in a specific time and space. With lower budgets, such 'speciality films' with 'limited audience appeal' (as the CMPDA would say) could turn a profit through distribution in the international circuit of art-house cinemas. Sales to European television were also becoming a more viable exhibition outlet, particularly as the number of stations expanded in the context of a general deregulation and privatization of European broadcasting. Finally, it is important to note that these films were not totally ignored by the American majors. *The Grey Fox*, for example, was distributed by United Artists Classics. Canadian producers of almost any ilk were drawn to the higher profits that might ensue from distribution through the American majors.[9]

Tampering with the Golden Goose

What role did the state attempt to play in relation to these trends? Reflecting concern over the abuses that had typified the tax-shelter boom, the Department of Communications' first major film policy initiative in the 1980s focused on the provisions of the capital cost allowance. In the summer of 1980, the Canadian Film and Video Certification Office circulated an 84-page discussion paper among industry representatives with the intention of tightening the definition of a 'Canadian' film. The minister of Communications, Francis Fox, announced the first modifications in December 1980. The 'points' system, involving the basic requirement that a film meet six out of ten points to classify as 'Canadian' remained in place. But as of 1 January 1981, all producer functions would have to be carried out by Canadians, and no points would be awarded in cases where a Canadian shared a creative position (e.g., screenwriter) with a non-Canadian.[10] In July 1981, Fox announced further revisions in a speech delivered at the annual convention of the Association des producteurs de films du Québec (APFQ). Effective 1 January 1982, two of the possible four points for the director and the screenwriter would be obligatory, as would one of the two possible points for principal performers. If one of the screenwriters was not Canadian then the author of the work on which the screenplay was based would have to be a Canadian citizen, and the work would have to have been published in Canada. The basic requirement of six out of ten points remained.

The modifications were in keeping with the change in investment priorities established by the CFDC a year earlier. Fox told Quebec producers that the changes were 'necessary to strike a balance between commercial viability and Canadian cultural content,' but it is clear that the government wanted to stop the private industry from using the capital cost allowance to fund ersatz Hollywood productions.[11] In an interview shortly before Fox's announcement, Ian McLaren, director of the cultural industries branch at the Department of Communications offered these incisive comments about the industry and the effect of the impending changes to the CCA:

The Capital Cost Allowance will no longer be able to be used for the kinds of international, commercial, American-type films that it has been used for in the past. I predict that the Harold Greenbergs, the Garth Drabinskys, will no longer use the CCA. I predict that they will align themselves much more closely with Hollywood. I predict that there'll be several producers who straddle both fences, like the Coopers and the Cohens; they will both not use it and use it for lower budget Canadian films ... There is already a tacit agreement on the part of producers that if they're using the CCA it has to be on films that are contributing to the Canadian film industry in some significant way. It also means that they are saying, 'we have to look at some way not to use the CCA to make the kinds of films we want to make.'[12]

McLaren's remarks turned out to be highly insightful, although, as we have seen, the trend he describes was already in progress. Tightening the provisions of the CCA accelerated the split in the industry. With support from American distributors, some producers were now able to finance productions without partaking of the tax shelter, and others were learning to 'straddle both fences,' as McLaren had put it.

But while the Department of Communications moved to tighten the qualifications for tax-sheltered films, the Department of Finance was rethinking the entire strategy of tax expenditures. No one, not least officials in the Department of Communications, anticipated the jolt delivered by Allan MacEachen's budget of 12 November 1981. In a budget that sought to close a number of corporate tax loopholes and reduce the ever-growing level of federal tax expenditures, Mac-Eachen announced that the capital cost allowance for Canadian films would be reduced to 50 per cent in both the first and second years. Furthermore, loans taken out to finance tax shelters would no longer be tax deductible. The measures were to take effect in less than two months, on 1 January 1982.[13] Once again the Department of Finance seemed to be working at cross purposes to the federal department responsible for the administration of Canadian cultural policy.

But the budget meant far more than that: it represented one of the few occasions when the Department of Finance seemed prepared to institute tax reforms that were consistent with the principle that 'a buck is buck.' From this perspective, the 1981 federal budget was a progressive, almost radical, document. Certainly, this was how it was viewed by the majority of Canada's business interests, who vehemently denounced the budget's overall intention. In the face of mounting pressure from Canadian capital, the Liberal government eventually 'revised' a number of the clauses that sought to reduce corporate and high-income tax advantages. For the feature film industry, which had learned to take advantage of Canada's regressive tax structure, the most pressing question was: what would happen to the arrangements for 1982 capital cost allowance productions?

Six days after the budget speech, representatives from every major film organization in the country met with NFB, CFDC, and Department of Communications officials.[14] The meeting resulted in an unanimous recommendation: that the 100 per cent capital cost allowance be extended for at least one year. It was the first time that the film industry had been able to reach a unanimous position on a question of public policy. Officials from the Department of Communications seemed as concerned and upset as the private-sector representatives.

Together they decided to broach the subject with the Department of Finance. The ACMPC supplied documents showing that over $140 million worth of production and $56 million worth of interim financing had been put on hold because of the budget. The point was made. Finance officials were convinced that the 100 per cent allowance was absolutely vital if capital cost allowance productions for 1982 were to go ahead as scheduled. MacEachen gave way. On 17 December, amidst a flurry of budget revisions, he announced that the 100 per cent tax shelter for films would be extended for one year.

Quiet Desperation

MacEachen's decision may have quelled the panic (for the time being), but it did nothing to re-establish confidence in the industry. The 'boom years' were well and truly over. Feature film production in Canada was in a serious slump. As the CFDC's annual report for 1982–3 noted, 'in the crucial economic area, the industry had been unable to develop a solid financial base.'[15] Clearly, the capital cost allowance had lost its allure. In 1982, only 17 theatrical or television features had been certified with budgets totalling $35 million, as opposed to 35 certified theatrical features with budgets totalling $85 million in 1981. Sales of public issues were limited to ten productions for the 1982 season (with nine for English-language films), and of these only 52 per cent of all available shares were sold to investors (only three films sold 100 per cent of their issues).[16] It was not all that surprising that the major films honoured at the 1983 Genie Awards – *The Grey Fox, Quest for Fire*, and *Une journée en taxi* – had all been produced in 1981. 1983 did not look much better. *Cinema Canada* reported that 'current feature film and films-for-television production in Canada is dominated by American developed and financed projects and with co-productions. Most indigenously Canadian projects are made-for-TV projects.'[17] Uncertainty over the future of the capital cost allowance provisions forced producers to look for alternate forms of finance or to drop production plans entirely. In 1983, only two feature films – *Blood Relations* and *Undercurrents* – were certified under the provisions of the capital cost allowance.[18]

In these circumstances, it was noteworthy that if there was a bright spot in the production of Canadian feature films, it was at the NFB. In 1982, the NFB had been involved in the production of Robin Phillips' *The Wars* and Don Owen's *Unfinished Business*. It had also entered into co-productions with a number of private French-Canadian producers. Claude Jutra's *La Dame en couleurs*, Francis Mankiewicz' *Les beaux souvenirs*, and Claude Fournier's *The Tin Flute* (1983), appeared to signal a new era of cooperation between public-

and private-sector forces.[19] One could hardly miss the irony of the situation. Time and again attempts had been made to move the NFB to the margin of theatrical and television productions, and time and again the Board had managed to reassert itself as a centre of creative productions. Each success, however, seems to have been followed by further challenges, and the decade of 'neoconservatism' would be no exception.

Public- and private-sector co-production was one new avenue being explored; the other was television. Feature film producers were now more eager than ever to obtain major funding from broadcasters, who had become an important source of film capital. Always narrow, the space between the two industries was growing narrower still. To symbolize the merger of these two spheres, people were beginning to speak of a 'program production industry.' There is no better example of this trend than the financial and production arrangements made for *Les Plouffe* (1981).[20] Produced by Denis Héroux and John Kemeny's International Cinema Corporation, *Les Plouffe* received one-fifth of its $5 million production budget from the CBC. It was in fact three projects in one: for television *Les Plouffe* was a six-hour mini-series; as a feature film there were two versions – one in French and one in English. Héroux and Kemeny had always been producers with a flair for innovation. *Les Plouffe*, like *Duddy Kravitz*, demonstrated their ability to produce Canadian films of quality and cultural sensibility. In the fall of 1982 Robert Cooper announced that the American pay-TV network Home Box Office would join the CTV Television Network as the principal financial backers of *The Terry Fox Story*.[21] The $2.5 million film would also qualify as a Canadian production under the revised provisions. When the film was released theatrically, it was distributed by Astral in Canada and by 20th Century–Fox internationally.

Opportunity Knocks? Pay TV in Canada

The increasing importance of television as a source of investment capital and exhibition outlet made the issue of pay television a particularly crucial one for the industry. The long-awaited hearings to determine the structure of Canadian pay TV took place at the CRTC between September and November 1981, and everyone involved in both film and television production hoped that the CRTC's decision would be a major boost to their respective industries. The CRTC had held its first hearings on pay TV in June 1977. At that time, it was presented with two options: a universal, publicly controlled, predominantly Canadian-content channel funded by a mandatory surcharge on all cable subscribers of between two to three dollars monthly; or a discretionary, privately controlled channel with predominantly American content. The CRTC decided it could not choose between the two. While the Commission felt that the first option 'established significant standards for future policy commitment,' it argued that the mandatory tax on all cable subscribers could not be approved without legislative support from government. The second option was more summarily rejected because of its fundamental opposition to the 'unequivocal' language of the Broadcasting Act with respect to Canadian-content standards.[22] In recommending further study of the various options, the CRTC also proposed its own solution to the problem: a private, discretionary system subject to stringent Canadian-content regulations and a levy on revenue to be channelled back into Canadian production.

At the 1981 hearings, 28 applicants came before the CRTC. Of the eight applications for a national service, seven proposed a privately controlled discretionary service, while the other, TeleCanada, proposed a universal service to be operated by a non-profit, private corporation.[23] Film industry representatives were divided on the question of which type of proposal should be endorsed. The CFDC, NFB, the Canadian Council of Filmmakers, and the Association of Canadian Television and Radio Artists (ACTRA) supported the principle of universality, while the major producer groups threw their support behind a discretionary service. Undoubtedly, almost everyone would have agreed with the CFDC's claim that 'pay-TV represents the last chance Canada may have to capture its own place in its own market by providing maximum access for both creators and consumers to Canadian film and video.'[24]

The CRTC reached its decision in March 1982. It did little to fulfil the optimism that had surrounded the hearings the previous fall. The Commission announced that it would license a competitive, discretionary system with two national networks, First Choice and Lively Arts Market Builders (which came to be known as C-Channel) and four regional networks. Canadian-content provisions were pegged at 30 per cent for the first year and were to rise to 50 per cent by year five. Canadian programming expenditures were set at between 15 to 50 per cent of overall revenues.[25] There was almost unanimous agreement among industry representatives and media observers that the decision to license a competitive system was a grave mistake: given the size of the Canadian market, a competitive system would make it almost impossible for the licensees to abide by their programming commitments – to attract subscribers and reduce overhead costs, the licensees would almost certainly rely on imported American films and television programs. Belatedly, the CRTC itself seemed to recognize the inherent weakness of its decision. In July, the Commission issued a major 'corrective' to its initial decision: the Canadian-content provisions would be applied not on a year-to-year basis but over the five-year span as a whole. For the new licensees, the correction was a blessing; for the program production industry, it was a curse. As Peter Lyman remarks in his review of the decision: 'It appears that pay-TV in Canada will continue the tradition of broadcasting as a conduit for American entertainment programming.'[26] Little that has happened since contradicts that view.

The Producers Council and an Industry Policy

Even before the CRTC's decision was made public, Canadian producers had decided to try to establish a more effective common front to deal with policy issues affecting the industry. Sustaining the organizational momentum brought about by negotiations over MacEachen's 1981 budget, the pell-mell of producer associations established the Producers' Council of Canada. By the spring, the Council had taken up the task of devising a comprehensive strategy for the development of the film industry, and they invited Canadian distributors to be part of the planning sessions.[27] This alone was a significant step: Canadian producers had finally acknowledged that the sorry state of Canadian distribution had to be addressed if the industry was to fully recover from its downturn. With the decline in tax-shelter-driven investment from outside the industry, producers were beginning to realize that a strong Canadian distribution sector would be an intelligent source of ideas and an important source of capital in the development of a more integrated and economically sound production sector.

The Producers' Council wasted little time in drawing up a list of policy proposals that covered both distribution and production. First, it wanted a three-tiered capital cost allowance system: projects that mustered ten of ten points would be permitted a 150 per cent tax write-off; the 100 per cent write-off would remain for films with six of ten points; while films with fewer points would be eligible for a 50 per cent write-off over two years. Second, the Council proposed the establishment of a new production fund to be generated by a levy on imported foreign films and/or a tax on cable companies. The money would be administered by the CFDC with one-third going to script development and films of 'national interest,' a second third going to 'demonstrably commercial projects,' and the final third to 'be divided between producers and distributors, awarding the success of their performance.'[28] To help Canadian distributors, the Council also recommended that in the case where government funds are used for production, distribution rights would have to be sold to a Canadian firm and that Canadian distributors should also be able to utilize the capital cost allowance for their operations.

If implemented, the proposals would continue the trend toward the privatization of production activities. To this end, the Council recommended that the

'CFDC's role ... be limited to administering the production fund according to criteria established by the private sector, having a free hand only in the disbursements made for script development and films of national interest.'[29] Furthermore, the Council had recommended that CBC productions be limited to information programming and that the NFB be transformed into a postgraduate film school. State-sponsored production agencies were still anathema to the country's private producers; public subsidy through tax expenditures, however, was not. The Producers' Council pegged the cultural future of Canada's feature film industry to the proposed capital cost allowance incentives. Although the point system had been tightened, it was doubtful whether Department of Communications officials were prepared to risk another round of tax-shelter-driven production. It was even less likely that the Department of Finance would go along with such a plan.

The Council's recommendations were made with the knowledge that Francis Fox was trying to put together new policies with regard to both television and feature film production. Aside from the recommendations of the Producers' Council, the Department of Communications had initiated its own review process, including a Federal Task Force on Distribution and Exhibition (chaired by producer Ron Cohen). In the months to follow, Fox would also receive the final draft of the Federal Cultural Policy Review Committee. In the meantime, like those who preceded him, Fox was also busy testing the resolve of the American distributors. In late May he ventured to Hollywood – with Ron Cohen, Harold Greenberg, David Silcox, and Ian McLaren – in a spirit of 'cooperation and consultation,' as his senior policy adviser put it.[30] The conversations included a discussion of ways in which the American majors could better integrate themselves with Canadian distributors (Astral's arrangement with Columbia and Fox was cited as a model for the future). Rumour had it that the policy announcements would come in early fall, but events initiated by another federal ministry and by one of Canada's most prominent feature film entrepreneurs would make the delay seem inconsequential.

Cineplex Odeon: Renegotiating Dependency?

Garth Drabinsky's Cineplex Corporation started operations in April 1979, when it opened an 18-screen theatre in Toronto's new Eaton Centre.[31] Eight years later, Cineplex Odeon Corporation had become the largest theatre circuit in North America: as of 1987, it controlled approximately 1,500 theatres in 475 locations. With the guidance of Nat Taylor (the same Nat Taylor who bought his first theatre in 1920), Drabinsky was to become Canada's N.L. Nathanson of the eighties. For a while, he did the old exhibition mogul one better. Not only was Cineplex Odeon the most powerful exhibitor in Canada, it was almost certainly the most powerful exhibitor in the United States as well. After its 1986 takeover of RKO's Century Warner Theatres, Cineplex controlled 40 per cent of the total screens in Manhattan. More than two-thirds of its theatre holdings were in the United States. Drabinsky's astonishing success reflected a new and important development in Canadian capitalism. A few Canadian capitalists – most notably in the financial and real estate sector – were working to shed their junior partnership with their counterparts in the metropole. They saw the American market as a sphere of opportunity where they could compete on an equal footing with their American brethren. Like the Reichmanns and Campeau, Drabinsky had little sense that Canadians were junior partners in the American empire.

Early on, however, it was by no means certain that Cineplex would survive. Although the Eaton Centre location did reasonably well exhibiting foreign films and move-over (or second-run mass appeal) pictures, the old arrangements between Famous Players and Odeon and the major American distributors made it almost impossible for Cineplex to access major first-run pictures. Dauntless, Cineplex continued to expand. By July 1982, it was operating 163 screens across Canada and the United States. But the expansion was costly, and by the end of 1982, the company reported losses of $15 million on sales of only $20 million. Drabinsky had gambled that if Cineplex expanded it would receive a decent share of the major distributors' first-run films. It didn't, and the company was on the verge of bankruptcy. Famous Players and Odeon had a stranglehold on the Canadian market. But the crucial point was – and this spoke volumes to the manifold contradictions of Canadian dependency – that this was emphatically not the situation in the United States, where the antitrust decrees had established a system of open bidding between the major distributors and theatre chains. When Cineplex opened the Beverly Center in Los Angeles in the summer of 1982, Drabinsky was able to bid for and receive the major distributors' first-run product. He wanted the same situation to apply in Canada. In the Canadian film industry, and from the standpoint of a Canadian interest, the era of free trade was oddly foreshadowed.

Drabinsky held a meeting with government officials from Consumer and Corporate Affairs in the summer of 1982 to draw their attention to the problem. He wanted the government to begin a combines investigation against the seven major motion picture distributors in Canada, and he supplied Lawson Hunter, the Director of Investigation and Research for the Combines Investigation Act, with all the information needed to make a case.[32] On 22 December 1982, Hunter applied to the Restrictive Trade Practices Commission with an order for the distributors to supply Cineplex with 'commercially valuable motion pictures.'[33] After the distributors attempted to have the order withdrawn on a legal technicality, they decided to enter into negotiations with Hunter rather than risk a public trial. On 7 June, the distributors agreed 'to make significant changes in their distribution practices' by allowing theatres to compete for their product on a picture-by-picture basis. Hunter told the press that the 'undertakings will mean the introduction of a completely new system of film distribution in Canada, benefitting the filmgoer, the exhibitors, and Canada's film producers and distributors.'[34]

Hunter's remarks probably reflected his belief that market competition was the best of all possible worlds, but there were good reasons to question his optimism. The decision would really have no direct effect on Canada's producers or distributors (in fact it could possibly hurt the distributors by making first-run Hollywood products more available to independent exhibitors), and it was quite possible that new bidding wars could result in increased ticket prices. As the only large-scale 'independent' exhibitor, Cineplex was clearly the major benefactor of the decision. As the interim and final reports of the Investigation and Research Branch showed, the new system of open bidding still favoured the more powerful market actors. From January 1984 to June 1984, independent exhibitors as a group increased their market share of first-run product from 11.9 per cent to 13.3 per cent, but the increase had really occurred in the market share controlled by Cineplex, which had gone from 5.3 per cent to 7.2 per cent. Smaller independent exhibitors complained that the major exhibitors were still receiving preferential treatment, and there was considerable evidence that this was indeed the case.[35] Hunter, however, was satisfied with the outcome. Given the terms of the initial application it was clear that Cineplex was now able to purchase 'commercially valuable motion pictures.'

But the point was almost academic. Cineplex had taken over Odeon theatres in May 1984, and by the summer it had withdrawn its application to continue the investigation. It no longer needed government protection. In fact, once the purchase of Odeon was completed, Cineplex actively sought to re-establish the old 'entente cordiale' between the major Canadian exhibitors (itself and Famous Players) and the Hollywood majors. The benefits that accrued to independent Canadian exhibitors and distributors (except Cineplex' own Pan-Canadian distributors) were next to nil.

More and more, Cineplex Odeon sought to expand its activities in the United States. In its drive to acquire another large American theatre circuit, Cineplex joined forces with MCA, the U.S. entertainment conglomerate that owns, among other things, Universal Studios. MCA paid close to $220 million for 50 per cent of the companies' shares. For Cineplex Odeon, the deal meant much-needed cash and yet more status; for MCA it meant guaranteed access to U.S theatres at a time when almost all the major studios had decided to ignore the old antitrust decrees of the 1940s and had started buying U.S. theatre chains with the tacit blessing of their friend in the White House, Ronald Reagan.[36]

At the time of the MCA deal, Drabinsky remarked: 'We're betting on this industry. It's a good opportunity to ride with them.'[37] And that was the point. Cineplex Odeon did little to support the production of new Canadian films; Drabinsky had parlayed his hand as a producer of films in the late 1970s (*The Silent Partner, The Changeling, Tribute*) and had found the experience wanting. In the late eighties, Cineplex Odeon made forays into the performing arts (restoring the Pantages Theatre in Toronto and mounting a $46.5 million production of *The Phantom of the Opera*) and signed a deal with Robert Redford to produce a number of low-budget independent films. Ultimately, Drabinsky's continuous drive for expansion left Cineplex Odeon debt-ridden. In a complex series of events, Drabinsky was driven from the company in December 1989 and the corporation, for all intents and purposes, fell under the control of MCA. The ride had ended with a jolt.

Applebaum-Hébert: The New Tone of Canadian Cultural Policy

The Report of the Federal Cultural Policy Review Committee, better known as the Applebaum-Hébert Report was released in November 1982, two years after its work had begun. Like the Massey Report, with which it was inevitably compared, Applebaum-Hébert was something of a landmark, though in terms of the evolution of a Canadian cultural policy a number of observers argued that it represented a step backward.[38] This was certainly true insofar as it is assumed that Canadian cultural policy moves forward by developing more elaborate state mechanisms to assist in the production and consumption of Canadian culture and to offset or curtail the inflow of foreign products. Applebaum-Hébert did not endorse these assumptions. Although the Report dutifully recorded the extent of foreign cultural penetration, it would not, as it put it, 'come down on the side of protectionism.'[39] As Albert Breton, one of the Committee members, explained in his minority comments, to 'discriminate is to give priority to nationalistic objectives to the detriment of arts and culture.'[40] If the free flow of cultural goods was one of the Committee's guiding principles, the other was its strong endorsement of the private sector as the proper vehicle for the growth of Canadian culture. With respect to the cultural industries, the Report took the view that culture had become first and foremost a business and that it had to be treated as such. It argued: 'There is clearly a very large sector of activity of which the primary function is to satisfy varying demands for entertainment and recreation, transmitting little from the past, leaving little residue in the form of future heritage and showing little conscious concern with the interpretation of society itself. From government it demands courses of action that involve at least as much industrial (or, more broadly, economic) policy, as cultural policy.'[41]

These assumptions guided the Committee through its chapter on the Canadian film industry. In this regard, Applebaum-Hébert is probably best remembered for its suggestion that the NFB get out of production entirely, to be 'transformed into a centre for advanced research and training in the art and science of film and video production.'[42] Relatedly, the Committee recommended that 'with the exception of its news operations, the CBC should relinquish all television production activities and facilities in favour of acquiring its television program material from independent producers.'[43] The Committee put its faith in Canada's private production community and in this sense it *did* endorse an old principle of Canadian public policy: not state control, as is often alleged, but public subsidy for private profit. The Report wanted to see the current capital cost allowance system maintained and it made a vague suggestion that the government should 'provide the Canadian-controlled film distribution industry with the economic strength to market Canadian films successfully.'[44] The option of quotas or levies was dismissed in eight lines; while the Committee argued that these were matters of provincial jurisdiction, it was obvious that such discriminatory measures would go against the basic principles it had established.

Private producers may have been pleasantly surprised that a government-appointed committee had so firmly endorsed their criticisms of public-sector production, but many others in both the film community and the general public were incensed at Applebaum-Hébert's recommendations concerning the NFB (and the CBC). Generally, the Report was criticized for the vagueness of its recommendations. As the chairperson of the CFDC, David Silcox, remarked: 'It's not as sophisticated as I would like it to be ... The film chapter just doesn't come to grips with what film is in our society ... (and) it doesn't provide a context for the country ... [it offers] no convincing arguments as to either changing priority or reallocating funds within the general area.'[45] Certainly, it would be hard to argue with Sandra Gathercole's conclusion that Applebaum-Hébert had endorsed 'an export-based strategy of industrialization which would increase and redirect public production funds from the publicly-mandated production agencies – CBC and NFB – to the private sector.'[46]

The Canadian Broadcast Program Development Fund: The TV Solution

It is not clear just how influential the Applebaum-Hébert Report was in the formation of the government's impending policy announcements on television and film production. The Department of Communications had been conducting its own policy reviews and had carried out its own informal talks with various industry groups. Regardless, there was a great deal of symmetry between the two. The first of a series of policy announcements occurred on 1 March 1983 in a document entitled *Towards a New National Broadcasting Policy*. It would have a dramatic impact upon the role of the CFDC and the film and television production industry.

In keeping with the emphasis of Applebaum-Hébert, Francis Fox explained that the new policy would 'make greater use of the private sector.'[47] While the document noted that 'new services from beyond our borders ... could undermine the present Canadian broadcasting and weaken our cultural integrity as a nation,' it did not recommend or condone new protectionist measures. The most important mechanism for the preservation of Canada's 'cultural integrity' would continue to be the shop-worn Canadian-content provisions as administered by the CRTC. Instead, the federal government would seek to increase the attractiveness and availability of Canadian programming, so that Canadians would have an opportunity to choose from programming 'which reflects Canadian cultural values,' 'and reinforces the cultural heritage of all Canadians.'[48]

The linchpin in the new federal strategy was a new fund to subsidize the cost of television production, specifically in the categories of drama, children's programming, and variety. The Canadian Broadcast Program Development Fund, as it was called, would dispense $35 million in 1983 and increase yearly until it reached $60 million in 1988. The Broadcast Fund was to be administered by the CFDC (soon to be renamed Telefilm Canada). Compared with the CBC's 1983 expenditures of over $900 million, or the NFB's appropriation of over $70 million, the new infusion of cash into the CFDC might be considered relatively insignificant, but from the perspective of the CFDC, the first-year budget alone represented an eightfold increase over its previous appropriation of $4.5 million. Moreover, because the CFDC was expected to assume no more than one-third of the cost of any given project, federal officials estimated that the Corporation would be partner to over $100 million worth of production activity in the first year, and over $180 million worth of activity in the fifth. Each project (including feature films) would have to be accompanied by an agreement from a public or private broadcaster to air the completed production during the hours of 7 and 11 p.m., within two years of its completion.[49] In no uncertain terms, the Broadcast Fund made Telefilm a major player in the production industry. Obviously, it also meant that there was an enormous incentive for Canadian feature film producers to shift their activities to the production of television features and other forms of television programming in the drama, children's, and variety categories.

TABLE 3
Broadcast Development Fund: Financial Participation in Production

		1985/6	1986/7	1987/8	1988/9
Number of projects	French	77	51	47	49
	English	72	62	61	64
	Total	149	113	108	113
Total budgets	French	73.5	N/A	68.4	59.7
	English	129.9	N/A	129.8	112.9
	Total	203.4	172.0	198.2	172.6
Total hours		498 hrs	437 hrs	637 hrs	570 hrs
Telefilm participation	French	25.0	18.1	28.3	22.7
	English	46.0	34.4	47.8	37.4
	Total	71.0	52.5	76.1	60.1
	(% of total budget)	(35%)	(30%)	(38%)	(35%)
Other gov't agencies	French	9.8	3.7	4.1	2.7
	English	3.2	3.6	3.0	3.4
	Total	13.0	7.3	7.1	6.1
	(% of total budget)	(6%)	(4%)	(4%)	(4%)
Broadcasters	French	8.3	7.4	16.5	13.3
	English	24.2	19.6	21.7	25.0
	Total	32.5	27.0	38.2	38.0
	(% of total budget)	(16%)	(16%)	(19%)	(22%)
Foreign	French	18.7	17.8	4.4	1.0
	English	31.0	18.6	22.4	27.4
	Total	49.7	36.4	26.8	28.4
	(% of total budget)	(24%)	(21%)	(14%)	(16%)
Producers	French	7.0	3.6	4.2	4.0
	English	10.3	7.7	6.0	5.5
	Total	17.3	11.3	10.2	9.5
	(% of total budget)	(8%)	(6%)	(5%)	(6%)
Private Cdn. investment	French	4.0	12.2	10.2	15.8
	English	13.5	22.0	26.1	9.0
	Total	17.5	34.2	36.3	24.8
	(% of total budget)	(8%)	(20%)	(19%)	(14%)
Cdn. distributors	French	0.3	0.2	0.5	0.0
	English	0.9	2.3	2.6	5.2
	Total	1.2	2.5	3.1	5.2
	(% of total budget)	(0%)	(1%)	(1.5%)	(3%)

Source: Telefilm Canada, *Annual Report*, 1985–90
Note: 'French' or 'English' refers to the first language used in production.

They did. At a ratio of one dollar to every two dollars of private investment, Telefilm had no trouble disbursing the first year's $35 million.[50] In 1987–8, it invested over $75 million in 108 projects (47 French, 61 English), consisting of over 600 hours of programming with cumulative budget of close to $200 million (see Table 3). English-language projects included: 'Danger Bay' (episodes 57 to 79), 'Mount Royal' (16 episodes), 'Cowboys Don't Cry,' 'Glory Enough for All,' 'Adderly' (episodes 12 to 22), 'Codco Comedy' (7 episodes), 'Degrassi Junior High' (episodes 14 to 26), 'Care Bears' (episodes 20 to 49), 'The Racoons,' (episodes 22 to 34), and 'The World Is Watching.' French-language projects included: 'Lance et compte' (episodes 27 to 39), 'Samedi de rire' (19 episodes), and 'La Maison Deschênes' (249 episodes). A year before the fund was due to expire, the federal government made the program permanent with an annual appropriation of $60 million.

In a very real sense the Canadian government had solved the problem of distribution and exhibition by gearing production activities to the regulated market of Canadian television. But the Broadcast Fund was not without its shortcomings.[51] While the proportion of available Canadian drama increased, private broadcasters did not join the new venture with enthusiasm. Over the first two years, CTV (the dominant national private network) accounted for barely one per cent of the broadcasters' commitment. Its decision to produce 'Mount Royal' (its answer to 'Dallas' and the CBC's 'Empire, Inc.') was announced only after it had been publicly roasted by the CRTC at its licence renewal hearings. Since then, the participation of private broadcasters has increased, but problems remain. Broadcasters in Canada continue to pay remarkably low licence fees to Canadian producers to telecast their programs. In most countries, the licence fee comes close to the cost of production; in Canada the fee is rarely greater than 20 per cent of the cost. Consequently, producers must plan to recoup the majority of their investment from foreign sales. Inevitably, Canadian producers sought closer links with foreign producers and distribution outlets to reduce the risks of production. 'Night Heat,' co-produced by Robert Lantos' Alliance and Grosso-Jacobson Productions in the U.S. with broadcasting licences from the Columbia Broadcasting System (CBS) and Canada's CTV, was an early example of this trend. Relatedly, Atlantis Films of Toronto has developed a strong corporate base by developing international television projects such as 'The Ray Bradbury Theatre.' By 1987 close to 80 per cent of Atlantis' revenues came from outside Canada, roughly 55 per cent from the United States and 25 per cent from Europe. 'Bradbury' is an example of just how complicated these deals may be. Bradbury (an American) wrote most of the scripts. The project came to Atlantis in 1984 from Home

Box Office (HBO) in the United States. It became an Atlantis-controlled project, and eventually produced in partnership with Granada TV in England and Canal Plus in France. In other deals, Atlantis had no equity stake whatsoever, but produced material on a service contract. Atlantis has also produced a number of half-hour dramas from Canadian short stories (one of them, *Boys and Girls*, won an Oscar in 1984). But as Michael MacMillan, one of the directors of Atlantis explains, there is constant pressure to produce 'American clone programming.' Or, as the CBC has noted: 'international saleability may be at variance with distinctiveness.'[52] At the very least, the Broadcast Fund had done little to resolve the ever-present tension between the industrial and cultural dimensions of Canadian cultural policy; instead it had given it a new dimension.

The Broadcast Fund also had the effect of shifting production priorities away from theatrical feature films. On those occasions when a package was produced under the Broadcast Fund for both theatrical and television release, as in the case of *Le Crime d'Ovide Plouffe* (1984), and *Joshua Then and Now* (1985), the resulting hybrid – usually a two-hour feature film and a television mini-series – was often less than satisfactory. As Denys Arcand, the director of the *Le Crime d'Ovide Plouffe*'s feature film segment, remarked: 'The movie scene in Canada is very trendy. Five years ago, the thing was to get in with the Americans at any cost. Now the trend is TV. So if you don't have a story that will fit neatly into six hours, forget it. The appetite for television desperately needs images, and they'll pay for any kind of series, even low-grade quality material. It is another one of our cultural disasters.'[53] Robert Lantos, producer of *Joshua Then and Now*, offered these comments: 'Hybrids are dangerous because if the primary purpose is to make a film for TV, it means the product has to be paced and constructed in a way that is diametrically opposed to what a feature film is. To try to make something work in two different mediums is a mistake.'[54]

The report of the Film Industry Task Force, which published its findings in November 1985, wholeheartedly concurred. The Broadcast Fund had worked wonders, but it had 'not provided significant impetus for the financing of Canadian feature films.'[55] And feature films were special:

Without doubt, fictional feature films are the most influential and prestigious of all forms of mass communication. The feature is to the twentieth century what the oral tradition, mythology and romantic literature represented to eras gone by. It is a form of storytelling perfectly suited to our time ...

Cinema remains an extraordinary means of self-affirmation, an unsurpassed expressed of national and cultural identity.[56]

Laden with unexamined and dated assumptions about the influence of the mass media, and the relative influence of different media, the report made its case for a new set of policies to support feature film production. It argued for a three-pronged 'industrial development strategy': (1) that the distribution of films and videos in Canada be by companies owned and controlled by Canadians; (2) that tax incentives be maintained and a new feature film fund established to support the capitalization of companies and the financing of films; and (3) that the government take measures to prevent all vertical integration of distribution and exhibition to the extent that such integration limits competition and freedom of trade in Canada.[57]

The federal government itself had said that the Broadcast Fund was 'only one aspect of a larger set of integrated policies now being developed.'[58] For the 'cultural integrity of the nation,' Canada had to have a feature film industry as well. The Task Force had offered a radical solution: if you want to ensure a stable supply of financial resources, establish conditions that will allow Canadian companies to control the distribution of all films and videos in Canada. All indications suggested that the government of Canada was about to address this final and fundamental issue.

The CFDC changed its name to Telefilm Canada in February 1984. Putting 'tele' before 'film' may have been in part an aesthetic decision – Filmtele does not exactly roll off the tongue – but nonetheless the new name confirmed the shift in emphasis toward television production. It was a strategy born of both administrative and political expediency. The Canadian-content provisions for television broadcasting – that 60 per cent of all programming and 50 per cent of the programming scheduled between 6 p.m. and midnight must be Canadian – establish a market and a demand for Canadian programming. Until the advent of the Broadcast Fund, broadcasters in Canada had to rely on their own financial resources to meet the quota, and of all types dramatic programming was the most expensive to produce. The Broadcast Fund thus helped defray the costs of producing the type of programming most valued by policy makers and individuals concerned with the status of Canadian culture. At the same time, the Broadcast Fund did little to irritate the American majors or the U.S. television industry.

But while the Broadcast Fund did increase the production of Canadian drama and fictional programming, it moved producers away from the theatrical venture or feature-length programming and, in its own way, encouraged a modified branch-plant television industry in Canada. Among others, 'Night Heat,' 'Adderly,' and '21 Jump Street,' were television's version of Porky's, Meat-

balls, and *The Neptune Factor* – cultural products made in Canada, often with the assistance of international partners, and oriented primarily for sale in the United States. One way or another, to paraphrase Garth Drabinsky, Canadians were along for the ride.

11 No More Borders

Culturally and economically, the potential of the Canadian film and video sector remains unfulfilled. Very few Canadian productions reach the vast majority of Canadians, let alone audiences in other countries. This uncomfortable reality bodes ill as we enter a new technological environment in which a flood of foreign productions into Canada is rapidly swelling into a tidal wave. We face, in short, a cultural crisis of undetermined proportions. We face an economic challenge of unmeasured magnitude.

– Francis Fox[1]

Introduction

Ministers of communication have never been short on rhetoric. Francis Fox offered his own contribution to that tradition as he introduced the federal government's National Film and Video Policy in May 1984. More than 50 years after the federal government first announced its intention to make broadcasting 'a great agency for communication of matters of national concern and for the diffusion of national thought and ideals,'[2] and more than 15 years after the CFDC had set about the task of building a viable feature film industry in Canada, there was still 'a crisis.' Perhaps it would always be so, and perhaps the crisis was in part a function of government policy. Nonetheless, the government was still intent upon shoring up the cultural ramparts, or at least appearing to do so.

Now, however, all efforts to protect and promote Canadian culture would take place in a new macro-economic context. One year after the announcement of the National Film and Video Policy the Royal Commission on the Economic Union and Development Prospects for Canada (otherwise known as the Macdonald Commission) published its recipe for Canada's economic future: a comprehensive, bilateral free-trade agreement with the United States.[3] The Commission had been established by the Liberal government in 1982, but its principal recommendation would be implemented by the new Progressive Conservative government of Brian Mulroney. The Canada–United States Free Trade Agreement was signed in October 1987.

The timing could not have been worse for the Department of Communications. It was preparing (again) to introduce legislation to deal with the American dominance of film and video distribution. Any policy of substance would run counter to the philosophy of the free trade deal, and would fly in the face of U.S. attempts to reduce its status as the Western world's largest debtor state. After aerospace technologies (weapons of war), the U.S. entertainment industry is the second most lucrative source of foreign revenues for the United States. In 1986, the United States had a cultural trade surplus with Canada of about $1.5 billion.[4] As a debtor nation, the United States could not afford to have one of its few international surpluses tampered with. How likely was it that the Canadian government would risk damaging its intimate trading relationship with the United States over the question of culture?

Distribution in Canada

According to reports in *Cinema Canada*, policy planners saw 'integration of a strong production sector with an equally strong distribution sector' as a primary objective of a new film policy.[5] As the Film Industry Task Force had argued, 'distribution occupies a strategic position in the industry. It supplies markets and finances production.'[6] As of 1981, 97 per cent of the profits from Canadian theatrical distribution went to foreign – mostly American – companies; by the middle of the decade, the American majors controlled over 90 per cent of the Canadian videocassette market.[7] With few exceptions, the American majors have been very reluctant to handle Canadian films; over 95 per cent of Canadian films are distributed by Canadian firms.[8] The consequences of this market profile are this: Canadian distributors exist on the margins of the industry; because they rarely get to distribute a 'blockbuster' film they cannot become active and full participants in the production of Canadian films. The Canadian film and video industry is severed at the head: most of the revenue that is generated flows to foreign sources. Hollywood depends on the flow of capital generated by its distributors. In Canada this capital flow is virtually absent.

In fact, the situation for Canadian independent distributors had become even worse in the early eighties. The American majors cut into two markets in which there had always been some space for independent exhibitors: the exploitation, or B-grade, features market, and the arts, or classics, market (a number of American majors had established new corporate wings, such as United Artists Classics, to capture a greater share of the latter).[9] In 1982, Columbia Pictures finalized a deal to distribute all of Gaumont's (the French giant in distribution, production, and exhibition) product in Canada. The deal, and others like it, was a serious blow to members of the Association Québécoise des distributeurs de films. As the Film Industry Task Force noted: 'the number of non-American films distributed by the Majors increased by 264 per cent in 1981 and 257 per cent in 1982 compared to figures from 1980. The market share held by Canadian and Quebec distributors decreased accordingly, as did their participation in production.'[10] Though the majors abandoned their classics divisions in the mid-1980s, primarily because of poor revenues and high overheads in the United States, other developments did not bode well for Canadian distributors. In 1986, Paramount signed a deal to buy the Canadian distribution rights for films from the DeLaurentis Entertainment Group and Atlantic Releasing, which until then had been distributed in Canada by independent Canadian firms.

Of course, the American majors were not the only source of trouble for Canadian distributors. The federal government had never insisted that films produced with its support, whether through the CFDC or the capital cost allowance, be distributed in Canada by Canadian firms. From 1968 to 1974, the CFDC had maintained its own regulation requiring that all projects be accompanied by a letter that guaranteed distribution. Even so, the CFDC did not insist on distribution through Canadian-owned firms. The policy worked well enough in Quebec because for the most part foreign distributors had little interest in obtaining and promoting Québécois films. Fuelled by the CFDC's money, Quebec's mini-production boom of the early 1980s was in part the result of an effective network encompassing producers and distributors. But the policy was far less successful in developing a strong English-Canadian distribution sector. With the introduction of the 100 per cent capital cost allowance and the shift in emphasis toward the production of English-language films for export, the CFDC dropped its requirement for distribution guarantees. The rush to package films for American distribution soon followed, and Canadian producers showed almost no inclination to put aside their short-term business considerations in an effort to help build a healthy Canadian distribution sector. Moreover, the production boom seriously undermined the operation of the Quebec film industry, still heavily dependent on CFDC funds, in part because it ruptured the close working relationship between producers and distributors necessary for stable commercial film production. Those Quebec distributors who survived did so on their ability to handle foreign films, but by the early 1980s even this niche was under attack.

Overall, the only Canadian-owned distributors who managed to hold their own through the late seventies and early eighties were firms vertically integrated with a production, and perhaps, exhibition wing. Cinépix, for example, was affiliated with Dal Productions and owned fourteen screens in Quebec through Cinema International Canada (although as we have already noted it did not handle *Meatballs*); New World Mutuel was affiliated with Pierre David's Productions Mutuelles; Astral Films was part of Greenberg's ever-expanding Astral–Bellevue-Pathé network; and Pan-Canadian was the distribution wing of Garth Drabinsky's growing empire, which included Cineplex Corporation and Tiberius Productions. Ironically, the corporate structures that included Cinépix and Pan-Canadian would have been illegal in the United States on the basis of the antitrust decisions of the 1940s. But in Canada even these firms were small players in the theatrical distribution network.

A Way Out

As we have seen, the Film Industry Task Force had recommended that all distribution of film and video in Canada be undertaken by Canadian-owned firms, who would pay 'fair remuneration' to producers 'in accordance with standard business practice.'[11] It was a very drastic recommendation. The American distribution firms had always considered Canada to be part of their domestic market. The Task Force's recommendation would shut the door completely.

Earlier, another Department of Communications' task force, chaired by producer Ronald Cohen, and devoted exclusively to the question of distribution, had made the following recommendations. Foreign distribution companies should 'only have the right to import and distribute motion pictures for which they possess world-wide distribution rights.'[12] It recommended further than only Canadian-owned distribution companies should be eligible for federal government funding as administered by the CFDC and that these companies could not import more than 60 per cent of their film line-up from any one foreign company. If implemented, the measures might help free up a significant number of foreign films for distribution by Canadian firms. The major distributors would no longer be able to operate as if Canada were part of the U.S. domestic market – they would no longer be able to go to Cannes and buy the 'North-American' rights to a film. Of course, much would depend on how the phrase 'world rights' was interpreted.

While not as radical as the Film Industry Task Force's recommendation, these measures would still alter the structure of film (and video) distribution in Canada and would entail direct confrontation with the long-established, American interests operating in the Canadian film industry. Experience had shown that such measures would not be taken lightly; it was safe to say that the American majors would fight them tooth and nail. Their introduction would be a test: a test of the resolve of the Canadian state to fundamentally challenge the structure of dependency, and a test of the resolve of the American empire to maintain the current balance of power. American-owned distributors could count on support from the imperial state, as they had on so many occasions before in dealings with so many other countries.

Bill 109: A Challenge from Quebec

By good luck or good management, the federal government did not have to take the lead in introducing legislation concerning distribution. That distinction was reserved for the province of Quebec, and federal officials seemed more than happy to watch the event as it unfolded in Quebec City. Efforts to change the distribution structure in Quebec dated back to the late seventies, but it was not until December 1982 that the Parti Québécois tabled its long-awaited Cinema Law – Bill 109 – in the National Assembly. With respect to distribution, Bill 109 was a bombshell. In its original form Bill 109 stated that all distribution firms operating in Quebec would have to be at least 80 per cent Canadian-owned, that all distributors operating in Quebec would have to share (with exhibitors) in a formula to contribute a certain portion of revenues to a provincial production fund, and that English-only releases could run for only 60 days before a dubbed French version would have to be made available.[13] Canadian independent distributors applauded the initiative, though there was some concern on the part of Quebec independents that the legislation as written did not give preference to Quebec-based distributors over others from outside the province. The American majors were furious. The MPAA's president, Jack Valenti, quipped that 'only Mozambique imposes stiffer controls on foreign films'; while the CMPDA's Millard Roth remarked that, if passed, the legislation 'would result in awakening the hostility of persons and organizations involved in the cinema industry, and will isolate Quebec, creating no new employment.'[14]

After the first round of hearings on the Bill, and after threats of possible counter-measures by the U.S. consulate, the Minister of Cultural Affairs, Clément Richard, introduced a number of significant revisions: first, in response to the concerns of Quebec independents, only an enterprise having its principal establishment in Quebec would be granted a general distributor's licence; second, non-Quebec firms that were operating in Quebec at the time the Bill was originally introduced (primarily the majors) would be allowed to distribute those films that they had produced or for which they had acquired world rights; third, all distributors in Quebec would be required to reinvest at least 10 per cent of gross revenues in Quebec-based productions.[15] Thus amended, Bill 109 was passed on 22 June 1983. The majors promised to be very uncooperative.

The federal government was no doubt hopeful that Quebec would settle its dispute with the American majors as quickly as possible and thereby establish a precedent it could follow. It was out of luck. All signs pointed to a lengthy period of preparation and review before Bill 109 would be implemented. Three new agencies – the Société générale du cinéma et de la vidéo, the Régie du cinéma et de la vidéo, and the Institut Québécois du cinéma – had to be set up. The Régie, which would have the responsibility of drafting the regulations concerning distribution, was not established until December 1983 and its members, which included André Guérin (its director) and Pierre Lamy, did not begin meeting until February 1984 (apparently because the building containing their offices was under renovation). The Régie was expected to hold another round of public hearings to determine the precise meaning of such terms as 'world rights' and 'producer.' At the same time, the Minister of Cultural Affairs had established a committee chaired by Guy Fournier and Millard Roth to draft a memorandum of understanding. The committee reached an agreement in September 1984. The Régie published its own regulations in May 1985. Public hearings were not held until September of that year. Quebec's showdown with the American majors was still a long way off. Francis Fox didn't have that long to wait.

The National Film and Video Policy

Shortly after Bill 109 was passed in the National Assembly in June 1983, and mindful of the federal government's own plan to introduce legislation concerning distribution, Jack Valenti, Millard Roth, and company held a meeting with Francis Fox in Montreal. Valenti suggested that 'the MPAA may prefer to close shop and remove their films from circulation rather than to conform to the new law.' To use the jargon of American jingoism, what the MPAA feared most was the 'domino effect' of the legislation. 'We live in a world environment,' Valenti explained, 'and measures like this could spread like a viral contagion through all the nations. We don't want that.'[16] Fox emerged from the meeting only to say that the two parties had established 'a working agenda with a view to improving things for the Canadian industry.'[17]

On 29 May 1984, with rumours of a federal election already in the air, Fox presented the National Film and Video Policy. It dealt with more (or less) than the question of distribution. Fox and his colleagues rejected Applebaum-Hébert's main recommendation with respect to the NFB. The Board would be allowed to continue as a production centre; it was, in the government's opinion, 'a synonym for excellence.'[18] In other respects, however, the Board's responsibilities were diminished. From this point onward, all government productions would be contracted-out, as would technical work of a commercial or industrial character. The Board would no longer handle its own international distribution, and its responsibilities in the area of still photos and archives would be transferred elsewhere. The policy paper maintained that these changes would give the NFB a 'more focused and effective mandate,' 'fulfilling the role of literary and intellectual essayist – an instrument for the highly-quality, in-depth, occasionally philosophical exploration of fundamental issues, trends, and concerns of importance to Canada and the world.'[19] It was just as true that the policy paper was continuing the trend toward the privatization of production.

The second thrust of the policy paper centred on the private sector and the attempt to establish 'a financially confident and economically viable Canadian film and video industry.'[20] Here the long-awaited announcement was woefully anticlimactic. The strategy was to build on existing programs, including the Broadcast Fund and the capital cost allowance, and to place new emphasis behind the marketing of Canadian film and video products at home and abroad. To symbolize the merger of film and television, and the government's intention to treat them as two sides of the same coin, the CFDC's new name – Telefilm Canada – was formally endorsed (the CFDC had announced the change of name in February 1984). To support feature film production through financing, script development, and marketing, Telefilm was given a budgetary increase of $7.75 million. Significantly, the policy paper was silent on the question of special support for the production of French-language films. One-third of the Broadcast Fund had been reserved for such productions, but there was no mention of such a scheme for the new film fund. The federal government may have decided that Quebec itself had the situation well under control, but the omission just as clearly suggests that federal concerns over the issue of Quebec independence had receded, given the defeat of the Quebec referendum on sovereignty-association. Certainly it was a sign of how unimportant feature films had become in terms of the federal government's stated desire to protect the nation's cultural integrity. But the central conclusion to draw regarding the film policy was this: the main focus was on the production of Canadian films for export, and in this regard it made more sense to give Telefilm and the production community as free a reign as possible – unencumbered by such unbusinesslike concerns as the future of Canadian bilingualism and biculturalism.

But what about the question of distribution? The policy paper reported that 'Canadian-made features win only two percent of the screen time in Canadian cinemas ... and are rarely distributed outside the country.' 'As matters now stand,' it concluded, 'the U.S. distribution industry determines what Canadian productions are seen by Canadians. That is simply unacceptable.'[21] Quebec's Bill 109 contained proposals that met the problem head-on. The federal government, on the other hand, saw 'negotiation [as] the preferred solution.'[22] It was as incredible as it was predictable. Because it had seen the trouble Bill 109 had caused the Parti Québécois, because a federal election itself was near, because it had already been informed of the fury and the possible 'counter-measures' that could result from protectionist measures, because it still believed that international distribution through the American majors was the preferred economic strategy: for all these reasons the Trudeau government had backed away from altering the structure of the distribution sector.

Cabinet had given Fox the authority to negotiate with the American majors, but what was it that Fox would ask for? According to the policy paper, Fox wanted the American majors to improve their distribution of Canadian-made films in both Canada and abroad; secondarily he wanted to find a way for Canadian-owned distribution companies to gain a greater share of the Canadian market.[23] There was absolutely no sign that the federal government was prepared to effectively challenge the American majors' control over distribution in Canada; in fact it could easily be argued that a 'successful' series of negotiations would only serve to stabilize and increase their control. In an open letter to Fox, Canada's independent distributors caustically remarked that the policy paper's section subtitled 'Private Sector Thrust – Towards a Stronger Industry' should have included an addendum that read: 'Towards a Stronger American [Film] Industry in Canada.'[24] Mercifully, the Liberal party, which had overseen Canada's cultural policy for almost the whole of the postwar period, would soon be driven from office. Fox would get to negotiate with the majors one more time, but not as a member of a Liberal federal government.

Negotiations in Quebec

Things were not going swimmingly in Quebec either. The Fournier-Roth memorandum of understanding was a coded capitulation. Its most important recommendation was that the term 'producer' apply only to the producer of a film originally produced in English, where that person has invested no less than one million dollars as payment for production *or* in consideration of distribution rights in North America.[25] Deciphered, it meant that the majors were prepared to relinquish distribution of foreign-language films to Quebec independents (unless it held the world rights to those films), but that otherwise it would be business as usual in Quebec (since the majors always spend more than a million dollars in the process of distribution). The minister rejected the draft agreement, as did the Régie.

In May 1985, the Régie published its own draft regulations. It stipulated that 'producer means any person holding at least 50 per cent of the financial interest in a film,' and that 'holder of world rights' meant 'any person who held the distribution rights for the film's country of origin, Canada, the United States, and the countries of Western Europe.'[26] As with the Fournier–Roth memorandum, financial interest seemed to include the costs of distribution. The Régie's measures were tougher, but not watertight: first, they made no mention of the film's language of origin; and second, because they did not include most of the world in the definition of 'world rights,' they made acquiring such rights much easier.

Public hearings on the final draft of Bill 109 began on 10 September and lasted four days. Valenti and company haggled over the proposals, though they made it abundantly clear that they had no trouble with the provision that the French subtitled or dubbed version of an English release be made available after 60 days. In fact the MPAA went even further and suggested that it was prepared to get out of the business of distributing non-English-language films in Quebec. The American distributors wanted to settle the issue without legislative measures. In Valenti's opinion, passage of the bill would 'make it very difficult, if not impossible, for the U.S. Majors to continue to do business in Quebec.'[27]

Valenti did not stay around to hear the other submissions. If he had, he would have heard Quebec distributors make the wholly rational suggestion that 'producer' be defined as that person or company that held a film's copyright on the first day of principal photography, and that the world meant the world. Remarkably, the recommendations were accepted, and while negotiations with the now incensed majors continued, the draft regulation went to Cabinet for approval. It was expected that Cabinet would ratify the regulations and institute Bill 109 before the Quebec election on 2 December.

It was not to be. According to Gérald Godin, the government's new minister of Cultural Affairs, Cabinet backed down on implementing Bill 109 after concerted pressure from the U.S. consulate and the MPAA.[28] Backed by the U.S. consulate, Valenti apparently threatened that the U.S. studios would 'pull out' if the bill was passed. Strongly worded letters were sent to both Premier René Lévesque and the federal Cabinet. As a Quebec policy adviser put it: 'The Americans always wanted the status quo, and that was it. For them, it is more the principle they are fighting against. They are afraid of the domino effect.'[29] The Parti Québécois itself was afraid of losing the election and a tactical boycott by the American majors would not have helped its chances. Even so, the party went down to defeat.

Given that the MPAA, like most Americans, considered the Parti Québécois to be one of the stranger aberrations of Canadian politics, they were probably quite surprised to learn that the new Liberal government in Quebec was still committed to Bill 109. With none other than Francis Fox as its chief negotiator, the Quebec government initiated another round of talks with the American majors. A deal was signed in late October 1986. The new deal was a compromise that the majors could live with. The term 'producer' now referred to anyone or any company who invested $4.5 million (Canadian) at any point in the life of a given film, including duplicating, advertising, and promotion.[30] The clauses concerning mandatory reinvestment in Quebec productions were left for future negotiations, as was the question of video distribution. Furthermore, the agreement would apply to all members of the MPEA as of 1 January 1987, which meant that at least four firms (Buena Vista, DeLaurentis, Orion, and Tri-Star) not eligible to distribute in Quebec under the original Cinema Act, could now do so. This extension of distribution privileges did not apply to Canadian firms from outside Quebec.

Because the majors typically spend between $3 and $10 million on duplicating, advertising, and promotion for the U.S. market alone, the deal did little to affect the status quo. It did give Quebec-based distributors better access to certain non-English-language films, something the American majors had already said they were prepared to give up (of course, the majors could still distribute non-English films for which they held 'world rights' or were a 'producer'). But the financial implications of the deal would be marginal. According to Michel Houle, if the terms of the agreement had applied in the previous two years, between 0.1 and 0.2 per cent of the majors' business would have been transferred to Quebec firms.[31]

Jack Valenti smugly announced that the deal was signed in recognition of Quebec's 'unique status' and that it should not be considered a precedent for other countries or other Canadian jurisdictions.[32] A more honest appraisal would be that the deal recognized the unique status of the American majors in Canada and that it had given that status a legislative or legal base.

A Federal Bill for Film and Video Distribution: Flora's Follies

Shortly after the MPAA and the Quebec government had reached an agreement on Bill 109, the federal government announced that it was about to introduce its own legislation on distribution.[33] On 17 February 1987, Minister of Communications Flora MacDonald revealed a proposal to limit the activities of foreign distributors only to those films or videos for which they held world distribution rights in all media. Perhaps eager to avoid the interpretive nightmare that had resulted from Bill 109, MacDonald made no mention of the term 'producers' rights.' According to the National Association of Canadian Film and Video Distributors, MacDonald's proposal would transfer approximately 7 per cent of the majors' revenues in Canada to Canadian-owned firms.[34]

Not all Canadian distributors were pleased with the announcement and the proposed legislation, not because it did not go far enough but because it went too far. Garth Drabinsky (whose Cineplex Odeon still operated Pan-Canadian Distributors) castigated the proposals, as he had those of the Film Industry Task Force. Though Pan-Canadian stood to gain some business if the legislation was passed, Drabinsky was far more concerned about damaging the cosy relationship with the U.S. majors. In September, at the Toronto Festival of Festivals, Drabinsky warned of dire consequences if the proposals became law: 'The American government will not sit idly by, given the significant lobbying clout of these companies, who are sure to demand either economic retaliation or the withdrawal of the legislation in consideration of concluding the broader free-trade agreement.'[35]

He was right. Jack Valenti moved quickly to signal his displeasure, mobilizing both President Reagan and the U.S. Senate to action in short order. Reagan reportedly denounced MacDonald's folly at a meeting with Mulroney in April; by June 1987, the Senate passed a resolution stating that 'discriminatory limitations on the ability of foreign companies to distribute motion pictures in Canada ... could result in an absolute bar to the successful completion ... of a Free Trade Agreement between the United States and Canada.'[36] MacDonald was losing the battle. On 15 October, a briefing paper to Clayton Yeutter, the U.S. trade ambassador, said Ottawa 'promised' to solve Jack Valenti's problem on film distribution within the next two weeks.'[37] The preliminary text of the free trade deal was signed shortly thereafter; MacDonald did not introduce the proposed legislation, though she maintained that some form of legislation would appear in the near future.

The new proposals were announced the following May. Not surprisingly, they were a pale imitation of the original proposal.[38] MacDonald now suggested that the Canadian rights for 'non-proprietary' films or videos would have to be negotiated and sold separately. In other words, the American majors could no longer buy the 'North American' rights to a film or video; instead, they would have to show that they had negotiated the Canadian rights separately. The main effect of the proposal would be more paper work for the majors. To ease the disappointment of Canadian distributors, the minister also announced a $17-million-a-year Film Distribution Fund to be administered by Telefilm. As Victor Loewy of Alliance/Vivafilm remarked: 'I suppose getting something is better than getting nothing.'[39] The Film Products Importation Act was tabled in the House in June 1988. By October, the 'free trade' election was on. MacDonald's bill died on the order paper. There would be no sequel.

In the Shadows of Free Trade

Throughout this period, federal officials staunchly maintained their commitment to Canadian culture. Indeed, because the issues of cultural sovereignty and national identity became a main bone of contention during the free trade negotiations, the rhetoric reached significant heights. The government argued time and again that the deal was just about trade and the need to secure access to the American market, that it had nothing whatsoever to do with culture, that at all costs Canada would be able to maintain its cultural identity because Canadian cultural policy would be protected. In December 1985, in a lengthy advertisement in the *New York Times*, Secretary of State Joe Clark remarked:

The protection of our distinct cultural identity is of singular importance to Canada. The Canadian government's intention to promote culture in Canada through direct financial support is not one of the things at issue in a trade negotiation. The question of whether or not specific Canadian cultural industries require special measures to assist them is a domestic issue that falls outside this sphere.[40]

American negotiators may have had some trouble understanding the Canadian concern for 'cultural sovereignty' but they certainly understood the need to protect and defend a most lucrative market for their cultural goods. At the outset of negotiations, William Merkin, deputy assistant U.S. trade representative, warned that the U.S. would insist upon 'Canadian cultural industries not being protected from ordinary commerce in a free-trade environment.'[41] In 1984, a U.S. sub-committee report entitled *Trade Barriers to U.S. Motion Pictures and Television, Prerecorded Entertainment, Publishing and Advertising Industries* argued that the U.S. government had failed 'to voice effectively its objections to trade barriers that are imposed by foreign governments under the guise of political or cultural concerns.' The first page of the report identified Canadian policies as a major irritant: 'for example, Canada places quotas on imported programming for "cultural" reasons, but, in effect, is protecting its government subsidized film and television production industry.'[42] In recent years, and aside from the MPAA, border broadcasters, Time Inc., and the publishing industry have registered vocal objections to proposed or existing Canadian policies.

With these grievances in mind, the American negotiating team had two objectives as it put culture 'on the table': first, and at the very least, to ensure that the political and economic costs to Canada of protectionist or discriminatory practices in the cultural industries remained unacceptably high; and second, to redress particular grievances in an attempt to expand the market for American cultural goods in Canada. As the president of the Business Council on National Issues, Thomas D'Aquino remarked: 'It is generally known that United States negotiators strongly pressed for inclusion of the cultural industries sector. And it is known that they wanted Canada to dismantle discriminatory postal rates, income tax provisions affecting border broadcasting, postal subsidies, and independent film distribution policy.'[43] To be sure, the American negotiators also understood the international implications of the treaty. Free trade in cultural goods is vital to the international competitiveness of the American economy; the Canadians could not be allowed to set an example that was otherwise.

Rhetoric aside, culture, and the cultural industries in particular, were on the table. In early 1986, the Canadian government established a Sectoral Advisory Group on International Trade on the Arts and Entertainment, chaired by Marie-Josée Raymond. Two prominent members of Canada's cultural industry, Philippe de Gaspé Beaubien of Telemedia and Ronald Osborne of Maclean-Hunter, joined government officials on the International Trade Advisory Committee. When the deal was signed the Tory government and its allies, such as the Business Council on National Issues, claimed victory: 'The Americans were held at bay,' wrote D'Aquino.[44] After the deal was ratified, Floral MacDonald told Canadian publishers: 'We have a free trade deal in agreement today because this Prime Minister, this Minister, and this government promised one thing: that Canada's right to determine its own culture would be respected in every degree.'[45]

The conclusions of D'Aquino and MacDonald, and the Tory government generally, regarding the victory on the issue of cultural policy is debatable. At first glance, Article 2005, which deals with cultural industries, does seem to preserve the status quo. The first clause explains that the cultural industries are exempt from the provisions of the agreement, except in terms of tariff elimination, divestiture of an indirect acquisition, the introduction of copyright payments for retransmission of American signals by Canadian cable companies, and the repeal of the print-in-Canada requirement for publications that qualify for advertising deductions under Bill C-58. None of these exceptions constitutes a dramatic concession in and of itself (though of course they do make it clear that culture was on the table). The second clause of Article 2005 is more interesting: 'Nothwithstanding any other provisions of this Agreement, a Party may take measures of equivalent commercial effect in response to actions that would have been inconsistent with this Agreement but for paragraph 1.'[46]

The precise meaning of Article 2005.2 and its potential impact upon future actions in the field of cultural policy is the subject of considerable disagreement. Canadian government officials have tried to argue that they have preserved the right to introduce new cultural programs and that the notwithstanding clause safeguards new initiatives from heavy-handed American reprisals by limiting the extent of retaliatory action to 'measures of equivalent commercial effect.' For instance, after the introduction of Bill C-58 in 1976, the American government retaliated by making the cost of attending conventions in Canada non-deductible from income tax; it was a $100 million blow to Canada's tourism industry, a 'commercial effect' at least 50 per cent higher than that of Bill C-58 on American interests. A reprisal of this type would violate the terms of the free trade agreement according to Canadian officials.

Not surprisingly, the Americans have settled on a slightly different interpretation of the clause. U.S. government documents note that Article 2005.2 'should encourage the adoption of nondiscriminatory policies in Canada,' and stress the importance of 'discouraging if at all possible the exercise of and reliance on' the cultural exemption clause.[47] A United States administrative action paper instructs the U.S. president to interpret the question of 'commercial effect' by taking into account world-wide U.S. interests. In other words, the United States could include the possibility of mirror legislation elsewhere in its assessment of 'damages.'[48] In a very real sense the notwithstanding clause simply preserves the status quo ante. The Canadian government can introduce new cultural policies and the U.S. government can retaliate. Still, it is hard to imagine how Canadian government officials can feel comfortable or satisfied by the clause. Retaliation is not confined to the cultural industries; the injured party may move against *any* area of commercial endeavour in order to satisfy its grievance. The Canadian government has apparently accepted the fact that future cultural policies may be subject to all manner of retaliation. Moreover, the clause is worded in such a way that the disputes-settlement mechanism established by the agreement is bypassed. The American government had argued repeatedly that Canadian-content requirements on television and radio, government-owned or subsidized production and distribution programs, Canadian tax laws (with respect to Bill C-58), and domestic purchasing preferences (in the case of educational books, for instance) constituted unfair trade barriers. It is hard to imagine how new Canadian cultural policy initiatives could be drafted without raising the spectre of U.S. retaliation, unless of course these policies abandon the attempt to promote and protect Canadian cultural goods. In this context, the decision to first delay and then emaciate the federal distribution deal makes perfect sense. As Susan Crean has remarked, given the satisfied claims of government leaders, 'we have to conclude that as little as three per cent and a maximum of twenty per cent is an acceptable definition of cultural sovereignty.'[49]

Business as Usual

Film and video makers in Canada have become accustomed to living in a climate of uncertainty. The last half of the eighties showed no signs of greater stability. In 1986, a year before Flora MacDonald's first attempt to introduce a distribution deal, then minister of Communications Francis Fox announced a five-year $65 million feature film fund to be administered by Telefilm Canada. The fund was designed to encourage theatrical productions, which had been marginalized as a result of the Broadcast Program Development Fund. In the first year of the Fund, Telefilm invested $16.2 million in 22 projects whose budgets totalled $40 million. Telefilm also signed a special deal with the National Film Board and private producers to co-produce six French-language feature films over the next two years.[50]

1986 turned out to be a year of optimism. According to an article by Martin Knelman in the *Report on Business Magazine*, a new breed of producers (more cautious, more financially sophisticated), and some favourable tax rulings from Revenue Canada, had coaxed private money back into the industry. In Telefilm-backed projects, 'the proportion of private investment has risen to 20% from 3% over a four-year period.'[51] Production totals for 1986 were estimated to be in the neighbourhood of $500 million, with over 50 per cent of the total representing productions made without the assistance of Telefilm.[52] This was also the year of Denys Arcand's *Decline of the American Empire*, which was nominated for an Academy Award in the Best Foreign Film category, Leon Marr's *Dancing in the Dark*, and Anne Wheeler's *Loyalties*. The boom continued into 1987; in Toronto alone production budgets totalled over $250 million, while in British Columbia total budgets reached a feverish $282 million.[53] This was also the year of Jean-Claude Lauzon's Genie Award–winning *Un Zoo la nuit* and Patricia Rozema's *I've Heard the Mermaids Singing*. These films, and other recent productions, such as Atom Egoyan's *Family Viewing* (1987), *Speaking Parts* (1989), and *The Adjuster* (1991); Bruce Macdonald's *Roadkill* (1989) and *Highway 61* (1992); Bill MacGillivray's *Life Classes* (1987); and Cynthia Scott's *The Company of Strangers* (1990), comprise a solid core of relatively low-budget feature films that have received widespread critical acclaim and do well in the niche market of 'art cinema.'

But, as we have come to expect, there was an underside to this latest boom. Much of the activity was a result of American film and television production in Canada. Taking advantage of both a cheaper dollar and lower-priced crews, these 'runaway shoots' were responsible for at least 50 per cent of the production activity; in B.C., as in the days of the quota quickies, the figure was closer to 95 per cent. At the same time, Canadian production firms were themselves gearing their projects to the American market, in particular as suppliers of 'off prime-time' or 'low-end' programming.[54] In no uncertain terms, the Canadian film and television industry was becoming dependent upon American capital and the American market for its continued health. It would seem that the production of a small amount of specifically Canadian cultural products is dependent upon the commercial viability of an industry whose primary orientation is U.S. demand. There is absolutely nothing surprising in this; indeed, it is in line with the advice and the expectations of many of the industry's most important players, from Ray Peck in the twenties, to Grierson in the forties, to Nat Taylor in the sixties, to Drabinsky in the eighties.

Still, nothing is guaranteed. With the boom underway, and the distribution bill still in the offing, the Department of Finance pulled the plug on the capital cost allowance. Its White Paper on Tax Reform, published in June 1987, reduced the CCA for Canadian films and videos to 30 per cent from 100 per cent over two years.[55] Peter Mortimer of the Canadian Film and Television Association noted that the change 'will result in a significant decline in the level of Canadian production and an upswing in American production ... The proposal is a disaster of epic proportions.'[56] The proposal took effect in 1988. That same year it was announced that Telefilm's budget would be frozen at 1989–90 levels through 1995–6.

During debate on the establishment of the CFDC in 1966, Jack Pickersgill had warned his Liberal colleagues that they had better be careful not to wind up making Hollywood pictures and paying for that privilege. Almost 20 years later, a good portion of Canada's film and television production is devoted to precisely this end. At the same time, more Canadian film and television drama of the type that is thought to express and develop cultural identity is being produced than ever before. This too is a function of government policy and the array of social forces that impinge upon the policy process. The aborted distribution bill, and the implications of the free trade agreement are not revolutionary events in the broadest sense; they point instead to the limitations of Canadian cultural policy, its insertion within a macro-economic strategy that in the final analysis has always privileged continentalism over nationalism. At this point it is hard to imagine a future that will look that much different from the past.

12 Vital Links: Culture, Nation, Dependency, and Beyond

Introduction

Of all peoples on earth, Canadians are the least able to understand the process of Americanization. America is total environment: it envelops us in a mist, penetrating every sphere of our cultural, political, economic, and social environment. For that very reason we seem to feel powerless, unwilling and unable to achieve the perspective necessary for an appraisal of our situation. It sometimes seems as superfluous to ask what should be done about the Americanization of this country as it is to ask what should be done about the weather.
                                                                    – Abraham Rotstein[1]

This study of Canada's feature film industry has brought us face to face with one of the most enduring themes of Canada's political, economic, social, and cultural history in the twentieth century: the pervasive presence of the American empire in Canada. Our exploration of Canadian feature film policy has charted only one aspect of this phenomenon in an effort to better understand how over time the relations of dependency have been established and sustained, challenged and modified. It has not been a study of Americanization per se, not if that term is meant to convey an intentional scheme to wreck the foundations of a separate Canadian identity or polity. Instead, it has been a study of how Canada – specifically various fractions of the Canadian state and the cultural sector – responded to the emergence of feature films as a revolutionary form of popular cultural expression in the twentieth century and to Hollywood's Herculean dominance over filmmaking as a cultural industry.

In 1900, Prime Minister Wilfrid Laurier predicted that the twentieth century would belong to Canada. As it turned out, Laurier was not much of a prophet. The twentieth century has belonged much more to the American film industry. As it began to spread itself around the world, Hollywood came to Canada, not in an effort to retool the Canadian psyche but in an effort to secure a new market for its cultural goods. It succeeded. Early Canadian film exhibitors (or theatre owners) were more than willing to earn a buck selling Hollywood to Canadians. Canadian audiences, for the most part, liked what they saw. It would be sheer folly to argue that the American film industry could, or should, have been repelled from the start. It would also be naïve to suggest that the terms of Hollywood's entry into Canada and the future course of the feature film industry in this country were determined solely by external forces bearing down on Canada's soul. The dynamics that have characterized the evolution of Canada's film industry are more nuanced than those of imperial imposition or colonial supplication; they are more a reflection of the social, economic, and political forces that constitute Canada than a mirror image of Uncle Sam. There has been and is, in the broadest sense, a politics of cultural dependency *in* Canada. The Canadian state has made significant choices regarding the balance between the American and Canadian film industries in Canada, and these choices have reflected domestic attitudes, interests, and strategies regarding the relationship between Canada and the United States. The ubiquity of American-produced culture in Canada is a point of fact. How Canadians have dealt with that presence is a reflection of the social practices that constitute Canada and its cultural space.

As we have seen, the dynamics of dependency in the film industry have changed over time. Until the late 1950s the near absence of feature filmmaking in Canada was not a cause for serious concern, neither for the industry, the state, nor the public. Until the mid-1960s, most movies about Canada were made by Hollywood in Hollywood. Since then a viable film and television production industry has emerged. Telefilm's budget is now over $150 million a year, and the independent production industry has reached annual production levels that hover around $500 million.[2] Even under the strictest rules of cultural and national purity, many of these productions could be said to interpret Canada to Canadians; some of them have found reasonable, even sizable, audiences both at home and abroad. Other productions have been designed for the American market or produced under the auspices of American firms; many of these too have found sizeable audiences in Canada. Without the vast array of public policies now in place, Canadian film and television drama would be a very endangered species; with these policies, the industry appears to have a sporting chance at survival.

Yet some things have changed little from the twenties to the nineties. Canadians continue to consume American film (and television) products at levels unparalleled by all but Americans themselves. According to a recent study of Ontario audiences, just less than three per cent of cinema time and just less than five per cent of home video time is spent watching Canadian material.[3] Hollywood's reach is global, but outside the United States its market grip is nowhere more firm than in Canada. While a vast array of state support mechanisms have certainly helped to create a critical mass of Canadian dramatic productions, most Canadians still experience these dramas as aberrations from the daily fare of film and television material that flows in from the mecca of all modern entertainment. It would be easy to conclude that, in terms of dramatic film and television production, Canadian cultural policy has failed to establish the conditions for shared cultural expression among Canadians, has failed to build a communicative space that reflects and articulates a dramatic sense of Canada as a nation. This book has been a study of that process of failure.

The Economics of Dependency

Any discussion of Canada–United States relations in the cultural sphere must be grounded in an understanding of the economics of production and distribution. Let us review the more salient points pertaining to the film and television industries. As the publicity that surrounds Hollywood is fond of pointing out, the production costs for theatrical films or dramatic television are high. In the U.S. the average cost of an hour of television drama can run to $1 million, while feature films average more than $20 million in production costs alone. One of the most noteworthy features of the American film and television industry is that its average production costs are easily the highest in the world. In Canada, by contrast, an average hour of domestically produced television drama costs roughly $500,000, while feature films average no more than $3 million.[4] The exorbitant cost of American film and television programming is, in the first instance, a function of its large and wealthy domestic market; in the second instance, it is part of Hollywood's competitive strategy to maintain its lead in the global marketplace. The typical rule of thumb when comparing Canada's market with that of the United States is that the latter is ten times larger; but in the case of cultural products, where language is an important constraint on audience appeal, the Canadian market is effectively smaller. Assuming that audience appeal is in part a function of higher production costs (and there is some evidence to suggest that it is), then all other things being equal, U.S. programs have an immediate competitive advantage over their Canadian competition.

But all other things are not equal. Because of market size many U.S. productions are able to recover their costs of production domestically, while only the most exceptional Canadian ones do so. Second, the costs of production are incurred mainly in making the first copy or print. The costs of reproduction, of duplicating the film or video for wide distribution, are, relatively speaking, almost nil. Thus producers and distributors have little reason not to seek as many markets as possible for the completed project. In the case of U.S. television exports, the most expensively produced material in the world is made available to foreign buyers at a small fraction of its original cost.[5] In the case of feature films, the added costs are associated with promotion and advertising. It is here that the enormous financial resources of the major distributors and the whole history of Hollywood as the entertainment capital of the world play such a key role. Promotion costs may run as high as production costs.[6]

In Canada, where advertising spillover is common, the costs of 'exporting' an American film are minimal, perhaps one reason why the American majors have long considered Canada to be part of their 'domestic' market. At the same time, Canadian buyers of American film and television products – whether theatre owners or broadcasters – have good reason to shop American. In the case of films, the risks are certainly smaller, in part because American distributors can underwrite large marketing campaigns, and in part because of the consumer demand for Hollywood films built up over time. For broadcasters, American dramatic television programs are a bargain when compared with in-house productions or with material purchased from independent Canadian producers. Even if advertising revenues for Canadian and American programming were the same, the latter would generate far more revenue. Very simply, insofar as culture is now a business, the relative cost of exporting (and importing) American cultural products makes it difficult for Canadian productions to compete on an equal footing.

This study has amply demonstrated this phenomenon with respect to the film industry. In the early years of the cinema, attempts at Canadian productions were sporadic, in large measure a function of the small and scattered market for feature films in Canada. As Hollywood was learning the value of the international marketplace for its product, there was no viable domestic production centre in Canada to challenge it. From the 1920s to the late 1950s, few Canadian producers or companies were interested in taking on the financial risks associated with making Canadian feature films. The two most successful English-Canadian companies, Associated Screen News and Crawley Films, survived and profited on the basis of newsreels, the duplication of foreign prints, and the production of industrial and theatrical shorts. As Ben Norrish, founder and general manager of Associated Screen News noted in 1920: '[Canada] had no more use for a large moving picture studio than Hollywood had for a pulp mill.'[7] More than 30 years later, Budge Crawley likewise maintained that a Canadian feature film industry did not make 'economic sense.'[8]

To the extent that the economics of comparative advantage determine contemporary cultural production, Norrish and Crawley were right. In Quebec, the brief flurry of feature film production during and after the Second World War was the exception that proved the rule. The war and German occupation devastated the French film industry, creating a vacuum in the Quebec market that was temporarily filled by Renaissance Films and the Quebec Productions Corporation. In the first instance then, market forces related to the production of feature films militated against the establishment of a stable, ongoing Canadian feature film industry.

At the same time, Canadian exhibitors – the Allens, N.L. Nathanson, and their ilk – learned quickly that their livelihood depended upon a stable flow of films from south of the border and the establishment of arrangements that guaranteed long-term supply. The weakness of Canadian anti-combines legislation, as evidenced by events surrounding the White Commission in the early thirties, made it easier for Canadian-based exhibitors to maintain their 'entente cordiale' with the American majors. Canadian-owned exhibition chains – including Odeon and Cineplex in their time – never sought anything more than a cosy place in the Hollywood nexus. Certainly, the combines investigation initiated by Garth Drabinsky in the early eighties was motivated far less by cultural nationalism than by a desire to secure better access to first-run Hollywood films. With very few exceptions, Canadian exhibitors (like private broadcasters) have collaborated with the American majors and facilitated the flow of transnational culture into Canada. Business acumen, not nationalist (or anti-nationalist) sentiment, is the basis of their actions.

As the business practices of the exhibition chains make plain, the pattern of dependency is not simply a function of markets performing according to textbook logic. The American majors moved early to secure their economic advantage by founding the Motion Picture Export Association. Ever since, they have used their market clout to secure favourable business arrangements in most of the markets in which they operate. What the Americans have reaped by virtue of their domestic market, they are ever ready to secure through oligopolistic and cartel-like practices in the global marketplace. When pressured in Canada – by the federal government after the Second World War, by Quebec's Bill 109, and by more recent federal proposals for a Film Products Importation Act – the American majors have reacted with an effective combination of political muscle and stealth to maintain their market share. In each case, they have also been able to find Canadian allies for their cause.

It would be wrong, however, to regard the economic dimensions of film production and trade as fixed over time. In the mid-fifties, Nat Taylor presciently noted how structural changes within the American film industry might affect the development of a feature film industry in Canada. In a series of articles in *Canadian Film Weekly*, Taylor detailed how the breakdown of the old studio system and the rise of television had increased the number of independent productions purchased and distributed by the American majors. Taylor was right. The trend has continued, as the introduction of cable television, videocassette recorders, and pay TV have dramatically increased the need for audio-visual products of all kinds. The majors have maintained their global dominance throughout this period by concentrating on distribution; they have become more and more willing to include independent productions in their business plans. As Taylor concluded, if Canadians could make films that were 'practically indistinguishable' from American ones, the majors might be eager to include them as part of their supply.[9] Taylor's *The Mask* (1961), Harold Greenberg's *The Neptune Factor* (1974) and *Porky's* (1981), Drabinsky's *The Changeling* (1980) and *Tribute* (1981), are some noteworthy examples of films that reflect the logic of Taylor's argument: Canadians could and should make feature films with the American market, the American majors, and the American public in mind. Co-ventures between American and Canadian firms, and American-led film and television productions in Canada (more and more common in the eighties and nineties), are a further extension of Taylor's logic.

As we have seen, Taylor's argument did not go unchallenged. In the sixties it was deeply at odds with the sentiment emerging within the Association professionnelle des cinéastes (APC) and the Directors' Guild of Canada (DGC). These two bodies came to see feature filmmaking as integral to the creation and expression of a national (or bi-national) culture. As the APC put it: 'Des peuples ont disparu à partir du moment où ils ont vécu par procuration, où ils ont vécu les rêves des autres, à partir du moment où ils ont été incapables de récréer l'image de leur univers, où ils sont allés chercher ailleurs toute leur mythologie.'[10] Taylor regarded such poetic justifications for feature filmmaking as misplaced idealism. But the two camps were not completely at odds. Taylor and the APC agreed on two things: first, that feature filmmaking should take place primarily in the private sector, apart from the political and bureaucratic limitations that might be imposed from within the CBC or NFB; and second, that without government assistance any attempt to build a feature film industry in Canada was doomed to failure. Taylor himself had noted in 1960: 'We shall have a production industry in Canada, a good and thriving one, if our government ever gets around to extending a helping hand.'[11]

Of course, there was to be profound disagreement over the precise form and content of government assistance. But one thing was clear: the supply of Canadian film and television productions would be a function of state intervention in conjunction with market forces, not market forces alone. In other words, economic variables alone do not provide a sufficient explanation of the dynamics that have characterized the history of the film industry in Canada. To complete the picture we must move to the terrain of politics, to the process whereby choices have been made regarding the extent and nature of state intervention.

The Politics of Dependency

In its 1990 annual report, the Department of Communications' goal is put simply as: 'Nation building: helping Canadians share their ideas, information and dreams.'[12] Cultural politics in Canada thus reflects a most essential concern of statecraft: the need to establish and maintain the cultural or communicative sense of the political unit qua nation. The debate has been about how best to achieve this objective. It has taken place on two planes: the first concerns the content of the cultural symbols and artefacts themselves, and whether certain products are more suited to the task of nation building than others; the second concerns the precise mechanisms that are required to ensure the existence of the appropriate channels of communication and production of the appropriate content. For the last two decades the debate has been complicated, some might say debilitated, by a further objective: the need to establish cultural industries that can compete in the global marketplace for cultural goods and contribute to Canada's economic growth.

It has been rightly said that there is something deeply ironic about Canadian cultural policy. On the one hand, the Canadian government has worked diligently to establish a technologically sophisticated and elaborate communications and cultural infrastructure. In itself this is a remarkable accomplishment given the country's sparse population and expansive geography. Not surprisingly, policy makers and government officials make frequent reference to Canada's envious communications infrastructure as a source, sometimes *the* source, of nation building. Sovereignty, in this view, is a function of the cultural linkages afforded by communications technology. On the other hand, as Robert Babe has argued, a careful analysis of the uses to which these infrastructures have been put shows that they have been 'deployed in manners supportive of continental integration; indeed, it may be fairly said that Canada as a nation persists despite, not because of, communication media.'[13] Even the establishment of CBC radio, which Prime Minister R.B. Bennett and others regarded as 'a great agency for the communication of matters of national concern and for the diffusion of national thought and ideals ... by which national consciousness may be fostered and sustained and national unity still further strengthened' was dependent upon foreign programming and music for much of its more popular content. As Paul Rutherford notes, 'what was variously called "mass" or "popular" culture, the culture of bubble gum and baseball and Hollywood, was everywhere.'[14] The development of sophisticated channels of communication in Canada has done little to alter the axis of communication from north–south (or south–north) to east–west. There is little in this study to challenge such a conclusion.

Indeed, as we begin to evaluate the politics of culture as they pertain to the film industry, the first question that needs to be addressed is why the state moved so late to support the establishment of a Canadian feature film industry. It would be wrong to suggest that the Canadian state did not have a film policy before the establishment of the Canadian Film Development Corporation (CFDC) in 1968. In fact, it had several. But common to all was a hands-off attitude toward the prevailing structure and practices of the feature film industry.

The establishment in 1917 of the Canadian Government Motion Picture Bureau (CGMPB) made the Canadian state something of a cinematic pioneer. But as we have seen, this state-operated film unit had a very limited mandate: the CGMPB was principally designed to attract investment and immigrants to Canada; it was only marginally interested in using film as a form of national education and even less interested in developing fictional feature-length films as part of its repertoire. It could be said that as an instrument of nation building the CGMPB was all about nuts and bolts. It had no desire and no mandate to pursue the development of the nation's soul.

Limited though it was, this policy orientation paralleled contemporary opinion regarding the cultural role of film as an extension or elaboration of Canadianism. While considerable public concern was expressed regarding the harmful effects of Hollywood films on the Canadian psyche, and while each province undertook some form of content regulation (or censorship), no organized movement outside the film industry put forth the case that Canada needed its own cinema. The dominant perspective, carried forward with such vehemence by Canada's cultural highbrows, looked upon feature films as culturally debilitating and pedestrian. The form itself was the problem – movies were movies were movies. Nationality was not a particularly important distinguishing criteria, though Hollywood films were almost unanimously regarded as the very worst of a bad lot. Against the onslaught of American values, some critics were prepared to argue that the British cinema might be an effective counterweight. The argument was made on and off throughout the twenties and into the thirties, though it was never carried forward with much passion or zeal. In retrospect, the attempt to establish a quota for British Empire pictures in Ontario was one of the last gasps of Canada's nineteenth-century colonial legacy, its ineffectiveness a sure sign that Canada's imperial centre had shifted.

Even the combines investigation conducted by Peter White, and the subsequent trial before Justice Garrow, cannot be considered a significant challenge to the basic structure of dependency. At issue was not the ability of Canadians to produce their own films, but the ability of independent Canadian exhibitors to have greater access to American ones. A guilty verdict would have temporarily destabilized the neatly structured relationship between Famous Players and the American majors, but it would not have changed the basic composition of the films that reached Canadian screens. In the period when dependency in the feature film industry was first established, it is fair to say that the production of Canadian feature films was a non-issue.

During this time the director of the CGMPB, Ray Peck, and other Canadians in the film business, notably Canadian-born Hollywood director Alan Dwan, suggested that Canada should pursue a simple branch-plant strategy and encourage the production of American films in Canada. Peck's views were perfectly in accord with one of the dominant features of the Canadian state's macro-economic policy: the encouragement and facilitation of American direct investment in Canada. In fact, Peck presented his case more vehemently once the British government had imposed a quota that discriminated in favour of films made in the Empire. Peck took the opportunity of a protected market to argue that because filmmaking was just like any other business (because it held no special place in terms of its cultural or social role), Hollywood might be encouraged to use Canada as a base from which to circumvent the intent of the British quota. For a while this was exactly what happened.

The arrival of John Grierson and the activities of the National Film Board of Canada (NFB) under his command can be regarded as a second variant of the state's approach to the question of a Canadian cinema. Like John Reith, the patriarch of the British Broadcasting Corporation, or Graham Spry, the messiah of public radio in Canada, Grierson argued that cultural production had a political purpose: that the cinema (in this case) should function as an instrument of national education and public purpose. Unlike the CGMPB and its emphasis on publicizing Canada abroad, the NFB's mandate was in part 'to interpret Canada to Canadians.' Grierson was a missionary. The NFB became his ministry. His sermons took the form of documentaries. From the beginning the NFB's films were didactic, when they were not simply propagandistic. Grierson drew a sharp distinction between films designed to educate and films designed to entertain. Hollywood films did the latter and Grierson detested them for it. As he put it, Hollywood films were 'lazy, weak, reactionary, vicarious, sentimental and essentially defeatist.'[15] Fictional films, remarked Grierson in 1970, were little more than 'temptation for trivial people.'[16] They were, in their very essence, unsuited to the Griersonian project. Like Peck then, but for his own set of reasons, Grierson was wary of the notion that Canada should have its own feature film industry: such films would be expensive to produce, and regardless of their cost could not serve the heady purposes of nation building. He too arrived at the conclusion that American firms should be encouraged to produce a few films in Canada or to make a few films about Canada without bothering to take the trip north. Ultimately, whatever credit Grierson deserves for his views and his influence upon the documentary tradition of filmmaking must be weighed heavily against his contempt for popular cultural forms.

In the immediate postwar period Grierson's proselytizing spirit and paternalistic ethic were codified in the Massey Report. As the first full-length review of the Canadian government's cultural policy, the Massey Report plainly revealed the élitist or highbrow, almost authoritarian, quality of Canada's early cultural policy. The Report drew a sharp distinction between art and entertainment, noting that only the former could serve the purposes of national cultural (or spiritual) development. In her own review of the Report, Hilda Neatby, one of its commissioners, charged that Canada was 'a nation of barbarians.'[17] Mass culture was the problem not the solution. Consequently, government assistance to produce feature films (barbarian in their very essence) would be a waste of both time and money.

Ideas matter, especially when they are the ideas of the dominant social and political forces. The antagonism toward mass culture, the combination of fear and loathing directed at the movies exhibited by Canada's cultural élite, played a determining role in limiting or shutting down the possibility of state support for feature filmmaking. For six years after the publication of the Massey Report, the 'arts' were still begging for public funds. If the state had money to spend, feature films would be near the bottom of the list of priorities. When the Canada Council was finally established in 1957, as a source of financial aid to the 'arts' in Canada, feature filmmaking was not one of the cultural activities deemed eligible for support.

Given the attitude represented by the Massey Report and Grierson, the Canadian Co-operation Project of the early postwar period (in which Hollywood promised to make a few films in Canada and insert a few choice phrases in other films to promote tourism) is not all that difficult to explain. The government was worried about its balance-of-payments deficit. C.D. Howe, chief architect of Canada's postwar economic policy, was worried about attracting American direct investment to Canada. Hollywood's offer of assistance (however nominal it turned out to be) was regarded as an amiable contribution to the cause. The dominant attitude consigned popular films to a lazy pastime, and Canada's producers showed almost no willingness to pursue the development of feature films. Within the context of the postwar environment the

Project was not much of a sell-out to American interests, because almost no one in Canada believed that there was a serious alternative to the near monopoly of Hollywood films in Canada *or* the need for one. Moreover, the establishment of the Canadian Co-operation Project serves as a reminder that cultural policy is framed within the context of the state's macro-economic policy. In this case the fit was nearly perfect.

So how to explain the emergence of the CFDC in 1968 and the decision finally to support the production of Canadian feature films? Abject cynicism would lead us to the CFDC's measly appropriation of $10 million and the conclusion that the CFDC had more to do with publicity than policy. But an evaluation of the period leading up to the establishment of the CFDC indicates that there was more at work here. First, as noted earlier in this chapter, industry spokespeople began to make the case that feature filmmaking deserved public support. While Nat Taylor's argument was based entirely on economic considerations, the APC and DGC noted the positive contribution that feature films might make to Canada's continuing efforts to foster a national identity. Though at odds over the precise nature of state intervention, each emphasized the importance of making the private sector the centre of production. Their demands were supported in principle by a number of state officials, including: Guy Roberge, the government film commissioner; Michael Spencer, the NFB's director of planning; and Maurice Lamontagne, secretary of state. Within the federal government itself, a stronger commitment to the principles of the Keynesian-welfare state was coupled with a new sense of urgency toward national cultural development. The impetus for this shift came, in part, from the events of Quebec's Quiet Revolution, and in part, from the new political demands of Canada's first postwar generation. Finally, and not least important, the Massey Report's view of popular culture's inferiority had been called into question; the speeches of Maurice Lamontagne, Canada's first 'minister of culture,' revealed a new orientation toward the development of Canada's cultural industries and popular culture as a means of establishing a national identity.

The establishment of the CFDC was part and parcel of the attempt to establish a greater Canadian presence in the area of 'mass' or 'popular' culture. It was a victory for a new version of Canadian cultural nationalism, but it was also a compromise – a renegotiation of dependent status, but not a break with it. The filmmakers themselves had argued that the proper way to develop Canadian feature film production was to introduce discriminatory measures that would reduce Hollywood's control over Canadian screens. Following the example of most other Western countries, the filmmakers proposed a combination of screen quotas and box-office levies to help sustain feature film production in the private sector. But the major Canadian interests within the private industry, including Canadian producers, did not support such an aggressive approach. Public subsidies for private production were one thing, public regulations that might alter the basic distribution and exhibition practices of the industry were quite another. As Nat Taylor so clearly argued, Canadian feature films would have to be good enough to make it on their own, without discriminatory measures. This was the path of least resistance – no one would be forced to show or watch Canadian films, and the American majors would not be forced to change their business practices or reduce their profits. This was also the path chosen by officials within the Canadian state. For a 'miserable ten million dollars,' as Secretary of State Judy LaMarsh put it, the CFDC seemed worth the risk.[18]

LaMarsh's remarks aside, there was apparently some justification for the belief that the Canadian state was about to embark on a more nationalist cultural strategy. LaMarsh's successor, Gérard Pelletier, served notice that the Liberal party had made the development of a comprehensive and rationally planned cultural policy a political priority. Under Pierre Juneau, the newly formed Canadian Radio-television Commission (CRTC) flexed its regulatory muscle by introducing more stringent Canadian-content provisions for broadcasters and by forcing foreign-controlled television broadcasters to sell to Canadian owners. But the optimism was short-lived, as was the attempt at planning a comprehensive cultural policy. The new CRTC regulations were not accompanied by a policy of public subsidies or loans to facilitate the production of high-quality independent Canadian television programming. Canada's private producers had already amply demonstrated their ability to side-step the pith and substance of the Canadian-content provisions (when they found it profitable to do so), and it was well known that Canadian television production was at a serious economic disadvantage when compared with the ready-made and cheaply priced exports from south of the border. Why, then, was there no CFDC-like institution for Canadian television productions? Why did it take more than a decade and a half for the federal government to introduce production subsidies for television projects? Certainly, Canada's private broadcasters seemed satisfied with the current arrangement, not least because the Canadian-content provisions were so loosely interpreted and applied. Ultimately, the Canadian state had established a situation in which Canadians – as broadcasters, and later as cable operators – could profit from the massive inflow of cheap American programs. The Canadianization of television ownership did little to Canadianize the content of television; indeed, its unintended consequence was to reinforce the internalization of dependency.[19] At the very least, given the rhetoric of state officials, one would have expected the Canadian state to develop a comprehensive policy encompassing film and television production. That it did not was a reflection of its own weak commitment to the principle of planning, and of the strength of vested interests in both fields of endeavour.

The CFDC was caught in a double bind from the very beginning. At one and the same time, it was expected to facilitate the production of films for profit and films for culture. CFDC officials expected a long period of trial and error, and they were originally prepared to take chances with young filmmakers and inexperienced producers. But the long-term goal of the Corporation was the development of a stable and commercially viable private sector. If the Corporation had a bottom line it was commercial success, not artistic integrity. Thus Gratien Gélinas, the CFDC's chairperson in the early 1970s, responded to Pelletier's emphasis on the need to develop 'la conscience nationale,' with a reminder that the CFDC would have to adapt to 'la rude philosophie des affaires.'[20] Unlike the NFB, the CFDC's mandate was not explicitly to interpret Canada to Canadians and, early on, CFDC officials made a point of noting that difference.

Ironically, in the first decade of its existence, the CFDC (together with the unsolicited help of the NFB's own forays into feature film production) did a lot more to help the production of films for culture than films for profit. This was more true in terms of the production of French-Canadian rather than English-Canadian films, but either way it was not in and of itself a measure of success according to the criteria of the CFDC. The films had to be seen by a large number of Canadians and some of them had to make money. Neither of these objectives was realized. Indeed, critical success without commercial success came to be regarded as a policy failure that made many state officials (especially those at the Treasury Board and in Finance) hostile to the Corporation's continuation. In their view, the industry had to become self-supporting. The policy had to be reassessed.

By the mid-seventies, there emerged three basic proposals to the problems being encountered. The Council of Canadian Filmmakers (CCFM) was the most vocal proponent of two of the three. The first proposal involved a clear break with the notion of private, commercial production. In 1974, the CCFM proposed a plan for the production of roughly 15 films a year to be fully supported through public subsidy. The CFDC dismissed the proposal out of hand, arguing that its mandate was to create a commercially viable private sector. In a fundamental sense, this proposal ran directly counter to the government's own growing commitment to the privatization of cultural production and to most of those currently engaged in private-sector production. That the proposal was never taken seriously was a clear sign that the Canadian state's cultural policy was fundamentally in accord with the interests of capital in the private sector who wanted Canada's cultural industries to be developed along the lines of private accumulation.

The second proposal involved the introduction of a combination of quotas and box-office levies that would improve access to Canadian screens and increase the financial base for support to private producers. Not least because it involved measures already in place in other capitalist-democratic countries, this proposal was taken more seriously by state officials and some Canadian producers. The CFDC itself supported the idea by 1973, although it seems that its executive director, Michael Spencer, was always more interested in a box-office levy than a quota. There is also evidence to suggest that secretaries of state Hugh Faulkner and John Roberts both believed that legislative measures should be taken. But again, there was opposition to the proposal. The major exhibitors in Canada – Famous Players and Odeon in the 1970s, and Famous Players and Cineplex Odeon in the 1980s – steadfastly opposed the introduction of quotas and levies; so too did the American majors. As the events that surrounded Roberts' proposal for a ten per cent tax on distributors demonstrate, there was also opposition from within the Canadian state. At that time, the Department of Finance exercised its de facto veto over the introduction of a discriminatory tax measure. But the basic point we must bear in mind is this: measures designed to discriminate against the operation of American interests and their Canadian allies in the private sector must be cleared at the highest reaches of the Canadian state. The introduction of quotas or levies could not be an administrative decision; it would be a political one of considerable magnitude. Because such measures ultimately involved direct confrontation with powerful and well-established American interests in Canada, they would be carefully evaluated within the context of ongoing negotiations and conflicts over bilateral issues. The history of these negotiations is essentially one of compromise not confrontation. The voluntary quotas negotiated by Faulkner and Roberts were designed to side-step a head-on clash with the American majors. And the events that surrounded the introduction of Quebec's Bill 109 and the federal government's proposed Distribution Bill amply demonstrated the difficulties created by a direct challenge to the American majors. These were two instances in which the American majors revealed the full force of the imperial relationship. While the negotiated settlement in Quebec marginally benefited Quebec-based Canadian distributors, it did not unduly harm the basic interests of the American majors in Canada.

The third approach to solving the commercial instability of Canadian feature filmmaking involved attempting to create an industry that could produce feature films for export, where the development of Canadian productions would be linked to the dynamics of the international marketplace. This orientation had underlined Nat Taylor's support for the development of a Canadian feature film industry; it was a view shared by the American distributors and many of Canada's producers. The Tompkins Report, prepared for the Secretary of State in the mid-seventies, argued as well for development along these lines when it suggested that Canadian films should aspire to the type of success achieved by Steven Spielberg's first box-office blockbuster, *Jaws* (1975). With the help of a new tax holiday for certified Canadian productions, and greater use of co-productions, the CFDC, under the guidance of Michael McCabe, presided over the first attempt to operationalize this strategy. The tax-shelter boom of 1978 to 1980 was a commercial and cultural disaster. In the rush to produce big-budget, Hollywood-style films, Canadian producers and the CFDC created an over-heated industrial structure that almost destroyed the production base in Quebec in its rush to ally itself with the American majors. Over-production was certainly a new phenomenon in the history of Canadian feature film production, but it was no less traumatic because of that. The first clear attempt to integrate the Canadian film industry into the international commercial marketplace was a failure. The boom went bust in 1981.

There has been a second, more successful, attempt at creating stable production houses able to produce market-oriented export products. There is no evidence that the new strategy was rationally planned by state officials; instead, it seems to have emerged from the pell-mell of policy decisions made in the early 1980s and, perhaps most important, from changes within the structure of the industry both at home and abroad. It had become increasingly difficult to maintain a clear distinction between television production and feature film production. The cinema still retains it allure and its status as a premier cultural institution – for purposes of marketing and publicity if for nothing else – but to speak of a film industry divorced from the television (or audio-visual) production industry is no longer a very useful analytic distinction. As a result of the introduction of videocassette recorders, expanded cable and satellite distribution, and the political decision by almost all states to allow a vast expansion in the number of audio-visual channels and services that enter the household, the major market for feature films is in the home. The integration of feature film and television production, and the proliferation of channels and services into the home, constitutes something of a mini-revolution in communications. For Canadian film policy a number of consequences are noteworthy: first, increasing privatization of motion picture viewing makes less viable a policy strategy based upon intervention at the point of theatrical exhibition; quotas or box-office levies are far less effective means of increasing access to Canadian films when consumers can bypass the theatre entirely and still see current feature films. In the new environment the equivalent policy options would be quotas and point-of-sale advertising or display regulations that discriminated in favour of Canadian productions, and a special tax earmarked for domestic production, to be applied to both video rental outlets and pay-per-view services. None of these would guarantee an increase in Canadian audiences for Canadian productions, and they would almost certainly encounter strenuous resistance. It would seem that Canadian productions will never constitute more than a small fraction of the total market for audio-visual productions.

But the structural changes to the audio-visual market have had other consequences. As CFDC officials noted in the early seventies, state support for dramatic television production could be considered a reasonable alternative to an emphasis on feature films and the cinema. In retrospect, the Canadian Broadcast Program Development Fund was a watershed development in the history of the CFDC and the relationship between the state and audio-visual production in Canada. Not only did it reorient the CFDC's activities toward the sphere of television (signified eloquently by the adoption of the neologism Telefilm Canada), it also led the newly named agency to support the production of independent television programming, which, when successful, helped establish a far more solid and stable industry base. Evidence suggests that the independent production industry achieved overall profitability in 1984–5, a year after the introduction of the Broadcast Fund.[21] Programs such as 'Night Heat' and 'Danger Bay' are examples of Canadian-originated series that have done well in foreign markets.

But these programs illustrate a further dimension of the new production environment. Both are co-ventures with American interests. 'Danger Bay' was produced with assistance from the Disney Channel in the United States, while 'Night Heat' was made by Alliance Films in Canada and Grosso-Jacobson Productions in the United States with a broadcasting licence from the CBS television network. Canadian-based Paragon Entertainment Corporation recently signed deals worth $40 million with ABC, CBS, Fox, Spelling TV, Tristar TV, and USA Network.[22] Co-venture and co-productions are now very much the norm for almost all forms of audio-visual drama, and the market power of Hollywood suggests that it will continue to play a leading role in program planning, production, and distribution, particularly for those designed for the U.S. market. In this respect, Canadian producers have become junior partners in a new, more transnational program industry.

Does this mean that ultimately the policy decisions of the Canadian government have been a success? Such a simple question cannot be answered simply. For one thing the criteria by which success should be measured have never been altogether clear. If we assume that success is characterized by the development of a stable domestic production industry that makes profitable and appealing audio-visual products, then, on this basis, there is cause for some optimism. In 1989, the total value of all productions in Canada reached $2.5 billion, an increase of 10 per cent in constant dollars over the years 1987 and 1988. Foreign production accounted for less than 10 per cent of total productions. Over the last five years, Canadians watched 30 per cent more English-language Canadian programming in prime time.[23]

But, as a recent report by Paul Audley on Canadian film and television production notes, growth rates have levelled off. The reduction of the capital cost allowance to 30 per cent has had a demonstrable braking effect, particularly in the production of feature films. In fact, feature films continue to constitute a troubled category of audio-visual production. Average production budgets dropped by one-half between 1988 and 1990 (from $4.0 million to $1.8 million) and the Canadian share of the feature film markets of theatres, home video, and pay TV are a paltry 6 to 7 per cent. Feature filmmaking remains 'a cottage industry.'[24] However, during this same period, some notable Canadian feature films have been made, proving once again that budgets alone do not determine critical reception. In other words, the policy has been a success only to the extent that it has facilitated the production of more television series. Feature films continue to be a weak link in the Canadian cultural chain, though year in and year out a few notable exceptions emerge. Perhaps that's the way it will always be.

The Culture of Dependency

Lurking beneath the surface of this analysis has been a question that is far more difficult to address, but that bears directly upon any evaluation of the success or failure of Canadian cultural policy. What is the relationship between the production, distribution, and consumption of culture and the articulation of individual and social attitudes and values? The common-sense assumption is that the relationship is quite linear, that the attitudes and values expressed through the media become the attitudes and values of the audience. This perspective falls in line with what media scholarship calls the 'transportation model of communication.' As James Carey has argued, the transportation model sees communication 'as a process of transmitting messages at a distance for the purpose of control. The archetypal case of communication then is persuasion, attitude change, behavior modification, socialization through the transmission of information, influence, or conditioning.'[25] Once this model is coupled with the assumption (or theory) that audiences are generally passive and open to persuasion (if only unconsciously), then the media become agents of considerable social power. The wrong messages will have disastrous social consequences.

It is fair to argue that a broad cross-section of Canadian opinion leaders understand the media and its relationship to audiences from this perspective, and that they principally have been concerned with messages that have to do with a category of attitudes and values known as national culture. From the Aird Commission to the present, a set of mathematic-like axioms has held sway: first, that the wholesale consumption of foreign cultural products is a national cultural disaster; and second, that national identity is a function of the production and consumption of Canadian cultural products. As one of the recent publications of the Department of Communications put it, cultural products are a 'vital link' to 'the very essence of our national identity.'[26] Culture is the bond that holds the nation together. The more Canadians consume foreign culture, the more they lose any sense of a separate national identity.

This line of reasoning reflects a set of propositions regarding the importance of nationalism that are not in any way unique to Canada. Since the rise of nationalism as a mobilizing social force, and the emergence of the nation-state as the paramount political unit, the need for some kind of symmetry between culture and polity has been virulently maintained.[27] Ideally, each state is supposed to coincide with a unique national culture. The distinction between state and nation is crucial here. The state is first and foremost a large administrative organization that claims the authority to carry out complex social tasks on behalf of all individuals who live within its boundaries.[28] A nation is more than an administrative unit, and it is more than a geographically defined zone. It is a culture; a culture that must be experienced and understood by its members; a culture that emerges from a sense of similarity, of belonging to a community; and a culture that involves a sense of difference from others. The basis for nationalism may be ethnicity, language, geography, or history alone or in combination; or it may be none of these, for ultimately the nation is a symbolic and political construction. It should be clear that a state can exist without a nation (and many have), but it is also true that the existence of a nation (or more appropriately the creation of one) that coincides with a state will dramatically increase its political legitimacy and authority. In fact, we have come to believe that a state is not fully developed unless it also embodies and articulates a nation, and that the articulation and embodiment of a nation is one of the highest forms of political endeavour.

Herein lies the problem for Canada. Canada is not only a state that governs over at least two nations (which define themselves first and foremost along linguistic lines), it is also a state that governs a populace exposed daily to the culture of a foreign nation and state. Moreover, in English Canada at least, there is almost no likelihood that Canadian cultural products will ever constitute more than a minority share of the culture consumed by Canadians. Furthermore, cross-over cultural consumption between the two language groups is negligible; each group consumes far more foreign culture than its consumes of the other's. Like Sisyphus, Canadian cultural policy faces a dauntless and seemingly hopeless task.

But what if there are reasons to challenge the basic assumptions regarding the process of communication and the role of nationalism as a cultural and social force? What if the relationship between the production, distribution, and consumption of culture and the articulation of individual and social attitudes and values is more complex than that proposed by a linear, transportation model of communication? And what if the emphatic concern over nationalism and national culture is more politically and socially problematic than is commonly assumed?

It would seem to be the case that the nationalist project, in Canada as elsewhere, is principally concerned with counteracting the influences of foreign 'mass' or 'popular' culture rather than the influences of foreign 'high' culture.[29] High culture is almost never criticized for its cosmopolitan character; indeed, cosmopolitanism is one of the defining (and virtuous) characteristics of high culture. We could draw the following conclusion: for some people some forms of foreign culture are acceptable, even desirable; while for other people other forms of foreign culture are unacceptable and vulgar. The problem for most cultural nationalists isn't foreign culture per se, it is foreign 'popular' culture and the passivity with which audiences are presumed to consume it.

We can take issue with this perspective in two ways. First, recent media scholarship has come to general agreement around the following point: audiences do not passively receive media messages; rather, they 'negotiate' and interpret them in various ways. Audiences are active, and the meaning of any media text ultimately resides in the interaction between text and reader.[30] In other words, whatever happens in the process of mediated communication, it is rarely, if ever, as simple as 'message sent equals message received.' It is, for example, conceivable that Canadians who watch the incessantly violent world of American television drama may conclude that Canada is a good place to be. A common theme of Canadian identity – that Canada is a more peaceful and law-abiding country – may be positively reinforced by the experience of watching and interpreting American television. Likewise, some Canadians who watch nostalgic depictions of Canadian pioneer life in the nineteenth century may find themselves completely unable to identify with such romantic constructions of national identity. It is, quite frankly, not that easy to know for certain what goes on in the minds of audiences as they consume cultural products.

Relatedly, the over-bearing concern regarding 'popular' culture can lead to its outright rejection. The popular itself can come to be seen as a source of cultural contamination, in part because, by a viciously circular logic, anything popular is suspect of being too American. We have seen evidence of this line of reasoning in connection with Grierson and the Massey Report, to name only two. It is certainly evident in the extent to which the state documentary is 'valorized as the "essential Canadian form".'[31] In a recent reassessment of the nationalist premise of Canadian broadcasting, Richard Collins argues that the result of this cultural conservatism is a television aesthetic that values 'miserable and ageing accents.'[32] At the very least, it leads to endless and fruitless debates regarding what is and what is not Canadian and a hopeless search for that perfect blend of form and content that might elevate, enrich, and encode the Canadian mind.

In the face of massive inflows of foreign cultural products, a cultural policy based on nationalism is not without its appeal. Plainly, the marketplace is no guarantee of cultural pluralism, especially when it is driven by multinational corporations that enjoy all the advantages of oligopoly, and a market (the United States) that enjoys the advantages of scale. The history of Canadian feature films is proof enough of that. But in and of itself nationalism is a poor rationale for continued attempts to create alternatives to the market power of Hollywood. Nationalism can easily become chauvinistic, xenophobic, parochial, and élitist. Nationalism makes for good rhetoric; it does not necessarily make for good politics. We do not need public support of cultural production in Canada to express a national identity. We have to stop the search for some romantic and overarching common cultural bond. Instead, we need public support for cultural production to explore the manifold and contradictory ways in which we exist as social beings in our every day lives. Against all odds, the best of Canadian cinema has done just that. We need more of it. And to get it, we need the support of public policies that are based on the principle that, when all is said and done, filmmaking is more than a business. We still need something more than Canada's version of Hollywood.

Notes

Chapter 1

1 An Account of James Freer's tour can be found in Peter Morris, *Embattled Shadows: A History of the Canadian Cinema 1895–1939* (1978), 30–2. The Canadian Pacific Railway was also an early sponsor of films to promote immigration. It established its own production facilities in 1903 and held gala première of its films at the Palace Theatre, London. Would-be immigrants were offered an opaque view of the Canadian Prairies, however, as the CPR instructed its film crews 'not to take any winter scenes under any conditions' (34).

2 Morris, *Embattled Shadows*, 128; emphasis in original.

3 Sir George Foster, Minister of Trade and Commerce, Canada, Parliament, House of Commons, *Debates*, 20 May 1918, 2267

4 'Canada Top Booster: Hollywood,' *Canadian Film Weekly*, 16 July 1953, 1

5 See Canada, Film Industry Task Force, *Canadian Cinema: A Solid Base* (1985).

6 Canada, Federal Cultural Policy Review Committee, *Report* (November 1982), 6

7 Canada, Royal Commission on National Development in the Arts, Letters and Sciences, *Report* (1951), 18, 50

8 'Touchstone for the CBC,' as quoted in K. Nordenstreng and H. Schiller, eds, *National Sovereignty and International Communication* (1979), xi

9 Dallas Smythe, *Dependency Road: Communications, Capitalism, Consciousness, and Canada* (1981), ix, xii

10 John Meisel, 'Escaping Extinction: Cultural Defence of an Undefended Border,' in David Flaherty and William McKercher, eds, *Southern Exposure: Canadian Perspectives on the United States* (1986), 152–3

11 See, for example, D. Lerner, *The Passing of Traditional Society* (1958), and the discussion in J.O. Boyd-Barrett, 'Cultural Dependency and the Mass Media,' Michael Gurevitch et al., eds., *Culture, Society and the Media* (1982).

12 'Playboy Interview with Marshall McLuhan: A Candid Conversation with the High Priest of Popcult and Metaphysician of the Media,' *Canadian Journal of*

Communication 14 (Special Issue) (1989), 107 and 128. The interview with McLuhan appeared in *Playboy* (March 1969) and provides the clearest presentation of his views. Unlike modernization theorists, McLuhan's assessment of the emerging global village was mixed. He suggests that 'uniformity and tranquility are not hallmarks of the global village, far more likely are conflict and discord as well as love and harmony' (128). Unfortunately, McLuhan never considers the possibility that this new pattern of communication may be structured unequally between the nations and peoples of the globe.

13 Landmark versions of the media imperialism thesis include: Herbert Schiller, *Mass Communication and American Empire* (1969); Anthony Smith, *The Geopolitics of Information: How Western Culture Dominates the World* (1980); Jeremy Tunstall, *The Media Are American* (1977); Armand Mattlelart, *Multinational Corporations and the Control of Culture* (1979). See also the essays in K. Nordenstreng and H. Schiller, eds, *National Sovereignty and International Communication* (1979). For useful critical reviews of this literature, see: J.O. Boyd-Barrett, 'Media Imperialism: Towards an International Framework for the Analysis of Media System,' in J. Curran et al., eds, *Mass Communication and Society* (1977); J.O. Boyd-Barrett, 'Cultural Dependency and the Mass Media,' (1982); Chin Chuan-Lee, *Media Imperialism Revisited: The Homogenizing of Television Culture* (1980); and John Tomlinson, *Cultural Imperialism* (1991).

14 Boyd-Barrett, 'Media Imperialism: Towards an International Framework' (1977), 117

15 Anthony Smith, *The Geopolitics of Information: How Western Culture Dominates the World* (1980), 52

16 Roger de la Garde, 'Is There a Market for Foreign Cultures?' *Media, Culture & Society* 9, no. 2 (1987), 191–2. See for example: Ien Ang, *Watching Dallas* (1985); Janice Radway, *Reading the Romance: Feminism and the Representation of Women in Popular Culture* (1984); John Fiske, *Television Culture* (1987); and Ellen Seiter et al., eds., *Remote Control: Television, Audiences & Cultural Power* (1989).

17 Herbert Schiller, *Mass Communication and American Empire* (1969), *Communication and Cultural Domination* (1976)

18 See, for example, J.O. Boyd-Barrett, 'Cultural Dependency and the Mass Media,' in Michael Gurevitch et al., eds, *Culture, Society and the Media* (1982); Chin Chuan-Lee, *Media Imperialism Revisited: The Homogenizing of Television Culture* (1980); and John Tomlinson, *Cultural Imperialism* (1991).

19 For a perceptive discussion of these questions see Abraham Rotstein, 'The Use and Misuse of Economics in Cultural Policy,' in Rowland Lorimer and Donald Wilson, eds, *Communication Canada: Issues in Broadcasting and New Technologies* (1988).

20 It is impossible to adequately summarize here the breadth of inquiries into the nature of the capitalist-democratic state. For useful overviews, see Martin Carnoy, *The State and Political Theory* (1984) and Bob Jessop, *Theories of the State* (1983).

21 As quoted in Marc Raboy, *Missed Opportunities: The Story of Canada's Broadcasting Policy* (1990), 40.
22 Bernard Ostry, *The Cultural Connection* (1978), 2 4, 5
23 Ibid., 176
24 Ibid., 178, 181
25 Ibid., 188
26 Ibid., 175
27 Ibid., 3
28 *Dependency Road: Communications, Capitalism, Consciousness, and Canada* (1981), ix, xii. See also, Smythe, 'Communications: Blindspot of Western Marxism,' *Canadian Journal of Political and Social Theory* 1, no. 3 (1977).
29 Smythe, *Dependency Road*, ix, 91
30 Ibid., 290
31 See Graham Murdock, 'Blindspots About Western Marxism: A Reply to Dallas Smythe,' *Canadian Journal of Political and Social Theory* 2, no. 2 (1978).
32 Susan Crean, *Who's Afraid of Canadian Culture?* (1976). See also Crean and Marcel Rioux, *Two Nations* (1983).
33 Crean, *Who's Afraid*, 267–8
34 Implicitly or explicitly, the best studies of Canadian broadcasting have worked from this perspective. See Marc Raboy, *Missed Opportunities* (1990); Robert Babe, *Canadian Television Broadcasting Structure, Performance and Regulation* (1979); Frank Peers, *The Politics of Canadian Broadcasting, 1920–1951* (1969); *The Public Eye: Television and the Politics of Canadian Broadcasting 1952–68* (1979).

Chapter 2

1 There is no shortage of works that describe and analyse the institutionalization of the cinema as a cultural form. See for example, Garth Jowett, *Film: The Democratic Art* (1976), and Tino Balio, *The American Film Industry* (revised, 1985). *Film Reader* 4 (1980) and the *Journal of Film and Video* 37, no. 1 (1985) both contain a series of interesting articles on the history of film and the writing of film history. Michael Chanan's *The Dream That Kicks* (1980) offers a particularly rich discussion of how nineteenth-century forms of middle-class and working-class culture influenced the origins of British cinema.
2 See Garth Jowett, *Film: The Democratic Art* (1976), 120 and passim, and Malcolm Dean, *Censored! Only in Canada* (1981).
3 For an excellent overview and critique of mass society theory see Alan Swingewood, *The Myth of Mass Culture* (1977)
4 As quoted in *Canadian Moving Picture Digest* (hereinafter *CMPD*), 29 June 1918, 7
5 Peter Morris, *Embattled Shadows: A History of Canadian Cinema 1895–1939* (1978), 18–24; Floyd Chalmers, 'The Story of the Allens,' *Maclean's* (15 February 1920)

6 Morris, *Embattled Shadows*, 26
7 David Clandfield, *Canadian Film* (1987), 3. Pierre Berton's *Hollywood's Canada: The Americanization of Our National Image* (1975) is a well-documented, often amusing, if not tragic, chronicle of the 575 movies Hollywood made about Canada between 1907 and 1956. The first Mountie movie, *The Cattle Thieves* was released in 1909. By 1929, Hollywood had made at least 250 movies about Canada's master police force (112). In case Hollywood's screenwriters have confused you, the RCMP motto is not 'Get your man' but 'Maintain the right.' In an article written in 1941 on Hollywood's portrayal of Canada, C.W. Jeffreys noted: 'The dead hand of the Hollywood formula only too frequently strangled both originality of plot and the realistic truth of history.' According to Jeffreys, Cecil B. De Mille's *North West Mounted Police* was a 'piebald' film, a 'masterpiece of misinformation,' and 'lying sentimental trash.' See 'History in Motion Pictures,' *Canadian Historical Review* 22, no. 4 (December 1941), 363, 368.
8 Thomas Guback, *The International Film Industry* (1969), 9
9 Thomas Guback, 'Hollywood's International Market,' in Tino Balio, ed., *The American Film Industry* (1985 revised), 471
10 Janet Staiger and Douglas Gomery, 'The History of World Cinema: Models for Economic Analysis,' *Film Reader* 4 (1980), 36
11 Ibid., 41
12 Ibid., 39
13 Morris, *Embattled Shadows*, 238
14 Ibid., 239
15 Morris, *Embattled Shadows*, esp. ch. 3
16 Ibid., ch. 4
17 Ibid., 55
18 *CMPD*, 5 January 1918, 4
19 Allan Dwan, 'Canada Has a Movie Future: But Certain Restrictions Must Be Removed,' *Maclean's* (1 February 1920), 74
20 For a discussion of ASN's activities, see D. Clandfield, *Canadian Film*, 10–11; and Morris, *Embattled Shadows*, 222–32
21 Morris, *Embattled Shadows*, 232
22 Sir George Foster, Minister of Trade and Commerce, Canada, Parliament, House of Commons, *Debates*, 20 May 1918, 2267
23 See Morris, *Embattled Shadows*, 60.
24 Ibid., 130
25 On the activities of the Bureau see Morris, *Embattled Shadows*, 131–7, 159–74; and Charles Backhouse, *Canadian Government Motion Picture Bureau 1917–1941* (1974). The Ontario government started its own Motion Picture Bureau in 1917. According to its first director, S.C. Johnson, the Bureau was to carry out 'educational work for farmers, school children, factory workers, and other classes' (Morris, 138). Like its federal counterpart, the Bureau was in the information business not the entertainment business. Safety stock was used,

since the main target of the Bureau's work was non-theatrical venues and, like the federal Department of Agriculture, the bulk of the Bureau's early films were directed toward rural communities and focused on new agricultural techniques. When the Bureau began producing its own films in 1923 there was some hope that they would receive more widespread theatrical distribution, but a combination of poor decision making and technical inferiority left the Bureau moribund by the early 1930s (see Morris, ch. 5)

26 See Backhouse, *Canadian Government Motion Picture Bureau*, 11; and House of Commons, *Debates*, 16 March 1927, 1257.

27 'Seeing Canada' *CMPD*, 15 February 1919, 13

28 See Morris, *Embattled Shadows*, 135–49. Pathescope survived on the basis of films commissioned by the Ontario Bureau, but when that Bureau began producing its own films in 1923, the company's fortunes declined precipitously.

29 Backhouse, *Canadian Government Motion Picture Bureau*, 7

30 House of Commons, *Debates*, 19 May 1924, 2294

31 Ibid., 5 June 1928, 3752–23; 16 March 1927, 1257

32 The macro-economic strategy of the federal government after the First World War involved the attraction of large-scale direct foreign investment in resource-extraction and manufacturing, the consolidation of those sectors where Canadian capital had established a foothold, and a general curtailment of labour strife. For discussions of this period see Tom Traves, *The State and Enterprise* (1979); and Glen Williams, *Not for Export* (1986).

33 To be sure, the pro-Empire and pro-Canadian sentiment exhibited in these films would have satisfied many an English-Canadian audience; however, it is not altogether clear how the newly arrived immigrant population and, perhaps more important, French Canadians reacted to the themes and values displayed.

The federal government was not the only institution that had seized upon the value of films as a propaganda technique. At the height of the 'red scare,' the Canadian Reconstruction Association sponsored *The Great Shadow*, a film about the infiltration of labour organizations by Bolshevik zealots. Several companies in Toronto were so impressed by the film's message that they handed out free tickets to their employees (Morris, *Embattled Shadows*, 67–9).

34 In Morris, *Embattled Shadows*, 163

35 Ray Peck to Capt H.V.S. Page, 3 March 1926, in Ontario Archives, RG 56, A.1, Box 1, British Films, 1926–1932 (emphasis added)

36 Williams, *Not for Export*, 80; and see, chap. 5.

37 See Morris, *Embattled Shadows*, 182–95.

38 See Robert Brady, 'The Problem of Monopoly,' *Annals of the American Academy of Political and Social Science* 254, (1947).

39 'Government Will Impose Reel Tax on Canadian Exhibitors.' *CMPD*, 11 May 1918, 6. Independent exhibitors formed a number of umbrella organizations during this period. The Motion Picture Exhibitors' Protection Association was formed in 1918. In 1926, the Motion Picture Theatre Owners' Association was established and affiliated with its American counterpart.

40 Thomas Scott, in *CMPD*, 24 August 1918, 30
41 See Kirwan Cox, 'Hollywood's Empire in Canada,' in Pierre Véronneau and Piers Handling, eds, *Self Portrait* (1980), 13.
42 See Ontario, Department of Labour, Investigation into an Alleged Combined in the Motion Picture Industry in Canada, *Report* (1931) (hereinafter White Report), ch. 4.
43 Ibid., ch. 4
44 Ibid., 74, 77
45 Ibid., 43
46 Ibid., 47
47 *CMPD*, 26 December 1926.
48 White Report, 180
49 Ibid., 105
50 Ibid., 12–28
51 In Cox, 'Hollywood's Empire in Canada,' 14
52 As quoted in White Report, 28
53 Ibid., 30
54 Ibid., 163
55 Ibid., 180
56 See Jowett, *Film: The Democratic Art*, ch. 10 and 465–72; Edward De Grazia and Roger Newman, *Banned Films: Movies, Censors and the First Admendment* (1982). For a useful discussion of film censorship in Canada see Malcolm Dean, *Censored! Only in Canada* (1981).
57 White Report, 212. Minutes from another MPDEC meeting conclude: 'Our relation with the Social Service Council of Ontario, the National Council of Women and other similar organizations have improved to such an extent that they believe that censorship in Canada has gone to extremes, so far as the motion picture is concerned. They are not quite prepared to vote censorship out of existence altogether, but they are almost ready to accept some compromises with the present system' (168).
58 White Report, ch. 13
59 See Col Cooper to Monteith, 13 June 1928, Ontario Archives, RG 56, A.1 Box, 2.
60 Lucien Cannon, House of Commons, *Debates*, 6 March 1919, 267
61 See Malcolm Dean, *Censored!*, ch. 2, especially 19–26.
62 Quoted in Morris, *Embattled Shadows*, 177
63 Simon Hartog, 'State Protection of a Beleaguered Industry,' in James Curran and Vincent Porter, eds, *British Cinema History* (1983), 59–73
64 Carl Berger, *The Sense of Power* (1970). As Sir George Foster explained: 'There has arisen, first in a dim sort of way but gradually gaining clearness and strength, the sense of power to be exercised within the Empire, of responsibilities to imperial duties, of attachments to imperial ideals, and of co-operation in the achievement of imperial destinies' (259–60). The imperialist objective, as Berger demonstrates, took on a rather precise objective: 'closer union of the

British Empire through economic and military co-operation and through political changes which would give the dominions influence over imperial policy' (3). It was an English-Canadian vision of grandeur, as antithetical to the various cultural and political projects of French Canada as it was to pressures for integration that emanated from the United States.

65 Dorothy Brown, 'The Unknown Movies,' *Queen's Quarterly* 36, (Summer 1929), 491. Brown appears to offer a contradiction to her own argument by pointing out that in Europe Chaplin was rightfully regarded as an 'artist' and not a 'low-brow' comic.

66 See White Report, ch. 8, 158–61, and for examples: George Mott, 'Criticizing the Movies,' *Canadian Bookman*, October 1928; Valance Patriarche, 'Canada's Movie Intelligence,' *Willison's Monthly*, July 1928; Ann Anderson-Perry, 'The Hollywood Menace,' *Chatelaine*, September 1931.

67 James Cowan, 'The Battle for Canadian Film Control,' *Maclean's* (15 October 1930), 48

68 In Morris, *Embattled Shadows*, 179

69 *CMPD*, 26 December 1925, 7

70 White Report, 156

71 See Cox, 'Hollywood's Empire in Canada,' 29 and passim, for discussion of the issues surrounding the introduction of quota legislation.

72 Cooper to Price, 17 March 1926, Ontario Archives, RG 56, A.1, Box 1, British Films

73 Cooper to Monteith, 1 October 1927, in Cox, 'Hollywood's Empire,' 29

74 John Boylen to Monteith, 11 February 1928, Ontario Archives, RG 56, A.1, Box 1, British Films

75 J.W. Stone to Monteith, 3 February 1928, Ontario Archives, RG 56, A.1, Box 1, British Films

76 Charles Roos to Monteith, 10 February 1928, Ontario Archives, RG 56, A.1, Box 1, British Films

77 Frederick Revell to E.A. Dunlop, June–July 1931, Ontario Archives, RG 56, A.1, Box 1, British Films

78 Cooper to Monteith, 4 February 1928, Ontario Archives, RG 56, A.1 Box 1, British Films

79 See White Report, 159–60; and Cox, 'Hollywood's Empire in Canada,' 31–2

80 White Report, 158

81 Ontario Archives, RG 3, 188/425, Orders-in-Council, 31 March 1931

82 *CMPD*, 4 April 1931, 4

83 *CMPD*, 4 July 1931, 8

84 Resolution passed at 27 June 1932 meeting of Allied Exhibitors of Ontario, Ontario Archives, RG 56, Series A.1, Box 5.4, Petitions, 1932–3

85 J.L. Murray to E.A. Dunlop, 26 March 1931, Ontario Archives, RG 56, A.1, Box 1, British Films

86 *CMPD*, 2 May 1930, 1

87 House of Commons, *Debates*, 19 May 1930, 2215
88 Ibid., 2216
89 Lloyd Reynolds, *The Control of Competition in Canada* (1940), xiii
90 Ibid., 131
91 See Tom Traves, *The State and Enterprise*, 82.
92 White Report, 230
93 Ibid., 232
94 Ibid., 106
95 Ibid., 106
96 'Open Letter to Bennett,' *CMPD*, 11 July 1931, 1. Ray Lewis came to have a financial stake in the exhibition of British pictures in Canada when, in October 1931, she became one of the major players in a deal to import the films of British International Pictures (see *CMPD*, 10 October 1931). The month before, Lewis ran full-page ads exhorting Canadian exhibitors to pledge at least 25 per cent screen time to British films. Curiously, Lewis became an unfriendly witness during the prosecution that resulted from the White Report.
97 'Ray presents,' *CMPD* (11 July 1931), 1.
98 *Mail and Empire*, 2 July 1931; see also, *Winnipeg Free Press*, 8 July 1931.
99 *Saturday Night* (18 July 1931), 1. Oddly, what most incensed *Saturday Night* was not so much the effect the combine had on the nature of the film industry in Canada as the fact that touring theatre companies were finding it increasingly difficult to rent or be given space in which to perform. Reflecting the élitist bias of so many of Canada's cultural critics, *Saturday Night* recommended that the provincial governments forgo prosecution and try to force Famous Players and its affiliates to provide access for live theatre companies. Like many Canadians, *Saturday Night* was not yet ready to evaluate the film industry and the plight of Canadian film production on their own terms. Its primary cultural concerns still focused on the traditional arts.
100 In Cox, 'Hollywood's Empire Canada,' 33
101 *CMPD* (25 July 1931), 1
102 Ibid.
103 'Canada to Have Film Independence,' *CMPD* (1 August 1931)
104 See 'Rex vs. Famous Players,' *Ontario Reports* 307, (1932), 343.
105 In Morris, *Embattled Shadows*, 57
106 Mae Huettig, 'Economic Control of the Motion Picture Industry,' in T. Balio, *The American Film Industry*, (1985) 285 (first published 1944)
107 See Frank Peers, *The Politics of Canadian Broadcasting 1920–1951* (1969), ch. 3.
108 House of Commons, *Debates*, 18 May 1932, 3035

Chapter 3

1 John Grierson, 'A Film Policy for Canada,' reprinted in Douglas Fetherling, ed.,

Documents in Canadian Film (1988), 55–56. (first published in *Canadian Affairs* 1, no. 11 (15 June 1944))

2 Ibid., 66
3 Ibid., 55
4 On the demise of the Canadian Government Motion Picture Bureau see Charles Backhouse, *The Canadian Government Motion Picture Bureau: 1917–1941* (1974), Peter Morris, *Embattled Shadows* (1978), especially 159–74.
5 McLean, as quoted in Gary Evans, *John Grierson and the National Film Board: The Politics of Wartime Propaganda* (1984), 52. For useful overviews of the NFB see also Marjorie McKay, 'History of the National Film Board of Canada,' unpublished manuscript NFB (1964) and D.B. Jones, *Movies and Memoranda* (1981).
6 Grierson had also become an adviser to the British government's Imperial Relations Trust. The Trust was working to strengthen relations between Britain and the Dominions in the likely event of war with Germany. Grierson had been asked by his British associates to prepare reports on film production in Australia, New Zealand, and Canada, with the intention of encouraging film centres in these countries to help the war effort. Given the importance of arousing support in the United States and the difficulties British films had in entering its market, a film centre in Canada with access to the U.S. market could prove particularly valuable.
7 Backhouse, *Canadian Government Motion Picture Bureau*, 26
8 Ibid., 27
9 Canada, Parliament, House of Commons, *Debates*, 7 March 1939, 1661–2. The major objections to the Act were voiced by Conservative members. J. Earl Lawson, who was to become president of Odeon, was particularly insistent that the Board would be a waste of money, and that the government would be better off contracting its films from private producers. See *Debates*, 7 March 1933, 1666.
10 Ibid., 7 March 1939, 1665
11 Ibid., 13 March, 1939, 1842
12 National Film Act, 1939, Section 9 (a)
13 See Piers Handling, 'The National Film Board in Canada: 1939–1959,' in P. Véronneau and P. Handling, eds, *Self Portrait* (1980), 44.
14 Evans, *John Grierson*, 3–4
15 Grierson, in Forsythe Hardy, ed., *Grierson on Documentary* (1946) 12; and Grierson, in Evans, *John Grierson*, 94
16 Grierson, in Hardy, *Grierson on Documentary*, 127, 140
17 Ibid., 219
18 Ronald Blumer, 'John Grierson: I Derive My Authority from Moses,' *Take One* 2, no. 9 (1970), 17
19 Grierson, in Hardy, *Grierson*, 157, 208, 244
20 Ibid., 205
21 Ibid., 126

22 Ibid., 127, 209; emphasis in original
23 Grierson, in Evans, *John Grierson*, 36
24 Grierson, in Stuart Hood, 'John Grierson and the Documentary Film Movement,' in James Curran and Vincent Porter, eds, *British Cinema History* (1983),
   104
25 Grierson, in Hardy, *Grierson*, 209–10
26 Grierson, in Rodrigue Chiasson, 'The CRTC Tapes,' *John Grierson and the
   NFB* (1984), 47
27 Grierson, in Hardy, *Grierson*, 105, 126
28 Grierson, in Peter Morris, *The National Film Board of Canada: The War Years*
   (1965), 5
29 'A Film Policy for Canada,' 55, 53
30 For two recent critical reappraisals of the Grierson legacy see Peter Morris, 'Rethinking Grierson: The Ideology of John Grierson,' in P. Véronneau et al., eds,
   Dialogue (1987); and Joyce Nelson, *The Colonized Eye: Rethinking the
   Grierson Legend* (1988).
31 Grierson, in P. Handling, 'The National Film Board of Canada 1939–1959,' in
   P. Véronneau and P. Handling eds, *Self Portrait* (1980), 44
32 Evans, *John Grierson*, 59
33 See ibid., 63; and "The End of a Perfect Set-up," *Canadian Moving Picture
   Digest*, 15 December 1945.
34 Evans, *John Grierson*, 71–6
35 Ibid., 76
36 Reg Whitaker, *The Government Party: Organizing and Financing the Liberal
   Party of Canada 1930–58* (1977)
37 For useful overviews of NFB wartime productions see Evans, *John Grierson*,
   especially chs 4 and 7; Jones, *Movies and Memoranda*, ch. 3; and Seth Feldman
   and J. Nelson, eds, *Canadian Film Reader* (1977), part II.
38 Evans, *John Grierson*, 169
39 Ibid., 224–5
40 C.W. Gray, *Movies for the People: The Story of the National Film Board of
   Canada's Unique Distribution System* (1973), 14. Gray provides an excellent
   summary of the Board's non-theatrical distribution network. See also Evans,
   John Grierson, ch. 5; Graham McInnes, 'Canada: Producer of Films,' *Queen's
   Quarterly* (Summer 1945); Len Chatwin, 'Canadians Cooperate to Show Films,'
   Canadian Film News (February 1950).
41 Gray, *Movies for the People*, 27; and Yvette Hackett, 'The National Film
   Society of Canada, 1935–51: Its Origins and Development,' in Gene Walz, ed.,
   Flashback: People and Institutions in Canadian Film History (1986)
42 Evans, *John Grierson*, 162
43 Gray, *Movies for the People*, 50–3
44 Ibid., 50
45 Evans, *John Grierson*, ch. 7
46 Grierson, 'Film Policy for Canada,' 58, 59, 62

47 See P. Morris, 'Backwards to the Future: John Grierson's Film Policy for
   Canada,' in G. Walz, ed., *Flashback* (1986), 25; and John Grierson, 'Relations
   with the United States Film Industry,' 31 October 1944, a confidential memorandum appended for the Minutes of the National Film Board, 28 December
   1944, reprinted in *Canadian Journal of Film Studies*, 1 no. 1 (1990)
48 See Evans, *John Grierson*, 200–15
49 Turnbull, in Ibid., 231
50 See Kirwan Cox, 'The Grierson Files,' *Cinema Canada*, no. 56 (June/July
   1979), 17.
51 House of Commons, *Debates*, 30 March 1944, 2017. For a useful overview of
   the political controversies that have surrounded the NFB see, Piers Handling,
   'Censorship and Scares,' *Cinema Canada*, no. 56 (June/July 1979).
52 See Evans, *John Grierson*, ch. 7. For an excellent discussion of the cold war in
   Canada and the Canadian government's internal security system, including a
   discussion of Grierson and the NFB, see Reg Whitaker 'Origins of the Canadian
   Government's Internal Security System, 1946–52,' *Canadian Historical Review*
   65, no. 2 (1984).
53 'How About a Victory Dinner?,' *Canadian Film Weekly* (2 January 1946). The
   banquet was held at the Beverly Hills Hotel on 17 December 1945. A number
   of Canadian film industry personnel were upset that a similar banquet was not
   held in Canada.

Chapter 4

1 Canada, Royal Commission on National Development in the Arts, Letters and
  Sciences, *Report* (1951), 50 (hereinafter Massey Report).
2 Harold Innis, 'Great Britain, the United States, and Canada,' *Essays in Canadian Economic History* (1956), 405
3 Ibid., 404
4 See Kirwan Cox, 'Hollywood's Empire in Canada,' in P. Véronneau and P.
  Handling, eds, *Self Portrait* (1980), 16–18; and Manjunath Pendakur, *Canadian
  Dreams and American Control: The Political Economy of the Canadian Film
  Industry* (1990), 95–101.
5 The split was described in 1976 by George Destounis, former president of
  Famous Players. See Cox, 'Hollywood's Empire in Canada,' 18; and Pendakur,
  Canadian Dreams, 99–101.
6 *Variety*, 10 April 1946.
7 See Pendakur, *Canadian Dreams*, 100–5. The *Canadian Moving Picture Digest*
  (hereinafter *CMPD*) had become a strong ally of the major chains and distributors. After the war, Ray Lewis, wrote: 'If we enjoy Dictatorship and Government control of our business, the best way to get it is to run to the Government
  for help every time we are faced with a problem, real or imaginary ... When
  this industry becomes so dumb, that those who trade with each other cannot
  solve their own trade problems, that will be the Evening of the Eclipse of Self-

Control and the Dawn of Dictatorship' ('Self-Control or Dictatorship,' *CMPD* (12 October 1946), 1).

8 See Pendakur, *Canadian Dreams*, 105–8.

9 On the Quebec film industry see P. Véronneau, 'The First Wave of Quebec Feature Films: 1939–59,' in P. Véronneau and P. Handling, *Self Portrait* (1980); P. Véronneau, ed., *Cinéma de l'époque duplessiste* (1979); and P. Véronneau, ed., *Le Succès est au film parlant français* (1979)

10 Véronneau, 'The First Wave of Quebec Feature Films,' 56

11 Thomas Guback, 'Theatrical Film,' in B. Compaine, ed., *Who Owns the Media?* (1979), 203. See also, Ernest Borneman, 'United States versus Hollywood: The Case Study of an Antitrust Suit,' in T. Balio, ed., *The American Film Industry* (1985, revised edition); and Michael Conant, 'The Paramount Decrees Reconsidered,' ibid.

12 As Guback notes: 'A motion picture is a commodity one can duplicate indefinitely without substantially adding to the cost of the first unit produced ... The economic and technological nature of a film compels the manufacturer and his agent, the distributor, to try to achieve the widest possible circulation for it. Extra prints represent little further investment, and it is in their interest to make many, distribute them widely, and attempt to recoup their total costs as quickly as possible' *The International Film Industry* (1969), 7–8. For an excellent, brief discussion of the industry's macro-economic structure see, Nicholas Garnham, 'The Economics of the U.S. Motion Picture Industry,' *Capitalism and Communication: Global Culture and the Economics of Information* (1990).

13 Herbert Schiller, 'Genesis of the Free Flow of Information Principles,' in A. Mattelart and S. Siegelaub, eds, *Communication and Class Struggle, Vol. 1: Capitalism, Imperialism* (1979), 347

14 'Johnston Report Sees Progress,' *Canadian Film Weekly* (hereinafter *CFW*), 3 April 1946

15 Eric Johnston, 'The Motion Picture as a Stimulus to Culture,' *Annals of the American Academy of Political and Social Science*, 254, (Nov. 1947), 102, 98. In a speech to independent U.S. exhibitors in 1946, Johnston remarked: 'In our hands, gentlemen, is the mightiest instrument for good so far devised by man. In our hands, is a new torch to enlighten the world ... Yes, you are the industry, an industry with a dream and a vision. It is a vision of education for democracy; of reviving democracy where it is dying, where it gasps for breath, where it is chained and fettered to the clammy walls of other concepts which ignore the rights and privileges of man. But to fulfil the dream and the vision, there is one indispensable condition for the motion picture. The screen must be free ... It must never be the plaything of politics or the tool of specious propaganda' 'Agreement – Not Compulsion,' *CFW* (25 December 1946), 34.

16 For a discussion of various attempts to establish domestic film industries through state intervention, see T. Guback, *The International Film Industry*, esp. chs 2 and 8.

17 The following discussion borrows heavily from Margaret Dickinson, 'The State

and the Consolidation of Monopoly,' in James Curran and V. Porter, eds, *British Cinema History* (1983).

18 House of Commons, *Debates*, 11 July 1946, 3362

19 'NFB Needs Curbs,' *Financial Post*, December 26, 1946

20 See the discussion in Piers Handling, 'Censorship and Scares,' *Cinema Canada*, no. 56 (June/July 1979), 28; and Gary Evans, *John Grierson and the National Film Board* (1984), 259.

21 'Canadian Producers Organize,' *CFW*, (5 June 1946)

22 As quoted in Harry Plummer, 'Have Canadian Films a Future?', *Canadian Business* (March 1947), 25

23 For a useful overview of Canada's postwar economic policies, see David Wolfe, 'The Rise and Demise of the Keynesian Era in Canada: Economic Policy, 1930–82,' Michael Cross and Gregory Kealy, eds, *Modern Canada* (1984).

24 'Little Change Seen in Canadian Film Tax,' *CFW* (17 September 1947), 1

25 Canada, Parliament, House of Commons, *Debates*, 28 May 1936, 3157

26 Ibid. 22 May 1941, 3069–82; and 15 July 1942, 4274–5

27 Ibid. 15 June 1941, 3563; and 6 December 1940, 739

28 'Keep More Rental $$ Here,' *CFW* (26 November 1947), 1

29 'Distribs Go Along with Ottawa,' *CFW* (3 December 1947), 1

30 McLean to McCann, 1 December 1947, Public Archives of Canada (hereinafter PAC), Canadian Co-operation Project, RG 20 vol. 575, File A338, 1

31 Ibid., 2 (emphasis in original)

32 Ibid., 3

33 E. Johnston to J.J. Fitzgibbons, 21 January 1948, in Maynard Collins, 'Cooperation, Hollywood and Howe,' *Cinema Canada*, no. 56 (June/July 1979), 35

34 'Industry-Gov't Said in Agreement,' *CFW* (28 January 1948), 1

35 'Rogell Will Shoot in Alberta,' *CFW* (4 February 1948). Rogell announced plans to produce two colour films, *Shadow of Time* and *Hiawatha*, for a total of $2.5 million.

36 House of Commons, *Debates*, 12 February 1948, 1163

37 Ibid., 20 February 1948, 1476, 1481

38 Ibid., 23 February 1948, 1494

39 Ibid., 23 February 1948, 1507

40 See J.J. Fitzgibbons to Spyros Skouras (president, 20th Century–Fox), 4 March 1948, PAC, Canadian Co-operation Project, vol. 575, File A338, 2.

41 McLean to Harmon, 31 May 1948, PAC, ibid., vol. 575, File A338, 1.

42 Ibid., 1

43 Gordon to M. MacKenzie (deputy minister Department of Trade and Commerce), 19 June 1948, PAC, ibid., vol. 575, File A338

44 Gordon to Howe, 24 June 1948, PAC, ibid., vol. 575, File A338, 2

45 Ibid., 3

46 'Donald Gordon Stresses FI Cooperation,' *CMPD* (26 June 1948), 8

47 See David Wolfe, 'Economic Growth and Foreign Investment: A Perspective on Canadian Economic Policy,' *Journal of Canadian Studies* 13, no. 1, (1978), 8.

48 For an entertaining and thorough review of the films made under the Canadian Co-operation Project, see P. Berton, *Hollywood's Canada* (1975), part 4.
49 Collins, 'Cooperation, Hollywood and Howe,' 36
50 Cox, 'Hollywood's Empire,' 24–6
51 'Quota Talk Bunk, says Ottawa,' *CFW* (2 February 1949), 1
52 Cox, 'Hollywood's Empire,' 26
53 '10% USA Foreign Rev from Canada,' *CFW* (1 July 1953), 1
54 'Canada Now a Ten Per Cent Territory,' *CFW* (16 July 1953), 7
55 See J.W. Pickersgill, *My Years with Louis St. Laurent* (1975), 139.
56 The other members of the commission were: Dr. N.A. Mackenzie, president of the University of British Columbia; Dr. Hilda Neatby, professor of history at the University of Saskatchewan, and Dr. Arthur Surveyor, a civil engineer from Montreal.
57 Massey Report, xvii
58 Ibid., xvii
59 Vincent Massey, *What's Past Is Prologue* (1963), 450
60 'Industry Brief for Royal Commission,' *CFW* (9 November 1949), 1; see also 26 October 1949; 11 May 1949.
61 Robert Winters to Prime Minister St. Laurent, 26 August 1949, PAC MG 26L, vol. 122, File: M75-1, 1949. See Whitaker, 'Origins of the Canadian Government Internal Security System,' *Canadian Historical Review* 65, no. 2, 171–3.
62 'Brief to the Royal Commission,' PAC, Massey Report, RG 33/28, vol. 23, no. 291, 2
63 Ibid., 67–9
64 Ibid., 65
65 'Minutes of Proceedings and Evidence,' PAC, Massey Report, vol. 23, no, 291 741
66 See 'Canadians Cooperate to Show Films,' *Canadian Film News* (February 1950) and 'Film Services in Canada,' *Food for Thought* (November 1950).
67 'Film Services in Canada,' *Food For Thought* (November 1950), 26
68 See 'Editorial,' *Canadian Film News* (February 1950), 3.
69 V. Massey, *On Being Canadian* (1948), 53. Massey's 1948 work bears a striking resemblance in structure and argument to the final report of the Royal Commission. 'No state today can escape some responsibility in the field to which belong the things of the mind,' Massey wrote (47)
70 Ibid., 52
71 'Submission of the AMPPLC,' PAC, Massey Report, vol. 3, no. 36A, 2
72 'Minutes of Proceedings and Evidence,' PAC, Ibid., vol. 3, no. 36A, 893
73 'Submission of the AMPPLC,' 19
74 'Supplement to Brief of AMPPLC: Feature Film Production,' ibid. After the losses incurred in the twenties, the Canadian financial community had steered clear of film ventures. When the government established the International Development Bank to provide the private sector with high-risk loans, film productions were excluded because the IDB had not been convinced that they had

'a reasonable prospect of earning power.' See 'No IDB Money in Dominion Production,' *CFW* (2 February 1949).

75 'Minutes of Proceedings,' PAC Massey Report, vol. 3, no. 36A, 905
76 K. Wilson and C. Bassett, 'Film Board Monopoly Facing Major Test?', *Financial Post* (19 November 1949), 17
77 House of Commons, *Debates*, 18 November 1949, 1976
78 See Maynard Collins, 'A View From the Top: Interview with Arthur Irwin,' *Cinema Canada*, no. 56 (June/July 1979).
79 House of Commons, *Debates*, 7 December 1949, 2850–4
80 See Collins, 'A View from the Top,' 38.
81 Robert Winters sent a letter to Massey on 5 April 1950 in which he distanced himself from the Woods Gordon Report by stating that he felt the Board's most important role was in distribution not production. See PAC, Massey Report, vol. 23, no. 291
82 Evans, *John Grierson*, 264
83 'Commons Committee Praises NFB,' *CFW* (9 July 1952), 1
84 See Gary Evans, *In the National Interest: A Chronicle of the National Film Board of Canada from 1949 to 1989* (1991), 23.
85 Massey Report, 4–5, 274. Art in the service of anti-communism was a theme close to the heart of Georges-Henri Lévesque. See 'The Answer to Communism,' *Food for Thought* (November 1950).
86 Ibid., 272
87 Ibid., 11
88 Ibid., 272
89 Ibid., 18
90 Ibid., 272
91 Ibid., 18
92 Ibid., 7
93 Ibid., 59
94 Ibid., 368
95 See Donald Buchanan, 'Documentary and Educational Films in Canada, 1935–50,' PAC, Massey Report, vol. 53
96 Massey Report, 50
97 Ibid., 58
98 Ibid.
99 'Canada Top Booster: Hollywood,' *CFW* (6 May 1953), 9
100 Leo Panitch, 'The Role and Nature of the Canadian State,' in Panitch, ed., *The Canadian State: Political Economy and Political Power* (1977), 18

Chapter 5

1 Nat Taylor, 'Our Business: The Feature Film Gamble,' *Canadian Film Weekly* (hereinafter *CFW*), (10 February, 1960), 3
2 See Stephen Clarkson, *Canada and the Reagan Challenge* (1982). On the rise

of nationalism in Canada in the 1960s see Philip Resnick, *The Land of Cain: Class and Nationalism in English Canada 1945–1975* (1977); and Janine Brodie and Jane Jenson, *Crisis, Challenge and Change: Party and Class in Canada* (1980), esp. 280–6.

3 William Coleman, *The Independence Movement in Quebec 1945–80* (1984)

4 For a useful review of the Canadian Film Awards, see Maria Topalovich, *The Canadian Film Awards: A Pictorial History* (1984)

5 'Canada Now Number 1 in U.S.A. $ Return.' 'CCP Assures Full Film, Money Flow,' *CFW* (2 May 1956), 1

6 Thomas Guback, *The International Film Industry* (1969), 170, 171

7 For a discussion of changes in the American film industry during this period see T. Balio, ed., *The American Film Industry* (1985), part IV, esp. 401–47.

8 See UNESCO, *Statistics on Film and Cinema: 1955–1977* (1981), Table 1. The UNESCO study points out that the trend toward decentralized production did not mean an end to the dominance of American firms in the global film trade. It states: 'But whatever the exact figures may be, it is not the number of films produced which makes the American film industry the most important and influential in the world ... [I]t is the U.S. which in almost any country has the lion's share of the number of films released' (9).

  In 1963, films produced in the United States (not those distributed by American companies) accounted for only 38.5 per cent of the total number of films that entered Ontario, as opposed to over 75 per cent a decade earlier. Films from Britain, Germany, Greece, and France made up a large portion of the rest. Figures do not of course reflect screen time or revenues but do suggest that production had become far more decentralized by the early 1960s. See 'U.S.A. Films Only 38.5 per cent of Ontario Total,' *CFW* (8 May 1963).

  Thomas Guback has shown how decentralized production itself did not necessarily diminish the American presence and American control of the films made. See, in particular, *The International Film Industry* (1969), chap. 9; and 'Film and Cultural Pluralism,' *Journal of Aesthetic Education* 5, no. 2 (1971).

9 Topalovich, *Canadian Film Awards*, 14

10 'CBC Story Re Film Industry,' *CFW* (9 November 1955), 3

11 See 'Our Business,' *CFW* (11 January 1956); and Hugh MacLennan, 'The Case for a Real Canadian Film,' *Saturday Night* (6 August 1955).

12 'Motion Picture Production in Canada,' *Canadian Forum* 36, no. 434 (March 1957)

13 See 'Chetwynd Views Production Future,' *CFW* (9 July 1958), 1; and Dean Walker, 'Film Industry Keeps Alive on TV Earnings,' *Canadian Business* (February 1958).

14 'To Shoot $1,500,000 TV Series Here,' *CFW* (11 July 1956), 1. See also, 'Big Surge in Canada TV Production,' *CFW* (27 March 1957), 1; 'TV Series Give Boost to Canada's Filmmakers,' *Saturday Night* (7 December 1957).

15 'CBC Big Brother to Our Filmmakers,' *CFW* (16 March 1960), 1

16 Dean Walker, 'Film Industry Keeps Alive on TV Earnings,' *Canadian Business* (February 1958), 112

17 'Busiest Year at Crawley,' *CFW* (2 April 1958), 1, 3

18 'Crawley Setting Production Pace,' *CFW* (11 January 1961), 1

19 'Can't See Canada Feature Industry,' *CFW* (11 June 1958), 1, 2

20 'Seven Feature Films Made in Canada,' *CFW* (24 July 1963). Crawley Films ventured back into feature films in 1972 with *The Rowdyman*. In 1975, Crawley's *The Man Who Skied Down Everest* won an Oscar for best feature-length documentary.

21 'Title: Films That Pass in the Night,' *CFW* (29 January 1964), 1

22 Crawley to *Financial Post* as quoted in *CFW* (9 October 1963), 3

23 For a brief outline of Nat Taylor's business career see 'Nat Taylor: The Mogul behind the Mogul,' *Report on Business Magazine* (December 1985), 45.

24 See 'Taylor-Roffman, Others in Production,' and 'Toronto International and Meridian Join Forces,' *CFW* (1 June 1960), 1, 19.

25 'Film Trade TV Holdings Growing in Numbers,' *CFW* (20 July 1960). Paul L'Anglais, J.A. DeSève, Paul Nathanson, and Famous Players had also become major shareholders in private television stations. See also 'L'Anglais Group Montreal French Winner,' *CFW* (30 March 1961); and Frank Peers, *The Public Eye: Television and the Politics of Canadian Broadcasting 1952–1968* (1979), 11, 13, and 43–4 especially for a discussion of Famous Players' involvement in private broadcasting.

26 'Taylor-Roffman, Others in Production,' *CFW* (1 June 1960)

27 'The Mask Bows in on Broadway,' *CFW* (8 November 1961), 1, 7

28 Other notable early efforts by English-Canadian producers eager to tap the American market include: *The Bloody Brood* (1958), produced and directed by Julian Roffman, with Yvonne Taylor (Nat Taylor's wife) as executive producer; *Devil's Spawn* (1959, the title was later changed to *Hired Gun*), produced by Lindsey Shonteff. Other efforts included: *A Cool Sound from Hell, Ivy League Killers, A Dangerous Age*. See 'Rundown on Canadian-Made Films,' *CFW* (1 March 1961); and 'Meridian Preps 1st Feature,' *CFW* (17 September 1958), 1.

29 'Seven Arts to Back 10 Feature Films,' *CFW* (18 July 1962); and 'Growth Great for 7 Arts,' *CFW* (25 July 1962). Seven Arts signed a 20-picture deal with MGM in 1962.

30 Ibid.; and 'Still Talking about Feature Production,' *CFW* (16 January 1963).

31 'NFB's Montreal Headquarters: Film Maker's Dream,' *CFW* (10 October 1956). For a general discussion of Film Board activities in the 1950s and early 1960s, see G. Evans, *In the National Interest* (1991), chs 2–5. See also Marjorie McKay, 'History of the National Film Board' (1964); and D.B. Jones, *Movies and Memoranda* (1981), esp. chs 5–8.

32 See especially Bruce Elder, 'On the Candid-Eye Movement'; Peter Harcourt, 'The Innocent Eye: An Aspect of the Work of the National Film Board of Canada'; and Derek Elley, 'Rhythm 'n' Truth: Norman McLaren,' in S. Feldman and J. Nelson, eds, *Canadian Film Reader* (1977); David Clandfield,

'From the Picturesque to the Familiar: Films of the French Unit at the NFB (1958–64),' in S. Feldman, ed., *Take Two* (1984); and Gary Evans, *In the National Interest*, ch. 4.

33 See Marjorie McKay, 'History of the NFB'; and especially parts one and two of the five-part series by Robert Boissonnault, 'Les Cinéastes québécois et l'Office national du film: une immersion totale dans un milieu anglophone (1945–55),' *cinéma québec* 2, no. 2, (October 1972), and 'Les Cinéastes québécois et l'Office national du Film: la séquence du film pour la télévision,' 2, no. 3, (November 1972).

34 In Boissonnault, 'Les Cinéastes québécois et l'Office national du film: une immersion totale dans un milieu anglophone (1945–55),' *cinéma québec* 2, no. 2, 20

35 Ibid., 21

36 For an excellent review of the press attacks see the dossier prepared by P. Véronneau, *L'Office national du film: l'enfant martyr* (1979).

37 *Le Devoir* (26 February 1957), in ibid

38 Boissonnault, 'Les Cinéastes québécois et l'Office national du film: la séquence du film pour la télévision,' *cinéma québec* 2, no. 3, 17–18

39 For a discussion of the cinéma direct movement and its influence on filmmakers at the Board, see the sources listed in fn. 32.

40 Clandfield, 'From the Picturesque to the Familiar,' 113

41 Also, Michel Euvrard and P. Véronneau, 'Direct Cinema,' in Véronneau and Handling, eds, *Self Portrait* (1980)

42 In R. Boissonnault, 'Les Cinéastes québécois et l'Office national du film: la séquence du cinéma direct,' *cinéma québec* 2, no. 4, (December/January 1973), 19

43 See McKay, 'The History of the NFB.' 143.

44 See Gary Evans, *In the National Interest*, 85–6, 87–8; and 'Drylanders Box-Office Surprise – Columbia,' *CFW* (23 October 1963).

45 See Natalie Edwards, 'Who's Don Owen? What's He Done, and What's He Doing Now?' in Feldman and Nelson, eds, *Canadian Film Reader* (1977), 163. It is worth noting that the reviews for Owen's film were generally more favourable in New York than in Toronto and Montreal.

46 For an excellent discussion of these two films see Peter Harcourt, '1964: The Beginning of the Beginning,' in Véronneau and Handling, eds, *Self Portrait* (1980).

47 Boissonnault, 'Les Cinéastes québécois et l'Office national du film: la séquence de long métrage,' *cinéma québec* 2, no. 5, (January–February 1973), 17

48 'Le Long Métrage Canadien est-il voue à l'amateurisme?' *La Presse* (31 July 1965), 2

49 Ibid.

50 Pierre Maheu, *Parti pris* (April 1964), as quoted in D.B. Jones, *Movies and Memoranda*, 109 (translation in Jones). See also, Gary Evans, *In the National Interest*, 99–102.

51 Peter Harcourt, 'The Years of Hope,' in Feldman and Nelson, eds, *Canadian Film Reader* (1977), 142–3

52 For a discussion of the early efforts of French-Canadian filmmakers in the private sector, see R. Boissonnault, 'Naissance d'une industrie "indépéndante" de cinéma,' *cinéma québéc* 2, no. 8 (May/June 1973); and Pierre Pageau, 'A Survey of the Commercial Cinema 1963–77,' in P. Véronneau and P. Handling, eds, *Self Portrait* (1980).

53 See 'Le Long Métrage Canadien est-il voue à l'amateurisme?' *La Presse*, (31 July 1965), 2. See also the interviews with Michel Brault, Gilles Groulx, Claude Jutra, Arthur Lamothe, and Jean-Pierre Lefebvre, *Cahiers du cinéma* (March 1966).

54 Jutra, as quoted in 'APC: Need Gov't Feature Aid Now,' *CFW* (26 February 1964), 2 (translation in *CFW*)

55 F.R. Crawley, 'Have Independent Films a Look-In,' *Saturday Night* (14 August 1951), 24

56 'Producers Study Eady Plan etc.,' *CFW* (29 January 1958), 1; and 'Producers to Prod Ottawa,' *CFW* (7 May 1958), 1

57 'Chetwynd Views Production Future,' *CFW* (9 July 1958), 1. Chetwynd reported that in 1956 there were 60 private production companies, which had a total production volume of $14 million and employed 1,500 people. The NFB, he reported, produced $28 million worth of film and had 900 employees.

58 'Can't See Canada Feature Industry,' *CFW* (11 June 1958), 1–2

59 For a discussion of the Canadian-content dispute, see F. Peers, *The Public Eye: Television and the Politics of Canadian Broadcasting 1952–68*, 219–24.

60 See 'Producers Prep Brief for BBG,' *CFW* (30 September 1959); 'Producers Want Gov't Aid,' *CFW* (18 November 1959).

61 See 'Production Plan Appeal to Ottawa,' *CFW* (19 November 1958), 2.

62 'Pratt Believes in Industry,' *CFW* (14 November 1962), 1

63 'Our Business,' *CFW* (30 June 1954), 2

64 Ibid., (14 October 1959), 3.

65 'Optimistic Views on Feature Film Production in Canada,' *CFW* (Christmas 1958), 13

66 Ibid.

67 'Our Business,' *CFW* (21 October 1959), 3

68 'Our Business,' *CFW* (24 May 1961), 3. Taylor's suggestion was in response to calls for an exhibition quota by Bob Milligan of IATSE Local 873 (see notes 75 and 76); and 'Our Business,' *CFW* (26 April 1961), 2

69 'Our Business,' *CFW* (10 February 1960), 3

70 'Form Canada Production Council,' *CFW* (25 October 1961). The Production Council should not be confused with the Motion Picture Industry Council, which still existed as the umbrella trade organization.

71 See 'Why Don't They Get Together,' *CFW* (25 March 1964), 1.

72 'Second Thoughts about Feature Film Import Tax,' *CFW* (12 December 1962)

73 'Do We Expect Too Much Too Soon from the Film Industry?' *Canadian Cinematographer* 3, no. 3 (March-April 1964)

74 See *Canadian Cinematographer* 3, no. 4 (May–June 1964); 3, no. 5 (July–August 1964); and 3, no. 6 (September–October 1964). Coté spoke of 'cultural colonialism' and suggested establishment of a government-sponsored film finance agency, an exhibition quota, and a box-office levy modelled after Britain's Eady Plan (see 3, no. 6, 4).

75 'Canada IA Local Boosts for Quota,' *CFW* (5 April 1961), 1

76 'MP's Given Quota pitch by IA Union,' *CFW* (9 April 1961), 1

77 The full title of the DGC's brief is: 'A Brief Urging the Development and Encouragement of a Feature Film Industry in Canada with Emphasis on the Need for Government Assistance in Finance and National Distribution Including a Specific Proposal for the Establishment of the "The National Film Distribution and Financing Scheme" and a Recommendation for Improved Participation by the Canada Council,' March 1964, 5.

78 The main briefs were entitled: 'Mémoire présenté au Secretaire d'État du Canada: vingt-deux raisons pour lesquelles le gourvernement du Canada doit favoriser la création d'une industrie de cinéma de long métrage au Canada et s'inquiéter des consequences economiques et culturelles de l'état actuel de la distribution et de l'exploitation des films,' February 1964; and 'Mémoire présenté au premier ministre du Québec: mesures d'ensemble que l'APC recommande au gouvernement du Québec pour favoriser le développement d'une industrie du cinéma de long métrage conformant aux intérêts économique et culturelles du Québec,' March 1964.

79 See 'Pour une direction générale (québécoise) des industries du cinéma,' *Le Devoir* (24 March 1964).

80 See 'Mémoire présenté premier ministre du Québec,' 4.

Chapter 6

1 Speech by Maurice Lamontagne at the occasion of the National Film Board's 25th Anniversary, 5 August 1964, Public Archives of Canada (hereinafter PAC), Lamontagne Manuscripts, MG 32 B32 vol. 1, file 8, 3–4.

2 See R. Bothwell et al., *Canada Since 1945: Power, Politics and Provincialism* (1981), 271–83. Of course these were still minor 'offences,' since Canada continued to support U.S. involvement in the Vietnam War through the Defence Production Sharing Arrangements. In 1965, Total U.S. defence procurement in Canada under the arrangement was $259.5 million, and the figures remained high throughout the war. See S. Clarkson, *Canada and the Reagan Challenge* (1982), 261.

3 For a thorough discussion of the *Time* and *Reader's Digest* case see I. Litvak and C. Maule, *Cultural Sovereignty: The Time and Reader's Digest Case in Canada* (1974).

4 See Bothwell et al., *Canada Since 1945*, 311 and passim.

5 For a general overview of the ongoing changes in Canada's cultural policy in the 1960s, see B. Ostry, *The Cultural Connection* (1978), ch. 4.

6 Jean Lesage, as quoted in Government of Quebec, Ministère des Affaires culturelles, *Pour l'évolution de la politique culturelle*, May 1976, 10

7 Ibid., 11

8 Ostry, *Cultural Connection*, 91

9 William Coleman, *The Independence Movement in Quebec 1945–1980* (1980), 200

10 Conseil d'orientation économique du Québec, *Cinéma et Culture* (1963), 45. The Bouchard Report on the Quebec Book Trade was released in January 1964; see Ostry, *Cultural Connection*, 92.

11 'Godbout: les cinéastes accueillent avec joie l'assistance au cinéma,' *Le Devoir* (15 October 1965). By way of contrast, Godbout described Lamontagne as 'un visionnaire.'

12 André Guérin, 'Le Québec et le projet de loi Fédérale d'aide au Cinéma,' l'Office du film du Québec (October 1966), 4, 18.

13 Coleman, *The Independence Movement in Quebec*, 156

14 Canada, Royal Commission on Publications, *Report* (1961), G. O'Leary Chair, 4

15 Canada, Royal Commission on Broadcasting, *Report* (1957), R. Fowler Chair, 8

16 See R. Bothwell et al., *Canada Since 1945*, 266.

17 Ibid., 289

18 Address by Pearson, 'Equal Partners in Confederation,' 17 December 1962, PAC MG 32, BG 32, vol. 11, part 4

19 'Le Rideau se lève,' *Le Devoir*, 4 February 1964; 'Now Canada Has a Cultural Governor,' *Toronto Daily Star* (18 July 1964)

20 In *Toronto Daily Star* (18 July 1964)

21 See Ostry, *Cultural Connection*, 100; and Lamontagne to House of Commons, *Debates*, 5 November 1964, 9810 passim.

22 'Address by Honourable Maurice Lamontagne Secretary of State of Canada to the Radio and Television Executives Club, 6 April 1964, PAC, Lamontagne Manuscripts, vol. 1, File: 6, 3

23 Ibid., 5

24 Ibid., 6

25 Address by the Honourable Maurice Lamontagne Secretary of State of Canada at the 1965 Seminar Canadian Conference of the Arts, 19 January 1965, PAC, Lamontagne Manuscripts, vol. 1, File: 10, 5–6

26 Ibid., 7

27 *Debates*, 13 November 1964, 10081

28 The Committee's work and much of the material related to government's decision with respect to the establishment of the CFDC can be found in PAC RG 6, vol. 824 (Secretary of State, Interdepartmental Committee on the Possible Development of Feature Film Production in Canada).

29 'A Plan for Government Assistance to the Canadian Feature Film Industry

Which Received the Concurrence in Principle of the National Film Board,' PAC, Interdepartmental Committee on Film Industry, RG 6, vol. 824, part 1

30 Ibid., 2
31 Some of the information in this section comes from a personal interview with Michael Spencer, conducted in Montreal, 30 January 1986.
32 'Canada Seeks British, French Coproductions,' *Canadian Film Weekly* (hereinafter *CFW*) (3 April 1963), 1
33 On the rise in importance of co-productions see T. Guback, *The International Film Industry* (1969), chap. 10.
34 'France-Canada Film Agreement,' *CFW* (6 November 1963), 7
35 'Canada-France Film Cooperation,' *CFW* (21 August 1963), 1
36 Lamontagne to G.G.E. Steele, undersecretary of state, 29 July 1964, PAC Lamontagne Manuscripts, vol. 11, part 2
37 See 'Recommendations made by the Secretary of State on the development of a feature film industry,' 30 July 1964, PAC, ibid., vol. 11, part 2.
38 Address by Maurice Lamontagne Secretary of State of Canada at the Occasion of the 25th Anniversary of the National Film Board, 5 August 1964, PAC, ibid., vol. 1, File: 8, 4–5
39 'Les cinéastes expriment leur vive satisfaction,' *Le Devoir* (7 August 1964)
40 'Money to Burn,' *Globe and Mail* (8 August 1964)
41 *Debates*, 5 August 1964, 6430
42 The full names of the studies are: 'Canadian Feature Film Production in the English Language'; 'L'industrie de production de long métrage d'éxpression française'; 'Film distribution: Practices, Problems and Prospects.' See PAC, Interdepartmental Committee on Film Industry, J1 vol. 824.
43 Spencer, 'Canadian Feature Film Production in the English Language,' 6 April 1965, PAC, Ibid, 31.
44 Ibid., 22
45 A Secretary of State official hinted that the government was trying to persuade its provincial counterparts to consider a box-office levy. He told the *Montreal Star*: 'In all other countries in the world, the money that comes from the box office goes back into film. Here it's used to build roads' ('NFB Chief Delighted, $5M Aid Forecast,' 6 August 1964); see also, 'Film Industry to Get $10M Ottawa Aid,' *Globe and Mail* (14 October 1965). Of course, while the federal government could not impose a box-office tax it could impose an export duty on film rental remittances and direct the money collected to the loan fund.
46 Interview with Spencer, 30 January 1986
47 See Spencer, 'Canadian Feature Film Production,' PAC, Interdepartmental Committee on Film Industry vol. 824; and Memo from Steele to Lamontagne, 29 July 1964, PAC, Lamontagne Manuscripts, vol. 11, part 2.
48 'Minutes of the 19th meeting of the Interdepartmental Committee,' May 1965, PAC RG 6 vol. 824, part 1
49 'Second Report of the Interdepartmental Committee,' PAC RG 6 vol. 824 part 2
50 Ibid., 4, 5
51 Ibid., 12

52 'Memorandum to the Cabinet: Development of Feature Film Production in Canada,' Ibid., PAC RG 6 vol. 824, part 2.

53 Ibid., 3

54 Ibid., 3

55 Memo, Steele to Lamontagne, 2 September 1955, PAC RG 6 vol. 848, 5020–1

56 'The Trials of Judy the Movie Maker,' *Globe and Mail* (10 September 1966); see also Judy LaMarsh, 'Close-Up on Bill C-204,' *Take One* 1, no. 1 (1966). LaMarsh reiterated the government's emphasis on the producer's responsibility to succeed without protectionist measures: 'We should not delude ourselves, however, on this basic point: Canadian producers will have to compete with foreign films for our market. Canadian productions will have to win respect – and audiences – on their own merits.' (5).

57 See 'Unhappy Squabbling behind Our Happy Birthday Party,' *Toronto Daily Star* (27 May 1965).

58 For a discussion of this point, see S. Crean, *Who's Afraid of Canadian Culture?* (1976) esp. 2–6 and passim; and Robin Endres, 'Art and Accumulation: The Canadian State and the Business of Art,' in Panitch, ed., *The Canadian State* (1977).

59 *Debates*, 3 February 1967, 12657

60 Ibid., 12657, 12663

61 Ibid., 27 January 1967, 12367–9

62 'The Trials of Judy,' *Globe and Mail* (10 September 1966)

63 *Debates*, 30 June 1966, 6632

64 *Debates*, 3 February 1967, 12655

65 'William Neville (executive assistant) to Secretary of State Judy LaMarsh, 13 July 1966.' See PAC RG 6, Acc. 85–86/184, Box 5, File: 177–104/0, pt. 2, Int. #4

66 See Nat Taylor, 'A Canadian Feature Film Industry: Part vii,' *CFW* (17 February 1965), 4.

Chapter 7

1 Kirwan Cox, 'Radical Surgery,' *Cinema Canada* (hereinafter *CC*), no. 13 (April–May 1974), 78

2 Michael Spencer and Undersecretary of State G.G.E. Steele were put in charge of getting the Corporation under way. Even before the legislation was passed, they had begun to consider choices for the position of executive director. Steele thought Budge Crawley might make a good candidate, while Spencer, who felt that Crawley's expertise lay too much in the field of documentary filmmaking, suggested that Nat Taylor or Sidney Newman would be better suited to the task. For chairperson, the more honorary of the two principal positions, LaMarsh was keenly interested in Jack McClelland, Canada's gregarious and flamboyantly nationalist publisher. McClelland turned the position down, and suggested that LaMarsh consider a foreigner since he felt there were no Canadians with

enough experience for the position. One year later, Cabinet settled on Georges-Émile Lapalme. The decision seems to have been taken to help forestall demands that the administration of half the Corporation's money be handed over to Quebec. As David Orlikow noted in the House, the rest of the CFDC's board of directors were 'all good Liberals,' with the exception of Michelle Favreau, who was a film critic at *La Presse*. The Cabinet left the choice of an executive director to the board. After a year as acting secretary, Michael Spencer was handed the position. He had received letters of support from the APC and the newly founded Association des producteurs de films du Québec. See 'Scene One Take One for the CFDC,'*Globe and Mail* (6 March 1968); and Public Archives of Canada (hereinafter PAC), RG 123, CFDC Records, Access 85–86/184, Box 5.1.

3 See Canada, Task Force on Broadcasting Policy, *Report* (1986), ch. 6.

4 See David Wolfe, 'The Politics of the Deficit.' in G.B. Doern ed., *The Politics of Economic Policy* (1986).

5 'Notes for the under-secretary of State for His Presentation of the CFDC Act and Related Government Policy to the First Meeting of the CFDC,' PAC RG 123 vol. 5, File: 263, 2 April 1968, 3

6 CFCD Act, Section 10, (2) (a)

7 'Notes for the under-secretary of State for his Presentation,' 6

8 See I. Litvak and C. Maule, *Cultural Sovereignty: The Time and Reader's Digest Case in Canada* (1974); and Paul Audley, *Canada's Cultural Industries* (1983), ch. 2.

9 See Frank Peers, 'Oh Say Can You See,' in Ian Lumsden, ed., *Close the 49th Parallel etc.: The Americanization of Canada* (1970), 141–2; and 'Famous Players Subsidiary Turned Down by CRTC,' *Canadian Film and Television Bi-Weekly* (hereinafter *CFTBW*) (23 April 1969), 12.

10 CFDC, *Annual Report 1968–9*, 7. The CFDC's fiscal year ends 31 March.

11 See Gary Evans, *In the National Interest* (1991), 122; 'Cameras Are Rolling in Canada's New Film Industry,' *Toronto Star* (2 August 1969); and 'Who Needs Bill C-204? Not the CBC or NFB,' *CFTBW* (18 January 1967).

12 See Harold Arthur, 'Thanks, Yanks, for All That You've Done,' *Saturday Night* (September 1966); and 'Local 644 Blacks Out NFB Theatrical Films,' *CFTBW* (1 February 1967); and 'PM Says Feature Films Government Perogative,' *CFTBW* (15 March 1967).

13 Canadian Society of Film Makers, as quoted in Ronald Blumer, 'NFB: Is This the End?' *Take One* 2, no. 3 (1969), 13. For a discussion of the NFB's production activities during this period, see D.B. Jones, *Movies and Memoranda* (1981), chs 8–10; and Gary Evans, *In the National Interest*, chs 6–9.

14 Michael Spencer, to the Parliamentary Standing Committee on Broadcasting, Films and Assistance to the Arts, 26 November 1968, 419–20 (emphasis added)

15 Lapalme, in Ibid., 415, 421, 429

16 Ibid., 433

17 Canada. CFDC, *Annual Report 1969–70*, 13

18 Laplame, to the Standing Committee, 26 November 1968, 418

19 Ibid., 418
20 Ibid., 434
21 During a news conference in the summer of 1968, Roy Firth, one of the board members of the CFDC, explained that the Corporation was not planning to invest in 'all-Canadian' projects only. He also emphasized the commercial imperative under which the CFDC was to operate, and said: 'Once we can assure distributors that we can produce commercially successful features for the world market, then we can perhaps take some chances with the obviously artistic projects' ('Feature Loan Corp. Sees $1M Grants in 1st Year,' *CFTBW* (3 July 1968), 1, 8).
22 Spencer to Standing Committee, 26 November 1968, 422
23 See Martin Knelman, *This Is Where We Came In* (1977), 10; CFDC, *Annual Report: 1968–9*; and 'Cameras Are Rolling in Canada's New Film Industry,' *Toronto Star* (2 August 1969). *Act of the Heart* was the second instalment in an Almond–Bujold trilogy that began with *Isabel* (1969) and ended with *Journey* (1972).
24 See 'Canada Proudly Presents: The Film Development Corporation, Whatever the Heck That Is,' *Montreal Star* (19 July 1969).
25 *Valérie* chronicles the adventures of a young woman who flees a convent, flirts with a biker, joins a commune, and becomes a topless dancer and prostitute before finding salvation in the form of a conventional marriage with a middle-aged widower. See Pierre Pageau, 'A Survey of the Commercial Cinema: 1963–1977,' in P. Véronneau, and P. Handling, eds, *Self Portrait* (1980), 151.
26 Ibid., 152; and David Clandfield, *Canadian Film* (1987), 73–5.
27 Canada, House of Commons, *Debates*, 13 October 1970, 84. The remarks were made by Léonel Beaudoin, a Créditiste Member of Parliament from Quebec.
28 Urjo Kareda, 'All Canadian Sex Movie,' *Toronto Star* (26 February 1971); and see 'A Skinful of Canadian Content,' *Montreal Star*, 15 August 1970.
29 See PAC RG 123, CFDC Records, vol. 6, File: 94, Int: 58. See also PAC, CFDC Records, vol. 1, File: 138. One of the letters read in part: 'I object strongly to the use of tax money for the production of films containing great footage of nudism and portraying to any extent acts of sexual perversion, as well as the exploitation of sex in any manner.'
30 CFDC, *Annual Report 1969–70*, 8–9. See also 'Corporation defends "sexploitation" films,' *Toronto Star* (30 January 1971).
31 Ibid., 9
32 See CFDC, *Annual Report 1971–2*.
33 CFDC, *Annual Report 1969–70*, 12 (emphasis added)
34 For a discussion of the 'crisis' in Hollywood in the late sixties, see Armand Mattelart, *Multinational Corporations and the Control of Culture* (1979), 193–6.
35 'CFDC Survives,' *Trade News North* (April 1978), 10
36 See Manjunath Pendakur, 'Cultural Dependency in Canada's Feature Film Industry,' *Journal of Communications* 31, no. 1 (Winter 1981), 50. After surveying the structure of distribution and exhibition, Pendakur concludes that the

'system is structured to exclude almost all Canadian films except by chance' (55) (emphasis in original). See also Pendakur's *Canadian Dreams and American Control* (1990), esp. 153–8.

37 CFDC, *Annual Report 1971–2*, 3
38 CFDC, *Annual Report 1972–3*, 6
39 Richard French, *How Ottawa Decides* (1980), esp. chs 1 and 2
40 See Bernard Ostry, *The Cultural Connection* (1978), 115.
41 'Film and Television: Tools for the Democratization of the Arts,' speech by Pelletier to the Associated Council of the Arts, 21 May 1969, 1. See also, 'Presto! Canada Has Its First Cultural Policy,' *Toronto Telegram* (13 February 1971).
42 Pelletier to Gélinas, 24 December 1969, PAC, CFDC Records, vol. 2, File: 170. Pelletier told *Actrascope* in December 1969: 'My greatest hope is for coordination between existing agencies. If the NFB, CBC, and CFDC can work out a way to coordinate their activities, much will be accomplished and many useful efforts saved.' See G. Pratley, 'In and Out of Cinema,' *CC*, no. 37 (January/February 1969), 5.
43 Pelletier to Gélinas, 24 December 1969, 3. See also Pelletier's remarks to the Standing Committee on Broadcasting, 18 March 1971.
44 Gélinas to Pelletier, 6 February 1970, PAC, CFDC Records, vol. 2, File: 170, 2 (emphasis added)
45 Ibid., 2, 3
46 In a letter to the author 20 August 1987, Pelletier wrote: 'Did the various agencies act more to protect their own turf than to assist the development of a cultural policy? Yes. Most agencies didn't feel the need for a cultural policy; they thought they had one already and were satisfied with the status quo ... I clearly remember that when we held our first meeting of all the agency heads (there had never been one before), most of the gentlemen involved were either quite agitated or totally sceptical about the usefulness of communicating with their colleagues.'
47 'General Statement on Canadian Film Development Corporation Policies,' April 1972, PAC, CFDC Records, vol. 1, File: 159, 1, 2
48 Ibid., 4
49 Ibid., 7
50 Pelletier to the Standing Committee on Broadcasting, 23 May 1972.
51 See Standing Committee on Broadcasting, 13 March, 27 March, and 29 April 1969.
52 Stanbury at the Standing Committee on Broadcasting, 13 March 1969, 1072
53 Toronto Filmmakers Coop, 'Proposals for Canada's Film Policy, a Brief to the Hon. Gérard Pelletier,' PAC, CFDC Records, vol. 1, File: 158, May 1972, 6–7.
54 Ibid., 33
55 Ibid., 42
56 Ibid., 40
57 Ibid., 35

58 'Our Business,' *Canadian Film Digest* (November 1971), 4
59 Ibid., 4
60 Notes for a speech by the Hon. G. Pelletier, 'The first phase of a federal film policy,' 4 July 1972, 2. The speech is reprinted in *CC*, no. 3 (July/August 1972).
61 Ibid., 4
62 Ibid., 1

Chapter 8

1 Claude Jutra, as quoted in Toronto Filmmakers' Coop, 'Proposals for Canada's Film Policy, a Brief to the Hon. Gérard Pelletier,' Public Archives of Canada (hereinafter PAC), RG 123, CFDC Records, vol. 1, file: 158 May (1972), 5
2 On the capital cost allowance and its relationship to the film industry see: 'Ottawa Buries Its Head While Film Industry Sickens,' *Globe and Mail* (17 March 1973); S. Daniel Lyon and M. Trebilcock, *Public Strategy and Motion Pictures* (1982), ch. 6; M.W. Bucovetsky, et al., *Tax Incentives for Film Production* (1982); Richard Wise, 'A Cineramic View of Motion Picture Film Investments,' *Canadian Tax Journal* 24, no. 2, (March/April 1976) and 'The New Rules for Motion Picture Tax Shelters,' *Canadian Tax Journal* 27, no. 3 (May/June 1979); Government of Canada, Canadian Film and Videotape Certification Office, *Statistical Bulletin 1974–83* (1985).
3 See 'Let's Be Realistic about Tax Write-Offs,' *Canadian Film Digest* (December 1972), 4.
4 See 'New Funds for Features,' *Cinema Canada* (hereinafter *CC*), no. 4 (October/November 1972), 7.
5 'English Language Films in Montreal,' *Canadian Film Digest* (February 1973), 8. See also 'Astral Bellevue-Pathé to Make Big-Budget Coproduction,' *CC*, no. 12 (February/March 1974). Greenberg told *Cinema Canada*: 'We want to win acceptance of Canada as a viable place to make movies and the best place to start is in partnership with Hollywood' (8).
6 Secretary of State, *Film Industry in Canada* (1977), 123 and passim.
7 See 'French Producers Have Frustrating Session with Secretary of State,' *Canadian Film Digest* (May 1973); 'Government Closes 60% Tax Loophole,' *Canadian Film Digest* (December 1973); Canadian Association of Motion Picture Producers, 'Brief to the Secretary of State,' 21 April 1973, PAC, CFDC Records, vol. 2, File: 171.
8 See 'Historic Meeting and Unanimous Vote to Form All-Canadian Guild,' *CC*, no. 7 (April/May 1973), 16. The CCFM began publishing a regular newsletter in *Cinema Canada*, as did a number of other film industry associations.
9 CCFM, 'Policy Statement on Feature Films,' *CC*, no. 12 (February/March 1974), 48.
10 Peter Pearson to the Parliamentary Standing Committee on Broadcasting, 25 April 1974, 5. Michael Spencer was also in attendance that day and the Committee asked him if the CFDC and the CCFM could get together and draw up a

list of specific proposals. Spencer and Pearson seemed to believe that they could strike an agreement on the need for new tax incentives, but they were doubtful whether a comprehensive position could be worked out. They were right. See also the exchange of letters between Spencer and Pearson in *CC*, no. 14 (June/July 1974). Pearson became executive director of Telefilm in 1985 and resigned in October 1987 amid allegations of political interference by the CFDC's chair, Pierre DesRoches.

11 See *CC*, no. 8 (June/July 1973), 8; and Secretary of State, *Film Industry in Canada*, 55.

12 See *CFDC Annual Report 1973–4*, 8; and *Annual Report 1974–5*, which states: 'The Corporation has often stated its support for quotas and levies, not on the grounds that they restrict the free flow of foreign films in Canada, but on the grounds of a guaranteed access to his own market for the Canadian producer' (9). Spencer himself leaned more toward the use of levies than quotas.

13 See 'Resume of a Meeting held 19 January 1972 in Montreal, on the possibility of forming a Cooperative for the distribution of Canadian films in the U.S.,' PAC, CFDC Records, vol. 4, File: 209.

14 'Extract from Minutes of 34th meeting of the CFDC,' 4–7 September 1972, PAC, CFDC Records, vol. 4, File: 209

15 See 'The Role of the CFDC in Feature Film Distribution,' 23 October 1972, PAC, CFDC Records, vol. 4, File: 209, 3. See also M. Spencer to Secretary of State, 'Distribution Policies of the CFDC,' 8 December 1972, PAC, CFDC Records, vol. 1, File: 159.

16 'Working Paper on Film Distribution,' January 1973, PAC, CFDC Records, vol. 4, File: 211, 3.

17 See *CC*, no. 9 (August/September), 1973.

18 See PAC, CFDC Records, vol. 3, File: 175, part 1.

19 'Minutes of preparatory discussion concerning the first meeting of the Film Advisory Committee,' 20 September 1972, PAC, CFDC Records, vol. 4, File: 209, 1

20 'Second Meeting of the Film Advisory Committee,' 22 November 1972, PAC, CFCD Records, File: 175, part 1, 3

21 'Synthesis of Discussions of the Film Advisory Committee,' 13–14 September 1975, PAC, CFCD Records, vol. 3, File: 175, pt. 2, 10–11

22 CCFM, 'Policy Statement on Feature Films,' *CC*, no. 12 (February/March 1974) 49

23 See 'Winnipeg Symposium: The Turning Point,' *CC*, no. 13 (April/May 1974).

24 'Radical Surgery,' *CC*, no. 13 (April/May 1974), 78

25 Secretary of State, Bureau of Management Consulting, 'Evaluation of the CFDC,' September 1974

26 Ibid., 35–7, 46

27 Ibid., 39

28 Ibid., 3

29 Spencer to Pearson, 9 May 1974, in *CC*, no. 14 (June/July 1974), 65

30 'Canada's Movie Industry in Critical Condition,' *Toronto Star*, 25 May 1974.

As usual, Spencer's remarks were well informed. During the summer election of 1974, Faulkner provided a hint of what phase two of the film policy would look like. At an open meeting in Peterborough, Faulkner told Kirwan Cox that the government was prepared to introduce a new capital cost allowance of 115 per cent for Canadian feature films, that it wanted to give the CFDC more leeway in funding distribution and promotion, and that quota negotiations with the provinces were about to commence. It would be another year before the policy was announced. See *CC*, no. 15 (August/September 1974), 6.

31 'The Film Industry in Ontario' (January 1973), in *CC*, no. 6 (February/March 1973). For reactions to the Bassett Report, see Kirwan Cox, 'Opinion,' ibid.; and Garth Drabinsky, who argued against the imposition of a quota in 'Editorial: Ontario Government Report,' *Canadian Film Digest* (February 1973).

32 See *CC*, no. 16 (October/November 1974), 60. See also, 'Canadian Films: A Fair Deal at Theatres,' *Globe and Mail* (14 September 1974).

33 'AMPPLC Guest Panel Comments on Aspects of Industry,' *Canadian Film Digest* (May 1973), 9. Some Ontario officials held a similar view, and like Vant were keenly interested in selling their province as a location for American film companies. See the remarks by Claude Bennett, Ontario's minister of Tourism, in Susan Crean, *Who's Afraid of Canadian Culture?* (1976), 93.

34 'Beyond Words: The Quebec Filmmakers Occupation of the Censorship Office,' *CC*, no. 18 (March/April 1975), 36

35 The ARFQ received letters of support from the Association des producteurs de films du Québec, the Association of Quebec Film Critics, the S.G.C.T.-O.N.F. section (the NFB's filmmakers' and technicians' union), the Montreal branch of ACTRA, and the CCFM.

36 See *CC*, no. 19 (May/June 1975), 6; and 'Numéro spécial: loi-cadre,' *cinéma québec* 4, no. 4 (1975).

37 Parliamentary Standing Committee on Broadcasting, 9 May 1975, 4, 5.

38 See *CC*, no. 21 (September 1975), 8. Although it seems clear that there was considerable support both inside and outside of the state for the new tax regulations, Joseph Beaubien, an official with the CFDC, explains that there were some last-minute events that finalized the decision. As he told *Variety*: 'I was in New York sometime in early 1975 and a Canadian producer told me that a group of Canadian investors were being rounded up all over the country's major cities to invest something between $10M and $15M in U.S. features for which they'd get Canadian tax write-off benefits. I came back, checked it out, found that was correct, and the CFDC went to the then Secretary of State and told him we had to give a better break to investors in all-Canadian features ... He said, "work out a definition that will make a distinction between Canadian and non-Canadian." The finance department said that it couldn't be done, but we pointed out that there was already a distinction on the books between non-Canadian and Canadian oil drilling' ('CFDC Enters Tenth Year,' *Variety* (23 November 1977), 35).

39 For the reactions of the CCFM and the Canadian Association of Motion Picture

Producers (CAMPP) see *CC*, no. 21 (September 1975), 18–19. Harry Blumson, president of Odeon, told the CBC that he had 'agreed to the arrangement under duress, that he interpreted the voluntary agreement to be literally voluntary, and that he would show only very commercial Canadian films in his theatres.' George Destounis, president of Famous Players told the *Vancouver Sun* that 'there is no way he is going to exhibit low budget $100,000 Canadian features' (ibid., 18).

40 Ibid., 8; and 'La SDICC cesserait ses opérations,' *Le Jour* (6 August 1975)
41 *CC*, no. 21 (September 1975), 19
42 Secretary of State, *Film Industry in Canada* (1977), 22–3
43 Ibid., 202
44 Ibid., 72
45 Ibid., 133
46 Ibid., 176
47 Ibid., 133
48 Ibid., 22
49 Ibid., 194
50 Ibid., 193
51 Standing Committee on Broadcasting, 29 April 1976, 7
52 CFDC, *Annual Report 1975–6*, 4
53 CFDC, *Annual Report 1976–7*, 4. The report noted that 'the steady appearance of numerous blockbusters from outside the country, makes it more and more difficult for modestly budgeted Canadian films to compete effectively.' (4).
54 Ibid., 4
55 Ibid., 5

Chapter 9

1 Canada, Parliament, Standing Committee on Broadcasting, Films and Assistance to the Arts, 11 April 1978, 11:13
2 'CMPDA Happy,' *Trade News North* (hereinafter *TNN*) (April 1978), 11
3 Roberts, Standing Committee, 11 April 1978, 11:4, 5
4 See Manjunath Pendakur, *Canadian Dreams and American Control* (1990), Table 12, 172.
5 'Interview: Michael McCabe,' *Cinema Papers*, December/January, 1980–81, 438, 440
6 CFDC, *Annual Report 1977–8*, 4
7 Martin Knelman, *This Is Where We Came In*, 166. For a review of the Canadian presence at Cannes in 1977, see Marc Gervais, 'Of Cannes, Canada, Robin Spry and Roberto Rosselini,' *Cinema Canada*, (hereinafter *CC*) no. 38–9 (June/July 1977).
8 CFDC, Annual Report 1977–8
9 Ibid., 5
10 Ibid., 6. The co-production treaty with France was renegotiated in 1974. Similar

treaties had been signed with Italy (1970), the United Kingdom (1975), and were soon to be signed with the Federal Republic of Germany (1978) and Israel (1978). For a brief discussion of how some of these treaties dealt with the question of Canadian involvement, and a good discussion of the general differences in the way in which the Secretary of State, the CFDC, Revenue Canada, and the CRTC approached the same issue for the purpose of designating a given film as 'Canadian,' see Joan Irving, 'Yes: But Is It Canadian ... Are You Canadian ... Are They Canadian?' *CC*, no. 37 (April/May 1977).

11 'CCFM,' *CC*, no. 37 (April/May 1977), 53
12 'The Heat's on in the CAMPPfire,' *CC*, no. 38–9 (June/July 1977), 10
13 'A Conversation with Hugh Faulkner,' *CC*, no. 28 (May 1976), 31
14 'Draft Film Policy,' *CC*, no. 32 (November 1976), 25
15 Ibid.
16 'Federal Policy in Three Months,' *CC*, no. 36 (March 1977), 8. Roberts had some personal connections with the film industry. David Perlmutter (Quadrant Films) who was president of the Canadian Association of Motion Picture Producers (CAMPP) had worked on Roberts' campaign during the last election.
17 On the introduction of Bill C-58 see the discussion in S. Crean, *Who's Afraid of Canadian Culture?* (1976), 224 and passim. For an account of how Bill C-58 affected advertising revenues for Canadian broadcasters, see: P. Audley, *Canada's Cultural Industries* (1983), 269–71; and Canada, Task Force on Broadcasting Policy, *Report* (1986), 461.
18 Congress first retaliated by making the cost of attending conventions in Canada non-tax-deductible. See S. Clarkson, *Canada and the Reagan Challenge* (1982), 235–6, 242. Clarkson estimates that this retaliation cost the Canadian convention and tourism industry $100 million, while Canadian advertising on U.S. border stations amounted to no more than $25 million in 1976.
19 See 'Roberts' Film Policy Didn't Clear Finance,' *TNN* (March 1978); and Sandra Gathercole, 'The Best Film Policy This Country Never Had,' *CC*, no. 47 (June 1978), 3.
20 'Roberts' Film Policy,' *TNN* (March 1978), 3
21 Odeon Theatres was purchased for $31.2 million by Michael Zahorchak and the Canadian Theatres Group in December (see *TNN*, December 1977). The new Canadian owners would make no commitment to increasing the exhibition of Canadian films.
22 'Roberts' Film Policy,' *TNN* (March 1978), 3
23 Standing Committee on Broadcasting, 24 November 1977, 1:21. Roberts also told the Committee that he expected to make his policy announcement on December 9. He was off by only five months.
24 For an excellent discussion of the planning system employed by the Department of Finance during the 1970s, see Richard French, *How Ottawa Decides: Planning and Industrial Policy-Making 1968–80* (1980), especially 27–32.
25 'A "major" offensive against nationalism,' *CC*, no. 34–5 (February 1977), 21. The article is a summary of the CMPDA's brief entitled: 'Position Paper Con-

cerning the Motion Picture Distribution Industry in Canada.' The CMPDA also submitted at least one other brief to the Department of Finance in the following year.

26 Ibid., 20
27 Ibid., 22, 23
28 Millard Roth, 'Filmmaker as Enterpreneur,' *TNN* (November 1977), 4
29 'A "major" offensive,' 23
30 'Gilken to Head Motion Picture Institute of Canada,' *CC*, no. 34–5 (February 1977), 8. The CMPDA had also decided to stop advertising in the nationalistically inclined *Cinema Canada*. To counteract the influence of *Cinema Canada*, the *Canadian Film Digest*, complete with ads from all the major distributors and a column by Nat Taylor, reappeared in December 1976. The *Digest* planned to begin regular publication in the spring, but the magazine folded. The CMPDA then sponsored the publication of *Filmworld*, starting in December 1977. After hearing of the CMPDA's plan to sponsor a general trade paper, the editors of *Cinema Canada* decided to establish *Trade News North* (which later became *Cinemag*). *Cinema Canada* and its offshoots have had to survive without the benefit of large-scale advertising by the American majors. See 'The War Within: Culture vs. Industry,' *CC*, no. 80 (December–January 1982), 24.
31 Personal interview with Millard Roth, executive director of the CMPDA, 27 September 1985. The headquarters of the CMPDA are located across the road from the Toronto office of the Department of Communications. Roth described the CMPDA as a 'uniquely structured trade association' that places a premium on internal unity and stability. Roth himself has been 'retained' as executive director for over 20 years.
32 'Real Risk of Retaliation,' *Cinemag* (October 1978), 10
33 Budge Crawley and George Destounis (president of Famous Players) reportedly liked the idea. Destounis was also on record as personally supporting some form of protectionist measures. Perhaps he saw the tax as a way of alleviating the pressure for an exhibition quota; nonetheless, his support is somewhat surprising. ' "Joplin" Sadness, "Man" Gladness for Crawley,' *Toronto Star* (23 November 1977).
34 'CCFM: Gathercole Steps Down,' *CC*, no. 38–9 (June/July 1977), 8; 'CCFM Heads Step Down,' *TNN* (December 1977), 3
35 'No Levy, No Quota – Roberts,' *TNN* (December 1977), 3
36 See 'Quebec Working Paper,' *TNN*, February 1978.
37 Standing Committee on Broadcasting, 11 April 1978, 11:6-8
38 Ibid., 11:16
39 Ibid., 11:33
40 'Roberts Defends Policy,' *TNN* (April 1978), 1
41 Ibid.
42 In Gathercole, 'The Best Film Policy,' 30. Progressive Conservative Member of Parliament David MacDonald, who had been the most vigilant parliamentary critic of the government's film policy over the last 12 years, remarked: 'This

policy to my mind is an almost 100 per cent write-off,' Standing Committee on Broadcasting, 11 April 1978, 11:21.

43 See 'S.O.S.: Mass Confusion,' *TNN* (March 1978), 1.

44 See, 'Michael Spencer: A Vote of Thanks,' *CC*, no. 46 (April/May 1978).

45 'McCabe: New CFDC Boss,' *TNN* (May 1978), 4

46 'New Proof That Nice Guys Finish Last,' *Maclean's* (18 May 1978), 86-7

47 'Le défi de Michel Vennat: créer une industrie viable,' *La Presse* (3 February 1979)

48 'McCabe: New CFDC Boss,' *TNN* (May 1978), 4

49 CFDC, *Annual Report 1978-9*, 4

50 Ibid.

51 Ibid., 5-6

52 See S. Daniel Lyon and Michael Trebilcock, *Public Strategy and Motion Pictures* (1982), 73-4; and Richard Wise, 'The New Rules for Motion Picture Tax Shelters,' *Canadian Tax Journal* 27, no. 3 (May-June 1979).

53 See Howard Goldberg, 'Reducing the Risk,' *CC*, no. 72 (March 1981).

54 See, for example, Susan Cole, 'Bay Street Gets into Movies,' *Canadian Business* (August 1979).

55 'John Turner in Film Financing,' *TNN* (December 1977)

56 See Table 2. As a study for the Institute for Policy Analysis reveals: 'Correcting for inflation does not alter the conclusion that budgets have grown considerably in real terms. In constant 1971 dollars, for example, average budgets in 1960-7 were about $220,000; in 1968-74 they were $340,000; and in 1975-80 they were about $710,000, with the 1979-80 average budget hovering around $1 million.' See M.W. Bucovetsky et al., *Tax Incentives for Film Production: The Canadian Experience* (1982), 13.

57 CFDC, *Annual Report 1979-80*, 7

58 'Study Focuses on Canadian Cultural Fact,' *Cinemag* (16 June 1980), 7

59 Paul Audley, *Canada's Cultural Industries* (1983), 237

60 These figures have been gathered from the CFDC's annual reports from 1978-9 through 1980-1.

61 'McCabe and Vennat in Hollywood: Meet Top Film Showmen,' *Variety* (17 January 1979)

62 Standing Committee on Broadcasting, 20 November 1979, 3:20

63 'Directors Demand CFDC Heads Roll,' *Cinemag* (March 1979), 3

64 'Les Réalisateurs blâment la direction de la SDICC,' *Le Devoir* (13 February 1979)

65 'Organizational News: CCFM,' *CC*, no. 43 (December-January 1978), 21

66 'Study Focuses on Canadian Cultural Fact,' *Cinemag* (16 June 1980), 7

67 'Movie Makers Trade Potshots,' *Montreal Star* (16 February 1979)

68 See 'Denis Héroux: La coproduction, c'est moi,' *CC*, no. 100 (October 1983), 14. For an excellent overview of Canada's coproduction history, see Michael Dorland, 'Quest for Equality: Canada and Coproductions,' *CC*, no. 100 (October 1983).

69 'CFDC to Recoup Second from Some French Productions,' *Cinemag* (July 1979), 4

70 'The CFDC: Money, Imagination, Persuasion,' *Saturday Night* (October 1979).

71 Claude Jutra, in 'Ten Hot Years,' *CC*, no. 83 (April 1982), 32. See also 'Interview: Beryl Fox with Cameo Appearance by Claude Jutra,' *CC*, no. 73 (April 1981).

72 Jay Scott, 'Burnout in the Great White North,' in S. Feldman, ed., *Take Two: A Tribute to Film in Canada* (1984), 32

73 The figures have been taken from various issues of *Cinema Canada* and *Cinemag*. See also Rick Salutin, 'The Canadian Film Boom Goes "Pop",' *This Magazine* (January-February 1980); and John Harkness, 'Notes on a Tax Sheltered Cinema,' *CC*, no. 87 (August 1982).

74 Martin Knelman, 'Shooting Games,' *Saturday Night* (March 1981), 57

75 Keith Burr, 'The North Lights Up,' *American Film* (December 1979), 69

76 In Salutin, 'The Canadian Film Boom Goes "Pop",' 32

77 See *Cinemag* (31 March 1980), 3. For a discussion of the founding of the Genie Awards see Connie Tadros, 'The 1983 Genies: Looking Back upon Tomorrow,' *CC*, no. 95 (April 1983), especially fn. 2.

78 See Manjunath Pendakur, *Canadian Dreams and American Control* (1990), 183–4; and Salutin, 'The Film Boom Goes "Pop",' 32.

79 'Universal Gets Running,' *Cinemag* (February 1979), 1. *Cinemag* reported that Universal paid $2.4 million for the rights. Keith Burr reported the figure as $2.6 million, noting as well that ABC paid $2.6 million for the television rights, while U.S. pay-TV rights were sold to Viacom for another $1 million. The film cost approximately $3 million. See 'The North Lights Up,' 67.

80 'Meatballs Sells Like Filet Mignon,' *Cinemag* (1 May 1979), 3; and 'Independent Distributors Meet Roberts,' *TNN* (June 1978), 1. Industry representatives informed Roberts that the American majors had booked Canadian screens well into the new year and that Canadian films were being used as fillers only.

81 'SOS to Act Soon,' *Cinemag* (February 1979), 3

82 For the position of the Independent and Canadian-Owned Motion Picture Distributors, see 'Market Unfree, Indies Ask Help from CFDC,' *Cinemag* (14 April 1980), 16; and ' "Urgent and Confidential": S.O.S. '78,' *Cinemag* (May 1980), 52. The initiatives in Quebec are well documented in the trade papers, especially *Cinemag* (from November 1978 to April 1981) and then *Cinema Canada*. See also a special issue of *cinéma québec* 6, no. 3 (1978).

83 'Statement on Film Policy,' 1 May 1979, 2. The speech concluded: 'I will continue to monitor developments in the industry to see if further steps are warranted, but at the moment the evidence of the past year suggests that our programs are working successfully towards the objectives I set out a year ago' (5).

In July, four major Canadian production houses, Film Consortium (Bill Marshall and Henk Van der Kolk), RSL Productions (Robert Lantos and Stephen Roth), Caroness Film Production (Ronald Cooper and Ron Cohen), and Jon Slan Productions, announced that they were thinking of establishing their own firm to distribute their product in Canada. Lantos suggested that Canadian independent distributors lacked 'imagination' and 'ingenuity,' and that they were thrown about 'like yo-yos.' The deal was never consummated. See 'Producers Re-Group to Join Indy Distribs,' *Cinemag* (July 1979), 3.

84 'Distribution: Federal Priority for 1979?' *Cinemag* (February 1979), 3
85 Bucovetsky et al. *Tax Incentives for Film Production*, 16–17, emphasis in original.
86 Lyon and Trebilcock, *Public Strategy and Motion Pictures*, 79
87 'Study Focuses on Canadian Cultural Fact,' *Cinemag* (16 June 1980), 7
88 See Lyon and Trebilcock, *Public Strategy*, Table 5, 81.
89 Richard Wise, 'Shelter in a Changing Climate,' *CC*, no. 68 (September 1980), 32
90 See 'Funds for Winners Only,' *The Globe and Mail* (31 March 1980); and CFDC, *Annual Report 1979–80*, 4–5.
91 CFDC, *Annual Report 1979–80*, 4
92 Ibid.
93 'Outgoing CFDC Head,' *Variety* (28 May 1980), 34. McCabe was not the only public official who exhibited a certain disdain toward the cultural dimension of Canada's film industry. Duncan Allen, Ontario's deputy minister of Industry and Tourism, told participants at the 1980 Toronto Film Festival's trade forum that 'he didn't care about Canadian content as long as you can sell it,' and that he 'had no quarrel with the people who want to turn University Ave. into Washington D.C.' (*Hollywood Reporter* (16 September 1980), 10). Allen's remarks were typical of those made by provincial officials trying to convince American productions to locate in their respective provinces.

Chapter 10

1 See Canada, Parliament, Standing Committee on Broadcasting, 8 November 1979, 1:46; House of Commons, *Debates*, 24 November 1978; and 'CCFM, News: An Election Review of Feature Film Priorities,' *Cinema Canada* (hereinafter *CC*), no. 55 (May 1979).
2 Canada, Parliament, Standing Committee on Broadcasting, 8 November 1979, 1:46, and Appendix 1, 1A: 13–14. With the intention of establishing a more coordinated approach to the development of Canada's cultural industries, MacDonald informed the Standing Committee in November 1979 that Cabinet was examining a proposal to establish a Canadian Cultural Industries Council. MacDonald's plan was to expand and transform the CFDC so that it would operate as an investment broker for all of the cultural industries. To this end, MacDonald also wanted to see the capital cost allowance provisions extended to cover the publishing and sound-recording industries. Legislation was to be announced sometime around Easter.
3 In 1984, revenues from videocassettes totalled some $530 million, while revenues from theatrical exhibition were approximately $400 million. See Canada, Film Industry Task Force, *Canadian Cinema: A Solid Base* (1985) 27.

4 'Department of Communications, An Overview' (1984), 11. For an excellent overview of the Department of Communications, see George Galt, 'Unscrambling the Future,' *Saturday Night* (October 1983). See also: L. Fortin and C. Winn, 'Communications and Culture: Evaluating an Impossible Portfolio,' in Bruce Doern, ed., *How Ottawa Spends: The Liberals, the Opposition and Federal Priorities: 1983* (1983); John Meisel, 'Flora and Fauna on the Rideau: The Making of Cultural Policy,' K. Graham, ed., *How Ottawa Spends 1988/89: The Conservatives Heading into the Stretch* (1988); Edward Comor, 'The Department of Communications under the Free Trade Regime,' *Canadian Journal of Communication* 16 no. 2 (1991).

5 'Struggling to Make the Big League,' *Financial Post* (16 May 1981), 21

6 'Big Nine Join to Form Producers Group, Lobby for Increased Commercial Clout,' *CC*, no. 74 (May 1981), 3. The founding companies were: Astral Film Productions, Dal Productions, Filmplan International, International Cinema Corporation, Paragon Motion Pictures, Robert Cooper Productions, RSL Films, Ronald I. Cohen Productions, and Tiberius Productions. The one holdout was Peter Simpson of Simcom Productions, who nevertheless 'endorsed their objectives 100 per cent.' Martin Bockner was named executive director of the ACMPC in November 1981.

7 Ibid., 3

8 This information is taken from various issues of *Cinema Canada*, 1981 to 1982.

9 Ibid.; see also articles by Marshall Delaney, Martin Knelman, and Jay Scott in Seth Feldman, ed., *Take Two* (1984).

10 S.D. Lyon and M. Trebilcock, *Public Strategy and Motion Pictures* (1982), 76

11 'Points Change, a Positive Contribution from Pay-TV, Says Fox,' *CC*, no. 75 (July 1981), 8

12 See 'Public Policy vs. Private Purpose,' *CC*, no. 74 (May 1981), 49.

13 'Budget Wreaks Havoc with Film Industry,' *CC*, no. 80 (December/January 1981), 3

14 'Industry Wins One Year Extension' and 'Industry Effort Spearheaded by Producers,' *CC*, no. 81 (February 1981), 3, 4

15 CFDC, *Annual Report 1982–3*, 5. These figures represent actual productions, rather than applications filed with the Canadian Film and Video Certification Office.

16 Ibid., 6; and 'Briefing Document Prepared by the CFDC for Its Appearance at the Standing Committee on Culture and Communications,' 8 April 1982, 2.

17 'TV dominates 1983 product,' *CC*, no. 94 (March 1983), 9

18 '1983: The Year of the American Compromise,' *CC*, no. 103 (January 1984), 5

19 See ibid. and, for example, 'Jutra Shoots Feature Le Silence at NFB,' *CC* no. 101 (November 1983), 28. Jutra's working title was *Le Silence* ... See also, 'APFQ Closer to Public Sector Dependence,' *CC*, no. 101 (November 1983), 25.

20 See Marc Gervais, 'Les Plouffe,' *CC*, no. 75 (July 1981), 26–7; and 'Interview with Gilles Carle,' *CC*, no. 74 (May 1981), 40–2.

21 'HBO Foots Bill for Terry Fox Pic,' *CC*, no. 78 (October 1981), 23; 'Thomas Gets Terry Fox Story for Cooper,' *CC*, no. 86 (July 1982), 5.

22 See S. Gathercole, 'Compromising the Country's Needs,' *Trade News North*, no. 4 (March 1978), 6.

23 See Peter Lyman, *Canada's Video Revolution: Pay TV, Home Video and Beyond* (1983), esp. ch. 5.

24 'CFDC – Should Be Universal,' *CC*, no. 79 (November 1981), 10

25 See 'CRTC License of First Choice Met with Surprise,' *CC*, no. 83 (April 1982), 3, 12–15; and Lyman, *Canada's Video Revolution*, 78.

26 Lyman, *Canada's Video Revolution*, 79. Just one year earlier, CRTC chairperson John Meisel had argued that the electronic media were the major 'agents of denationalization and of the Americanization of our climate,' adding that satellite transmission in particular could lead to the 'complete annihilation of what remains of a distinct Canadian culture ... and, in the final analysis, of an independent Canadian state.' Perhaps the comments were mere hyperbole? But in light of CRTC's pay-TV decision, they were also bitterly ironic. See S. Clarkson, *Canada and the Reagan Challenge* (1982), 228.

27 'Industry Wins One Year extension,' *CC*, no. 81 (February 1982), 4; and 'ACMPC invites distribs to talk policy,' *CC*, no. 83 (April 1982), 3

28 'Producers Suggest Guidelines for Survival,' *CC*, no. 85 (June 1982), 3

29 'Producers Suggest Guidelines,' *CC*, no. 85 (June 1982), 3

30 'Minister Meets Majors, Talks of Cooperation and Change,' *CC*, no. 85 (June 1982), 3

31 See David Olive, 'Garth Drabinsky's Empire,' *Report on Business Magazine* (December 1985); Kenneth Kidd, 'Cineplex's Expanding Garth,' *Toronto Star* (10 August 1986), F1; Joseph Lampel and Jamal Shamsie, 'Garth's Dominion: A Case Study of the Cineplex Odeon Empire,' *Cinema Canada*, (October 1989); Manjunath Pendakur, *Canadian Dreams and American Control* (1990), ch. 7.

32 An important revision to the Combines Investigation Act, passed in 1976, made Drabinsky's case almost watertight. Under section 13.2 of the Act, the director of investigation and research could bring an order against a supplier of commodities if 'a person is substantially affected in his business or is precluded from carrying on business due to his inability to obtain adequate supplies of a product anywhere in a market on usual trade terms.' In other words, unlike the trial that resulted from the findings of the White Report (see Chapter 2), the director of investigation and research did not have to prove that the combine was not in the public interest. See Canada, Combines Investigation Act (1978), 27–8.

33 For a synopsis of events, see Canada, Department of Consumer and Corporate Affairs, Director of Investigation and Research, 'Report to the Restrictive Trade Practices Commission on the Operation of the Undertakings Given by Six Major Motion Picture Distributors, 11 March 1984, 1 and passim.

34 See ibid., and the press release reprinted in ibid. Appendix 2.

35 Ibid., Appendix 2, 2. Director of Investigation and Research, 'Final Report to the Restrictive Trade Practices Commission on the Operation of the Undertakings Given by the Six Major Motion Picture Distributors, 11 July 1984. And see

'Combines Deal Six Months Old – Blind-Bidding Biggest Problem,' *CC*, no. 103 (January 1984), 29.

36 See Alexander Cockburn, 'The Mission; Reagan, Hollywood and the American Empire,' *The Nation* (18 April 1987). Universal, it should be noted, was not a part of the original consent decrees.

37 'U.S. Media Giant Taking Major Stake in Cineplex Odeon,' *Globe and Mail* (18 January 1986), 1

38 For useful reviews of Applebaum-Hébert, see Sandra Gathercole, 'Refusing the Challenge,' *Canadian Forum* (February 1983); and Susan Crean, 'Understanding Applebert,' *Canadian Forum* (April 1983).

39 Canada, Federal Cultural Policy Review Committee, *Report* (1982) (hereinafter, Applebaum-Hébert), 6.

40 Ibid., 362. Breton approaches the question of cultural policy from the perspective of a neoclassical economist, and his views seem to have been particularly influential in the Report's recommendations. See also Albert Breton, 'Introduction to an Economics of Culture: A Liberal Approach,' UNESCO, *Cultural Industries* (1982).

41 Applebaum-Hébert, 32

42 Ibid., recommendation 64, 264

43 Ibid., recommendation 67, 292

44 Ibid., recommendation 62, 260, and recommendation 63, 262

45 Silcox, as quoted in Gathercole, 'Refusing the Challenge,' 40. In December 1982, Silcox moved to the arts and culture branch of the Department of Communications.

46 Ibid., 9

47 As quoted in Marc Raboy, *Missed Opportunities* (1990), 286.

48 Canada, Department of Communications, *Towards a New National Broadcasting Policy* (1983), 3

49 One-third of the fund was to be reserved for the production of French-language programming. In 1985, provincial over-the-air broadcasters were made eligible for the fund, and documentaries were added to the list of eligible program formats. Telefilm was also given permission to take up to 49 per cent of the costs in totally Canadian production. In 1986, pay-TV licensees were added to the list of eligible 'broadcasters.'

50 Canada, Telefilm, *Annual Report 1984–5*, 10. Not surprisingly, the CBC became the most important investor in the broadcasting community. For example, in 1985, it was estimated that the CBC was responsible for 80 per cent of the productions underway. In the first year of the fund's operation the CBC was involved in 57 projects, while CTV, the next most important participant, was involved in only 6. Major financial support also came from foreign sources. In the first 26 months of the fund's operation, foreign investment totalled $90 million, a figure very close to the CFDC's own investment. Recently signed television co-production treaties helped fuel this latter trend. See Canada, Film Industry Task Force, *Canadian Cinema: A Solid Base*, 30, 33; 'Film Industry Boom Bogs Down,' *Globe and Mail* (31 August 1985), E3.

51 See discussion in Government of Canada, Task Force on Broadcasting Policy, *Report*, (1986), ch. 14.

52 Ibid., 371, 373. See also: Tom Perlmutter, 'Strategies for Survival,' *Cinema Canada*, no. 158 (June 1988); and John Haslett Cuff, 'It's Take One for Huge Film Factory,' *The Globe and Mail* (26 March 1987), C1.

53 Matthew Fraser, 'Riding the TV Bandwagon,' *Globe and Mail* (10 November 1984), E1. See also Matthew Fraser, 'Film Industry's Boom Bogs Down,' *Globe and Mail*, 31 August 1985, E3; and the interview with Telefilm executive director, Peter Pearson, 'Television Is Everything Says Broadcast Fund head Pearson,' *CC*, no. 108 (June 1984).

54 'Riding the TV Bandwagon,' *Globe and Mail* (10 November 1984), E1. Lantos felt that *Joshua Then and Now*, whose financial backers included the CBC, the CFDC, Rogers Cable Systems, and 20th Century–Fox (its theatrical distributor), had transcended this problem. A better example, completed at almost the same time, would probably be *My American Cousin*, directed by Sandy Wilson and produced by Peter O'Brian with the CBC as its television broadcaster.

55 Canada, Film Industry Task Force, *Canadian Cinema: A Solid Base* (1985), 30

56 Ibid., 26, 39

57 Ibid., 9–12

58 Canada, Department of Communications, *Towards a National Broadcasting Policy*, 3

Chapter 11

1 Canada, Department of Communications, *National Film and Video Policy* (1984), 3

2 From the oft-quoted speech of Prime Minister Bennett on the establishment of public broadcasting in Canada in 1932, Canada, Parliament, House of Commons, *Debates*, 18 May 1932, 3035

3 Canada, Royal Commission on the Economic Union and Development Prospects for Canada, *Report*, (1985)

4 See David Crane, 'Battle Lines Drawn for Cabinet Battle over Cultural Future,' *The Toronto Star* (5 August 1986) A1, A8.

5 'Fed Film Policy This Month,' *Cinema Canada* (hereinafter *CC*), no. 94 (March 1983), 5

6 Canada, Film Industry Task Force, *Canadian Cinema: A Solid Base* (1985), 8

7 Ibid.

8 Canada, Department of Communications, *Vital Links: Canadian Cultural Industries* (1987), 45

9 For an excellent discussion of the plight of Canada's independent distributors, see: Virginia Kelly, 'Lament for an Industry,' *CC*, no. 81 (February 1982), 24–7; and 'Against All Odds,' *CC*, no. 144 (September 1987), 10–15. See also, Strativision Inc., 'The Structure and Performance of the Canadian Film and Distribution Sector,' 1985, prepared for the Department of Communications.

10 See Canada, Film Industry Task Force, *Canadian Cinema: A Solid Base*, 29; and 'Majors tighten control in Canada,' *CC*, no. 86 (July 1982), 3. Of the ten original members of the Association of Independent and Canadian-Owned Motion Picture Distributors, only two – Pan-Canadian and Astral – have survived.

11 Film Industry Task Force, *Canadian Cinema*, 9

12 'Majors to Be Limited in Distribution,' *CC*, no. 95 (April 1983), 3

13 See 'Radical Recommendations for Quebec's Industry: Law Expected,' *CC*, no. 88 (September 1982), 3; 'New Structures, Indigenous Distribs, Highlight Quebec Film Bill,' *CC*, no. 93 (February 1983), 3. For an excellent discussion of Bill 109 and its relationship to Canada's free-trade negotiations with the United States, see Joyce Nelson, 'Losing It in the Lobby,' *This Magazine* (October/November 1986). The most comprehensive assessment of Bill 109 and the negotiations between the American majors and the Quebec government is Michel Houle, 'Analysis of the Agreement Reached October 22, 1986, between the Minister of Cultural Affairs of Quebec and the Motion Picture Export Association – Submitted to Telefilm Canada,' reprinted as 'Power Protects,' *CC* (March 1987).

14 In Nelson, 'Losing It in the Lobby,' 18, 19

15 Houle, 'Power Protects,' 17. The minister also announced that subtitled French versions could be used in lieu of dubbed versions. The minister was also working on plans to establish a 150 per cent capital cost allowance for films produced in Quebec. See 'Quebec 150% Shelter Wide Open for Under 75 Min. Programs,' *CC*, no. 103 (January 1984), 29.

16 'Valenti Lunches with Fox in Effort to Avoid Viral Spread,' *CC*, no. 100 (October 1983), 4

17 'The Canadian Domino,' *CC*, no. 100 (October 1983), 5

18 Canada, Department of Communications, *National Film and Video Policy* (1984), 10

19 Ibid., 13

20 Ibid., 19

21 Ibid., 38, 39

22 Ibid., 40

23 Ibid., 41

24 See ' "Unthinkable and Inexcusable" State Distributors in Open Letters,' *CC*, no. 110 (September 1984), 35; and 'Industry Unanimous in Rejecting Distribution Policy,' ibid, 33. In the pages of *Cinema Canada* producers voiced their support for Canadian-owned distributors, but it is not exactly clear how genuine that support was. Immediately after Francis Fox' announcement, both Stephen Ellis, president of the Canadian Film and Television Association, and Peter O'Brian, president of the Canadian Association of Motion Picture Producers, told the *Toronto Star* that they agreed with Fox' decision to proceed through negotiations. Perhaps they were later convinced otherwise by Canadian distributors, or perhaps they were practising their own version of double-talk.

See 'Canada's New Film Policy Delights Movie Industry,' *Toronto Star* (30 May 1984), B1.

25 Houle, 'Power Protects,' 17
26 Ibid.
27 'Valenti Threatens Pull-Out If Law Enacted,' *CC*, no. 123 (October 1985), 53; and 'Quebec Hearings Support Ouster of Majors As Regular Distributors,' *CC*, no. 124 (November 1985), 44
28 See Nelson, 'Losing It in the Lobby,' 22; and 'Furor Erupts over Quebec's Backing Down on Film Law,' *Globe and Mail* (12 December 1985).
29 In 'Furor Erupts over Quebec's Backing Down,' *Globe and Mail* (12 December 1985)
30 'Quebec Signs Landmark Film Deal,' *Globe and Mail* (24 October 1986), D9; 'Quebec Signs with the Majors,' *Cinema Canada: News Update*, no. 1, (10 November 1986), 1; and Houle, 'Power Protects'
31 Houle, 'Power Protects,' 21
32 Valenti, as quoted in 'Quebec Signs Landmark Film Deal,' *Globe and Mail* (24 October 1986), D9. See also Michael Bergman, 'New Deal, Bad Deal,' *Cinema Canada: News Update*, no. 1, (10 November 1986), 2.
33 See 'A Proposal to Cut Canada into the Film-Distribution Pie,' *The Sunday Star* (15 February 1987); 'Canadian Film Licensing Proposal Draws Cautious Response in U.S.,' *Globe and Mail* (21 February 1987); Pendakur, *Canadian Dreams* (1990), 264–6; and 'Distribution Now,' *CC* (December 1987).
34 Pendakur, *Canadian Dreams*, 266.
35 ' "Capricous" Laws Scare Off Film Cash, Drabinsky Says,' *The Sunday Star* (13 September 1987), A21; Astral-Bellevue, which holds various sub-licensing agreements with American distributors, and runs a profitable film and video duplication business in Canada, was also apparently edgy about the proposed legislation.
36 Pendakur, *Canadian Dreams*, 271
37 See 'MacDonald Shrugs Off "Valenti's problem",' *Globe and Mail* (27 October 1987), D8; and Sid Adilman, 'Surprise, Surprise Hollywood Wins Distribution Battle,' *Toronto Star* (21 November 1987), D1.
38 'MacDonald Policy Seeks to Help Film Industry,' *Globe and Mail* (6 May 1988), A1
39 'New Film Fund a Disappointment,' *Globe and Mail* (10 May 1988), A19; and see Michael Bergman, 'The Distribution Gag,' *CC*, no. 153 (June 1988); Michael Bergman, 'The Real Cost of the Federal Distribution Bill,' no. 157 (November 1988); and, Tom Perlmutter, 'The Politics of Film Distribution,' *The Canadian Forum* (February/March 1989)
40 'Canada: Economic Update,' *New York Times* (10 December 1985)
41 Steve Globerman and Aidan Vining, 'Canadian Culture under Free Trade,' *Canadian Business Review* (Summer 1986), 18
42 Ibid., 19
43 Thomas D'Aquino, 'Ten Myths about the Deal,' *Policy Options* (December 1988), 33

44 Ibid.
45 Flora MacDonald, as quoted in 'Association of Canadian Publishers Wary of Free Trade Agreement,' *Quill and Quire* (August 1988), 18
46 Canada, Department of External Affairs, *Canada–United States Free Trade Agreement*, Minister of Supply and Services (1988)
47 See 'Association of Canadian Publishers: Brief,' House of Commons, Legislative Committee on Bill C-130 An Act to Implement the Free Trade Agreement between Canada and the United States, 'Minutes of Proceedings and Evidence,' 1988, 15A:3.
48 See House of Commons, Legislative Committee on Bill C-130, 'Minutes,' 23:42, 10:64.
49 Susan Crean, 'Reading between the Lies: Culture and the Free Trade Agreement,' *This Magazine* (May 1988), 32; see also Michael Bergman, 'Trick–or–Treaty?,' *CC*, no. 149 (February 1988).
50 Telefilm Canada, *Annual Report 1986–7*, 13
51 Martin Knelman, 'Hollywood North: The Sequel,' *Report on Business Magazine* (April 1987), 64
52 'Film, TV Productions Post Boom Year,' *Globe and Mail* (27 December 1986), B1
53 Sid Adilman, 'Toronto Film Boom Reaches New Heights,' *Toronto Star* (16 January 1988), F3; Stephen Godfrey, 'B.C. Film Boom Has Craft Unions at Odds,' *Globe and Mail*, (25 May 1988), C9
54 John Haslett Cuff, 'It's Take One for Huge Film Factory,' *Globe and Mail* (26 March 1987), C1
55 Michael Bergman, 'Bye Bye Tax Shelter,' *Cinema Canada* no. 143 (July–August 1987), 6
56 'Filmmaker Outraged by Tax Reforms,' *Sunday Star* (21 June 1987), A1

Chapter 12

1 Abraham Rotstein, 'Binding Prometheus,' in Ian Lumsden, ed., *Close the 49th Parallel etc.: The Americanization of Canada* (1970), 210
2 See Canada, Telefilm Canada, *Annual Report 1988–9*.
3 'Ontario Film Industry Worth Billions,' *Globe and Mail* (11 July 1990), C3
4 See the discussion in C. Hoskins and R. Mirus, 'Reasons for the U.S. Dominance of the International Trade in Television Programs.' *Media, Culture & Society* 10 no. 4 (1988); and C. Hoskins and S. McFadyen, 'The U.S. Competitive Advantage in the Global Television Market: Is It Sustainable in the New Broadcasting Environment.' *Canadian Journal of Communications* 16, no. 2 (1991).
5 As Hoskins and Mirus note: 'So we have the paradox that the most expensive programming in the United States becomes available to broadcasters abroad at low prices not related to costs but to the demand characteristics of the importing market. Examples of maximum prices paid per half hour for U.S. series in 1985 are Italy, $48,000, Canada, $20,000, Federal Republic of Germany $18,000,

U.K. $14,000, France $10,000, Japan $7,000' ('Reasons for the U.S. dominance,' 511).

6 Film projects in which Telefilm invests are now required to have a minimum marketing budget of $100,000. By way of contrast, Oscar-winning *Driving Miss Daisy* (1989) had a promotional budget of $10 million, which equalled its production cost. See 'Telefilm: A Big Boon, A Bigger Bust,' *Globe and Mail* (5 May 1990), C1.

7 As quoted in Peter Morris, *Embattled Shadows* (1978), 232

8 'Can't See Film Industry,' *Canadian Film Weekly* (11 June 1958), 1

9 Nat Taylor, 'Our Business,' *Canadian Film Weekly* (14 October 1959), 3

10 'Pour Une Direction générale (québécoise) des industries du cinéma,' *Le Devoir* (24 March 1964).

11 Nat Taylor, 'Our Business,' *Canadian Film Weekly* (10 February 1960), 3

12 Canada, Department of Communications. *Annual Report 1989–90*, (emphasis in original)

13 Robert Babe, *Telecommunications in Canada: Technology, Industry and Government* (1990), 7

14 Bennett, in House of Commons, *Debates*, 18 May 1935, 3035; Paul Rutherford, *When Television Was Young: Prime Time Canada 1952–67* (1990), 13

15 John Grierson, as quoted in Peter Morris, *NFB: The War Years* (1965), 3

16 Ronald Blumer, 'John Grierson: "I Derive My Authority from Moses," ' *Take One* 2 no. 9 (1970), 17

17 Hilda Neatby, as quoted in Paul Rutherford, *When Television Was Young*, 14. Rutherford offers a brief but highly incisive discussion of Canada's cultural intelligentsia in the 1940s and 1950s (13–26).

18 Canada, House of Commons, *Debates*, 3 February 1967, 12657

19 Numerous studies of Canada's broadcasting system have noted that each increase in the number of private Canadian broadcasting outlets leads to an increase in the percentage of foreign television programming available and viewed. See, for example, Robert Babe, *Canadian Television Broadcasting: Structure, Performance and Regulation*, 1979

20 Pelletier to Gélinas, 24 December 1969, and Gélinas to Pelletier, 6 February 1970, PAC RG 123, CFDC Records, vol. 2, File 170

21 See Paul Audley and Associates, 'Film and Television Production in Canada: Trends to 1989 and Projections to 1995,' March 1991, 6, Table 3.

22 'U.S. Deals Thrust Paragon into Television Spotlight,' *Globe and Mail* (11 March 1992), B1

23 Paul Audley and Associates, 'Film and Television Production'

24 Ibid., 25

25 James Carey, 'Mass Communication Research and Cultural Studies: An American View,' in James Curran et al., eds, *Mass Communication and Society* (1977), 412

26 Canada, Department of Communications. *Vital Links: Canada's Cultural Industries* Ottawa: Minister of Supply and Services Canada, 1987, 6

27 For recent critical discussions of nationalism, see Eric Hobsbawm, *Nations and Nationalism since 1780: Programme, Myth, Reality* (1990); Phillip Schlesinger, 'On National Identity: Some Conceptions and Misconceptions,' *Social Science Information* 26, no. 2 (1987).

28 Max Weber's classic definition of the state is 'a human community that (successfully) claims the *monopoly of the legitimate use of physical force* within a given territory.' In H. Gerth and C.W. Mills, eds, *Fram Max Weber: Essays in Sociology* (1964), 78 (emphasis in original).

29 A similar argument is made in two recent studies of Canadian broadcasting: Richard Collins, *Culture, Communications and National Identity: The Case of Canada Television* (1990); and Paul Rutherford, *When Television Was Young* (1990).

30 For an excellent collection of essays on the question of audience reception, see Ellen Seiter et al., eds, *Remote Control: Television, Audiences and Cultural Power*, (1989). See also references cited in Chapter 1, note 16

31 Scott Forsyth, 'The Failure of Nationalism and Documentary: Grierson and Gouzenko,' *Canadian Journal of Film Studies* 1 no. 1 (1990), 75

32 Richard Collins, *Culture, Communication and National Identity*, 344

Bibliography

Much of the material for this work has been drawn from the following trade periodicals:

Canadian Cinematographer (1961–6)
Canadian Film Digest (1971–3)
Canadian Film and Television Bi-Weekly (1965–9)
Canadian Film Weekly (1945–65)
Canadian Moving Picture Digest (1917–48)
Cinema Canada (1967–90)
Cinemag (1978–81)
Trade News North (1977–8)

L'Action nationale. 'Une loi cadre pour le cinéma québécois en 1975 où un nouveau traité de capitulation face à Ottawa' (February 1975)
Adilman, Sid. 'Surprise, Surprise Hollywood Wins Distribution Battle.' *Toronto Star* (21 November 1987)
– 'Toronto Film Boom Reaches New Heights.' *Toronto Star* (16 January 1988)
Allen, Robert. 'Motion Picture Exhibition in Manhattan: Beyond the Nickelodeon.' *Cinema Journal* 18 (2), 1979
Anderson, Benedict, *Imagined Communities: Reflections on the Origin and Spread of Nationalism*. London: Verso, 1983
Anderson-Perry, Ann. 'The Hollywood Menace.' *Chatelaine* (September 1931)
Ang, Ien. *Watching Dallas: Soap Opera and the Melodramatic Imagination*. London: Methuen, 1985
Arthur, Harold. 'Thanks, Yanks, for All That You've Done, or Why There Isn't a Canadian Feature Film Industry, Unless a Big American Union Called IATSE Is Forced to Reassess its Role.' *Saturday Night* (September 1966)
L'Association des réalisateurs de films du Québec. 'La culture et le cinéma au Québec: un mémoire présenté au premier ministre, M. René Lévesque.' *cinéma québec* 6 (3), 1978

L'Association professionnelle des cinéastes. 'Mémoire présenté au Secrétaire d'État du Canada: vingt-deux raisons pour lesquelles le gouvernement du Canada doit favoriser la création d'une industrie de cinéma de long métrage au Canada et s'inquiéter des consequences économiques et culturelles de l'état actuel de la distribution et de l'exploitation des films.' Public Archives of Canada, RG 6, Secretary of State, Interdepartmental Committee on Film Industry, February 1964
– 'Mémoire présenté au premier ministre du Québec: mesures d'ensemble que l'APC recommande au gouvernement du Québec pour favoriser le développement d'une industrie du cinéma de long métrage conforment aux intérêts économiques et culturelles du Québec.' March 1964
Audley, Paul, and Associates. 'Film and Television Production in Canada: Trends to 1989 and Projections to 1995.' A study commissioned by the Alliance of Canadian Cinema, Television and Radio Artists (ACTRA) and Communications Canada with support from the Ontario Film Development Corporation and the National Film Board, March 1991
Audley, Paul. *Canada's Cultural Industries: Broadcasting, Publishing, Records and Film.* Toronto: Lorimer, 1983
Babe, Robert. *Canadian Television Broadcasting: Structure, Performance and Regulation.* Ottawa: Economic Council of Canada, 1979
– *Telecommunications in Canada: Technology, Industry, and Government.* Toronto: University of Toronto Press, 1990
Backhouse, Charles. *Canadian Government Motion Picture Bureau 1917–41.* Ottawa: Canadian Film Institute, 1974
Balio, Tino, ed. *The American Film Industry.* rev. ed. Madison: University of Wisconsin Press, 1985
Beattie, Eleanor. *A Handbook of Canadian Film.* 2d. ed. Toronto: Peter Martin Associates, 1977
Berger, Carl. *A Sense of Power.* Toronto: University of Toronto Press, 1970
Bergman, Michael. 'New Deal, Bad Deal.' *Cinema Canada: News Update,* no. 1 (10 November 1986)
– 'Bye Bye Tax Shelter.' *Cinema Canada,* no. 143 (July/August 1987)
– 'Trick – or – Treaty?' *Cinema Canada,* no. 149 (February 1988)
– 'The Distribution Gag.' *Cinema Canada,* no. 153 (June 1988)
– 'The Real Cost of the Federal Distribution Deal.' *Cinema Canada,* no. 157 (November 1988)
Berton, Pierre. *Hollywood's Canada: The Americanization of our National Image.* Toronto: McClelland and Stewart, 1975
Blumer, Ronald. 'NFB: Is This the End?' *Take One* 2 (2), 1969
– 'John Grierson: I Derive My Authority from Moses.' *Take One* 2 (3), 1970
Boissonnault, Robert. 'Les Cinéastes québécois et l'ONF: une immersion totale dans un milieu anglophone, ou la periode 1945–55.' *cinéma québec* 2 (3), 1972
– 'Les Cinéastes québécois et l'ONF: la séquence du film pour la télévision.' *cinéma québec* 2 (3), 1972
– 'Les Cinéastes québécois et l'ONF: la séquence du cinéma direct.' *cinéma québec* 2 (4), 1973

- 'Les Cinéastes québécois et l'ONF: la séquence du long métrage.' *cinéma québec* 2 (5), 1973
- 'Les Cinéastes québécois et l'ONF: Naissance d'une industrie indépendante de cinéma.' *cinéma québec* 2 (8), 1973
Borneman, Ernest. 'United States vs. Hollywood: The Case Study of the Anti-Trust Suit.' In Tino Balio, ed., *The American Film Industry*. rev. ed. Madison: University of Wisconsin Press, 1985
Bothwell, Robert, et al. *Canada Since 1945: Power, Politics, and Provincialism*. Toronto: University of Toronto Press, 1981
Boyd-Barrett, Oliver. 'Media Imperialism: Towards an International Framework for the Analysis of Media Messages.' In James Curran et al., eds., *Mass Communication and Society*. London: Arnold, 1977
- 'Cultural Dependency and the Mass Media.' M. Gurevitch et al., eds., *Culture, Society and the Media*. London: Methuen, 1982
Brady, Robert. 'The Problem of Monopoly.' *Annals of the American Academy of Political and Social Science* 254 (1947)
Breton, Albert, 'Introduction to an Economics of Culture: A Liberal Approach.' UNESCO, *Cultural Industries: A Challenge for the Future of Culture*. Paris: UNESCO, 1982
Brodie, Janine, and Jane Jenson. *Crisis, Challenge and Change: Party and Class in Canada*. Toronto: Methuen, 1980
Brown, Dorothy. 'The Unknown Movies.' *Queen's Quarterly* 36 (1929)
Bucovetsky, M., et al. *Tax Incentives for Film Production: The Canadian Experience*. Working Paper no. 8215. Toronto: Institute for Policy Analysis, 1982
Burr, Keith. 'The North Lights Up.' *American Film* (December 1979)
Cahiers du cinéma. 'Canada: un cinéma de la disposition.' (March 1966)
Canada, Royal Commission on Radio Broadcasting. *Report*. Ottawa: King's Printer, 1929
- Royal Commission on National Development in the Arts, Letters and Sciences. *Report*. Ottawa: King's Printer, 1951
- Royal Commission on Broadcasting. *Report*. Ottawa: Queen's Printer, 1957
- Royal Commission on Publications. *Report*. Ottawa: Queen's Printer, 1961
- Advisory Committee on Broadcasting. *Report*. Ottawa: Queen's Printer, 1965
- Federal Cultural Policy Review Committee. *Report*. Ottawa: Minister of Supply and Services, 1982
- Film Industry Task Force. *Canadian Cinema: A Solid Base*. Ottawa: Minister of Supply and Services, 1985
- Royal Commission on the Economic Union and Development Prospects for Canada. *Report*. Ottawa: Minister of Supply and Services, 1985
- Task Force on Broadcasting Policy. *Report*. Ottawa: Ministry of Supply and Services, 1986
Canada, Canadian Film Development Corporation (CFDC). *Annual Reports*, 1967–82
Canada, Department of Communication (DOC). *The Department of Communications: An Overview*. Ottawa: Minister of Supply and Services, Canada, 1984

– *Instant World: A Report on Telecommunications in Canada*. Ottawa: Information Canada, 1971
– *Towards a New National Broadcasting Policy*. Ottawa: Minister of Supply and Services Canada, 1983
– *The National Film and Video Policy*. Ottawa: Minister of Supply and Services Canada, 1984
– *Vital Links: Canadian Cultural Industries*. Ottawa: Minister of Supply and Services Canada, 1987
– Canadian Film and Videotape Certification Office. *100 per cent Capital Cost Allowance for Certified Canadian Films and Videotapes: Review of the Certification Program*. Ottawa: Minister of Supply and Services, 1980
– Canadian Film and Videotape Certification Office, *Statistics Bulletin: 1974–1983*, Ottawa: Minister of Supply and Services, 1985
Canada, Department of Consumer and Corporate Affairs, Director of Investigation and Research. 'Report to the Restrictive Trade Practices Commission on the Operation of the Undertakings given by the Six Major Motion Picture Distributors,' Ottawa, March 1984
– 'Final Report to the Restrictive Trade Practices Commission on the Operation of the Undertakings Given by Six Major Motion Picture Distributors.' Ottawa, July 1984
Canada, Department of External Affairs. *The Canada–U.S. Free Trade Agreement*. Ottawa: Minister of Supply and Services, 1988
Canada, Department of Labour. *Investigation into an Alleged Combine in the Motion Picture Industry*. Ottawa: King's Printer, 1931
Canada, Secretary of State. *Film Industry in Canada*. Ottawa: Minister of Supply and Services, 1977
– Notes for speeches by secretaries of state Maurice Lamontagne, Gérard Pelletier, Hugh Faulkner, and John Roberts
– Bureau of Management Consulting. *Evaluation of the Canadian Film Development Corporation*. September 1974
Canada, Parliament, House of Commons. *Debates*, 1919–1988
– Legislative Committee on Bill C-130 an Act to Implement the Free Trade Agreement Between Canada and the United States. *Minutes of Proceedings and Evidence*, 1988
– Standing Committee on Broadcasting, Films and Assistance to the Arts. *Minutes of Proceedings and Evidence*, 1966–79
– Standing Committee on Communications and Culture. *Minutes of Proceedings and Evidence*, 1979–88
Canada, Public Archives (PAC)
– Records of the Department of Trade and Commerce, Canadian Co-operation Project, RG 20 B1 Vol. 575
– Submissions and Hearings of the Royal Commission on National Development in the Arts, Letters and Sciences, RG 33/28
– Records of the Secretary of State, Proceedings and Correspondence of the Interde-

partmental Committee of the Government of Canada on the Possible Development
of Feature Film Production in Canada, RG 6, vol. 824, 848
- Manuscripts of Maurice Lamontagne (1962–65), MG 32, B32
- Records of the Canadian Film Development Corporation, RG 123
- Records of the Royal Commission on Corporate Concentration, RG 33/113
Canada, Telefilm Canada. *Annual Reports*, 1983–90
Canadian Motion Picture Distributors Association. 'Position Paper Concerning
Motion Picture Distribution in Canada.' (1976)
- 'A Submission to the Federal Department of Finance.' (July 1978)
- 'A Report on the Distribution of Feature Films in Canada.' (September 1980)
Carey, James. 'Mass Communication Research and Cultural Studies: An American
View.' In James Curran, ed., *Mass Communication and Society*. London: Arnold,
1977
Carnoy, Martin. *The State and Political Theory*. Princeton: Princeton University
Press, 1984
Chalmers, Floyd. 'The Story of the Allens.' *Maclean's* (15 February 1920) Chanan,
Michael. *The Dream That Kicks: The Prehistory and Early Cinema in Britain*.
London: Routledge, 1980
Chanan, Michael. *The Dream That Kicks: The Prehistory and Early Years of Cinema
in Britain*. London: Routledge, 1980
Chatwin, Len. 'Canadians Cooperate to Show Films.' *Canadian Film News*
(February 1950)
Chuan-Lee, Chin. *Media Imperialism Reconsidered: The Homogenizing of Television
Culture*. Beverly Hills: Sage, 1980
cinéma québec. 'Numéro spécial "loi-cadre": pour décoloniser le cinéma québécois'
4 (4), 1975
Clandfield, David. 'From the Picturesque to the Familiar: Films of the French Unit at
the NFB (1958–64).' In Seth Feldman, ed., *Take Two*. Toronto: Irwin Publishing,
1984
- *Canadian Film*. Toronto: Oxford University Press, 1987
Clarkson, Stephen. *Canada and the Reagan Challenge*. Toronto: Lorimer, 1982
Coatsworth, E.A. 'Motion Picture Production in Canada.' *Canadian Forum* 36 (434),
1957
Cockburn, Alexander. 'The Mission: Reagan, Hollywood and the American Empire.'
The Nation (18 April 1987)
Cole, S. 'Bay Street Gets into Movies.' *Canadian Business* (August 1979)
Coleman, William. *The Independence Movement in Quebec 1945–1980*. Toronto:
University of Toronto Press, 1984
Collins, Maynard. 'Cooperation, Hollywood and Howe.' *Cinema Canada*, no. 56
(June/July 1979)
- 'A View From the Top: Interview with Arthur Irwin.' *Cinema Canada*, no. 56
(June/July 1979)
Collins, Richard. *Culture, Communication and National Identity: The Case of Cana-
dian Television*. Toronto: University of Toronto Press, 1990

- 'National Culture: A Contradiction in Terms?' *Canadian Journal of Communication* 16 (2), 1991
Comor, Edward. 'The Department of Communications under the Free Trade Regime.' *Canadian Journal of Communications* 16 (2), 1991
Conant, Michael. 'The Paramount Decrees Reconsidered.' In Tino Balio, ed., *The American Film Industry.* rev. ed. Madison: University of Wisconsin Press, 1985
Council of Canadian Filmmakers. 'CCFM Policy Statement on Feature Films.' *Cinema Canada*, no. 12 (February/March 1974)
- 'Submission to the Royal Commission on Corporate Concentration.' Public Archives of Canada, RG 33/113, Royal Commission on Corporate Concentration, April 1976
Cowan, James. 'The Battle for Canadian Film Control.' *Maclean's* (1 October 1930)
- 'Is There a Chance for Empire Films?' *Maclean's* (15 October 1930)
Cox, Kirwan. 'Radical Surgery.' *Cinema Canada*, no. 13 (April/May 1974)
- 'The Grierson Files.' *Cinema Canada*, no. 56 (June/July 1979)
- 'Hollywood's Empire in Canada.' In P. Véronneau and P. Handling, eds., *Self Portrait*. Ottawa: Canadian Film Institute, 1980
Crane, David. 'Battle Lines Drawn for Cabinet Battle over Cultural Future.' *Toronto Star* (5 August 1986)
Crawley, F.R. 'Have Independent Films a Look-In.' *Saturday Night* (14 August 1951)
Crean, Susan. *Who's Afraid of Canadian Culture?* Toronto: General Publishing, 1976
- 'Understanding Applebert.' *Canadian Forum* (February 1983)
- 'Reading between the Lies: Culture and the Free Trade Agreement.' *This Magazine* (May 1988)
Crean, Susan, and M. Rioux. *Two Nations.* Toronto: James Lorimer, 1983
Cuff, John Haslett. 'TV's Baby Boom.' *Globe and Mail* (12 July 1986)
- 'It's Take One for Huge Film Factory.' *Globe and Mail* (26 March 1987)
Curran, James, ed., *Mass Communication and Society.* London: Arnold, 1977
Curran, James, and V. Porter, eds. *British Cinema History.* London: Wiedenfeld and Nicolson, 1983
D'Aquino, Thomas. 'Ten Myths about the Deal.' *Policy Options* (December 1988)
Dean, Malcolm. *Censored! Only in Canada.* Toronto: Virgo Press, 1981
De Grazia, Edward, and Richard Newman. *Banned Films: Movies, Censors and the First Amendment.* New York: R.R. Bowker, 1982
De la Garde, Roger. 'Is There a Market for Foreign Culture?' *Media, Culture and Society* 9 (2), 1987
Delaney, Marshall. 'You Should Know How Bad This Film Is. After All, You Paid For It.' *Saturday Night* (September 1975)
Dickinson, Margaret. 'The State and the Consolidation of Monopoly.' In James Curran and Vincent Porter, eds., *British Cinema History.* London: Wiedenfeld and Nicolson, 1983
Directors' Guild of Canada. 'A Brief Urging the Development and Encouragement of a Feature Film Industry in Canada with Emphasis on the Need for Government

Assistance in Finance and National Distribution including a Specific Proposal for the Establishment of the "National Film Distribution and Financing Scheme" and a Recommendation for Improved Participation by the Canada Council.' Public Archives of Canada, RG 6, Secretary of State, Interdepartmental Committee on Film Industry, March 1964

Dorland, Michael. 'Quest for Equality: Canada and Coproductions.' *Cinema Canada*, no. 100 (October 1983)

Drabinsky, Garth. *Motion Pictures and the Arts in Canada*. Toronto: McGraw-Hill Ryerson, 1976

Dwan, Allan. 'Canada Has a Movie Future: But Certain Restrictions Must be Removed.' *Maclean's* (1 February 1920)

Dzeguze, K. 'New Proof That Nice Guys Finish Last.' *Maclean's* (15 May 1978)

Edgerton, Gary. *American Film Exhibition and an Analysis of the Motion Picture Industry's Market Structure*. New York: Garland, 1983

Edwards, Natalie. 'Who's Don Owen? What's He Done, and What's He Doing Now?' In Seth Feldman and Joyce Nelson, eds., *Canadian Film Reader*. Toronto: Peter Martin Associates, 1977

Elder, Bruce. 'On the Candid-Eye Movement.' In S. Feldman and J. Nelson, eds., *Canadian Film Reader*. Toronto: Peter Martin Associates, 1977

Elley, Derek. 'Rhythm 'n' Truth: Norman McLaren.' In Seth Feldman and Joyce Nelson, eds., *Canadian Film Reader*. Toronto: Peter Martin Associates, 1977

Endres, Robin. 'Art and Accumulation: The Canadian State and Business of Art.' In L. Panitch, ed., *The Canadian State: Political Economy and Political Power*. Toronto: University of Toronto Press, 1977

Euvrard, Michael, and Pierre Véronneau, 'Direct Cinema.' In P. Véronneau and P. Handling, eds., *Self Portrait*. Ottawa: Canadian Film Institute, 1980

Evans, Gary. *John Grierson and the National Film Board: The Politics of Wartime Propaganda*. Toronto: University of Toronto Press, 1984

– *In the National Interest: A Chronicle of the National Film Board of Canada from 1949 to 1989*. Toronto: University of Toronto Press, 1991

Famous Players Ltd. 'Submission of Famous Players Ltd. to the Royal Commission on Corporate Concentration.' Public Archives of Canada, RG 33/113, Royal Commission on Corporate Concentration, 1976

Feldman, Seth, ed. *Take Two: A Tribute to Film in Canada*. Toronto: Irwin, 1984

Feldman, Seth, and Joyce Nelson, eds. *Canadian Film Reader*. Toronto: Peter Martin and Associates, 1977

Ferras, Michael. 'Towards a National Film Industry: A View of the CFDC.' MA Thesis, Carleton University, 1983

Fetherling, Douglas, ed., *Documents in Canadian Film*. Peterborough: Broadview Press, 1988

Film Council, 'A Brief History of the American Film Industry.' In A. Mattelart and S. Sieglaub, eds., *Communication and the Class Struggle: Volume One*. New York: International General Publishing, 1979

Fiske, John. *Television Culture*. London: Routledge, 1987

Forsyth, Scott. 'The Failure of Nationalism and Documentary: Grierson and Gouzenko.' *Canadian Journal of Film Studies* 1 (1), 1990

Fortin, L., and C. Winn. 'Communications and Culture: Evaluating and Impossible Portfolio.' In Bruce Doern, ed., *How Ottawa Spends*. Ottawa: Carleton University Press, 1984

Fraser, Matthew. 'Riding the TV Bandwagon.' *Globe and Mail* (19 November 1984)

– 'Film Industry Boom Bogs Down.' *Globe and Mail* (31 August 1985)

French, Richard. *How Ottawa Decides: Planning and Industrial Policy-Making 1968–1980*. Toronto: Lorimer/Canadian Institute for Economic Policy, 1980

Galt, G. 'Unscrambling the Future.' *Saturday Night* (October 1983)

Garnham, Nicholas. *Capitalism and Communication: Global Culture and the Economics of Information*. London: Sage, 1990

Gathercole, Sandra. 'Film: Confronting the Monolith.' *Canadian Forum* (September 1977)

– 'Compromising the Country's Needs.' *Trade News North*, no. 74 (March 1978)

– 'The Best Film Policy This Country Never Had.' *Cinema Canada*, no. 47 (June 1978)

– 'Refusing the Challenge.' *Canadian Forum* (February 1983)

– 'As the Grapefruit Grows: A Short Critical History of Canadian Film Policy.' *Cinema Canada*, no. 94 (March 1983)

– 'Changing Channels.' *Canadian Forum* (November 1985)

Gerth, H., and C.W. Mills, eds., trans. *From Max Weber: Essays in Sociology*. London: Routledge, 1983

Gervais, Marc. 'Of Cannes, Canada, Robin Spry and Robert Rosselini.' *Cinema Canada*, nos. 38–9 (June/July 1977)

– 'Les Plouffe.' *Cinema Canada*, no. 74 (May 1981)

Globerman, Steven. *Cultural Regulation in Canada*. Montreal: The Institute for Research on Public Policy, 1983

Globerman, Steven, and Aidan Vining. 'Canadian Culture under Free Trade.' *Canadian Business Review* (Summer 1986)

Goldberg, Howard. 'Reducing the Risk.' *Cinema Canada*, no. 72 (March 1981)

Gomery, Douglas. 'The Movies Become Big Business: Public Theatres and the Chain Store Strategy.' *Cinema Journal* 18 (2), 1979

Gordon, David. 'Why the Majors Are Major.' *The Journal of the Producer's Guild of America* 16 (2), 1974

Grant, George. *Lament for a Nation*. Toronto: McClelland and Stewart, 1965

Gray, C.W. *Movies for the People: The Story of the National Film Board of Canada's Unique Distribution System*. Montreal: National Film Board, 1973

Grierson, John. 'A Film Policy for Canada.' Reprinted in D. Fetherling, ed., *Documents in Canadian Film*. Toronto: Broadview Press, 1988

– 'Relations with the United States Film Industry.' 31 October 1944. A confidential memorandum appended to the Minutes of the National Film Board, 28 December 1944. Reprinted in *Canadian Journal of Film Studies* 1 (1), 1990

Guback, Thomas. *The International Film Industry.* Bloomington: Indiana University Press, 1969
– 'Film and Cultural Pluralism.' *Journal of Aesthetic Education* 5 (2), 1971
 'Cultural Identity and Film in the European Economic Community.' *Cinema Journal* 14 (1), 1974
– 'Film as International Business.' In A. Mattelart and S. Sieglaub, eds., *Communication and the Class Struggle: Volume 1.* New York: International General, 1979
– 'Theatrical Film.' In B. Compaine, ed., *Who Owns the Media?* White Plains NY: Knowledge Industry Publications, 1979
– 'Hollywood's International Market.' In T. Balio ed., *The American Film Industry.* rev. ed. Madison: University of Wisconsin Press, 1985
Guérin, André. 'Le Québec et le projet de loi Fédérale d'aide au cinéma.' Office du film du Québec (October 1966)
Gurevitch, Michael, et al., eds. *Culture, Society and the Media.* London: Methuen, 1982
Hackett, Yvette. 'The National Film Society of Canada, 1935–51: Its Origins and Development.' In Gene Walz, ed., *Flashback: People and Institutions in Canadian Film History.* Montreal: Mediatexte, 1986
Handling, Piers. 'Censorship and Scares.' *Cinema Canada* no. 56 (June/July 1979)
– 'The NFB in Canada 1939–69.' In P. Véronneau and P. Handling, eds., *Self Portrait.* Ottawa: Canadian Film Institute, 1980
Harcourt, Peter. 'The Years of Hope.' In S. Feldman and J. Nelson, eds., *Canadian Film Reader.* Toronto: Peter Martin and Associates, 1977
– 'The Innocent Eye: An Aspect of the Work of the National Film Board of Canada.' In S. Feldman and J. Nelson, eds., *Canadian Film Reader.* Toronto: Peter Martin and Associates, 1977 (first published 1965)
– 'Film Making as a Cottage Industry.' *Canadian Forum* (August 1979)
– '1964: The Beginning of the Beginning.' In P. Véronneau and P. Handling, eds., *Self Portrait.* Ottawa: Canadian Film Institute, 1980
Hardy, Forsyth, ed. *Grierson on Documentary.* London: Faber and Faber, 1946
Harkness, John. 'Notes on a Tax-Sheltered Industry.' *Cinema Canada,* no. 87 (August 1982)
Hartog, S. 'State Protection of a Beleaguered Industry.' In James Curran and V. Porter, eds., *British Cinema History.* London: Wiedenfeld and Nicolson, 1983
Hobsbawn, Eric. *Nations and Nationalism Since 1780: Programme, Myth, Reality.* Cambridge: Cambridge University Press, 1990
Hood, Stuart. 'John Grierson and the Documentary Film Movement.' In James Curran and V. Porter, eds., *British Cinema History.* London: Wiedenfeld and Nicolson, 1983
Hoskins, Colin, and R Mirus. 'Reasons for the U.S. Dominance of the International Trade in Television Programs.' *Media, Culture and Society* 10 (4), 1988
Hoskins, Colin, and Stuart McFadyen. 'The U.S. Competitive Advantage in the Global Television Market: Is It Sustainable in the New Broadcasting Environment?' *Canadian Journal of Communication* 16 (2), 1991

Houle, Michel. 'Power Protects.' *Cinema Canada*, no. 139 (March 1987)
Huettig, Mae. 'Economic Control of the Motion Picture Industry.' In Tino Balio, ed., *The American Film Industry*. rev. ed. Madison: University of Wisconsin Press, 1985
Innis, Harold. *Essays in Canadian Economic History*. Toronto: University of Toronto Press, 1956
Irving, Joan. 'Yes: But Is It Canadian ... Are You Canadian ... Are They Canadian?' *Cinema Canada*, no. 37 (April/May 1977)
Irwin, Arthur. 'A View from the Top.' *Cinema Canada*, no. 56 (June/July 1979)
Jefferys, C.W. 'History in Motion Pictures.' *Canadian Historical Review* (9 December 1941)
Jessop, Bob. *Theories of the Capitalist State*. Oxford: Martin Robertson, 1982
John Grierson Project – McGill University, eds. *John Grierson and the NFB*. Toronto: ECW Press, 1984
Johnston, Eric. 'The Motion Picture as a Stimulus to Culture.' *Annals of the American Academy of Political and Social Science* 254 (November 1947)
Jones, David. *Movies and Memoranda: An Interpretive history of the National Film Board of Canada*. Ottawa: Canadian Film institute/Deneau, 1981
Jowett, Garth. *Film: The Democratic Art*. Boston: Little, Brown, 1976
Kelly, Virgina. 'Lament for an Industry.' *Cinema Canada*, no. 81 (February 1982)
– 'Against All Odds.' *Cinema Canada*, no. 144 (September 1987)
Kidd, Kenneth. 'Cineplex's Expanding Garth.' *Toronto Star* (10 August 1986)
Knelman, Martin. *This Is Where We Came In*. Toronto: McClelland and Stewart, 1977
– 'Shooting Games.' *Saturday Night* (March 1981)
– 'Hollywood North: The Sequel.' *Report on Business Magazine* (April 1987)
LaMarsh, Judy. 'Close-Up on Bill C-204.' *Take One* 1 (1), 1966
Lampel, Joseph, and Jamal Shamsie. 'Garth's Dominion.' *Cinema Canada*, (October 1989)
Lerner, David. *The Passing of Traditional Society*. New York: Free Press, 1958
Lévesque, Georges-Henri. 'The Answer to Communism.' *Food for Thought* (November 1950)
Litvak, I., and C. Maule. *Cultural Sovereignty: The Time and Reader's Digest Case in Canada*. New York: Praeger, 1974
– *Canadian Multinational Media Firms and Canada–United States Relations*. Ottawa: Institute of International Affairs, 1982
Lorimer, Roland. 'Towards Canadian Cultural Industries: Problems and Prospects.' *Media Information Australia* (November 1981)
Lorimer, Roland, and Donald Wilson, eds. *Communication Canada: Issues in Broadcasting and New Technologies*. Toronto: Kegan and Woo, 1988
Lyman, Peter. *Canada's Video Revolution: Pay TV, Home Video and Beyond*. Toronto: James Lorimer, 1983
Lyon, S.D., and M. Trebilcock. *Public Strategy and Motion Pictures: The Choice of Instruments to Promote the Development of the Canadian Film Production Industry*. Toronto: Ontario Economic Council, 1982

McCabe, Michael. 'Interview.' *Cinema Papers* (16 March 1981)

McInnes, Graham. 'Canada: Producer of Films.' *Queen's Quarterly* (Summer 1945)

McKay, Marjorie. 'History of the National Film Board.' Unpublished manuscript. Montreal: NFB Archives, 1964

MacLennan, Hugh. 'The Case for a Real Canadian Film.' *Saturday Night* (August 1955)

McLuhan, Marshall. 'Playboy Interview with Marshall McLuhan: A Candid Conversation with the High Priest of Popcult and Metaphysician of the Media.' Reprinted in *Canadian Journal of Communication* 14 (Special Issue, Fall 1989)

Magder, Ted. 'A "Featureless" Film Policy: Culture and the Canadian State.' *Studies in Political Economy*, no. 16 (1985)

– 'From No Films to Telefilm: Feature Films and the Canadian State.' *Transactions of the Royal Society of Canada*, series V, volume IV, 1989

Massey, Vincent. *On Being Canadian*. Toronto: Dent and Sons, 1948

– *What's Past Is Prologue*. Toronto: Macmillan, 1963

Mattelart, Armand. *Multinational Corporation and the Control of Culture*. Brighton: Harvester Press, 1979

Meisel, John. 'Escaping Extinction: Cultural Defence of an Undefended Border.' In D. Flaherty and W. McKercher, eds., *Southern Exposure: Canadian Perspectives on the United States*. Toronto: McGraw-Hill Ryerson, 1986

– 'Flora and Fauna on the Rideau: The Making of Cultural Policy.' In K. Graham, ed., *How Ottawa Spends 1988–9: The Conservatives Heading into the Stretch*. Ottawa: Carleton University Press, 1988

Monaco, Eitel. 'The Financing of Film Production in Europe.' *Cinema Journal* 14 (1), 1974

Morris, Peter, *The National Film Board of Canada: The War Years*. Ottawa: Canadian Film Institute, 1965

– *Canadian Feature Films, 1913–40*. Ottawa: Canadian Film Institute, 1970

– *Embattled Shadows: A History of Canadian Cinema 1895–1936*. Kingston: McGill-Queen's University Press, 1978

– 'Backwards to the Future: John Grierson's Film Policy for Canada.' In Gene Walz, ed., *Flashback: People and Institutions in Canadian Film History*. Montreal: Mediatexte, 1986

– 'Rethinking Grierson: The Ideology of John Grierson.' In P. Véronneau et al., eds., *Dialogues*. Montreal: Mediatexte, 1987

Mott, George. 'Criticizing the Movies.' *Canadian Bookman*, October 1928

Murdock, Graham. 'Blindspots about Western Marxism: A Reply to Dallas Smythe.' *Canadian Journal of Political and Social Theory* 2 (2), 1978

Nelson, Joyce. 'Losing It in the Lobby.' *This Magazine* (October/November 1986)

– *The Colonized Eye: Rethinking the Grierson Legend*. Toronto: Between the Lines, 1988

Nordenstreng, K., and H. Schiller, eds., *National Sovereignty and International Communication*. Norwood, NJ: Ablex, 1979

Offe, Claus. *Contradictions of the Welfare State*. Boston: MIT Press, 1984

Olive, D. 'Garth Drabinsky's Empire.' *Report on Business Magazine* (December 1985)

Ontario Department of Labour. Investigation into an Alleged combine in the Motion Picture Industry in Canada, *Report*. 1931

– 'Rex vs. Famous Players.' *Ontario Reports*, no. 307 (1932)

– Ministry of Industry and Tourism. *The Film Industry in Ontario*. 1973

– Select Committee on Economic and Cultural Nationalism. *Final Report on Cultural Nationalism*. 1975

Ontario Public Archives. Records of the Treasury Department. Early Correspondence on Motion Picture Regulation 1913–34. RG 56 Series A.1

Ostry, Bernard. *The Cultural Connection*. Toronto: McClelland and Stewart, 1978

Pageau, Pierre. 'A Survey of the Commercial Cinema: 1963–1977.' In P. Véronneau and P. Handling, eds., *Self Portrait*. Ottawa: Canadian Film Institute, 1980

Painchaud, Robert. 'Government and Cultural Affairs 1867–1977.' In R. Byers and R. Redford, eds., *Canada Challenged: The Viability of Confederation*. Toronto: Canadian Institute of International Affairs, 1979

Panitch, Leo. *The Canadian State: Political Economy and Political Power*. Toronto: University of Toronto Press, 1977

– 'Class and Dependency in Canadian Political Economy.' *Studies in Political Economy*, no. 6, (1981)

Park, Julian, ed. *The Culture of Contemporary Canada*. Cornell: Cornell University Press, 1957

Patriarche, Valance. 'Canada's Movie Intelligence.' *Willison's Monthly* (July 1928)

Peers, Frank. 'The Nationalist Dilemma in Canadian Broadcasting.' In Peter Russell, ed., *Nationalism in Canada*. Toronto: University of Toronto Press, 1966

– *The Politics of Canadian Broadcasting, 1920–51*. Toronto: University of Toronto Press, 1968

– 'Oh Say, Can You See?' In I. Lumsden, ed., *Close the 49th Parallel etc.: The Americanization of Canada*. Toronto: University of Toronto, 1970

– *The Public Eye: Television and the Politics of Canadian Broadcasting 1952–68*. Toronto: University of Toronto Press, 1979

Pendakur, Manjunath. 'Cultural Dependency in Canada's Feature Film Industry.' *Journal of Communications* 31 (1), (Winter 1981)

– 'Film Policies in Canada: In Whose Interests?' *Media, Culture & Society*, no. 3 (1981)

– *Canadian Dreams and American Control: The Political Economy of the Canadian Film Industry*. Detroit: Wayne State University Press, 1990

Perlmutter, Tom. 'Strategies for Survival.' *Cinema Canada*, no. 158 (June 1988)

– 'The Politics of Film Distribution.' *The Canadian Forum* (February/March 1989)

Pickersgill, J. *My Years with Louis St. Laurent*. Toronto: University of Toronto Press, 1975

Plumer, Harry. 'Have Canadian Films a Future?' *Canadian Business* (March 1947)

Québec. Conseil d'orientation économique du Québec. *Cinéma et Culture* (November 1963)

- Ministère des 'Affaires culturelles. *Pour l'évolution de la politique culturelle* (May 1976)
- Raboy, Marc. *Missed Opportunities: The Story of Canada's Broadcasting Policy.* Montreal: McGill-Queen's University Press, 1990
- Radway, Janice. *Reading the Romance: Feminism and the Representation of Women in Popular Culture.* Chapel Hill: University of North Carolina Press, 1984
- Resnick, P. *The Land of Cain: Class and Nationalism in English Canada 1945–1975.* Vancouver: New Star, 1977
- Reynolds, Lloyd. *The Control of Competition in Canada.* Cambridge, MA: Harvard University Press, 1940
- Rotstein, Abraham. 'Binding Prometheus.' In Ian Lumsden, ed., *Close the 49th Parallel etc.: The Americanization of Canada.* Toronto: University of Toronto Press, 1970
- 'The Use and Misuse of Economics in Cultural Policy.' In R. Lorimer and D. Wilson, eds., *Communication Canada.* Toronto: Regan and Woo, 1988
- Rutherford, Paul. *When Television Was Young: Primetime Canada 1952–67.* Toronto: University of Toronto Press, 1990
- Salutin, Rick. 'The Canadian Film Boom Goes Pop.' *This Magazine* (January–February 1980)
- Schiller, Herbert. *Mass Communication and American Empire.* New York: Augustus M. Kelly, 1969
- *Communication and Cultural Domination.* White Plains, NY: International Arts and Sciences Press, 1976
- 'Genesis of the Free Flow of Information Principles.' In A Mattelart and S. Sieglaub, eds., *Communication and the Class Struggle: Volume 1.* New York: International General, 1979
- Schlesinger, Phillip. 'On National Identity: Some Conceptions and Misconceptions.' *Social Science Information* 26 (2), 1987
- Scott, Jay. 'Burnout in the Great White North.' In S. Feldman, ed., *Take Two: A Tribute to Film in Canada.* Toronto: Irwin, 1984
- *Midnight Matinees.* Toronto: Oxford University Press, 1985
- Seiter, Ellen, et al., eds. *Remote Control: Television, Audiences and Cultural Power.* London: Routledge, 1989
- *Sight and Sound.* 'States and Cinemas.' 36 (1), 1967/8
- Simeon, Richard. 'Studying Public Policy.' *Canadian Journal of Political Science* 9 (4), 1976
- Smith, Anthony. *The Geopolitics of Information: How Western Culture Dominates the World.* London: Faber and Faber, 1980
- Smythe, Dallas. 'Communications: Blindspot of Western Marxism.' *Canadian Journal of Political and Social Theory* 1 (3), 1977
- *Dependency Road: Communications, Capitalism, Consciousness, and Canada.* Norwood, NJ: Ablex, 1981
- Spencer, Michael. 'Speech Delivered to the Annual Conference of the University of Windsor Film Association.' *University of Windsor Film Association Journal* 27 (3), 1975

- 'Inside the Wagon Train: A Cautionary Tale. U.S.–Canada Film Relations 1920–86.' *Cinema Canada*, no. 131 (June 1986)

Spry, Robin. 'Beyond Words: The Quebec Filmmakers' Occupation of the Censorship Office.' *Cinema Canada*, no. 18 (April/May 1975)

Staiger, Janet. 'Dividing Labour for Production Control: Thomas Ince and the Rise of the Studio System.' *Cinema Journal* 18 (2), 1979

Staiger, J., and Gomery, D. 'The History of World Cinema: Models for Economic Analysis.' *Film Reader* no. 4 (1980)

Stockbridge, Sally. 'Monopoly Capitalism — The Case of the Australian Film Industry.' *Australian Journal of Screen Theory*, nos. 5–6 (1978)

Stokes, Peter. 'The Role of Government in the Feature Film Industry.' Unpublished manuscript. Kingston: Queen's University, School of Public Administration, 1978

Strativision Inc. 'The Structure and Performance of the Canadian Film and Distributon Sector.' Prepared for the Department of Communication (October 1985)

Strick, J.C. 'The Economics of the Motion Picture Industry.' *Philosophy of The Social Sciences* 8 (1978)

Swingewood, Allan. *The Myth of Mass Culture*. London: MacMillan, 1977

Taylor, Nat. 'Our Business.' *Canadian Film Weekly* (regular column, various dates)

Tomlinson, John. *Cultural Imperialism*. Baltimore: Johns Hopkins University Press, 1991

Topalovich, Maria. *The Canadian Film Awards: A Pictorial History*. Toronto: Academy of Canadian Cinema, 1984

Toronto Filmmakers' Coop. 'Proposals for Canada's Film Policy: A Brief to the Honourable Gérard Pelletier.' Public Archives of Canada (PAC) RG 123, CFDC Records, vol. 1, File: 158, 1972

Traves, Tom. *The State and Enterprise*. Toronto: University of Toronto Press 1979

Tunstall, Jeremy. *The Media Are American*. London: Constable, 1977

UNESCO. *Statistics on Film and Cinema: 1955–77*. Paris: UNESCO, 1981

- *Cultural Industries: A Challenge for the Future of Culture*. Paris: UNESCO, 1982

Véronneau, Pierre, ed. *Le Succès est au film parlant français* (Histoire du cinéma au Québec, 1). Montreal: Cinémathèque québécoise, 1979

- *Cinéma de l'époque duplessiste* (Histoire du cinéma au Québec, 2). Montreal: Cinémathèque québécoise, 1979

- *L'office nationale du film: l'enfant martyr*. Montreal: Cinémathèque québécoise, 1979

Véronneau, Pierre, and Piers Handling, eds., *Self Portrait: Essays on the Canadian and Quebec Cinemas*. Ottawa: Canadian Film Institute, 1980

Walker, Dean. 'Film Industry Keeps Alive with TV Earnings.' *Canadian Business* (February 1958)

Walker, D. 'Interview with Michael Spencer.' *Canadian Photographer* (September 1973)

Walz, Gene, ed. *Flashback: People and Institutions in Canadian Cinema*. Montreal: Mediatexte, 1986

Wasko, Janet. *Movies and Money: Financing the American Film Industry.* Norwood, NJ: Ablex, 1982

Whitaker, Reg. *The Government Party: Organizing and Financing the Liberal Party of Canada 1930–58.* Toronto: University of Toronto Press, 1977

– 'Origins of the Canadian Government's Internal Security System, 1946–52.' *Canadian historical Review* 65 (2), 1984

Williams, Glen. *Not for Export.* Toronto: McClelland and Stewart, 1982

Williams, Raymond. *Communications.* Harmondsworth: Penguin, 1962

– *Television: Technology and Cultural Form.* London: Fontana, 1974

– *Culture.* Glasgow: Fontana, 1981

Wilson, K., and Bassett, C. 'Film Board Monopoly Facing Major Test.' *Financial Post* (19 November 1949)

Wise, Richard. 'A Cineramic View of Motion Picture Film Investments.' *Canadian Tax Journal* 24 (2), 1976

– 'Motion Pictures as a Tax Shelter.' *CA Magazine* (October 1977)

– 'The New Rules for Motion Picture Tax Shelters.' *Canadian Tax Journal.* 27 (3), (May/June 1979)

– 'Shelter in a Changing Climate.' *Cinema Canada,* no. 68 (September 1980)

Wolfe, David. 'Economic Growth and Foreign Investment: A Perspective on Canadian Economic Policy.' *Journal of Canadian Studies* 13 (1), 1978

– 'Rise and Demise of the Keynesian Era in Canada: Economic Policy 1930–1982.' In M. Cross and G. Kealy, eds., *Modern Canada.* Toronto: McClelland and Stewart, 1984

– 'The Politics of the Deficit.' In G.B. Doern, ed., *The Politics of Economic Policy.* Volume 40, Background Studies prepared for Royal Commission on the Economic Union and Development Prospects for Canada, Toronto: University of Toronto Press, 1986

Woodcock, George. *Strange Bedfellows: The State and the Arts in Canada.* Vancouver: Douglas & McIntyre, 1985

Woodside, K. 'Tax Incentives vs. Subsidies: Political Considerations in Governmental Choice.' *Canadian Public Policy* (Spring 1979)

Index